Jesus in the Divine Providence

Jesus in the Divine Providence

Thomas Cromwell

East West Publishing
Washington, DC

Copyright © 2022 by Thomas Cromwell

All rights reserved. No part of this book may be reproduced, stored in a retrieval system, or transmitted in any form or by any means—electronic, mechanical, photocopy, recording, or any other—except in the case of brief quotations embodied in critical articles and reviews, without the prior permission of the publisher.

Although the author and publisher have made every effort to provide accurate, up-to-date information, they accept no responsibility for alternate opinions, beliefs or inconvenience sustained by any person using this book.

East West Publishing, Washington, DC
JesusInTheProvidence.com

Library of Congress Control Number: 2022921881

ISBN Paperback: 978-1-7374418-7-8
ISBN Hardcover: 978-1-7374418-8-5
ISBN eBook: 978-1-7374418-9-2

Published on December 19, 2022
Printed in the United States of America

IM32

Contents

Preface ix

Introduction xiii

PART I
Providential Preparations For The Messiah

1 The Mission of the Messiah 1
Replacing Adam as God's Sinless Son

2 The Cain-Abel Paradigm 11
The Key to Understanding Providential History

3 Jesus: God or Man? 18
Addressing Christological Confusion

4 Did Jesus Pre-Exist His Birth? 30
The Role of Predestination in the Providence

5 Jesus Embodied the Mosaic Law 36
The Transition From Servant to Son

6 The Tabernacle and Temple Foreshadowed the Messiah 43
Establishing a Tradition of Obedience to Abel

7 Jesus Belongs to the Order of Melchizedek 50
The Messiah is Both High Priest and King

8 Was Mary the Mother of God? 57
Seeking a Sinless Woman to Replace Eve

9 Providential Women Risk all to Restore Eve 65
  An Old Testament History Leading to Mary

10 Jesus Inherited the Missions of Moses and David 85
  Combining the Roles of Priest and King

11 Preparing a Nation and the World for the Messiah 95
  Central and Supporting Providential Developments

PART II
The Providence Betrayed In The Crucifixion

12 Jesus' Difficult Early Life 110
  His Family Failed to Support Him

13 The Sermon on the Mount 126
  Teaching the Way of Abel

14 Parables and Miracles to Open Minds and Hearts 136
  A Stubborn People Rejected Jesus' Message

15 Jesus' Mastery of the Spirit World 142
  Cain and Abel Spirits and Angels Influence Our Lives

16 Persecution by Israel's Political Establishment 152
  Herod and Pilate had Jesus Tortured and Killed

17 Persecution by Israel's Religious Establishment 158
  The Wise Men of the Temple Rejected Jesus

18 The Doubting Mind of John the Baptist 166
  The Crucial Mission of Elijah Went Unfulfilled

19 The Catastrophic Consequences of John's Failure 182
Moses and Elijah Confirm a Change in Jesus' Mission

20 Betrayal By His Disciples 192
Satan Invaded the Inner Circle of Jesus

21 The Tragic Death of Jesus on the Cross. 201
Cain-type Forces Conspired to Kill Christ

PART III
Christians Inherit A Providential Mission From Jesus

22 Consequences of the Crucifixion 214
The Creation of an Otherworldly Kingdom

23 The Meaning of Salvation Through the Cross 224
Why the Kingdom of Heaven Remains Elusive

24 Inheriting the Mission of Jesus 238
The Path to Becoming One with Christ

25 Inheriting the Mission of Israel. 251
Christians Must Learn from the Israelites' Mistakes

26 The Providence Unfolds Through Christianity 258
Preparing for the Second Coming of Christ

27 Christianity as Global Abel 271
The Challenge to Save a Cain-Dominated World

28 The Role of Christianity in Conflict and War............. 283
The Importance of Discerning Cain from Abel

29 Christianity and Judaism 301
Becoming An Abel-Type Younger Brother

30 Christianity and Islam............................308
Becoming An Abel-Type Older Brother

31 Christianity and Marxism.........................323
Becoming a Resolute Abel to Defeat Cain

32 Christianity and Science 348
Humanism Spurs Both Reformation and Renaissance

33 Thy Kingdom Come on Earth......................361
Culmination of the Divine Providence

Acknowledgments....................................374
Table of Contents in Detail 378
Index..390

Preface

For most of human history, people believed that the earth was flat and that the sun rotated around it. This was a perfectly reasonable belief based on what they observed when looking at the horizon and the daily passage of the sun across the sky.

The first people to question this belief were Greek astronomers who studied the motion of celestial bodies and used newly-invented instruments to measure distances and interpret phenomena such as the solar and lunar eclipses. The most important of these was Aristarchus of Samos (310-230 BC), who came up with the revolutionary theory that ours is a heliocentric rather than geocentric solar system. However, he was too far ahead of his time and his theory was largely ignored.

Almost two millennia passed before the Polish astronomer and mathematician Nicolaus Copernicus (1473-1543 AD) reintroduced this heliocentric idea. A brilliant scholar and master of several scientific disciplines, Copernicus was also a canon in the Catholic church. When his heliocentric theories were introduced to Pope Clement VII in 1533, they were well received, and when his main work, De revolutionibus orbium coeletium (On the Revolutions of the Celestial Spheres) was published on his death in 1543 it was dedicated to Pope Paul III.

However, the Catholic hierarchy would soon move to denounce the revolutionary theory of Copernicus, which the Roman Inquisition did in 1615. This decision was largely aimed at another great Renaissance polymath, the Italian Galileo Galilei (1564-1642), who had embraced the Copernican theory. The Inquisition condemned him for "vehement suspicion of heresy". To avoid torture and execution, he renounced heliocentrism, but Pope Urban VIII anyway ordered him to remain under house arrest, which lasted until his death.

But Copernicus was a contemporary of Martin Luther, the most important figure in the Protestant Reformation. A close colleague of Luther, Philipp Melanchthon, arranged for the astronomer Georg Rheticus to become a student of Copernicus, and it was Rheticus who arranged for the first publication of the seminal work of Copernicus. Both Luther and Copernicus were influenced by the Christian humanists, notably Petrarch and Erasmus, pointing to the intertwined nature of the two great transformative movements of that era: the Renaissance and Reformation.

Thus the Copernican revolution would not be stopped, and when Isaac Newton (1642-1727) proved the validity of heliocentrism mathematically, what had once been heresy was on an irreversible path to becoming orthodoxy. Today we know for a certainty that Aristarchus, Copernicus and Newton were correct.

With our minds long since unchained from unquestioned beliefs, from superstition and religious dogma, we are free to choose explanations of the universe that make the most sense, based on evidence, logic and experimentation. When we look at our earth and our sky, we see the very same things that have always been visible to the naked eye, but we now know so much more than our ancient forebears about the structure and function of our universe. With this ever greater knowledge, science and technology have flourished and the world we live in has been transformed in a myriad good ways.

What does this revolution in knowledge have to do with the topic of this book, Jesus in the Divine Providence?

Our contention is that a similar revolution is needed in the way that we understand Jesus. In the same way that Aristarchus and Copernicus observed the very same universe as everyone else but, with the help of science, were able to interpret what they saw in a way that rightly challenged established beliefs, so too we must look with new eyes at the Biblical account of Jesus that is widely accepted as the truth by most Christians.

We are suggesting that the missing 'science' needed to see Jesus in a true light is the Divine Providence. In other words, it is not possible to recognize Jesus for who he really was—and is—without the perspective of the original Divine purpose for the creation, the reason for the human fall, the need for human salvation from the dominion of Satan, and the historical process that led up to the advent of Jesus as the Messiah.

The Divine Providence is the invisible hand of God that guides humanity to the fulfillment of our original purpose. The better we understand it, the better we can understand Jesus, our own purpose and the mission Christians have inherited from Jesus.

Christians have waited for 2,000 years for Christ to return and establish the Kingdom of Heaven on earth. However, without a providential understanding of the nature of Jesus and the significance of his life ending in his crucifixion it is not possible to know how a second advent of Christ can be realized and what we can do as Christians to prepare for it.

This book offers a new, providential perspective on the nature, purpose and life of Jesus, and what this understanding means for every individual and for the world.

Introduction

Jesus Seen From a Providential Perspective

In the preface to this book we suggested that looking at Jesus from a providential perspective would shed a new and necessary light on his unique nature and special place in history. That perspective derives from understanding the Divine Providence, which is the original and unchanging purpose of our Creator working itself out over time.

The aim of the providence is the establishment of a world of goodness and love in which all people are at one with God and live in harmony with one another. The original Garden of Eden embodied this ideal, but it was destroyed due to the disobedience of the first humans, Adam and Eve. Providential history traces God's work to free humanity from the dominion of Satan that resulted from the alienation of the first family and its descendants from the Creator. Thus the goal of the providence is to raise up sinless replacements for Adam and Eve who can establish a new Eden, the Kingdom of Heaven on earth.

Jesus was the most important person in providential history. After millennia of providential preparation for a savior, Jesus came as a second Adam to establish the Kingdom of Heaven on earth. It is this mission of Jesus that is the key to understanding him and his impact on the world.

As the Biblical account of the Fall reveals, one salient feature of the providence is that it requires the cooperation of human beings, who are endowed with the potential to achieve perfection but only on condition that they exercise their free will in accordance with the Divine purpose. Thus although God's purpose and will are unchanging, their realization in the perfection of individuals and society is subject to men and women fulfilling their God-given responsibilities.

As we will elaborate in this book, the best way to understand God's purpose for the creation is to compare it to the desire of parents who want children who will grow to adulthood and share in a world of love and joy. Fallen nature makes the realization of this ideal extremely difficult.

The difficulty of getting sinful people to fulfill their responsibilities was demonstrated at the very beginning when Cain, the eldest son of Adam and Eve, killed his innocent younger brother, Abel, in a fit of selfish jealousy and resentment. With this dark and murderous behavior establishing a pattern for Satanic dominion of the world, it would take many millennia of slow and painful progress—spearheaded by a series of Godly leaders, such as Noah, Abraham, Moses and the prophets—before a people capable of receiving a second Adam could be guided into forming a providential nation.

It is against this background that we must examine the significance of Israel's rejection of Jesus as the Messiah. Didn't the conspiracy to kill Jesus pursued by the religious and political leaders of Israel amount to a repetition of Cain's murder of Abel? If so, what impact did that have on Jesus' mission to replace Adam? Indeed, wasn't the crucifixion of Jesus the reason the Kingdom of Heaven on earth was not established by Jesus and remains a distant hope even today?

The Three Parts of This Book

The chapters of this book delve into the many issues related to the Divine Providence as described above. They are organized in three parts to help the reader recognize the three stages of the providence that are most pertinent to this narrative.

The first part looks at the significance of Jesus as the long-awaited Messiah of the Old Testament prophesies, but also as the fruit of a millennia-long process of spiritual evolution and enlightenment necessitated by the disobedience of Adam and Eve in the Garden of Eden. It examines the mission of Jesus as a 'second Adam' whose advent followed a prolonged period of preparation during which chosen individuals and tribes had to set certain conditions of obedience that reversed the disobedience of our first ancestors. Although these preparations were concentrated in Israel, they were part of a worldwide period of enlightenment.

The second part looks at the life of Jesus in terms of his mission to replace Adam and the responsibility of Israel to embrace and follow him as the Messiah. Here we look at the behavior of his immediate family and his close relatives in the family of John the Baptist, at the resistance of Israel's establishment leaders to the person and message of Jesus, and at the betrayal of those close to Jesus that paved the way to the cross.

The third part looks at the impact of the cruel treatment of Jesus by Israel and how this led to Israel's loss of its privileged position as the nation chosen to receive the Messiah. It traces the creation and evolution of Christianity, which inherited the mission to establish a new Israel to receive a second advent of Christ. It interprets major events, such as the emergence of Islam, Marxism and modern science, in the light of the providence and role of Christianity in the world today.

The Need to Complete the Biblical Narrative

The Divine Providence discussed in this book is the very root of life and our existence. It therefore precedes and transcends all scriptures and beliefs as well as all the human divisions, whether of religion, race or nationality. We are all God's children.

The Bible covers a central providence leading to the advent of Jesus, but it does not explain the providential role of other religions and spiritual movements, such as those that rose in Asia several centuries before Jesus. It also does not recognize the role of classical Greece with its discoveries that would form the foundations for Western Civilization and the development of science.

Finally, the Bible's narrative ends with the lives of the earliest followers of Jesus, notably the 12 disciples and the apostle Paul, leaving us without a scriptural basis for understanding the providence as it has developed over the past 2,000 years.

Thus in this book we have endeavored to supplement the Gospel narratives with a providential interpretation of Old and New Testament scriptures, and applied the same interpretive perspective to our discussion of the last two millennia of providential history.

PART I

PROVIDENTIAL PREPARATIONS FOR THE MESSIAH

Chapter 1

The Mission of the Messiah

Replacing Adam as God's Sinless Son

Adam and Eve and the Need for a Messiah

The Bible recounts the story of Adam and Eve being created as the first humans in the idyllic Garden of Eden. However, the story soon turned into a tragedy when they disobeyed the one rule given them and—in symbolic language—ate of the fruit of the Tree of the Knowledge of Good and Evil. This disobedience led to their alienation from the Creator and the establishment of a human lineage under the dominion of Satan who—as the archangel Lucifer—had tempted them into disobedience. This tragedy is called the Fall, and its effects were inherited in the fallen nature of humankind, a nature that all of us experience as an obstacle to living a virtuous life. It would soon manifest in Adam and Eve's family when their first son, Cain, in a fit of jealous rage killed his younger brother, Abel. The dominion of evil over good as represented by this murder represents the reality of the world under the influence of the Fall.

This account of the first family comes to us from pre-history yet it resonates with what we know about human nature and the long history of conflict and suffering that has dominated the human experience ever since. Yet against this miserable historical backdrop, the Bible tells a story of hope, of a Divine Providence that was frustrated by the Fall but is unchanging in its good purpose—the realization of a world in the image of the unchanging and perfect Creator.

As the Biblical story unfolds, pre-history becomes a history tracing the advances made by the providence. Thus while humanity has grown from a single family until people populate every region of the globe, multiplying in a seemingly random fashion, a central providence has continued to proceed towards the goal of replacing Adam and Eve with a man and woman capable of becoming one with God and fulfilling the original purpose for the creation. The hope of humanity lies in the success of this providence and the creation of a sinless world to replace the sinful world we inherited from the first family.

Major Biblical figures in this central providence included members of Noah's family; Abraham, Isaac and Jacob; Judah, Joseph, Moses, Aaron and Joshua; priests like Samuel; King David and prophets like Elijah, Isaiah and Jeremiah; Ezra the scribe and Nehemiah the governor of Jerusalem. The Second Adam that all these important leaders were preparing for is called the Messiah in Hebrew, a term the Jews used for the promised deliverer of Israel. (In the Greek language Septuagint version of the scriptures, the Messiah is referred to as Christ, or the anointed one.)

Divine Providence and Human Responsibility

The history of preparations for a Second Adam spans millennia. Why is this? Why couldn't an almighty God intervene in history at will? The answer lies in the very nature of the relationship between God and humankind, and the Divine principles that govern it. We humans are created with free will so that we have the potential to love and experience joy, which is the purpose for the creation and our existence in the first place. Free will comes with responsibility and therefore represents an endowment of co-creatorship with God. Used wisely, free will is the key for human beings to achieve their purpose and become one with the Creator, a state of being in which they can fulfill their potential for love with other people and nature.

It is because of free will and the shortcomings of human beings in fulfilling their God-given responsibilities that the historical process of the providence has been drawn out over so many centuries. God is a perfect being and therefore the Divine principles that govern the creation are likewise perfect. Indeed, our hope lies in this perfection since it guarantees the ultimate success of the providence because our Creator always accomplishes the full measure of Divine responsibility. However, it also means that the providence can advance only when we do our part. This is true for individuals as well as for families, societies and nations. The fallen nature inherited from Adam and Eve always makes this difficult—as we saw with Cain's inability to overcome his resentment and anger—and thus the providence has been postponed again and again because of the shortcomings and failures of the people chosen by God to advance the providence.

In the Fall we saw that free will was abused by Adam and Eve in disobedience to the Divine purpose and will, contravening the Divine principles. The result was catastrophic. As sinless beings, Adam and Eve had the nature to know God intimately and to respond fully to Divine love and law. In their disobedience, however, they were alienated from their Creator and lost the nature they needed to reach full maturity as God's children. Their children inherited this alienation and the world has suffered in spiritual darkness ever since.

The Nature and Mission of the Messiah in the Divine Providence

The Messiah replaces Adam as a sinless son of the Creator. Endowed with Adam's original purity, he is able to reverse the mistakes of Adam, raise a bride in the place of Eve, establish a sinless family, and serve as the savior of all humankind. But in a world in which evil is dominant, none of these accomplishments comes without his personal investment of blood, sweat and tears. One way to look at his work is to compare the Messiah to a heavenly farmer who comes to earth to plant the seeds of the Kingdom of Heaven, the world that embodies the nature of the original, sinless creation. For the farmer to reap a harvest, the soil must be fertile and well watered. The fertile soil is the hearts and minds of the people chosen for the providence, and they are watered by the truth of creation and the providence, which is revealed most fully by the Messiah.

Thus the hope for humanity that is embedded in the providence finds its fulfillment in the advent of the Messiah and the creation of the Kingdom of Heaven. Preparing the ground for his arrival was the work of providential individuals, families, tribes and nations, down through history, a providential history prolonged because of all the shortcomings of those chosen for that mission. Thus while the mission of the Messiah is to restore the mistakes of Adam and create the Kingdom of Heaven on earth, the mission of those sent to prepare the way for the Messiah is to assure his success so that all can enjoy the benefits of a Godly world.

Ending the Dominion of Evil and Sin

We live in a world dominated by sin, making it difficult to imagine any other reality. Yet if we believe the Creator to be absolutely good in nature and unchanging in purpose we must also believe that our destiny is likewise unchangingly good. All sin is destructive and deadly in purpose, but it is also behavior that is inconsistent with the Divine principles of creation, and therefore not ultimately durable. This is a second reason to give us hope: evil has no foundation in truth and must therefore pass. The problem is that all people are born with a fallen nature which makes us incapable of recognizing clearly—and eliminating fully—the tendencies to evil that we are born with. Only a sinless person can recognize and do away with evil, which is why we need the Messiah.

Thus the most important mission of the Messiah is to overcome evil and liberate fallen humanity from the dominion of Satan, the source of all evil and sin. This is not a magical process in which fallen man is transformed into sinless man by simply believing in the Messiah; it is a process of salvation through which fallen men and women unite with the Messiah by receiving his teaching, obeying his instructions, following his example and inheriting his nature. As a person fully at one with God, the Messiah fulfills his salvific responsibilities perfectly. He has the authority to dispense grace and forgiveness of sins so that if we do our part, we can truly be liberated from our sinful nature and follow the Messiah into the ideal world of the Kingdom of Heaven.

The Mission of Israel

The principles by which God made and governs all people require our free exercise of choice in accordance with Divine Providence if we are to fulfill our original purpose in a world under the dominion of God. The Creator does not impose Divine will on human beings. Thus the success of the mission of Jesus as Messiah was in the hands of the Jews of Israel. It was their responsibility to use their knowledge of the Mosaic Law and the words of the prophets to recognize and follow Christ. God would not violate the Divine principles that govern the creation and recreation of human beings to impose on Israel the messianic providence centered on Jesus.

Among the main providential people who had laid the foundation for Israel to receive the Messiah were members of Noah's family, Abraham's family, Moses, the prophets and others. When Jesus came, he explained his mission to the Jews in terms of their existing beliefs. But he also made it clear that their understanding of the Mosaic Law was insufficient; that they needed a much deeper conception of their Heavenly Father and the Divine Providence if they were to fulfill their responsibilities as chosen people and receive the blessings of salvation.

Nevertheless, it was almost impossible for a sinful person living in an evil-dominated world to recognize, accept and follow the sinless Messiah, which is why the preparation of Israel to receive the chosen one had been so long drawn out and painstaking. This also explains why so few of the Israelites did understand and follow Jesus when he came, while the religious and political establishments rejected him altogether, and finally had him killed.

Israel's Notion of Salvation Through the Messiah

For the people of Israel, the Messiah was expected as someone who would save them from their enemies, a kingly figure who would inherit the throne of David, drive away their many foes, and usher in a new era of peace. The advent of this savior was foretold by some of their major prophets:

> For to us a child is born, to us a son is given; and the government will be upon his shoulder, and his name will be called "Wonderful Counselor, Mighty God, Everlasting Father, Prince of Peace." Of the increase of his government and of peace there will be no end, upon the throne of David, and over his kingdom, to establish it, and to uphold it with justice and with righteousness from this time forth and for evermore. The zeal of the Lord of hosts will do this. (Isaiah 9:6-7)

In the long history of the Jewish people, the descendants of Jacob, David was the first successful ruler of a United Kingdom of Israel, and his son, Solomon, would see Israel's wealth and power reach its zenith. On Solomon's death, however, the kingdom was divided, north and south, and idolatry would eventually lead to the destruction of both: the Northern Kingdom of Israel was conquered by the Assyrians and its ten tribes scattered, while the Southern Kingdom of Judah was overrun by Nebuchadnezzar II. Jerusalem and the Temple were destroyed and the people of Judah were taken into exile in Babylon. The hopes of Israel were crushed:

> How lonely sits the city that was full of people! How like a widow has she become, she that was great among the nations! She that was a princess among the cities has become a vassal. She weeps bitterly in the night, tears on her cheeks; among all her lovers she has none to comfort her; all her friends have dealt treacherously with her, they have become her enemies. (Lamentations 1:1-2)

But liberation would come to the Jews in captivity and they were permitted to return to Jerusalem where the walls and the Temple were rebuilt. The last prophet of Israel before Jesus was Malachi, and he foretold the coming of the Messiah as a messenger who would purify the priesthood and restore Jerusalem to its blessed status:

> Behold, I send my messenger to prepare the way before me, and the Lord whom you seek will suddenly come to his temple; the messenger of the covenant in whom you delight, behold, he is coming, says the Lord of hosts. But who can endure the day of his coming, and who can stand when he appears? For he is like a refiner's fire and like fullers' soap; he will sit as a refiner and purifier of silver, and he will purify the sons of Levi and refine them like gold and silver, till they present right offerings to the Lord. Then the offering of Judah and Jerusalem will be pleasing to the Lord as in the days of old and as in former years. (Malachi 3:1-4)

> For I the Lord do not change; therefore you, O sons of Jacob, are not consumed. From the days of your fathers you have turned aside from my statutes and have not kept them. Return to me, and I will return to you, says the Lord of hosts. (Malachi 3:6-7)

However, there were conditions the people of Israel would have to fulfill for the Messiah to be able to complete his mission. The Levites would have to submit to the purification of the messenger and the Israelites would have to return to God if they wanted God to return to them. If they did, theirs would once more be a blessed nation:

> Then all nations will call you blessed, for you will be a land of delight, says the Lord of hosts. (Malachi 3:12)

The Christian Notion of Salvation Through the Messiah

For most Christians the purpose of the Messiah was not to restore Israel to the glory of David's era, but to sacrifice his life on behalf of fallen humanity so that all people can be free from sin and assured a place in the Kingdom of Heaven. They point to passages like the following in Isaiah that seem to suggest a path of suffering was necessary for Christ:

> He was despised and rejected by men; a man of sorrows, and acquainted with grief; and as one from whom men hide their faces he was despised, and we esteemed him not. Surely he has

> borne our griefs and carried our sorrows; yet we esteemed him stricken, smitten by God, and afflicted. But he was wounded for our transgressions, he was bruised for our iniquities; upon him was the chastisement that made us whole, and with his stripes we are healed. (Isaiah 53:3-5)

This prophesy might be interpreted to mean that since we are healed through the suffering of Christ, he had to die on the cross to save us from our sins. However, this interpretation of its meaning ignores the providential purpose of Jesus: replacing Adam as the sinless son of God. Saint Paul discussed this providential purpose in detail:

> Therefore as sin came into the world through one man and death through sin, and so death spread to all men because all men sinned—sin indeed was in the world before the law was given, but sin is not counted where there is no law. Yet death reigned from Adam to Moses, even over those whose sins were not like the transgression of Adam, who was a type of the one who was to come. But the free gift is not like the trespass. For if many died through one man's trespass, much more have the grace of God and the free gift in the grace of that one man Jesus Christ abounded for many. And the free gift is not like the effect of that one man's sin. For the judgment following one trespass brought condemnation, but the free gift following many trespasses brings justification. If, because of one man's trespass, death reigned through that one man, much more will those who receive the abundance of grace and the free gift of righteousness reign in life through the one man Jesus Christ. (Romans 5:12-19)

And Paul summed up Jesus' mission as a second Adam:

> For as in Adam all die, so in Christ all will be made alive. (I Corinthians 15:22)

So Jesus was the second Adam, a man who replaced the first man as the fountainhead of a pure, Godly lineage, free from the dominion of Satan.

As such Jesus not only inherited the original, sinless nature of Adam, but also Adam's mission to be an obedient son of God. This meant Jesus had to replace Adam as a sinless man, reverse the disobedience of Adam and overcome the temptations of Satan. This was the extremely difficult task Jesus had to fulfill to qualify as the Messiah. Second, he had to win over the people of Israel to accept and support him in his mission so that Israel could fulfill its providential mission in the plan for salvation of the world. Very few of the Israelites did accept Jesus and, as we will demonstrate, his rejection by Israel would have far-reaching negative consequences.

Messianic Expectations and Jesus
Jesus did not start his life as a victorious Messiah, but as a son of a carpenter's family that lived in Nazareth, a modest town in the Galilee region of Israel. Starting out from this humble beginning he was faced with the monumental task of winning over Israel for the providence. The key people responsible for helping him included his family, John the Baptist, his disciples and Israel's religious and political establishments. Looking back at that time from the perspective of a believer in Christ today, one would assume that those who knew Jesus would have gladly given up their own lives to follow him, and that Israel would have willingly united with him to fulfill its destiny as the chosen nation.

But it was not so. We will show that the key people and institutions who were to receive and support Jesus all failed to fulfill their responsibilities. Jesus was left to fend for himself against a hostile Jewish establishment. His death was not the joyful fulfillment of centuries of Divine preparation, but a repetition of Cain killing Abel, as we will explain in the next chapter.

Christians believe that Jesus was the Messiah and that they have now replaced the Jewish people as those blessed to be the first to receive salvation. However, they need to understand that if this belief is to be realized they must avoid making the same mistake as the Jews did in taking their privileged position as a chosen people for granted. Over the 2,000 years since Jesus walked the earth Christians have enjoyed the blessings of the salvation they receive from Jesus' sacrifice on the cross. But they have not overcome their own sin nor managed to rid the world of evil. The mission of the Messiah has yet to be fulfilled.

Chapter 2

The Cain-Abel Paradigm

The Key to Understanding Providential History

The First Family

The story of the first family comes to us from beyond the limits of historical records. As such its value lies not in its literal accuracy but in the truth it reveals about creation, the nature of man and woman, and the reason for human alienation from the Creator. It is a depiction of the starting point for the Divine Providence that has unfolded over the course of human existence. As such, we can learn from it the manner in which the Creator works to reverse the alienation of humankind so as to recreate a sinless family as a new starting point for a human lineage that is free from the corruption of evil.

We know from Genesis that the human race emerged from the first family deeply infected with evil and that therefore something catastrophically bad must have occurred in the Garden of Eden. Instead of growing up to embody the image of God, our ancestors came to exhibit the characteristics of the rebellious, predatory and murderous archangel Lucifer, subsequently known as Satan. The first family was plunged into spiritual darkness and their children, Cain and Abel, became the archetypes of the nature of fallen humanity. We need to unravel the mystery of this tragedy that took place at the dawn of our existence in order to understand how God has been working to reverse its consequences and save humanity from the dominion of Satan.

The origin of evil is explained in Genesis as occurring when Eve was tempted by Lucifer into disobeying God's instruction to Adam and Eve:

> You may freely eat of every tree of the garden; but of the tree of the knowledge of good and evil you shall not eat, for in the day that you eat of it you shall die. (Genesis 2:16-17)

Lucifer was in the position of an angelic servant to the children as they grew to maturity. Although trusted by God, he evidently envied Adam, wanting Eve for himself. He abandoned his rightful position when he tempted Eve to "eat of the tree", in other words seducing her into an unprincipled sexual relationship. As a rebellious creature, Lucifer became Satan by taking advantage of Eve's youth and innocence with the first lie—the promise that eating the fruit would give her Divine knowledge:

> Now the serpent was more subtle than any other wild creature that the Lord God had made. He said to the woman, "Did God say, 'You shall not eat of any tree of the garden'?" And the woman said to the serpent, "We may eat of the fruit of the trees of the garden; but God said, 'You shall not eat of the fruit of the tree which is in the midst of the garden, neither shall you touch it, lest you die.'" But the serpent said to the woman, "You will not die. For God knows that when you eat of it your eyes will be opened, and you will be like God, knowing good and evil." (Genesis 3:1-5)

Eve did not become God-like. Instead, she lost her relationship with her Creator. She then turned to Adam for succor, seducing him into a sexual relationship that was premature and which plunged them into the darkness of fallen nature. They were now ashamed of themselves and sought to hide from their Creator. They had lost their position as the first, sinless children of God, and they were now unable to raise children as part of a Godly family.

Thus evil entered the world in the form of selfish sexual desire channeled into predatory behavior towards an innocent victim who was deceived into disobedience by the first lie.

Cain and Abel Inherited Fallen Nature

The children of Adam and Eve were doomed to inherit this evil from their parents. They too were in spiritual darkness, but to differing degrees. The elder son, Cain, inherited the primary burden of his parents' legacy of disobedience, while the second son, Abel, was endowed with a nature better able to understand and respond to the Creator. This relative difference in goodness between them was the means by which God could work to separate evil from good and use Abel's better nature to enlighten Cain so that together they could overcome evil.

The difference between them became evident when they were called to make sacrifices. Cain's offering was rejected by God, while Abel's was accepted. As the letter to Hebrews explains:

> By faith Abel offered to God a more acceptable sacrifice than Cain, through which he received approval as righteous, God bearing witness by accepting his gifts; he died, but through his faith he is still speaking. (Hebrews 11:4)

Cain was filled with Luciferian jealousy towards Abel. He resented his rejection, blaming his circumstances for his situation and, eventually, murdering his brother to 'get even'. This was a repetition of Lucifer's spiritual murder of Adam and Eve. But it did nothing to improve the situation for Cain. In fact it made the situation for Cain worse, since he was burdened with guilt and exiled from his own family. Fallen nature was planted more deeply into human lineage and the third son, Seth, was chosen to take the place of Abel in the providence. It would be many centuries before a new central family could be chosen out of Seth's lineage, that of Noah.

The Cain-Abel Paradigm

Thus Cain and Abel became the archetypes of evil and good, respectively. Over time, the Cain-type character would emerge as unfaithful, selfish, irresponsible, predatory, unjust and murderous. By contrast, Abel would emerge as faithful, unselfish, responsible, sacrificial, just and willing to give up his life to defeat evil and save Cain.

As the better brother, Abel represented the hope of eventually restoring human beings to their rightful position as sinless children of the Creator. In other words, the character and behavior of Abel provides a path that the Divine Providence takes towards the fulfillment of its ultimate purpose: a world at one with the Creator.

One way to look at this process is that Abel's task is to restore the position of the elder son as God's representative in the family, the descendant who is qualified to be the parent of a Godly lineage. As such, Abel works to restore man to the position of Adam before the fall. This is the path of salvation. As we shall see, Jesus labored as the first perfect Abel to enlighten the people of Israel, his Cain, so that they could accept him as the Second Adam, the Messiah.

Cain's Falsehoods Precede Abel's Truths in the Providence

The first family demonstrated the pattern of the elder son being most influenced by Satan, based on his parents having shown a preference for Lucifer over God. As the first fruit of the illicit union of Adam and Eve, Cain was claimed by Satan. There is a limit to what Satan can take from God and thus Satan's claim on Cain enabled God to claim Abel for the providence. This meant that as the younger brother Abel could enjoy a closer relationship with God than Cain.

The first family was established, then, under the dominant influence of Lucifer, or Satan. In a world under the dominion of Satan, the appearance of Cain and a false, Cain-type facsimile of God's purpose and ideal typically precedes the appearance of Abel with a true representation of God's purpose and ideal. This pattern is repeated: a Cain-type person appears before their Abel counterpart; a Cain-type family appears before its Abel-type counterpart; a Cain-type tribe appears before its Abel-type counterpart; and a

Cain-type nation appears before its Abel-type counterpart. The same pattern applies in all aspects of life, including ideologies, political and economic systems and types of government.

Thus the false appears before the true, seeking to deceive people and lead them astray in an effort to prevent them from recognizing and following Abel, God's true representative. We will see this pattern repeated again and again as we trace the path of the Divine Providence.

Cain Can and Should Become Abel

Cain and Abel represent relative positions of evil and good, respectively. As such they can change—Cain can become Abel and Abel can become Cain. Indeed, the purpose of salvation is for everyone to become Abel-like. The Cain-Abel paradigm that we are discussing here is based on the events that unfolded in the first family and which established a pattern of evil dominating good. To reverse this inherited status quo, Abel has to help Cain become Abel-like.

Thus it is through the externalization of the struggle between good and evil that manifests in the Cain-Abel paradigm that a way is opened to achieve internal purification. All of us are burdened with Cain-type natures that must be overcome by our Abel-type natures if we are to become Abel-type figures in the world. However, the way we become Abel-type individuals is through learning to practice Abel-type behavior towards our family members, people in our community and our nation.

Thus internal change towards good is developed through practicing goodness towards others, and the practice of goodness towards others is made possible through the development of a good character. Put a little differently, the practice of goodness is essential for the development of a good character, and a good character is essential for the practice of goodness. Spiritual growth comes from the give and take between these internal and external developmental processes.

In providential history there are some examples of Cain becoming Abel. For example, when Ham, the second son of Noah, demonstrated his faithlessness in the matter of Noah's drunkenness, he lost his Abel position to his elder brother Shem, who had been in the Cain position but consequently became the Abel ancestor of the providence, a position confirmed when Abraham was born in his lineage.

Most of us are not part of a central providence, but all of us have an original nature that is in the image of God and which functions as our internal Abel through conscience. It struggles with its Cain counterpart, our fallen nature, so it must be strengthened so that it can become dominant within us. Thus the purpose of our life is to strengthen our Abel-type nature and make it dominant over our Cain-type nature.

This process is at the heart of becoming a spiritually mature, Abel-type person in the world, a person who can respond to the Divine Providence and the Abel-type figures sent to lead it, and can contribute to liberating humanity from the Satanic curse of fallen nature. Most important, it prepares us to meet and follow the absolute Abel, who is Christ, the savior, so that we can become part of the salvific providence centered on Christ. The Cain-Abel paradigm shows the way for us to accomplish this.

The Importance of Personal Responsibility

The hallmark of Abel-type behavior is taking responsibility. Why is this so important? Lucifer, Eve and Adam all failed to fulfill their responsibilities. They did not do what they were created to do, but rather chose to follow the path of self-indulgence and self-gratification, in disobedience to their Creator. The result was a world of suffering distant from God.

As any parent can understand, the loss of children is cause for the greatest pain, and thus we need to recognize that behind the providence there is a Heavenly Parent wanting above all else to see their children saved from misery and death. However, as we experience in our families, the children always have their own responsibility to do what is right. The parents can only educate and encourage, they cannot take the place of their children and do what is right on behalf of their children. This is an immutable principle of the creation.

Both Cain and Abel have responsibilities before God. Thus while God uses Abel to bring the truth to humankind and to lead the way in doing good, Cain's responsibility is to overcome his natural envy and bitterness towards Abel and to accept and support his brother. When they both fulfill their responsibilities, the providence advances. As history shows, when Abel wins, everybody wins, including Cain as well as Abel, but when Cain wins, everybody loses, including Cain.

Jesus' Mission as Absolute Abel

As the providence advances through the reconciliation of Cain and Abel on Abel's terms, it also expands. Thus it starts with individuals, then includes families and tribes, and finally reaches the national level. The goal is to prepare the way for a national Abel who can then make his nation a global Abel.

This is a way to understand Jesus. He came on the foundation of victories by Abel as described in the Old Testament. Before him there had been many Abel-type figures in Israel (notably the virtuous judges, kings and prophets), but he was the first Abel-type person who was sinless and therefore exemplified an absolute, perfect standard of virtue.

The difficult course of his life can best be understood as a contest between Jesus and the Cain-type forces arrayed against him in Israel. The outcome was not the establishment of the Kingdom of Heaven on earth awaited by the chosen people, but the murder of Jesus by those he came to save, the creation of a new religion, Christianity, and the subsequent destruction of Israel itself.

Thus salvation through Christ comes from his spiritual victory over Satan, represented by the Cain-type forces of Israel. Evil was not driven from the world and the Cain-Abel paradigm has continued to operate throughout the centuries that followed his death. This history will be examined in detail later in this book.

Chapter 3

Jesus: God or Man?

Addressing Christological Confusion

An Age-Old Question Divides Christians

Who was the historical Jesus? Was he God incarnate? Was he part God, part man? Was he 'just' a man? The identity of Jesus has puzzled and often divided Christians. It has also been a central point of contention between Christianity, on the one hand, and Judaism and Islam on the other. After all, the Jews were not expecting to be saved by God, but by a man, the Messiah. And Muslims recognize only one, invisible God, who cannot be incarnated and cannot be divided.

The Gospels tell of a man who was born to a woman, Mary, and grew through boyhood until he started his public mission at the age of 30. Like all other humans, he got tired, thirsty and hungry. At the last supper he shared a meal with his disciples, and later that night wept as he cried out in prayer to his invisible, Divine Father. When he was beaten, he bled, and when the weight of the cross was too heavy for him to carry to his place of crucifixion someone else had to carry it for him. Finally, when crucified and pierced through his side with a spear by the Romans, he died an agonizing death.

The greatness of Jesus lies in the fact that he was and is a man, albeit a man of unique purity and goodness who was able to overcome all the temptations and attacks from a hostile nation without losing his faith and devotion to God. And because he has always been a man and lived as a man, through his example all human beings have the hope of attaining a similar state of grace and unity with our Creator.

Yet the Gospels and Acts of the Apostles also describe Jesus as someone who appeared after his crucifixion, who walked and talked with his core disciples, and ate a meal with them. One of his disciples, Thomas, was allowed to touch Jesus' crucifixion-inflicted wounds, to confirm that it was indeed Jesus. How could this be if Jesus was an ordinary man who had just died?

The true nature of Christ is not only of importance to Christians today, it has been the cause of confusion and divisions in the church almost from the outset. Early church fathers debated the nature of Jesus as well as that of his mother Mary. After all, if Jesus was God, wouldn't that make Mary the mother of God? These issues were of primary importance to the early church councils, which began in Nicaea in 325 AD.

The church sought to adopt a unified theology by issuing statements of faith on behalf of its councils. The first such statement is called the Nicene Creed. Other councils would follow and serve as major markers in the progress of Christian theology. Very often, theological dogmas were debated and adjusted at these councils. Major early councils after Nicaea were held at places like Constantinople, Ephesus and Chalcedon. Later, the Roman Catholic Church used councils to convict heretics—for example, John Hus was sentenced to burn at the stake at the Council of Constance. They were also used to initiate reforms—the Counter-Reformation was initiated at the Council of Trent.

The Holy Trinity

In response to challenges from some of the earliest branches of Christianity, such as Gnosticism, Manicheism and Nestorianism, the mainstream church leaders developed the concept of a Holy Trinity, enshrining it in official doctrine.

The term "Trinity" does not appear in the Bible, neither is there a trinitarian theological construct presented in scriptures. It is simply a church invention created to explain what has always been a mystery. The church fathers tried to explain the existence of a "Godhead" comprised of three "persons": the Father, Son and Holy Spirit. And while these three persons are discreet, with separate functions, they form part of a single whole (a relationship sometimes described as three in one and one in three).

As the Catholic Catechism puts it:

> The Trinity is One. We do not confess three Gods, but one God in three persons, the "consubstantial Trinity". The divine persons do not share the one divinity among themselves but each of them is God whole and entire: "The Father is that which the Son is, the Son that which the Father is, the Father and the Son that which the Holy Spirit is, i.e. by nature one God."[1]

It's not clear how this statement is a clarification. It seems to say that although there are differences among the three persons of the Trinity, actually there aren't. Truthfully, the concept of the Trinity does not help dispel the mystery of the relationship among God, Jesus and the Holy Spirit; it actually deepens it by confusing the discreet identity and purpose of each. The logical explanation is that God is the Creator Parent, or Father, Jesus the perfected human son in the place of fallen Adam, and the Holy Spirit is the manifestation of the Creator's spirit working in human affairs to advance the providence, in particular representing the motherly heart of God.

A sinless man embodies the image of the Creator, but is not the Creator. Thus perfected humans embody attributes of the Divine but are not God. Which is why Jesus is so important in the Divine Providence, since he was the first person after the Fall of Adam and Eve to be born sinless and therefore capable of living a morally perfect life. It had taken thousands of years of enlightenment and painstaking spiritual growth for a suitable environment to be created for Jesus, whose mission was to restore the mistakes made by another man, Adam.

---

1. Catholic Catechism Paragraph 253, Quoting the Council of Toledo XI.

Thus while the Trinitarian concept is intended to help unify theological belief among Christians, differences in the interpretation of its meaning have often been at the heart of long-lasting and sometimes bitter disputes. For example, it was just such a disagreement over the Trinity that provided the theological basis for the Great Schism in 1054. The Eastern Orthodox Churches believed that the Holy Spirit was an emanation of God alone while the Western Catholic Church believed in what is called the Filioque: the notion that the Holy Spirit is an emanation of both Father and Son.

How Can We Resolve This Confusion?

If the concept of a Holy Trinity only adds to confusion about the true identity of Jesus, how can we best resolve that confusion? There are several scripture-based perspectives that shed a great deal of light on Christology, including words spoken by God about Jesus, words spoken by Satan about him, words spoken by angels to Mary and Joseph about him, words spoken by Old Testament prophets about him, words spoken by Jesus' disciples about him, and words Jesus used to describe himself. All of these words simply confirm that Jesus was a man, the son of God. However, he was no ordinary man. His character and mission were unique in history.

Most important, we have the perspective of Divine Providence, which makes clear that the failings of Adam had to be 'paid for' and reversed by another man. This is where we will start.

A Providential Perspective

The identity and purpose of Jesus come into sharp and unequivocal focus when viewed through the lens of Divine Providence.

First: God is the sole Creator of the universe, who made humankind in the Divine image. Thus while the creation, and human beings in particular, embody the image of the Creator, there is always a clear distinction between them.

Second: Jesus came as a man to restore the position of Adam as the sinless man created as a 'child' of the Creator. Only a perfectly moral man could replace the original, sinless Adam.

Third: The advent of Jesus was not a random event. It was the culmination of a millennia-long process of purification and enlightenment that began in Adam's family after the Fall, and led to creation of the necessary conditions for Jesus to be born with the mission to restore Adam.

This explains why the life of Jesus was so difficult. Despite his purity and goodness, as with all Abel-type figures before him, he had to overcome a host of difficulties in order to accomplish his mission. To restore the fallen Adam, Jesus had to reverse the disobedience of Adam and obey God, whatever the personal cost. By doing so, he showed the way for all people to separate from Satan and become one with God.

When looked at from this viewpoint, Jesus is clearly a man, albeit a uniquely moral man. Scriptures support this conclusion.

Jesus In the Words of God

Nowhere in the Bible is God reported to have said that Jesus was also God. Indeed, the only words about Jesus attributed to the Creator in the New Testament identify Jesus as the beloved son of God. This occurs twice: once when John baptized Jesus and a second time after Jesus met Moses and Elijah in spirit.

At the baptism of Jesus by John, God's voice is heard:

> And lo, a voice from heaven, saying, "This is my beloved Son, with whom I am well pleased." (Matthew 3:17)

And again, on a later occasion, after Jesus met Moses and Elijah on the Mount of Transfiguration, Peter asked Jesus if he and the other two disciples with him, James and John, should make shelters for Jesus, Moses and Elijah. At that moment God manifested and told the disciples who Jesus was:

> [Peter] was still speaking, when lo, a bright cloud overshadowed them, and a voice from the cloud said, "This is my beloved Son, with whom I am well pleased; listen to him." (Matthew 17:5)

As the son of God Jesus was endowed with Divine characteristics that enabled him to have a profound union with the Creator. This made him a true man, not God. Children inherit their nature from their parents, and thus human beings are 'children of God' since they were made in the image of the Divine:

> So God created man in his own image, in the image of God he created him; male and female he created them. (Genesis 1:27)

As descendants of Adam and Eve we too inherit the image of God as our original nature:

> I say, "You are gods, sons of the Most High, all of you; nevertheless, you shall die like men, and fall like any prince." (Psalm 82:6-7)

When God called Jesus "beloved son" it confirmed that Jesus had fulfilled the responsibility originally given to Adam and Eve. Thus Jesus was the first true son of God.

Jesus In the Words of Satan

Even Satan testified to the identity of Jesus as the son of God. When Jesus was fasting for 40 days, Satan tempted him:

> And the tempter came and said to him, "If you are the Son of God, command these stones to become loaves of bread." (Matthew 4:3)

And again:

> Then the devil took him to the holy city, and set him on the pinnacle of the temple, and said to him, "If you are the Son of God, throw yourself down; for it is written, 'He will give his angels charge of you,' and 'On their hands they will bear you up, lest you strike your foot against a stone.'" (Matthew 4:5-6)

Frequently when Jesus confronted a person possessed by a demon, the demon would identify Jesus as the son of God:

> Whenever the impure spirits saw him, they fell down before him and cried out, "You are the Son of God." (Mark 3:11)

Jesus In the Words of Angels

The Bible recounts how Mary was told that her son would be a great man:

> And the angel said to her, "Do not be afraid, Mary, for you have found favor with God. And behold, you will conceive in your womb and bear a son, and you shall call his name Jesus. He will be great, and will be called the Son of the Most High; and the Lord God will give to him the throne of his father David, and he will reign over the house of Jacob for ever; and of his kingdom there will be no end." (Luke 1:30-33)

Later, when Mary's husband Joseph questioned her pregnancy, an angel reassured him:

> But as he considered this, behold, an angel of the Lord appeared to him in a dream, saying, "Joseph, son of David, do not fear to take Mary your wife, for that which is conceived in her is of the Holy Spirit; she will bear a son, and you shall call his name Jesus, for he will save his people from their sins." (Matthew 1:20-21)

Jesus In the Words of Old Testament Prophets

There are a number of prophecies in the Old Testament that are generally interpreted by Christians to anticipate the coming of Jesus. Although none of them explicitly refer to a figure with the name of Jesus, or even to a person whose life was essentially the same as that of Jesus, this is nevertheless a central element of Christian faith. Christians believe that Jesus fulfilled Old Testament references to a much-awaited Messiah, the Hebrew term for a savior king who would sit on the throne of David in the messianic age.

If Christians are correct in identifying Jesus as the fulfillment of Messianic expectations, this only strengthens our contention that Jesus was clearly a man, albeit a man anointed by God to rule Israel. Indeed, to be anointed by God means you are a creation of God, and not God.

Furthermore, the passages believed by Christians to anticipate Jesus clearly identify him as a man. Some anticipate the savior as a great king who sits on David's throne; others as a man of suffering. In both cases, the scriptures are about a man:

> But you, O Bethlehem Ephrathah, who are little to be among the clans of Judah, from you shall come forth for me one who is to be ruler in Israel, whose origin is from of old, from ancient days… And he shall stand and feed his flock in the strength of the LORD, in the majesty of the name of the LORD his God. And they shall dwell secure, for now he shall be great to the ends of the earth. (Micah 5:2-4)

> For to us a child is born, to us a son is given; and the government will be upon his shoulder, and his name will be called "Wonderful Counselor, Mighty God, Everlasting Father, Prince of Peace." Of the increase of his government and of peace there will be no end, upon the throne of David, and over his kingdom, to establish it, and to uphold it with justice and with righteousness from this time forth and for evermore. (Isaiah 9:6-7)

> He was despised and rejected by men; a man of sorrows, and acquainted with grief; and as one from whom men hide their faces he was despised, and we esteemed him not. Surely he has borne our griefs and carried our sorrows; yet we esteemed him stricken, smitten by God, and afflicted. (Isaiah 53:3-4)

Thus whether you believe Jesus came to rule Israel from David's throne or to die on the cross to save us from sin, the prophecies anticipating the Messiah refer to a man and not God.

Jesus In the Words of his Disciples

The closest disciples of Jesus recognized him as the son of God. When Jesus asked his disciples to tell him who they thought he was, his most important disciple, Simon Peter, said:

> You are the Christ, the Son of the living God. (Matthew 16:16)

Much of John's Gospel is devoted to explaining the relationship between God, the Father, and Jesus, the son. In the penultimate chapter of his Gospel, John explains his purpose for writing it:

> Now Jesus did many other signs in the presence of the disciples, which are not written in this book; but these are written that you may believe that Jesus is the Christ, the Son of God, and that believing you may have life in his name. (John 20:30-31)

At Pentecost, 50 days after the crucifixion, Saint Peter told a crowd in Jerusalem:

> Men of Israel, hear these words: Jesus of Nazareth, a man attested to you by God with mighty works and wonders and signs which God did through him in your midst, as you yourselves know—this Jesus, delivered up according to the definite plan and foreknowledge of God, you crucified and killed by the hands of lawless men. (Acts 2:22-23)

And:

> Let all the house of Israel therefore know assuredly that God has made him both Lord and Christ, this Jesus whom you crucified. (Acts 2:36)

Saint Stephen, the first Christian martyr, explained the death of Jesus as just the latest in a long history of the Jewish people persecuting God's representatives:

> You stiff-necked people, uncircumcised in heart and ears, you always resist the Holy Spirit. As your fathers did, so do you. Which of the prophets did not your fathers persecute? And they killed those who announced beforehand the coming of the Righteous One, whom you have now betrayed and murdered, you who received the law as delivered by angels and did not keep it. (Acts:7:51-53)

Saint Paul discussed the nature of Jesus many times in his letters. In a letter to his own close disciple, Timothy, he put it most succinctly:

> For there is one God, and there is one mediator between God and men, the man Christ Jesus. (1 Timothy 2:5)

Paul also recognized that Jesus came as a man to restore the position of the first man, Adam:

> For as in Adam all die, so also in Christ shall all be made alive. (1 Corinthians 15:22)

And Paul said that through Jesus we can be adopted from our fallen lineage into the lineage of God, the pure lineage of original man:

> But when the set time had fully come, God sent his Son, born of a woman, born under the law, to redeem those under the law, that we might receive adoption to sonship. (Galatians 4:4-5)

Jesus In his Own Words

At no point did Jesus claim to be God. On the contrary, he made it clear that he was not God. Here are some relevant passages from the gospels.

> And as he was setting out on his journey, a man ran up and knelt before him, and asked him, "Good Teacher, what must I do to inherit eternal life?" And Jesus said to him, "Why do you call me good? No one is good but God alone." (Mark 10:17-18)

When Philip asked Jesus to show the disciples the Father, Jesus explained that the invisible Creator was in effect made visible in Christ, the perfect image of the Father, and that he was acting on behalf of the Father:

> He who has seen me has seen the Father; how can you say, "Show us the Father"? Do you not believe that I am in the Father and the Father in me? The words that I say to you I do not speak on my own authority; but the Father who dwells in me does his works. Believe me that I am in the Father and the Father in me;

> or else believe me for the sake of the works themselves. (John 14:9-11)

Thus the way to the Father is through Jesus:

> Jesus said to him, "I am the way, and the truth, and the life; no one comes to the Father, but by me. If you had known me, you would have known my Father also; henceforth you know him and have seen him." (John 14:6)

And Jesus taught his disciples to pray to their Heavenly Father, not to him:

> Pray like this: Our Father who art in heaven, Hallowed be thy name. Thy kingdom come, Thy will be done, On earth as it is in heaven. (Matthew 6:9-10)

As his death drew near, Jesus prayed desperately in the Garden of Gethsemane to his Heavenly Father for a way forward that would not lead to the cross, but also accepting the will of God:

> And going a little farther he fell on his face and prayed, "My Father, if it be possible, let this cup pass from me; nevertheless, not as I will, but as thou wilt." (Matthew 26:39)

According to the Gospels of Mark and Matthew, on the cross Jesus cried out to his Father in anguish, repeating David's lament in the first line of Psalm 22:

> And about the ninth hour Jesus cried with a loud voice, "Eli, Eli, lama sabachthani?" that is, "My God, my God, why hast thou forsaken me?" (Matthew 27:46)

Like David, Jesus was a man. Unlike David, Jesus was without sin. Yet David would die in his sleep while Jesus died in the midst of immeasurable pain and suffering.

Jesus Had to be a Man

All of these scriptural references support the providential understanding of who Jesus was and is. He was anointed by God to replace the original man, Adam, who had been created in the image of the Divine but who had failed to fulfill his responsibility as a son of the Creator. Jesus had the nature of Adam before the Fall, but unlike all those who went before him in the providence, he fulfilled the responsibilities of a true son. This is why he was the way, the truth and the life, and continues in this role to this day.

Only a man can restore the failures of another man, and it was Jesus' struggle to restore the many Cain-type individuals and institutions that surrounded him that made him such a unique and great man. Jesus was not God, but he uniquely exemplified, and continues to exemplify, what a true, Godly man should be.

Chapter 4

Did Jesus Pre-Exist His Birth?

The Role of Predestination in the Providence

The Meaning of "the Word"

John's Gospel opens with a passage that has caused considerable confusion regarding the nature of Jesus:

> In the beginning was the Word, and the Word was with God, and the Word was God. He was in the beginning with God; all things were made through him, and without him was not anything made that was made. (John 1:1-3)

"Word" here is translated from the Greek word *logos*. This term is often taken by Christians to mean Christ. Thus some versions of the Bible substitute "Christ" for "Word" in translating logos, or offer notes explaining that "Word" in this passage means Christ or Jesus.[1] However, this is conflating two very different things: the Divine concept of a perfect embodiment of Godly nature as opposed to the historical person of Jesus.

Before creation there is logos, the conception of creation—ideation translated into being through the process of creation. Our Creator is omni-

---

1. At least one version of the New Testament, the Living Bible (TLB), replaces "Word" with "Christ". The New Life Version (NLV) puts "Christ" in parenthesis next to "Word". Many more include notes that offer the explanation that the author John meant Christ or Jesus when he used the term "Word". These versions include: ERV, EXB, Holman, ICB, NAB, NCB, NCV and NMB.

scient, omnipresent and omnipotent. These attributes of infinite being cannot exist in a finite being. Thus the genius of our creation is that men and women embody Divine nature to the maximum extent possible for finite beings. We cannot be God, but we can be the most perfect image of God that is possible. The rest of creation exists in the image of human beings and was created to provide an environment to sustain the life of humankind.

The original man and woman, Adam and Eve, were created with the potential to become the perfect, sinless embodiments of the image of God, the exquisite incarnation of the logos:

> So God created man in his own image, in the image of God he created him; male and female he created them. (Genesis 1:27)

Thus they could have become the children of God in the sense that in maturity they would have shared essential characteristics with the Creator and would have enjoyed an intimate relationship of love with the Creator. The society they would have established would have been heavenly and their relationship with the rest of the creation a model of good stewardship.

However, perfecting the image of God required Adam and Eve to exercise their free will in obedience to the instructions they were given by their Creator. As the Bible recounts, this they failed to do and consequently they became profoundly alienated from God, never achieving the status of true son and daughter of the Creator. For their descendants, the ideal of sinless man and woman living in a perfect world became little more than a figment of the imagination and the subject of myth.

Jesus Embodied the *Logos*

Yet despite the grievous consequences of the Fall of Adam and Eve, the image of our Creator remains imprinted on our original nature. It cries out to us through our conscience. It searches for a perfect man and woman, for an absolute Abel that can liberate us from our fallen nature. For the descendants of Abraham, that Abel figure became known as the Messiah, the man to save Israel from its enemies.

Jesus was born into this world as the Messiah, a new, sinless Adam who embodied the logos. John confirms this in his Gospel:

> And the Word became flesh and dwelt among us, full of grace and truth; we have beheld his glory, glory as of the only Son from the Father. (John 1:14)

The laws of the universe were not altered to accommodate Jesus' birth, and thus, like all men and women, he had a father and mother. He began life in Mary's womb and after his birth had to grow in maturity and wisdom to be able to fulfill his potential as the son of God and Messiah. Thus he only started his public mission at age 30 after gaining a deep understanding of the scriptures and the people of Israel. He needed an unrivaled wisdom to overcome the unprecedented difficulties he was faced with without compromising his purity or deviating from his Divinely mandated course.

When Israel ultimately rejected Jesus and had him put to death, his body was killed but his eternal sinless spirit entered the Spirit World—the destiny for all people. Thus the complete embodiment of logos that Adam and Eve were originally destined to fulfill was realized in the perfected spirit of Jesus, but its completion on earth was postponed. Many followers of Christ have had profound experiences with Jesus since his crucifixion, testifying to his ongoing providential spiritual ministry.

Predestination

This understanding of Jesus is reinforced by the principle of predestination, a concept that is often misunderstood. Predestination should be understood as the original purpose for creation. Thus all creation exists with a causal purpose to fulfill. This purpose is Divine and therefore immutable. The purpose of creation was always for a sinless man and woman to establish an ideal world on earth—the Kingdom of Heaven. Thus after the Fall of Adam and Eve this purpose was predestined to be fulfilled by another man and woman. The mission of Jesus was, then, to be a second, sinless Adam.

The Divine purpose encapsulated in the logos is unchanging, but after the Fall of Adam and Eve the time, place and manner of its realization have changed again and again as fallen nature has continued to stand in the way of the Divine Providence. If Adam and Eve had not fallen, there would have been no need for this providence, because the Divine purpose would have been fulfilled in the first family.

Predestination and Personal Responsibility

Many Christians—as well as many members of other faiths—believe that their lives are predestined. In other words, that their destiny is predetermined, good or bad, and therefore cannot be altered by anything they do. This is fundamentally erroneous, for two reasons. First, Divine purpose and the providence that flows from it are always for good only, since the Creator is only good. Second, the most basic law of creation is that human beings have a responsibility to participate in shaping their own destiny. Thus fatalism is fallacious.

The implication is that while the predestination of Divine Providence is absolute, its fulfillment is subject to our response to it. This has always been the case as we can see from the story of the first family. Adam and Eve were created sinless but through disobedience failed to create the ideal world purposed by God. The Messiah was to replace Adam but the success of his mission depended on his acceptance by Israel.

For us too, then, our predestined purpose to be part of the providence and the Kingdom of Heaven on earth does not guarantee a place in Heaven for us. Rather this providence represents an opportunity for us that can be realized based on two conditions. First, that the individuals predestined to establish the Kingdom receive the support necessary for them to succeed and, second, that we do our part in providing that support.

Being Responsible Requires Spiritual Maturity

A spiritually immature person is unable to fulfill the Divinely-mandated responsibilities of men and women. This was true in the Garden of Eden and has remained true until today. As the Biblical story indicates, Adam and Eve never reached full spiritual maturity before they used their bodies in disobedience to God, establishing the basic pattern of fallen behavior that we have all inherited. This fallen inheritance prevents us from attaining our own ultimate destiny as sons and daughters of God and necessitates the intercession of a sinless Messiah to establish the standard for a sinless life and to show us the way to achieve it.

We are all confronted with choices, throughout our lives. Becoming mature means learning to make the right choices, demonstrating the faith, commitment and responsibility of Abel rather than the faithlessness, resentment and irresponsibility of Cain. So long as we are dominated by Cain-type fallen nature we cannot become mature and fulfill our original purpose.

The essence of spiritual maturity is the dominance of 'mind over body', that is of the human spirit over the human body. However, it should be recognized that the body is the necessary counterpart to the spirit such that spiritual growth occurs as the body learns to conform to the direction it receives from the spirit, which in turn must learn to understand and follow Divine guidance. For sinless people, such as Adam and Eve before the Fall and Jesus, that guidance can be direct. For the rest of us with a fallen nature that is unable to know God fully, that guidance must come from a sinless intermediary, the Messiah. Jesus often spoke about his intimate relationship with God, such as in this passage in John's Gospel:

> Do you not believe that I am in the Father and the Father in me?
> The words that I say to you I do not speak on my own authority;
> but the Father who dwells in me does his works. (John 14:10)

Predestination After the Crucifixion

What then is the significance of Jesus' death on the cross from the viewpoint of predestination? First and foremost it meant that Jesus could not establish the Kingdom of Heaven. Because an ideal world was originally to be created by man and woman on earth, with the help of their bodies, its recreation by the Messiah also had to be created on earth first. When Jesus lamented his death on the cross at the hands of the people of Israel, he pleaded with God to forgive them for their ignorance. He was the only person who truly understood the consequences of this end to his life. Not only were the messianic expectations of Israel thwarted by his premature death, but the suffering of humanity as a whole was immeasurably increased.

Jesus himself pointed to the need for a Second Coming of Christ to complete the work of the Messiah, as we discuss in detail in the last chapter of this book. This means that the predestined purpose of the Messiah was not completed in Jesus' time, and has remained the unfulfilled goal of the providence after the crucifixion of Christ. It also implies that our personal destinies as children of God cannot yet be realized. The best we can do is follow Jesus in living sacrificially to prepare for a second coming of Christ and the eventual establishment of the Kingdom of Heaven on earth, thereby contributing to the ongoing Divine Providence.

Chapter 5

Jesus Embodied the Mosaic Law

The Transition From Servant to Son

The Law Prepared Israel for the Messiah

For all the goodness and virtue contained in the Mosaic Law, obedience to it alone could never achieve the realization of God's ideal on earth. Only men and women who embody the divinity of God can transform the world into the Kingdom of Heaven. Thus one way to understand the purpose of Jesus is that he came to reveal the deeper meanings of the law. The Israelites needed to understand that the laws they had received from Moses were not an end in themselves but a guide to living a Godly life in preparation for receiving, following and emulating the Messiah.

The relationship between Creator and creation is governed by Divine principles, but the Divine purpose for these principles is what shaped them. That purpose is the loving coexistence between God as parent and human beings as children. It is also the purpose behind the Divine Providence. Jesus taught, and demonstrated in his own life, that the application of Mosaic Law should be governed by this purpose. He was often criticized by Israel's religious establishment for violating the law, but he responded by providing a providential context for interpreting the law. For example, he responded this way when accused of violating the sabbath:

> One sabbath he was going through the grainfields; and as they made their way his disciples began to pluck heads of grain. And

the Pharisees said to him, "Look, why are they doing what is not lawful on the sabbath?" And he said to them, "Have you never read what David did, when he was in need and was hungry, he and those who were with him: how he entered the house of God, when Abiathar was high priest, and ate the bread of the Presence, which it is not lawful for any but the priests to eat, and also gave it to those who were with him?" And he said to them, "The sabbath was made for man, not man for the sabbath; so the Son of man is lord even of the sabbath." (Mark 2:23-28)

The Evolution of Divinely-Inspired Laws

The first law was given to Adam and Eve. They were told they could eat of any tree in the Garden of Eden except The Tree of the Knowledge of Good and Evil. If they had obeyed this restriction, they would have grown to maturity and a state of enlightenment and oneness with their Creator that would have precluded the need for a system of laws. Their failure to adhere to this single instruction resulted in their alienation from the Creator and descent into profound ignorance.

In this state of spiritual and intellectual darkness, our first ancestors were in no position to understand and follow Divine laws. Thus the scriptures describe God's interactions with humans beings as based on specific instructions to specific people and specific times.

Thus, for example, Cain and Abel were told to make offerings; Noah was told to build an Ark; Abraham was told to sacrifice animals, circumcise the males in his household, and then sacrifice his son Isaac. If obedient, these central figures in the providence would be given further instructions. This process continued until Moses was told to liberate the Hebrews from slavery in Egypt. Once he had led the 12 tribes with their 600,000 families out of Egypt, he ascended Mount Sinai, where he was given the Ten Commandments.

The First Legal System

The Ten Commandments were the basis for a system of laws to govern the Israelites as they prepared to enter Canaan and establish a nation to receive the Messiah. Thus from Sinai onwards, Jewish obedience to God went beyond following specific instructions, such as circumcision, to following what became known as the Mosaic Law. The Ten Commandments were supplemented by a host of laws stipulating proper attendance to the Tabernacle (and later the Temple), the role of the Levites in performing rituals, rules for moral behavior, and detailed punishments for various crimes—to be dispensed by the Levites. (Many of these rules are laid out in Leviticus.)

Thus obedience to the Mosaic Law became the foundation of Jewish faith and the basis for their justification before God. Pre-Mosaic practices, such as circumcision, were not discarded but incorporated into the system of laws and requirements of Judaism. The purpose of the law was to separate the chosen people from the rest of the fallen world so that they would be able to receive the sinless Messiah. Separating Noah's family through the flood had the same purpose. It had also been the purpose for circumcision, which represented purifying Abraham's family and lineage of the influence of the sexual sin that caused the Fall.

The limitations of the Mosaic Law were always evident. This was not due to a lack of severity in punishments which, for example, prescribed death for adultery:

> If a man commits adultery with the wife of his neighbor, both the adulterer and the adulteress shall be put to death. (Leviticus 20:10)

And death was the punishment for blasphemy and murder:

> He who blasphemes the name of the Lord shall be put to death; all the congregation shall stone him; the sojourner as well as the native, when he blasphemes the Name, shall be put to death. He who kills a man shall be put to death. (Leviticus 24:16-17)

The problem was the Israelites' resistance to the law. The scriptures describe how Moses constantly had to chastise his fellow Jews for their faithlessness and disobedience. They frequently demonstrated a lack of faith in the providence that was leading them to establish a new nation in Canaan; they craved the idols they had left behind in Egypt; and they failed to keep their lineage pure by marrying members of non-Jewish tribes. Once in Canaan, idolatry and intermarriage with non-Jews continued to delay the creation of a single nation to receive the messiah, and eventually led to the destruction of the kingdoms of Israel and Judah, the destruction of the Temple, and the Babylonian exile.

Although chastened by this catastrophe, on returning to Jerusalem the people once more engaged in idolatry and intermarriage. To purify them, the scribe Ezra read the scriptures and he and the governor, Nehemiah, made the people pledge to obey the law and purify their families by putting away any non-Jewish spouses. The reconstruction of Jerusalem and the Temple and the recommitment of the people to follow the law came some four centuries before Jesus, and were in preparation for his messianic mission.

The Radical Teachings of Jesus

In his Sermon on the Mount, Jesus explained that his mission was to fulfill the Law, not to do away with it:

> Think not that I have come to abolish the law and the prophets; I have come not to abolish them but to fulfil them. For truly, I say to you, till heaven and earth pass away, not an iota, not a dot, will pass from the law until all is accomplished. Whoever then relaxes one of the least of these commandments and teaches men so, shall be called least in the kingdom of heaven; but he who does them and teaches them shall be called great in the kingdom of heaven. For I tell you, unless your righteousness exceeds that of the scribes and Pharisees, you will never enter the kingdom of heaven. (Matthew 5:17-20)

Jesus clearly wanted the people to understand that he had not come to destroy the foundation of their faith as Jews, but rather to help them understand that the law fulfilled was very different from the law as practiced by the religious leaders of their time. This was a radical position that threatened the religious establishment. Instead of heeding Jesus and seeking his guidance as the Messiah, they remained entrenched in their beliefs and practices, and they worked to turn the people against him, eventually arranging for him to be executed by the Roman rulers.

After Jesus had been killed, Stephen, the first Christian martyr, condemned the Jews for failing to make the transition from faith in the Law to belief in Christ:

> You stiff-necked people! Your hearts and ears are still uncircumcised. You are just like your ancestors: You always resist the Holy Spirit! Was there ever a prophet your ancestors did not persecute? They even killed those who predicted the coming of the Righteous One. And now you have betrayed and murdered him—you who have received the law that was given through angels but have not obeyed it. (Acts 7:51-53)

After the Messiah appeared in Israel, the need to follow the Mosaic Law in preparation for the Messiah was superseded by the obligation to follow Jesus, the living embodiment of the law. Jesus not only understood the law itself better than the Jewish religious leaders, he understood what they could not fully know: its true intent. History had shown that the law alone was insufficient for creating a Godly nation, but Israel's leaders were nevertheless unwilling to abandon their positions of power and privilege to follow Jesus so that the Divine Providence could advance.

A New Understanding of Circumcision

The letters of Saint Paul and other early Christian leaders seek to explain the providential transition from the era of Mosaic Law, centered on the Tabernacle and Temple, to the era of Christ, centered on the person and life example of Jesus. This transition can perhaps best be understood through the change in meaning regarding circumcision, which under the law was a necessary condition for belonging to the chosen people and a physical marker of that identity. This change was necessitated by the broadening of the providence from its pre-Jesus focus on the descendants of Abraham to its post-crucifixion inclusion of any person on earth who accepted and followed Jesus.

An early decision on the matter of circumcision by the Christian leaders meeting in Jerusalem was made after Peter had been guided by a vision to convert Gentiles as well as Jews to the new faith. It was revealed to him that they were equally qualified to receive salvation, even though they were not circumcised. Out of this meeting a policy was established that specifically exempted Gentiles from the need to be circumcised as a condition for joining the new faith. (Acts 15:1-29)

For the apostle Paul this was a foundational principle for his evangelizing, which he carried out primarily among non-Jews. He pointed out that Abraham received the blessing of God and the promise that he would father nations before he was told to circumcise his household, implying that circumcision was not a precondition for God to bless Abraham and his offspring. Paul explained how the advent of Christ meant Gentiles could now share the blessings that had previously been exclusive to Abraham's chosen lineage:

> Before the coming of this faith, we were held in custody under the law, locked up until the faith that was to come would be revealed. So the law was our guardian until Christ came that we might be justified by faith. Now that this faith has come, we are no longer under a guardian. So in Christ Jesus you are all children of God through faith, for all of you who were baptized into Christ have clothed yourselves with Christ. There is neither Jew nor Gentile, neither slave nor free, nor is there male and female, for you are all one in Christ Jesus. If you belong to Christ, then you are Abraham's seed, and heirs according to the promise. (Galatians 3:23-29)

Thus, as Stephen had said, the true meaning of circumcision was not cutting of foreskin but cutting off fallen nature so as to be pure "in heart and ears" and thus open to the workings of the Creator. After Christ's death on the cross, his followers adopted this notion as justification for accepting non-Jews into the new faith. Again from Paul:

> For he is not a real Jew who is one outwardly, nor is true circumcision something external and physical. He is a Jew who is one inwardly, and real circumcision is a matter of the heart, spiritual and not literal. His praise is not from men but from God. (Romans 2:28-29)

Differences Between Moses, the Prophets and Jesus

The core difference between the law given by Moses and the supplemental messages of prophets when compared with the teachings of Jesus lies in the uniquely sinless nature of Jesus. His intimacy with the Creator enabled him to know the deep meanings and hidden purposes of God, unlike his Old Testament predecessors who were limited in their understanding by their fallen nature. Hebrews describes this difference:

> In the past God spoke to our ancestors through the prophets at many times and in various ways, but in these last days he has spoken to us by his Son, whom he appointed heir of all things, and through whom also he made the universe. The Son is the radiance of God's glory and the exact representation of His being, sustaining all things by His powerful word. (Hebrews 1:1-3)

And Hebrews specifically compares Moses as a servant of God to Jesus as God's son:

> Now Moses was faithful in all God's house as a servant, to testify to the things that were to be spoken later, but Christ was faithful over God's house as a son. (Hebrews 3:5-6)

Chapter 6

The Tabernacle and Temple Foreshadowed the Messiah

Establishing a Tradition of Obedience to Abel

The Tabernacle Was in the Image of the Messiah

The goal of the Divine Providence is to raise up a new, sinless Adam and Eve who can establish a new Garden of Eden in which God exercises an absolute dominion of good. In the providence centered on Abraham's family, the new Adam was the Messiah, the sinless man whom the Israelites expected to be their savior. It was he who would establish a new Eden as the Kingdom of Heaven on earth.

As we have discussed, to lay the foundation for the Messiah to come, Abel was separated from Cain by being put in a position closer to God than his brother, enabling him to understand and support the providence and help Cain to separate from evil. In the history of the providence, when those in the position of Cain accepted the greater goodness of those in the position of Abel—and submitted to them—the preparations for the Messiah advanced. When they failed to unite with their Abels the providence was delayed.

Moses was an Abel figure who was chosen to liberate the Israelites from their captivity in Egypt and to lead them to the "Promised Land" of Canaan, where the 12 tribes were supposed to establish a nation to receive the Messiah. To be able to fulfill his mission Moses was given direct instructions from God about how to convince Pharaoh to let the Israelites leave (and follow Moses out of Egypt) and a revelation of the fundamental laws needed to govern the lives of the people—the Ten Commandments.

After living for four centuries in pagan Egyptian society, the Israelites were far from ready to receive the Messiah. They first had to separate themselves from Egypt's Cain-type environment and embrace the Abel-type way of life that Moses introduced to them. Moses was not a second, sinless Adam, but he was God's instrument in establishing the law and the Tabernacle, a structure representing the Messiah to come. Both the law and the Tabernacle served as durable, Abel-type representations of the Messiah. By learning to live in obedience to them the Israelites could prepare to receive the actual Messiah.

Thus after Moses received the Ten Commandments from God, he was also given detailed instructions for erecting the Tabernacle. It was to be a tent-like sanctuary that could be carried with the people while they transited from Egypt to the promised land of Canaan. It was designed with an outer section, called the Holy Place, and an inner section, called the Holy of Holies—a structure which foreshadowed, respectively, the body and spirit of the Messiah.

It was the inner sanctum which housed the Ark of the Covenant, containing the two tablets inscribed with the commandments (representing God's word), manna (representing God's grace) and the staff of Aaron (representing God's authority). Initially only Moses was allowed to enter the Holy of Holies, and later only the chief priests were permitted to enter. And it was here that Moses met "face to face" with God:

> Thus the Lord used to speak to Moses face to face, as a man speaks to his friend. (Exodus 33:11)

It was through the Tabernacle that God's word and providential purpose were communicated to the Israelites, first through the medium of Moses, and after his death by the chief priests, who were descendants of his brother Aaron.

To impress the Israelites with the importance of the Tabernacle, the

Holy Spirit of God that had guided them from Egypt in the form of a pillar of cloud by day and fire by night, came to rest on the Tabernacle:

> For throughout all their journeys the cloud of the Lord was upon the tabernacle by day, and fire was in it by night, in the sight of all the house of Israel. (Exodus 40:38)

The Tabernacle was the first place on earth where God established a sustained presence after Adam and Eve had corrupted the Garden of Eden by their disobedience to God, thereby granting dominion of the world to Satan. For the Israelites to retain their position as the chosen people of God's providence, they had to follow the Divine instructions that came to them through the Tabernacle.

The Levites Were Responsible to Uphold God's Word

Moses was of the tribe of Levi. Because of his great faith and obedience to God, he was chosen to lead the Israelites out of captivity in Egypt. And because only members of his tribe had remained loyal to him while he was on Mount Sinai receiving the Ten Commandments, the Levites were chosen as a priestly class to serve the rest of the Israelites:

> For the Lord said to Moses, "Only the tribe of Levi you shall not number, and you shall not take a census of them among the people of Israel; but appoint the Levites over the tabernacle of the testimony, and over all its furnishings, and over all that belongs to it; they are to carry the tabernacle and all its furnishings, and they shall tend it, and shall encamp around the tabernacle. When the tabernacle is to set out, the Levites shall take it down; and when the tabernacle is to be pitched, the Levites shall set it up. And if any one else comes near, he shall be put to death. The people of Israel shall pitch their tents by their companies, every man by his own camp and every man by his own standard; but the Levites shall encamp around the tabernacle of the testimony, that there may be no wrath upon the congregation of the people of Israel; and the Levites shall keep charge of the tabernacle of the testimony." (Numbers 1:47-53)

There were additional providential reasons for the choice of the Levites, explained in Chapter 12. For our purposes here, it should be noted that they were granted a special position in Israel. They did not receive territory in the Promised Land of Canaan, but they did enjoy privileges in select cities and they were granted the right to receive tithes from the rest of the people.

Most important, with these special privileges came special responsibilities. They were to represent God's word to the people, and to live according to that word as model citizens of the chosen nation. In other words, they were supposed to embody Abel-type values and teach them to the rest of Israel, in preparation for the Messiah who would be the full and perfect embodiment of the Tabernacle and the word.

The Temple Replaced the Tabernacle

The Tabernacle was replaced with a permanent structure when Solomon—starting in the fourth year of his reign—built the Temple in Jerusalem. The Temple was modeled on the Tabernacle, with the Ark located in the Holy of Holies that was itself located within the Holy Place.

Solomon's Temple would remain the main place of worship for the Jews for the four centuries of the divided kingdoms. This period came to an end in 587 BC when Nebuchadnezzar II of Babylon invaded Judah, laid waste to Jerusalem, ransacked the Temple and took the Israelites into captivity.

After living in exile for some 70 years, the Jews were allowed by Cyrus the Great to return to Jerusalem from Babylon and other parts of the Achaemenid Empire. Solomon's Temple was rebuilt under the leadership of Nehemiah, who had been allowed to leave Susa, the Achaemenid capital, for this purpose. This restoration of the Temple was accompanied by a recommitment of the Jewish people to obey the Mosaic Law and fulfill their obligations to the Temple.

The building of this Second Temple and the recommitment to the law enabled Israel to reclaim its position as the nation chosen to receive the Messiah, who appeared in the person of Jesus some 400 years after Nehemiah.

The Tabernacle and Temple Had to be Kept Pure

The responsibility of the Levites was transferred from the Tabernacle to the Temple. The Levites had to protect the purity of both structures because they were where God and the people of Israel met, and where God communicated with the people through Moses and, later, the chief priests. Thus the Levites were responsible for Israel fulfilling the conditions of faith and obedience that enabled it to retain its special place in the providence as the nation chosen to receive the Messiah.

The slightest violation of the law was to be dealt with severely by the Levites. Even the smallest disobedience would set a condition for Satan to corrupt and destroy God's foundation on earth that was embodied in the Tabernacle and Temple. As history would show, the Temple was under constant attack from Cain-like forces seeking its destruction.

As history has also shown, the seeds of destruction are all too often planted by those chosen to be in the Abel position within society but who are not fully aware of their providential importance—or are unwilling to accept the responsibility of their Abel position—and therefore make mistakes that have repercussions they cannot imagine. In the case of Solomon's Temple, those seeds were planted by Solomon himself, who introduced a wave of idolatry to Israel when he participated in the worship of some of the false gods venerated by his hundreds of wives and concubines. The punishment for this mistake was the division of the United Kingdom of Israel established by Solomon's father, David, into two rival kingdoms, Israel and Judah.

As we have noted, the Temple itself would later be destroyed by the Babylonians. However, despite this clear punishment for idolatry, when the Temple was rebuilt by Nehemiah following the return of the Jews from their exile in Babylon, it was not kept pure. In the four centuries before Jesus appeared, Israel suffered several invasions and the Temple was defiled with pagan idols. It was the conquest and occupation of Jerusalem, and the placement of pagan gods in the Temple by the Seleucid ruler Antiochus IV in 168 BC, that finally prompted an all-out rebellion of the Israelites against these invaders, led by the Maccabees.

The Temple Was Corrupted at the Time of Jesus

At the time of Jesus, the Second Temple and the ceremonies and sacrifices conducted in it were at the very heart of the Jewish faith. Herod the Great had made many improvements to its structure and to the walls of Jerusalem that protected it. But the Levites would prove to be unable to maintain the Temple's purity in preparation for receiving the Messiah, who was in their midst.

When Jesus did appear as the Messiah, he found corruption in the Temple, corruption that showed the Levites were not living up to their responsibilities as stewards of this most holy place in Israel:

> The Passover of the Jews was at hand, and Jesus went up to Jerusalem. In the temple he found those who were selling oxen and sheep and pigeons, and the money-changers at their business. And making a whip of cords, he drove them all, with the sheep and oxen, out of the temple; and he poured out the coins of the money-changers and overturned their tables. And he told those who sold the pigeons, "Take these things away; you shall not make my Father's house a house of trade." (John 2:13-16)

Finally the Actual Messiah Appeared

The Mosaic Law had been supplemented over time by the words of the prophets and other Abel-type figures responsible for the providence. But the law as interpreted by the Levites—the chief priests, scribes, Pharisees and Sadducees—could never compare with the truth that flowed from the perfect Messiah himself, and was embodied in the way he lived. Thus the obedience of the Israelites to the Temple had to be transferred to the Messiah.

As we will explain in detail in later chapters, the Levites bore the greatest responsibility to make this transfer of obedience possible, but they did not recognize Jesus as the Messiah on whom the Tabernacle and Temple had been modeled. Therefore they never understood their responsibility to prepare the people to receive and follow Jesus in place of the Mosaic Law and the Temple.

At one point, Jesus explained to the Jews that the Temple was nothing more than a representation of himself as the Messiah:

> "Destroy this temple, and in three days I will raise it up." The Jews then said, "It has taken forty-six years to build this temple, and will you raise it up in three days?" But he spoke of the temple of his body. When therefore he was raised from the dead, his disciples remembered that he had said this; and they believed the scripture and the word which Jesus had spoken. (John 2:19-22)

Chapter 7

Jesus Belongs to the Order of Melchizedek

The Messiah is Both High Priest and King

One of the most mysterious figures in the Bible is Melchizedek [Mel·chiz·e·dek], king of Salem, who blesses Abraham before the great patriarch is anointed by God as father of the providence. Melchizedek is a Greek word meaning priest-king. The only other member of the "Order of Melchizedek" mentioned in the Bible is Jesus, who is David's heavenly lord referenced in Psalm 110 as "a priest forever, after the order of Melchizedek." Jesus himself confirmed that he is this 'lord', and Hebrews explains that belonging to this order signifies a status above tribal or national identity, above the Levitical priesthood or the secular monarchy of Israel. The Messiah belongs to this order as the savior who is both high priest and king.

The First Reference to Melchizedek

As with so many individuals in the Bible, we do not know very much about the original Melchizedek, the contemporary of Abraham. The meeting we know about occurred when Abraham returned from his victory over several minor kings who had kidnapped his nephew, Lot. Traveling with Lot and a small army bearing the spoils of war, he encounters Melchizedek:

> And Melchizedek king of Salem brought out bread and wine; he was priest of God Most High. And he blessed him and said,

> "Blessed be Abram by God Most High, maker of heaven and earth; and blessed be God Most High, who has delivered your enemies into your hand!" And Abram gave him a tenth of everything. (Genesis 14:18-20)

Salem is usually understood to mean Jerusalem, although this was centuries before David made Jerusalem the capital city of Israel and the home for the Temple. Melchizedek was the king of Salem but also a person of great spiritual stature. He was qualified to bless Abraham and to receive tithes from Abraham. As the Book of Hebrews explains:

> It is beyond dispute that the inferior is blessed by the superior. (Hebrews 7:7)

Abraham recognized the importance of Melchizedek, and offered tithes to God through him. Taking from Hebrews again, this tithing was a precursor of tithing by the Israelites to God through the Levites:

> One might even say that Levi himself, who receives tithes, paid tithes through Abraham, for he was still in the loins of his ancestor when Melchizedek met him. (Hebrews 7:9-10)

Abraham met Melchizedek after Ishmael had been born but before the birth of Isaac. Giving a tithe was a condition that Abraham made to receive the substantial blessing of God as the ancestor of a chosen people and nation:

> After these things the word of the Lord came to Abram in a vision, "Fear not, Abram, I am your shield; your reward shall be very great." But Abram said, "O Lord God, what wilt thou give me, for I continue childless, and the heir of my house is Eliezer of Damascus?" And Abram said, "Behold, thou hast given me no offspring; and a slave born in my house will be my heir." And behold, the word of the Lord came to him, "This man shall not be your heir; your own son shall be your heir." And he brought him outside and said, "Look toward heaven, and number the

stars, if you are able to number them." Then he said to him, "So shall your descendants be." And he believed the Lord; and he reckoned it to him as righteousness. (Genesis 15:1-6)

Melchizedek was, then, the substantial representative of the Divine. By submitting to him, Abraham qualified to become the central figure of the substantial lineage used by God to restore humanity to its state before the Fall. This lineage would run through his son Isaac to Jacob and Jacob's twelve sons, who became the twelve tribes of Israel. A secondary line would run from Lot through Lot's daughter and her son Moab, who was the ancestor of Ruth. Boaz and Ruth were the parents of Obed who was the father of Jesse who was the father of David, the providential ruler of the twelve tribes of Israel united in a single kingdom.

The Second Reference to Melchizedek

A millennium later, once David had established the first United Kingdom of Israel with Jerusalem as its capital, the name Melchizedek appears again. This time, David is told that his lord sits on the right hand of God, and that he belongs to the Order of Melchizedek:

> The LORD says to my lord: "Sit at my right hand, till I make your enemies your footstool." ...The LORD has sworn and will not change his mind, "You are a priest for ever, after the order of Melchizedek." (Psalm 110:1,4)

Christians interpret "my lord" as Jesus, the anticipated Messiah, who was to be a priest-king, that is, the man to lead Israel as both high priest and king. Jesus confirmed his identity as "my lord", and thus his belonging to the Order of Melchizedek, when he responded to Pharisees who said that Christ would be the son of David:

> Now while the Pharisees were gathered together, Jesus asked them a question, saying, "What do you think of the Christ? Whose son is he?" They said to him, "The son of David." He said to them, "How is it then that David, inspired by the Spirit,

calls him Lord, saying, 'The LORD said to my Lord, Sit at my right hand, till I put thy enemies under thy feet'? If David thus calls him Lord, how is he his son?" (Matthew 22:41-45)

The Third Reference to Melchizedek

The Messiah was long expected as the person to inherit the throne of David. This was not a symbolic position but literally the seat of power occupied at that time by the Herodian dynasty. At the same time, the Messiah is the person who overcomes evil and leads the way to reunion with God through the priestly functions of teaching and Godly example. Thus the Messiah belongs to the Order of Melchizedek, a status above the Levitical priesthood and the Davidic monarchy. This is explained in the New Testament Book of Hebrews:

> Now if perfection had been attainable through the Levitical priesthood (for under it the people received the law), what further need would there have been for another priest to arise after the order of Melchizedek, rather than one named after the order of Aaron? (Hebrews 7:11)

Thus Jesus came in the role of both internal and external savior of Israel, fulfilling the promise of the covenants made by God with his Abrahamic ancestors. As the Messiah, Jesus was uniquely to combine spiritual and secular leadership so that he could lead Israel to fulfill its providential purpose, both for Abraham's descendants and for the rest of the world.

Thus as Abraham had submitted to Melchizedek so too Abraham's descendants were to submit to Jesus. This they refused to do. Instead they rejected him both as high priest and king. The Bible recounts that Herod and his soldiers mocked Jesus as king:

> And Herod with his soldiers treated him with contempt and mocked him; then, arraying him in gorgeous apparel, he sent him back to Pilate. (Luke 23:11)

And the Roman soldiers under Pilate did likewise:

> Then the soldiers of the governor took Jesus into the praetorium, and they gathered the whole battalion before him. And they stripped him and put a scarlet robe upon him, and plaiting a crown of thorns they put it on his head, and put a reed in his right hand. And kneeling before him they mocked him, saying, "Hail, King of the Jews!" And they spat upon him, and took the reed and struck him on the head. And when they had mocked him, they stripped him of the robe, and put his own clothes on him, and led him away to crucify him. (Matthew 27:27-31)

This mockery continued when the Roman soldiers nailed a derisive sign above the head of Jesus on the cross:

> And over his head they put the charge against him, which read, "This is Jesus the King of the Jews." (Matthew 27:37)

But despite the best efforts of the religious and political establishments in Israel to destroy him, Jesus never lost faith. Thus, although his enemies were able to have his body killed, they could never destroy his spiritual foundation as savior and high priest. This became the hope of his followers:

> So when God desired to show more convincingly to the heirs of the promise the unchangeable character of his purpose, he interposed with an oath, so that through two unchangeable things, in which it is impossible that God should prove false, we who have fled for refuge might have strong encouragement to seize the hope set before us. We have this as a sure and steadfast anchor of the soul, a hope that enters into the inner shrine behind the curtain, where Jesus has gone as a forerunner on our behalf, having become a high priest for ever after the order of Melchizedek. (Hebrews 6:17-20)

Comparing Jesus to traditional Levitical priests, Hebrews adds:

> The former priests were many in number, because they were prevented by death from continuing in office; but [Jesus] holds his priesthood permanently, because he continues for ever. Con-

sequently he is able for all time to save those who draw near to God through him, since he always lives to make intercession for them. (Hebrews 7:23-25)

The Return of Melchizedek

We have a Biblical record of two men identified as Melchizedek: the King of Salem at the time of Abraham and Jesus. Both are transcendent of the limits of tribal or national identity and both are Abel-type figures representing the Divine Providence to chosen people in a Cain-type world. In combining the roles of high priest and king, they represent the need for the Kingdom of Heaven to be established on earth. Recognizing that their work is not complete, we can assume that the second coming of Christ will once again combine both spiritual and temporal aspects of the providence to restore the Garden of Eden on earth. This purpose was clear in the Old Testament prophecies regarding the coming Messiah, and is clear in the prophecies regarding the return of Christ:

> But in those days, after that tribulation, the sun will be darkened, and the moon will not give its light, and the stars will be falling from heaven, and the powers in the heavens will be shaken. And then they will see the Son of man coming in clouds with great power and glory. And then he will send out the angels, and gather his elect from the four winds, from the ends of the earth to the ends of heaven. (Mark 13:24-27)

And in Matthew, Jesus says:

> When the Son of man comes in his glory, and all the angels with him, then he will sit on his glorious throne. Before him will be gathered all the nations, and he will separate them one from another as a shepherd separates the sheep from the goats. (Matthew 25:31-33)

We can expect the return of Christ to differ from the first advent, although the goal is the same. Once again those prepared to receive Christ will be tested, as the chosen nation of Israel was tested at the first advent. As the disciples of Christ, Christians now occupy the privileged position as the first people to receive a returned Christ. As Christians, however, we should not take this privilege for granted. It is an enormous responsibility to fulfill. And we should not be bound by our assumptions as to where, when and how the second coming will unfold, and who from the Order of Melchizedek we will have to follow.

Chapter 8

Was Mary the Mother of God?

Seeking a Sinless Woman to Replace Eve

Whatever confusion about the identity of Jesus was created by the theory of the Holy Trinity (discussed in Chapter 3), it did confirm his divinity. However, if Jesus was divine, what could be concluded about the mother who gave him birth? This was an issue as problematic for the Church fathers as was the identity of Jesus himself. Their conclusion was to describe Mary as the "Mother of God". This identity would be codified as a central article of faith for Catholics and Orthodox Christians in particular. Quoting from the Catholic Catechism:

> He was begotten from the Father before all ages as to his divinity and in these last days, for us and for our salvation, was born as to his humanity of the virgin Mary, the Mother of God.[1]

The logical question this belief engenders is: How could Mary be the Mother of God if she herself was from a fallen lineage?

Neither the Holy Trinity nor the belief that Mary was the Mother of God has a foundation in the Gospels. Significantly, only the Gospel of Luke has details of the circumstances surrounding the birth of Jesus. Thus there are few scriptures to reference in trying to understand this most important

---

1. Catholic Catechism Paragraph 467, Quoting the Council of Chalcedon.

moment in the providence. In Luke's account, Mary was told by the angel Gabriel that she would give birth to Jesus even though at the time she was only engaged to be married to Joseph. She was reassured that she would conceive when the Holy Spirit visited her and the power of the "Most High" would "overshadow" her:

> In the sixth month the angel Gabriel was sent from God to a city of Galilee named Nazareth, to a virgin betrothed to a man whose name was Joseph, of the house of David; and the virgin's name was Mary. And he came to her and said, "Hail, O favored one, the Lord is with you!" But she was greatly troubled at the saying, and considered in her mind what sort of greeting this might be. And the angel said to her, "Do not be afraid, Mary, for you have found favor with God. And behold, you will conceive in your womb and bear a son, and you shall call his name Jesus. He will be great, and will be called the Son of the Most High; and the Lord God will give to him the throne of his father David, and he will reign over the house of Jacob for ever; and of his kingdom there will be no end." And Mary said to the angel, "How shall this be, since I have no husband?" And the angel said to her, "The Holy Spirit will come upon you, and the power of the Most High will overshadow you therefore the child to be born will be called holy, the Son of God." (Luke 1:26-35)

The Immaculate Conception

This account is understood by most Christians to mean that Mary was impregnated by the Holy Spirit, in what is called the immaculate conception. This event made Mary unique among women and Jesus a man like no other in history. The Gospels do not elaborate on her qualifications to be the mother of Christ except to note that she was a virgin at the time of her visitation. We can assume that Mary was chosen because of her lineage and purity, but she was not a sinless person—Jesus, not Mary, is the starting point of sinless humanity after the Fall.

But what does impregnation by the Holy Spirit mean? Luke 1:35 says: "The Holy Spirit will come upon you, and the power of the Most High will overshadow you." We know, of course, that human conception occurs through sexual relations between a man and a woman. This is the Godly natural order. Why would the conception of Jesus take place in any way other than the way designed by God? Wouldn't it make more sense to interpret "the Holy Spirit will come upon you, and the power of the Most High will overshadow you" as meaning that Mary would experience an overwhelming spiritual force guiding her to the right man to be the father of Jesus?

Clearly Mary was blessed with a very pure lineage, but Joseph was not qualified to father Jesus. Only through Divine guidance could Mary know where to turn to fulfill her providential mission as the mother of the Messiah.

Luke continues his account by repeating the words of the angel who told Mary that her cousin Elizabeth had already conceived a son, despite having been barren all her life:

> "And behold, your kinswoman Elizabeth in her old age has also conceived a son; and this is the sixth month with her who was called barren. For with God nothing will be impossible." And Mary said, "Behold, I am the handmaid of the Lord; let it be to me according to your word." And the angel departed from her. (Luke 1:36-38)

Zechariah and Elizabeth Supported Mary

Immediately after receiving this message from Gabriel, Mary left her home in Nazareth to visit her cousin in Judea:

> In those days Mary arose and went with haste into the hill country, to a city of Judah, and she entered the house of Zechariah and greeted Elizabeth. (Luke 1:38-40)

And Elizabeth recognized the special mission of Mary as the mother of 'her Lord', the Messiah, as soon as they met:

> And when Elizabeth heard the greeting of Mary, the babe leaped in her womb; and Elizabeth was filled with the Holy Spirit and

> she exclaimed with a loud cry, "Blessed are you among women, and blessed is the fruit of your womb! And why is this granted me, that the mother of my Lord should come to me? For behold, when the voice of your greeting came to my ears, the babe in my womb leaped for joy." (Luke 1:41-44)

Thus Elizabeth, who was pregnant with John the Baptist at the time, recognized the Divine intervention in the life of Mary and the importance of accepting it, however unusual and impossible it might seem. She commended Mary for her faith:

> And blessed is she who believed that there would be a fulfilment of what was spoken to her from the Lord. (Luke 1:45)

Elizabeth's husband, the priest Zechariah, had also been visited by Gabriel who informed him that his barren wife would give birth to a providential son, who was to be called John, and who would "be filled with the Holy Spirit, even from his mother's womb." (Luke 1:15)

Initially Zechariah doubted this message, much as Abraham had doubted Sarah's ability to have a son. He was chastised for this faithlessness by being unable to speak during Elizabeth's pregnancy, which was also the time when Mary stayed with his family. When John was born, Zechariah was able to speak again. He was filled with the Holy Spirit and testified to the importance of the child to be born of Mary:

> And his father Zechariah was filled with the Holy Spirit, and prophesied, saying, "Blessed be the Lord God of Israel, for he has visited and redeemed his people, and has raised up a horn of salvation for us in the house of his servant David, as he spoke by the mouth of his holy prophets from of old, that we should be saved from our enemies, and from the hand of all who hate us; to perform the mercy promised to our fathers, and to remember his holy covenant, the oath which he swore to our father Abraham, to grant us that we, being delivered from the hand

of our enemies, might serve him without fear, in holiness and righteousness before him all the days of our life." (Luke 1:68-75)

And Zechariah prophesized that his own son John who would become a prophet and "go before the Lord [Jesus] to prepare his ways":

And you, child, will be called the prophet of the Most High; for you will go before the Lord to prepare his ways, to give knowledge of salvation to his people in the forgiveness of their sins, through the tender mercy of our God, when the day shall dawn upon us from on high to give light to those who sit in darkness and in the shadow of death, to guide our feet into the way of peace. (Luke 1:76-79)

Mary stayed in the house of Zechariah for three months. By that time John was due and Mary would have been certain of her pregnancy and ready to return home to prepare for the birth of Jesus.

Two Providential Families Prepared for the Birth of Jesus

The Biblical passages quoted above describe a Divine plan for Joseph and Mary, Zechariah and Elizabeth. These four key people were all visited by the angel Gabriel to tell them of God's plan, and all of them accepted their own roles in it. As if to confirm their shared providential mission, Elizabeth even testified that John leapt in her womb when Mary first came to their home, guided there by the Holy Spirit and thus confirming that this unusual arrangement was blessed by God.

These passages also reveal the vital part in the Divine plan that John—who was born six months before Jesus—had to play by supporting the mission of Jesus. This was important since John came from a Levitical family, with the recognition and respect that brought with it. Jesus, by contrast, came from a lowly carpenter's family. He would hardly be expected to be a prophet for Israel, let alone the Messiah expected to ascend the throne of David.

As for Mary, this account confirms her as a woman of faith. Despite her earlier reservations about conceiving Jesus when she had not yet consummated her marriage to Joseph, she accepted the word of Gabriel and allowed herself to be guided by the Holy Spirit in pursuing a difficult and unconventional path to pregnancy and motherhood. For his part, Joseph deserves credit for keeping this providential arrangement confidential by accepting Jesus as a son of his own.

Mary's later life as the mother of both Jesus and several other children raises some questions about her role in the providence, and these will be addressed in Chapter 12. For now, we recognize in her a pure young woman who obeyed the call of God and, as the mother of Jesus, came to represent the feminine aspect of our Creator to believers in Christ.

Mary Risked Her Life to Follow Divine Instructions

The problem with all human births after the fall was the presence of fallen nature in the parents, a nature they passed on to their children such that all humanity was born with what is called original sin—an inheritance of the fallen nature of Adam and Eve. Thus the internal dimension of the centuries of preparation for the Messiah was purification of the lineage so that he could be born free of the original sin. There are a number of Old Testament accounts of unusual sexual relationships—in fact immoral relationships by Judaic and Christian standards—which nevertheless produced providential individuals.

All these cases feature providential women who sacrificially engaged in sexual relations with providential men for the sake of preserving and purifying the central lineage chosen to bring forth a savior, or Messiah. By doing this, they did the opposite of Eve who engaged in a selfish and illicit relationship with Lucifer, and then with Adam. They thereby made a condition to reverse the fall and cleanse the human lineage of Satanic influence. This was not sex for pleasure, but sex for the salvation of fallen humankind. (See the next chapter for a detailed discussion of this topic.)

This was the case with Mary, too, who obeyed the call of God to accept the providential will by allowing the Holy Spirit to guide her to the man whose lineage was destined to produce the Messiah. This was an act of supreme sacrifice, contravening the Mosaic Law and putting Mary at risk of censure or death for the crime of adultery.

Mary Substitutes for a Second Eve

The elevation of Mary to the status of Mother of God by some Christians is understandable. The original mind of human beings seeks not only a perfected Adam, but also a perfected Eve, since together they embody the image of the Creator more fully than they can as individuals. This is because Divine nature has both male and female characteristics, as proven by the existence of male and female in the creation. Thus restoration of a sinless Adam as he was before the fall must ultimately be accompanied by restoration of a sinless Eve as well.

We are all born with a nature that incorporates the male and female attributes of our Creator, but which manifest differently in men and women. Men are endowed with sexual organs that align with their predominantly male characteristics, while women have sexual organs that align with their predominantly female characteristics. On the physical level this differentiation makes procreation possible. On the spiritual, psychological and emotional levels, this difference is the basis for the development of conjugal love, which brings a man and woman into oneness and enables them to be responsible co-creators of new life—the good parents of good children.

Jesus never married and never indicated who was to be Eve to his Adam. Thus many Christians have substituted Mary for this Second Eve, looking to her to be their spiritual mother. And many Christians have experienced a tender love from Mary, a love that has helped them understand and embrace Christ. Usually those with the most powerful spiritual experiences with Mary have been young and innocent, such as the girl to whom Mary appeared many times at Lourdes, and the children who were visited by her at Fatima. Their purity enabled them to receive direct guidance from Mary.

The Holy Spirit as Divine Mother

The term Holy Spirit is used in various ways in the Bible. In a general sense, it is the spirit of God. However, in certain situations at least, the Holy Spirit plays a more specific role as a manifestation of the feminine, motherly aspects of the Creator. It was this feminine personification of the Divine that visited Mary to guide and strengthen her in accomplishing her providential purpose despite the inherent danger of conceiving and giving birth to Jesus in a non-conventional way. And it was this Holy Spirit that descended on the disciples at Pentecost, moving their hearts and those who followed them to embrace the resurrected Jesus.

In the absence of a restored Eve in the providence, we can continue to look to the Holy Spirit to guide us rightly down the providential paths that are our destiny. And on a spiritual level we can look to the Holy Spirit to provide the loving embrace we need from our Heavenly Mother. Over the centuries of Christian history, Mary has often come to embody this Holy Spirit as a comforter. This is a great providential role, but it does not make Mary the mother of God.

Chapter 9

Providential Women Risk all to Restore Eve

An Old Testament History Leading to Mary

Since the purpose of the providence is to restore the positions of sinless Adam and Eve, many of the most significant events in providential history have to do with representatives of Adam and Eve reversing the behavior that resulted in the Fall by obeying the words of God and rejecting the seductions of Lucifer. Eve had been responsible for the first human mistakes when she heeded the rebellious archangel's lies and entered into an illicit sexual relationship with him, a mistake that led to the spiritual death of Adam and Eve and the alienation of human beings from their Creator. Thus the conditions to restore the Fall require women in the position of Eve to obey God by carrying out extremely difficult missions at the risk of their lives. These missions typically have involved using their sex to advance the providence in ways that contravened the mores of their time and are undoubtedly sinful from the perspective of the Mosaic Law and Christian morality, thus inviting condemnation and possibly death.

Mary came on the foundation laid by the providential women who lived before her, and her own story can best be understood in the context of the ongoing providence to restore the fallen lineage of Adam and Eve by reversing Eve's mistakes. She heeded the words of the good angel, Gabriel, even though this meant her taking actions that on their face violated the Mosaic Law. Thus she risked condemnation and likely death for adultery in order to conceive and give birth to Jesus according to the Divine will. This chapter describes some of the Old Testament individuals and events that established a foundation for Mary to be victorious in reversing the fallen behavior of Eve, so that she could give birth to a sinless son, Jesus.

Abraham, Sarah and Hagar

After Abraham left Haran with his beautiful wife Sarah to establish his family in a land to be shown to him, he twice asked her to pretend to be his sister rather than his wife, to avoid being killed by the rulers in whose territory they were traveling. The first time was in Egypt:

> Now there was a famine in the land. So Abram [later Abraham] went down to Egypt to sojourn there, for the famine was severe in the land. When he was about to enter Egypt, he said to Sarai [later Sarah] his wife, "I know that you are a woman beautiful to behold; and when the Egyptians see you, they will say, 'This is his wife'; then they will kill me, but they will let you live. Say you are my sister, that it may go well with me because of you, and that my life may be spared on your account." (Genesis 12:10-13)

Sarah was obedient to Abraham and the higher purpose he represented. She was taken by the Pharaoh of the time, but the Egyptian ruler's household was afflicted with plagues and the Pharaoh came to realize who she really was and returned her to Abraham before harm could be done:

> But the LORD afflicted Pharaoh and his house with great plagues because of Sarai, Abram's wife. So Pharaoh called Abram, and said, "What is this you have done to me? Why did you not tell me that she was your wife? Why did you say, 'She is my sister,' so that I took her for my wife? Now then, here is your wife, take her, and be gone." And Pharaoh gave men orders concerning him; and they set him on the way, with his wife and all that he had. (Genesis 12:17-20)

In her faith and obedience to the providence, Sarah restored the failure of Eve: she resisted the temptations of Pharaoh (representing Lucifer) and was safely reunited with Abraham (representing Adam), thus conditionally separating their family from the dominion of Satan. This took great courage on her part, since she risked either being forced to remain with Pharaoh, or being killed by him out of his anger at being deceived by Abraham.

Sarah was unable to have children, so she told Abraham that to continue his lineage he should have a child by her servant, Hagar:

> Now Sarai, Abram's wife, bore him no children. She had an Egyptian maid whose name was Hagar; and Sarai said to Abram, "Behold now, the LORD has prevented me from bearing children; go in to my maid; it may be that I shall obtain children by her." And Abram hearkened to the voice of Sarai. So, after Abram had dwelt ten years in the land of Canaan, Sarai, Abram's wife, took Hagar the Egyptian, her maid, and gave her to Abram her husband as a wife. And he went in to Hagar, and she conceived; and when she saw that she had conceived, she looked with contempt on her mistress. And Sarai said to Abram, "May the wrong done to me be on you! I gave my maid to your embrace, and when she saw that she had conceived, she looked on me with contempt. May the LORD judge between you and me!" But Abram said to Sarai, "Behold, your maid is in your power; do to her as you please." Then Sarai dealt harshly with her, and she fled from her. (Genesis 16:1-6)

Despite Sarah's anger and Abraham's decision to send Hagar away, this was not the providential destiny for Hagar and her son to be, Ishmael:

> The angel of the LORD found her by a spring of water in the wilderness, the spring on the way to Shur. And he said, "Hagar, maid of Sarai, where have you come from and where are you going?" She said, "I am fleeing from my mistress Sarai." The angel of the LORD said to her, "Return to your mistress, and submit to her." The angel of the LORD also said to her, "I will so greatly multiply your descendants that they cannot be numbered for multitude." And the angel of the LORD said to her, "Behold, you are with child, and shall bear a son; you shall call his name Ishmael;

because the LORD has given heed to your affliction." (Genesis 16:7-11)

The reaction of Sarah to Hagar's arrogance is understandable, but it was inconsistent with her own original intention to give children to Abraham to preserve his lineage and represented a lack of faith on her part. Her anger with Abraham over Hagar's attitude—and blaming him for it—created a separation between them in this all-important providential family. They would once more have to go through a process of separation from Satan through Sarah overcoming another test of faith. This occurred in Gerar, the land of King Abimelech:

> From there Abraham journeyed toward the territory of the Negeb, and dwelt between Kadesh and Shur; and he sojourned in Gerar. And Abraham said of Sarah his wife, "She is my sister." And Abimelech king of Gerar sent and took Sarah. But God came to Abimelech in a dream by night, and said to him, "Behold, you are a dead man, because of the woman whom you have taken; for she is a man's wife." Now Abimelech had not approached her; so he said, "Lord, wilt thou slay an innocent people? Did he not himself say to me, 'She is my sister'? And she herself said, 'He is my brother.' In the integrity of my heart and the innocence of my hands I have done this." Then God said to him in the dream, "Yes, I know that you have done this in the integrity of your heart, and it was I who kept you from sinning against me; therefore I did not let you touch her. Now then restore the man's wife; for he is a prophet, and he will pray for you, and you shall live. But if you do not restore her, know that you shall surely die, you, and all that are yours." (Genesis 20:1-7)

Sarah once again showed great courage in putting herself at risk for the sake of the providence. And because she once more overcame the temptations of Lucifer, now in the person of Abimelech, and was restored to Abraham undefiled, Abraham was able to intercede on behalf of Abimelech so that he could be blessed by God as a good archangel:

Providential Women Risk all to Restore Eve

> Then Abraham prayed to God; and God healed Abimelech, and also healed his wife and female slaves so that they bore children. For the LORD had closed all the wombs of the house of Abimelech because of Sarah, Abraham's wife. (Genesis 20:17-18)

Thirteen years after the birth of Ishmael to Hagar, when Abraham was 99 and Sarah 90, God appeared to Abraham and revealed that even though Sarah was barren she would be the mother of nations and kings:

> And God said to Abraham, "As for Sarai your wife, you shall not call her name Sarai, but Sarah shall be her name. I will bless her, and moreover I will give you a son by her; I will bless her, and she shall be a mother of nations; kings of peoples shall come from her." Then Abraham fell on his face and laughed, and said to himself, "Shall a child be born to a man who is a hundred years old? Shall Sarah, who is ninety years old, bear a child?" And Abraham said to God, "O that Ishmael might live in thy sight!" God said, "No, but Sarah your wife shall bear you a son, and you shall call his name Isaac. I will establish my covenant with him as an everlasting covenant for his descendants after him. As for Ishmael, I have heard you; behold, I will bless him and make him fruitful and multiply him exceedingly; he shall be the father of twelve princes, and I will make him a great nation. But I will establish my covenant with Isaac, whom Sarah shall bear to you at this season next year." (Genesis 17:15-21)

Having never been able to conceive, Sarah was naturally incredulous at the news:

> The Lord said, "I will surely return to you in the spring, and Sarah your wife shall have a son." And Sarah was listening at the tent door behind him. Now Abraham and Sarah were old, advanced in age; it had ceased to be with Sarah after the manner of women. So Sarah laughed to herself, saying, "After I have grown old, and my husband is old, shall I have pleasure?" The Lord said to Abraham, "Why did Sarah laugh, and say, 'Shall I indeed bear a child, now that I am old?' Is anything too hard for the Lord? At

the appointed time I will return to you, in the spring, and Sarah shall have a son." (Genesis 18:10-14)

Despite the incredulity of Abraham and Sarah, she did conceive and within a year gave birth to a son of her own, Isaac. But she was unable to overcome her resentment towards Hagar and Ishmael, and demanded that Abraham send them away:

> And the child grew, and was weaned; and Abraham made a great feast on the day that Isaac was weaned. But Sarah saw the son of Hagar the Egyptian, whom she had borne to Abraham, playing with her son Isaac. So she said to Abraham, "Cast out this slave woman with her son; for the son of this slave woman shall not be heir with my son Isaac." And the thing was very displeasing to Abraham on account of his son. But God said to Abraham, "Be not displeased because of the lad and because of your slave woman; whatever Sarah says to you, do as she tells you, for through Isaac shall your descendants be named. And I will make a nation of the son of the slave woman also, because he is your offspring." So Abraham rose early in the morning, and took bread and a skin of water, and gave it to Hagar, putting it on her shoulder, along with the child, and sent her away. And she departed, and wandered in the wilderness of Beersheba. (Genesis 21:8-14)

From a providential point of view, it would have been better for Sarah to share the parental heart of Abraham, who loved both of his sons, Ishmael (representing Cain) and Isaac (representing Abel). The separation of Cain from Abel that led to Cain murdering his brother, undoubtedly was the result of Adam and Eve failing to show their children the love of God that embraced both of their sons. Sarah was to restore Eve's failings in this respect. If Isaac and Ishmael could have been raised together in a loving family (and their playing together indicated there was a real hope for that), the enmity and division that emerged between their families and descendants might have been avoided. This would have prevented the history of resentment between these two branches of Abraham's family which we see to this day in the bitterness and conflicts between Jews and Christians, on one hand, and Muslims on the other. (The 12 sons of Ishmael became 12 tribes whose descendants include the Arabs, to whom Mohammed was sent as a prophet in the 7th century AD.)

The reluctance of providential parents to help Cain unite with Abel was repeated at the time of Jesus. John the Baptist was in the position of elder half-brother to Jesus, and thus was to unite with him and support him. Although his parents were told of this by Gabriel, there is no record of them actually helping John understand and support Jesus as needed, as we shall discuss in detail in Chapter 18. Furthermore, apparently Mary also was unable to get her six children who came after Jesus to devote themselves to serving Jesus, nor to get John to fulfill his mission.

Thus Sarah established a pattern of demonstrating faith that enabled the providence to advance, but after the miracle of Isaac she faltered in her faith by rejecting her Cain son instead of embracing him and his mother with the parental heart of God. This limitation in understanding and uniting with Divine purpose and love meant Sarah could not restore fallen Eve fully to her position before the Fall. This shortcoming would often prevent providential women from completing their missions.

Isaac, Rebekah, Esau and Jacob

When Abraham made a mistake in performing a sacrifice of birds, he was told to sacrifice his son, Isaac. Although this act if carried out would have prevented the realization of the providence through Isaac promised to Abraham, the boy trusted his father who was determined to carry it out. At the last moment an angel stayed the hand of Abraham, who was shown a sheep to sacrifice in Isaac's place. Because of his own faithful obedience, Isaac was qualified to inherit Abraham's providential position as father of faith.

Later, after Sarah had died, Isaac sent a servant to find a wife for him in Haran, the ancestral home of Abraham. He returned with Rebekah, the granddaughter of Abraham's Aramean brother, Nahor, and they were married. Like his parents before him, Isaac lived in Gerar, the land of King Abimelech, and like his father he warned Rebekah to pretend to be his sister, fearing that he would be killed by men wanting her because of her beauty:

> So Isaac dwelt in Gerar. When the men of the place asked him about his wife, he said, "She is my sister"; for he feared to say, "My wife," thinking, "lest the men of the place should kill me for the sake of Rebekah"; because she was fair to look upon. When he had been there a long time, Abimelech king of the Philistines looked out of a window and saw Isaac fondling Rebekah his wife. So Abimelech called Isaac, and said, "Behold, she is your wife; how then could you say, 'She is my sister'?" Isaac said to him, "Because I thought, 'Lest I die because of her.'" Abimelech said, "What is this you have done to us? One of the people might easily have lain with your wife, and you would have brought guilt upon us." So Abimelech warned all the people, saying, "Whoever touches this man or his wife shall be put to death." (Genesis 26:6-11)

Like her late mother-in-law Sarah, Rebekah showed great courage in risking her life. And, like Sarah, she suffered from being barren. However, after twenty years of marriage, Isaac's prayers were granted and Rebekah was finally able to conceive:

> And Isaac prayed to the Lord for his wife, because she was barren; and the Lord granted his prayer, and Rebekah his wife conceived. The children struggled together within her; and she said, "If it is thus, why do I live?" So she went to inquire of the Lord. And the Lord said to her, "Two nations are in your womb, and two peoples, born of you, shall be divided; the one shall be stronger than the other, the elder shall serve the younger." When her days to be delivered were fulfilled, behold, there were twins in her womb. The first came forth red, all his body like a hairy mantle; so they called his name Esau. Afterward his brother came forth, and his hand had taken hold of Esau's heel; so his name was called Jacob. (Genesis 25:21-26)

Esau as the eldest was in the Cain position, replacing Ishmael, while Jacob represented Abel, inheriting the position of his father Isaac. In Malachi, God expresses his preference for Jacob as the son to lead the providence:

> "Is not Esau Jacob's brother?" says the LORD. "Yet I have loved Jacob but I have hated Esau." (Malachi 1:2-3)

Following the tradition of his time, Isaac favored his older twin, Esau, However, Rebekah held the providential perspective, favoring Jacob:

> When the boys grew up, Esau was a skillful hunter, a man of the field, while Jacob was a quiet man, dwelling in tents. Isaac loved Esau, because he ate of his game; but Rebekah loved Jacob. (Genesis 25:27-28)

When Isaac was old and practically blind, he planned to bless Esau, as was the custom for the older son. However, Rebekah intervened on behalf of Jacob:

> Now Rebekah was listening when Isaac spoke to his son Esau. So when Esau went to the field to hunt for game and bring it, Rebekah said to her son Jacob, "I heard your father speak to your brother Esau, 'Bring me game, and prepare for me savory food, that I may eat it, and bless you before the LORD before I die.' Now therefore, my son, obey my word as I command you. Go to the flock, and fetch me two good kids, that I may prepare from them savory food for your father, such as he loves; and you shall bring it to your father to eat, so that he may bless you before he dies." (Genesis 27:7-10)

This stratagem worked, and Jacob, who had already secured the birthright from a hungry Esau, in exchange for food, received the blessing from his father. Furious to discover this, Esau swore to kill Jacob:

> Now Esau hated Jacob because of the blessing with which his father had blessed him, and Esau said to himself, "The days of mourning for my father are approaching; then I will kill my

brother Jacob." But the words of Esau her older son were told to Rebekah; so she sent and called Jacob her younger son, and said to him, "Behold, your brother Esau comforts himself by planning to kill you. Now therefore, my son, obey my voice; arise, flee to Laban my brother in Haran, and stay with him a while, until your brother's fury turns away; until your brother's anger turns away, and he forgets what you have done to him; then I will send, and fetch you from there." (Genesis 27:41-45)

Heeding his mother's advice, Jacob did flee to Haran, where he prospered and established a family that would be pivotal in the providence. Thus what Rebekah did to help Jacob might seem to be abetting immoral behavior, she contributed to the providence which called for Jacob to reverse the murder of Abel by Cain, and to claim a victory for God's side. Time would tell that Jacob was indeed in the Abel position as his 12 sons became the 12 tribes that formed the nation of Israel, to which the Messiah would be sent. Rebekah played a key role in Jacob avoiding death and fulfilling his mission.

Jacob, Leah and Rachel

In Haran, while exiled from his home in Canaan, Jacob served his Cain-type uncle Laban for seven years in order to win the hand of his daughter, Rachel. However, when he woke after his wedding night, he realized that he had been tricked—under cover of darkness Laban had sent Leah to him in place of Rachel. Discovering this after the marriage was already consummated, Jacob persevered in serving Laban for another seven years until he also won Rachel. He worked yet another seven years to accumulate wealth that his uncle refused him, despite his 14 years of service.

Leah would bear Jacob six sons: initially Reuben, Simeon, Levi and Judah, and then after a barren period Issachar and Zebulun. While Rachel was initially barren—and like Sarah and Rebekah before her she was put in the position of making a condition to restore Eve's misuse of love and sex—she overcame the resentment she felt towards Leah by allowing her servant, Bilhah, to have two sons on her behalf, Dan and Naphtali. During Leah's barren period she also allowed her servant, Zilpah, to have two sons, Gad and Asher. When Rachel was finally able to conceive, she bore Joseph and then Benjamin. Rachel was carrying Benjamin as the family returned from Haran, and she died upon his birth. She literally gave her life so that the providence could advance through Jacob's lineage.

On returning to his homeland, Jacob had to overcome an angel who tested his faith and resolve by wrestling with him through the night, but then blessed him with a new name, Israel. Jacob then reconciled with Esau by offering his brother the wealth he had accumulated in Haran, bowing before him like a servant. So Jacob was a victorious Abel. He overcame Esau representing Cain, Laban representing the fallen angel Lucifer, and he subjugated a good angel representing Lucifer before the Fall, even though he had suffered an injury to his thigh from the angel. (It should be noted that human beings are children of God while angels are servants, therefore angels are to serve men and women. One aspect of the Fall was Lucifer's reversal of this heavenly hierarchy.)

Jacob's twelve sons became the twelve tribes of the chosen nation of Israel, to whom the Messiah was sent. By Christian standards of morality Jacob's behavior in deceiving Esau and Isaac and in having children from four women was wrong. Nevertheless, history showed that he played a pivotal role in the providence. Furthermore, although his two wives experienced jealousy towards each other they ultimately fulfilled their providential roles by both giving birth to sons of Jacob and by instructing their servants to have sons with Jacob on their behalf.

Judah and Tamar

One of the most unusual accounts of a woman risking her life for the sake of the providence is that of Tamar and all of the efforts she made to secure the lineage of Judah, despite the danger of being killed for her trouble.

The importance of Judah was established when Jacob, nearing the end of his life, chose Judah, his fourth son, to be the leader of the 12 tribes:

> Judah, your brothers shall praise you; your hand shall be on the neck of your enemies; your father's sons shall bow down before you. Judah is a lion's whelp; from the prey, my son, you have gone up. He stooped down, he couched as a lion, and as a lioness; who dares rouse him up? The scepter shall not depart from Judah, nor the ruler's staff from between his feet, until he comes to whom it belongs; and to him shall be the obedience of the peoples. (Genesis 49:8-10)

Judah married a Canaanite woman, Shua, and had three sons with her: Er, Onan and Shelah. Tamar, a Jewess, was married to Er, but there were problems:

> And Judah took a wife for Er his first-born, and her name was Tamar. But Er, Judah's first-born, was wicked in the sight of the Lord; and the Lord slew him. Then Judah said to Onan, "Go in to your brother's wife, and perform the duty of a brother-in-law to her, and raise up offspring for your brother." But Onan knew that the offspring would not be his; so when he went in to his brother's wife he spilled the semen on the ground, lest he should give offspring to his brother. And what he did was displeasing in the sight of the Lord, and he slew him also. Then Judah said to Tamar his daughter-in-law, "Remain a widow in your father's house, till Shelah my son grows up"—for he feared that he would die, like his brothers. (Genesis 38:6-11)

However, Tamar was determined to preserve the lineage of Judah and when she realized that Judah would not give his third son to her in marriage, she devised a plan to have a child by him directly:

> And when Tamar was told, "Your father-in-law is going up to Timnah to shear his sheep," she put off her widow's garments, and put on a veil, wrapping herself up, and sat at the entrance to Enaim, which is on the road to Timnah; for she saw that Shelah was grown up, and she had not been given to him in marriage. When Judah saw her, he thought her to be a harlot, for she had

covered her face. He went over to her at the road side, and said, "Come, let me come in to you," for he did not know that she was his daughter-in-law. She said, "What will you give me, that you may come in to me?" He answered, "I will send you a kid from the flock." And she said, "Will you give me a pledge, till you send it?" He said, "What pledge shall I give you?" She replied, "Your signet and your cord, and your staff that is in your hand." So he gave them to her, and went in to her, and she conceived by him. Then she arose and went away, and taking off her veil she put on the garments of her widowhood. (Genesis 38:13-19)

Tamar had taken a great risk in doing this, and was in danger of being killed:

> About three months later Judah was told, "Tamar your daughter-in-law has played the harlot; and moreover she is with child by harlotry." And Judah said, "Bring her out, and let her be burned." As she was being brought out, she sent word to her father-in-law, "By the man to whom these belong, I am with child." And she said, "Mark, I pray you, whose these are, the signet and the cord and the staff." Then Judah acknowledged them and said, "She is more righteous than I, inasmuch as I did not give her to my son Shelah." And he did not lie with her again. When the time of her delivery came, there were twins in her womb. And when she was in labor, one put out a hand; and the midwife took and bound on his hand a scarlet thread, saying, "This came out first." But as he drew back his hand, behold, his brother came out; and she said, "What a breach you have made for yourself!" Therefore his name was called Perez. Afterward his brother came out with the scarlet thread upon his hand; and his name was called Zerah. (Genesis 38:24-30)

Thus as Jacob had to overcome his older twin Esau to reverse Cain's dominion over Abel, so too Perez had to overcome Zerah, which he did while still in Tamar's womb. It was Perez, then, who became the Abel-type ancestor of the lineage that led to David. And it was to Tamar's credit that she was willing to risk the censure of her people and even her life to fulfill her providential role. Again, her behavior was immoral by Israelite and Christian standards but out of her lineage would come the leadership of the chosen people.

Lot and his Two daughters

Although the central providence ran from Abraham through Isaac to Jacob, a secondary providential lineage ran from Abraham through Ishmael to his 12 sons and tribes, and a third providential lineage ran from Abraham through his nephew Lot. As Lot was escaping from the angry people of Sodom with his wife and two daughters, his wife disobeyed the instructions they had received and looked back at the city as it was being destroyed. She was immediately turned into a pillar of salt. Fearful that the people of Sodom would pursue him and his daughters, Lot hid in a cave with them. The daughters' mother was dead as were their two married sisters, who had perished in Sodom. Thus they were concerned that their father would not now be able to have a male lineage. They got their father drunk and took turns sleeping with him. Both became pregnant and had sons, called Moab and Ben-Ammi:

> And the first-born said to the younger, "Our father is old, and there is not a man on earth to come in to us after the manner of all the earth. Come, let us make our father drink wine, and we will lie with him, that we may preserve offspring through our father." So they made their father drink wine that night; and the first-born went in, and lay with her father; he did not know when she lay down or when she arose. And on the next day, the first-born said to the younger, "Behold, I lay last night with my father; let us make him drink wine tonight also; then you go in and lie with him, that we may preserve offspring through our father." So they made their father drink wine that night also; and the younger arose, and lay with him; and he did not know when she lay down or when she arose. Thus both the daughters of Lot were with child by their father. The first-born bore a

> son, and called his name Moab; he is the father of the Moabites to this day. The younger also bore a son, and called his name Ben-Ammi; he is the father of the Ammonites to this day. (Genesis 19:31-38)

These incestuous relationships contravened moral norms, although this took place four centuries before the advent of Moses and the establishment of the first Divinely inspired moral/legal code, the Mosaic Law. The daughters acted not out of sexual desire but to advance the providence. They were vindicated when, centuries later, out of Moab's lineage came Ruth, who married Boaz. Their grandson Jesse fathered David, the key figure in establishing a national foundation for the Messiah.

Boaz and Ruth, Obed, Jesse and David

Ruth was the widow of a son of Elimelech and Naomi, who were Ephrathites (a clan of the Ephraimites) who left their home in Bethlehem—a town near Jerusalem—for Moab, to escape a famine in Judea. Their ancestor was Ephraim who as the younger of twin sons born to Joseph—his older brother was Manassas—had been blessed by Jacob. The branch of Ephraim's tribe in Bethlehem inherited the blessing that originally belonged to Jacob's oldest son Reuben but was passed to Joseph and then Ephraim when Reuben committed a serious sexual sin:

> The sons of Reuben the firstborn of Israel (he was the firstborn, but when he defiled his father's marriage bed, his rights as firstborn were given to the sons of Joseph son of Israel; so he could not be listed in the genealogical record in accordance with his birthright, and though Judah was the strongest of his brothers and a ruler came from him, the rights of the firstborn belonged to Joseph). (1 Chronicles 5:1-3)

This transfer of the rights of the firstborn in the family of Israel (Jacob) repeated the transfer of the rights of the firstborn that took place in the family of Isaac, when Esau lost the birthright to his younger twin Jacob. According to Genesis 48:13-19, Jacob retained his Abel-type authority until his death. Thus although Joseph remained faithful to his father, it was Jacob who decided which of Joseph's twin sons would be the main inheritor of Joseph's Abel status in the family. Much later, Jeremiah would confirm the special favor God granted Ephraim, even though his tribe became part of the Cain-type Northern Kingdom of Israel during the period of divided kingdoms:

> Is Ephraim my dear son? Is he my darling child? For as often as I speak against him, I do remember him still. Therefore my heart yearns for him; I will surely have mercy on him, says the LORD. (Jeremiah 31:20)

Which brings us back to the story of Boaz and Ruth. When Naomi's husband and two sons died in Moab, Naomi decided to return to her home in Bethlehem. Her widowed daughter-in-law Ruth insisted on going with her, even though it meant leaving her family and tribe to live with strangers. By doing this she was sacrificing the comforts of living with her own people, the Cain-type descendants of Lot—son of the Cain-type older brother of Abraham—to join the Abel-type lineage of Abraham, Isaac and Jacob:

> But Ruth said, "Entreat me not to leave you or to return from following you; for where you go I will go, and where you lodge I will lodge; your people shall be my people, and your God my God; where you die I will die, and there will I be buried. May the LORD do so to me and more also if even death parts me from you." And when Naomi saw that she was determined to go with her, she said no more. (Ruth 1:16-18)

Ruth's heart of determination, even at the cost of her life, proved providential. Like Rebekah before her, who made the sacrifice to leave her home in Haran to become the wife of Isaac and mother of Jacob, Ruth's sacrifice enabled her to play a central role in the providence unfolding in the home of Boaz, a relative of Naomi living in Bethlehem. Boaz was another member of the Ephrathite clan, according to Ruth 2:1 and 3, and 1 Chronicles 2:5-11. Through his father Salma and ancestor Perez he was also a descendant of Judah. So Boaz combined the lineages of Judah and Joseph, the two most Abel-type sons of Jacob. Guided by Naomi, Ruth took an opportunity to stay with Boaz one night and, although he was much older, the next day he decided to take her as his wife. He reported his intention to marry Ruth to the elders:

> "Also Ruth the Moabitess, the widow of Mahlon, I have bought to be my wife, to perpetuate the name of the dead in his inheritance, that the name of the dead may not be cut off from among his brethren and from the gate of his native place; you are witnesses this day." Then all the people who were at the gate, and the elders, said, "We are witnesses. May the Lord make the woman, who is coming into your house, like Rachel and Leah, who together built up the house of Israel. May you prosper in Ephrathah and be renowned in Bethlehem; and may your house be like the house of Perez, whom Tamar bore to Judah, because of the children that the Lord will give you by this young woman." (Ruth 4:10-12)

Interestingly, in approving Boaz's marriage to Ruth, the elders referred to two other out-of-the-ordinary families in the central providence as models that Boaz and Ruth should follow: the families of Jacob and Judah, which we have discussed. Thus Obed their son combined the Abel-type Ephrathite/Judahite line of his father with the Cain-type Moabite line of his mother. This providential lineage was inherited by Obed's son Jesse and grandson David. Ruth's commitment to serve the providence was the key to laying a foundation for the success of David.

Esther and King Ahasuerus

Esther was a member of the Jewish community of exiles from Judah who lived in Susa, the Persian capital of the Achaemenid Empire. Esther is beloved among the Jewish people because of her sacrificial behavior as the woman who won the heart of King Ahasuerus (Xerxes 1) and as his wife was able to save her people.

The chief of Ahasuerus' court, Haman, had persuaded the king to issue an edict that all Jews in his kingdom be killed. Esther's father, Mordecai, asked her to intercede with the king. This was difficult to do, since the king's rule was that any of his wives who wished to see him had to be invited to do so by him. Approaching him without an invitation risked being put to death. Esther, however, found a way to please the king:

> On the third day Esther put on her royal robes and stood in the inner court of the king's palace, opposite the king's hall. The king was sitting on his royal throne inside the palace opposite the entrance to the palace; and when the king saw Queen Esther standing in the court, she found favor in his sight and he held out to Esther the golden scepter that was in his hand. Then Esther approached and touched the top of the scepter. And the king said to her, "What is it, Queen Esther? What is your request? It shall be given you, even to the half of my kingdom." (Esther 5:1-3)

Her only request was that the king and Haman attend a banquet that she was holding in his honor. At the banquet, she revealed to the king the scheme of Haman to get rid of the Jews and steal their possessions. The king was angered and commanded that Haman be executed and his position given to Mordecai. Esther then begged the king to reverse his edict to kill the Jews:

> Then Esther spoke again to the king; she fell at his feet and besought him with tears to avert the evil design of Haman the Agagite and the plot which he had devised against the Jews. And the king held out the golden scepter to Esther, and Esther rose and stood before the king. And she said, "If it please the king, and if I have found favor in his sight, and if the thing seem right before the king, and I be pleasing in his eyes, let an order be written to revoke the letters devised by Haman the Agagite, the son of Hammedatha, which he wrote to destroy the Jews who are in all the provinces of the king. For how can I endure to see

> the calamity that is coming to my people? Or how can I endure to see the destruction of my kindred?" Then King Ahasuerus said to Queen Esther and to Mordecai the Jew, "Behold, I have given Esther the house of Haman, and they have hanged him on the gallows, because he would lay hands on the Jews. And you may write as you please with regard to the Jews, in the name of the king, and seal it with the king's ring; for an edict written in the name of the king and sealed with the king's ring cannot be revoked." (Esther 8:3-8)

Saving the Jews in exile was of critical importance to the providence, and Esther's bravery would soon be rewarded. The third son of Ahasuerus was Artaxerxes I, who took power in Susa after Darius 1. Among his servants was the Jew Nehemiah. In 444 BC Nehemiah got permission from the king to leave Susa with a group of exiled Jews and return to Jerusalem to rebuild the city walls and the Temple, which had been destroyed in the sack of Jerusalem by the Babylonians in 597 BC. Artaxerxes trusted him so much that he not only allowed him to go to Jerusalem but also appointed him governor of Judea, a province of the Achaemenid Empire.

Nehemiah was successful in his reconstruction activities, and worked together with the scribe Ezra to reawaken the spirit of the Jews in Jerusalem by reading the scriptures to them and getting them to recommit to the word. Ezra had also been permitted to return to Jerusalem from exile by Artaxerxes:

> Now after this, in the reign of Artaxerxes king of Persia, Ezra... went up from Babylonia. He was a scribe skilled in the law of Moses which the LORD the God of Israel had given; and the king granted him all that he asked, for the hand of the LORD his God was upon him. (Ezra 7:1, 6)

Thus the importance of Esther risking her life to save the exiled Jews of the Achaemenid Empire cannot be overstated. This passage about the completion of reconstruction of the Temple sums up its significance well:

> They finished their building by command of the God of Israel and by decree of Cyrus and Darius and Artaxerxes king of Persia; and this house was finished on the third day of the month of Adar, in the sixth year of the reign of Darius the king. And the people of Israel, the priests and the Levites, and the rest of the returned exiles, celebrated the dedication of this house of God with joy. (Nehemiah 6:13-16)

Mary Inherited These Women's Foundation

These are the stories of some of the women who played a critical role in the providence leading to the advent of Jesus. All of them set an example for Mary by overcoming enormous difficulties, with many risking their lives in obedience to God. As the mother of the Messiah, Mary bore the greatest responsibility of them all.

Chapter 10

Jesus Inherited the Missions of Moses and David

Combining the Roles of Priest and King

How Did Jesus Represent Moses and David?

The Gospel of Matthew begins with a genealogy that shows the lineage of Jesus running from Abraham to Joseph, Mary's betrothed, through the major providential figures Abraham, Isaac, Jacob, Judah and David. But a central Christian belief, based on the Gospels, is that Jesus was not the son of Joseph but of the virgin Mary, who was impregnated under the authority of the Holy Spirit. Before conceiving Jesus, Mary was visited by the angel Gabriel, who told her:

> The Holy Spirit will come on you, and the power of the Most High will overshadow you. So the holy one to be born will be called the Son of God. (Luke 1:5)

As we have noted, Mary was the cousin of Elizabeth, the Levite wife of the Levite priest Zechariah. It is likely, then, that Mary was also a Levite. There is no genealogy for Mary provided in the Bible, but in Luke's Gospel the fact that Jesus was not actually the son of Joseph, a descendant of David and Judah, is made clear. Luke's genealogy for Joseph passes through Heli to ancestors that include David, Judah, Jacob, Abraham, Noah and Adam. It begins:

> Jesus, when he began his ministry, was about thirty years of age,

> being the son (as was supposed) of Joseph, the son of Heli...
> (Luke 3:23)

The "as was supposed" of course relates to the fact that the public would have known Jesus as the son of Joseph whereas Christians 'in the know' would have known that Joseph was not the actual father of Jesus, but his step-father. It must have been very difficult for Joseph to accept the position he was put in, especially when Mary became pregnant with Jesus. However, it was undoubtedly important for Joseph, as the representative of Judah and David, to stay with Mary and accept Jesus as his son, thereby supporting the providence of God and protecting the mother and child from the stigma of an out-of-wedlock birth.

Matthew records Joseph planning to quietly divorce Mary, but being encouraged by an angel to remain with her and protect her:

> Now the birth of Jesus Christ took place in this way. When his mother Mary had been betrothed to Joseph, before they came together she was found to be with child of the Holy Spirit; and her husband Joseph, being a just man and unwilling to put her to shame, resolved to divorce her quietly. But as he considered this, behold, an angel of the Lord appeared to him in a dream, saying, "Joseph, son of David, do not fear to take Mary your wife, for that which is conceived in her is of the Holy Spirit; she will bear a son, and you shall call his name Jesus, for he will save his people from their sins." (Matthew 1:18-21)

The Importance of Being a Descendant of Levi and Moses

According to the Biblical record, then, we do not know who the real father of Jesus was and hence what his lineage was. However, for Mary there is every indication that she was a Levite. There is also a high likelihood that she went to her cousin Elizabeth's home to meet the Levite whom the Holy Spirit wanted her to accept as the father of her child. Thus only the family of Zechariah and Mary knew who the father of Jesus was and therefore exactly how he was connected through blood lineage to the providential figures of the Old Testament era.

At the time of Moses, his tribe, the Levites, was chosen by God to represent all the first-born of Israel whom God had claimed as his own when they left Egypt:

> "And you shall appoint Aaron and his sons, and they shall attend to their priesthood; but if any one else comes near, he shall be put to death." And the LORD said to Moses, "Behold, I have taken the Levites from among the people of Israel instead of every first-born that opens the womb among the people of Israel." (Numbers 3:10-12)

The Levites were chosen to be the priestly tribe under Moses' older brother Aaron because they had remained faithful to Moses and God when the other tribes had worshipped an Egyptian idol at Mount Sinai. (The reason for this choice and the anointing of the Levites is explained in detail in Chapter 12.)

Being of Levitical ancestry was important for Jesus insofar as he was to fulfill a priestly role in his mission as Messiah. This meant restoring the role of sinless man before the Fall and creating a family free from the dominion of Satan. The family of this Second Adam and Second Eve would then become the ancestors of a new, sinless lineage. This was the core mission of the Messiah, trumping his secondary role as heir to David's throne.

The Importance of Being a Descendant of Judah and David

The importance of the genealogies of Matthew and Luke was to satisfy the Jewish belief that the Messiah, or Christ, would be descended from David, the king of Israel most beloved by God and looked up to with the greatest respect by the people of Israel. As Messiah, he was to be anointed as the savior of the Jewish people and king of the nation of Israel. As prophesized:

> For to us a child is born, to us a son is given, and the government will be on his shoulders. And he will be called: Wonderful Coun-

selor, Mighty God, Everlasting Father, Prince of Peace. Of the greatness of his government and peace there will be no end. He will reign on David's throne and over his kingdom, establishing and upholding it with justice and righteousness from that time on and forever. (Isaiah 9:6-7)

Who was David and why was he important to Israel? David was a member of the tribe of Judah, who were descendants of the fourth son of Jacob and Leah. Judah had been designated by Jacob to lead his 11 brothers, known as Israelites after their father received the new name, Israel. Thus the head of the tribe of Judah was the leading figure in the central providence, the person most responsible for securing a victory for Abel over Cain and restoring the Adamic lineage. The tribe of Judah was given a choice location in the promised land when the tribes first arrived from Egypt with Joshua, after spending 40 years in the wilderness.

However, for the first four centuries the Jews spent in Canaan they were not a single nation. This made them vulnerable to attack by their many enemies, and eventually their pleas for a king were answered when the prophet Samuel anointed Saul the first king of the United Kingdom of Israel. But Saul proved to be a man of many faults who failed to make Israel into a nation that could receive the Messiah:

> The LORD said to Samuel, "How long will you grieve over Saul, seeing I have rejected him from being king over Israel? Fill your horn with oil, and go; I will send you to Jesse the Bethlehemite, for I have provided for myself a king among his sons." (1 Samuel 16:1)

Samuel could not find the chosen king among the sons of Jesse until he asked to see the youngest, David, who was tending sheep. When David came in from the fields, Samuel was told by God that this boy would be king:

> Now he was ruddy, and had beautiful eyes, and was handsome. And the LORD said, "Arise, anoint him; for this is he." Then

> Samuel took the horn of oil, and anointed him in the midst of his brothers; and the Spirit of the LORD came mightily upon David from that day forward. (1 Samuel 16:12-13)

Meanwhile, Saul, who had lost God's blessing, became a dark and tragic figure. Nevertheless, David befriended Saul's son Jonathan and served the king faithfully, beginning by entertaining him but then becoming the most valuable soldier in his army when, even as a youth he killed the nemesis of Israel, Goliath. Jealous of David and his popularity in Israel, Saul dedicated much of his time and energy trying to kill him. But David was always able to escape, sometimes miraculously. Eventually Saul killed himself after losing a battle, and David was made king.

David was Abel to Saul's Cain, and was the first successful ruler of the United Kingdom of Israel, the nation chosen by God to receive the Messiah. He made Jerusalem his capital and brought the Ark of the Covenant there, to be replaced by the Temple, which was built by his son, Solomon. Throughout his life he fought the enemies of Israel, constantly enlarging its boundaries, such that when Solomon inherited David's throne Israel reached the zenith of its power, wealth and prestige.

In the Psalms, David expressed his great love for God. This is most beautifully articulated in Psalm 23:

> The Lord is my shepherd, I shall not want;
>   he makes me lie down in green pastures.
> He leads me beside still waters;
>   he restores my soul.
> He leads me in paths of righteousness
>   for his name's sake.
> Even though I walk through the valley of the shadow of death,
>   I fear no evil;
> for thou art with me;
>   thy rod and thy staff,
>   they comfort me.

> Thou preparest a table before me
>> in the presence of my enemies;
> thou anointest my head with oil,
>> my cup overflows.
> Surely goodness and mercy shall follow me
>> all the days of my life;
> and I shall dwell in the house of the Lord
>> for ever.

And God loved David. Even after the great king had long since passed into the Spirit World, God would treat Israel with patience and forgiveness for the sake of David. For example:

> Now in the eighteenth year of King Jeroboam the son of Nebat, Abijam began to reign over Judah. He reigned for three years in Jerusalem. His mother's name was Maacah the daughter of Abishalom. And he walked in all the sins which his father did before him; and his heart was not wholly true to the Lord his God, as the heart of David his father. Nevertheless for David's sake the Lord his God gave him a lamp in Jerusalem, setting up his son after him, and establishing Jerusalem; because David did what was right in the eyes of the Lord, and did not turn aside from anything that he commanded him all the days of his life, except in the matter of Uriah the Hittite. (1 Kings 15:1-5)

Thus even though David had sinned when he sent Uriah to his death in order to take Uriah's wife, Bathsheba, for himself, he was the model of a faithful king of a united Israel and for his sake God would forgive many sins by the kings who followed him once Solomon's reign ended and the kingdoms were divided, north and south. Because of Solomon's many failings related to his taking 700 wives and 300 concubines, and worshipping some of their idols, the kingdom of David came to represent the high point in the history of Israel. Thus for the Jews, the Messiah who was to inherit the throne of David was to be a king of David's caliber at least, a man of

God capable of defeating all of Israel's enemies and fulfilling the promise of the chosen nation.

Jesus' Disciples Said he was Descended from King David

Many of Jesus' disciples and followers considered him the descendant, or 'son', of David. Three of the Gospel writers use the term son of David—Matthew, ten times; Mark and Luke, four times each. (John's Gospel does not use the term.) Importantly for the Christian Church as it formulated its doctrines, Saint Paul called Jesus the descendant of David. Below are some samples of these scriptures. From the Gospels:

> The book of the genealogy of Jesus Christ, the son of David, the son of Abraham. (Matthew 1:1)
>
> Most of the crowd spread their garments on the road, and others cut branches from the trees and spread them on the road. And the crowds that went before him and that followed him shouted, "Hosanna to the Son of David! Blessed is he who comes in the name of the Lord! Hosanna in the highest!" (Matthew 21:8-9)
>
> And when he heard that it was Jesus of Nazareth, he began to cry out and say, "Jesus, Son of David, have mercy on me!" And many rebuked him, telling him to be silent; but he cried out all the more, "Son of David, have mercy on me!" (Mark 10:47-48 and Luke 18:38-3)

From the letters of Saint Paul:

> Paul, a servant of Jesus Christ, called to be an apostle, set apart for the gospel of God which he promised beforehand through his prophets in the holy scriptures the gospel concerning his Son, who was descended from David according to the flesh and designated Son of God in power according to the Spirit of holiness by his resurrection from the dead, Jesus Christ our Lord. (Romans 1:1-4)

> Remember Jesus Christ, risen from the dead, descended from David, as preached in my gospel, the gospel for which I am suffering and wearing fetters like a criminal. (2 Timothy 2:8-9)

But Jesus Rejected the 'Son of David' Identity

Jesus himself, however, rejected the notion that the Messiah was the 'son of David', warning both the people of Israel and his disciples about that belief, and explaining that the position of the Messiah was higher than any previously held by a man, referring to the words of David himself, in Psalm 110:

> Now while the Pharisees were gathered together, Jesus asked them a question, saying, "What do you think of the Christ? Whose son is he?" They said to him, "The son of David." He said to them, "How is it then that David, inspired by the Spirit, calls him Lord, saying, 'The Lord said to my Lord, "Sit at my right hand, till I put thy enemies under thy feet"'? If David thus calls him Lord, how is he his son?" And no one was able to answer him a word, nor from that day did any one dare to ask him any more questions. (Matthew 22:41-46)

The Gospels of Mark and Luke also record this exchange, making it highly likely that it took place:

> And as Jesus taught in the temple, he said, "How can the scribes say that the Christ is the son of David? David himself, inspired by the Holy Spirit, declared, 'The LORD said to my Lord, "Sit at my right hand, till I put thy enemies under thy feet."' David himself calls him Lord; so how is he his son?" (Mark 12:35-37 and Luke 20:41-44)

A Providential Perspective

As we have shown, for the Jewish people the Messiah was to be a king in the lineage of David. The disciples knew this and in order to win the Jews to a belief in Jesus as Christ they sometimes claimed that Jesus was the "son of David." You could say this claim was for public consumption, because the scriptures provide no evidence that Jesus was in the lineage of David. In fact, the scriptures emphatically state that Jesus was not the son of Joseph, who was a descendant of David. The Gospels say that Jesus was the son of Mary and 'the Holy Spirit'.

However, from a providential perspective, Jesus was indeed a descendant of David, insofar as he was, like David before him, the central figure of God's providence in his time. Furthermore, as Psalm 110 anticipated, Jesus was at a higher level than David, whose mission had been to prepare the nation of Israel to receive the Messiah. At the time of Jesus' advent, the throne of David was occupied by the Herodian dynasty under the aegis of the Roman Empire. This was the throne the Messiah was to ascend.

David and Solomon wielded far greater political, economic and military power than Jesus ever did, but it was to prepare the way for Messiah that they had been so blessed. The people of Israel never understood that Jesus was the awaited Messiah because his life was so greatly different from that of a mighty king. Only Jesus fully understood this and he suffered greatly trying to teach the people that he was their Messiah even though there were radical differences between their expectations and the reality of his life.

Despite these Messianic expectations in Israel, the most important providential role of Jesus as savior was as the man who would restore the relationship of human beings with their Divine Creator—the relationship that had been lost in the Fall. This was a spiritual and priestly role that could be fulfilled only through the sinless birth of Christ.

The lineage prepared for this was that of Moses and the Levites—the tribe chosen by God to serve as priests to the people of Israel. Hence a qualification for Mary to be chosen as mother of Jesus was her Levitical ancestry. However, Mary was chosen not only because of her lineage but even more importantly because of her purity of heart and her willingness to risk her reputation and even her life in order to follow the instructions of Gabriel.

From the point of view of Israel's establishment, however, the father of a household determined the tribal affiliation of the children.[1] Joseph was a member of the tribe of Judah. Thus, since Jesus was known to the world as a son of Joseph and Mary, his disciples claimed that he was indeed in the lineage of David and Judah.

Jesus came as the Messiah to be both high priest and king of Israel on the foundation of two Abel-type lines from Jacob's family: the priestly role being from Levi through his descendant Moses, and the kingly role being from Judah—the son chosen by Jacob to lead the twelve tribes of Israel—through his descendant David. This combined lineage prepared Jesus to be a priest-king after the Order of Melchizedek, as explained in Chapter 7.

For the people of Israel, the Messiah's role as king was most important. For Christians, Jesus' role as priest was most important. To understand his providential role fully, we need to recognize that Jesus came as both priest and king.

---

1. Interestingly, scholars believe that the system of matrilineal rather than patrilineal descent and inheritance that is prevalent in today's Judaism originated around the time of Jesus. Based on the genealogies that Matthew and Luke provided for Joseph, this system was not in place before Christ.

Chapter 11

Preparing a Nation and the World for the Messiah

Central and Supporting Providential Developments

As we have indicated, the Biblical history that traces God's work to save all humanity from the dominion of Satan, beginning with Adam's family and continuing to the advent of Jesus and the birth of Christianity, is the story of the central providence. Although there is insufficient space in this book to cover in detail the central and supporting providential events that prepared the way for Jesus to fulfill the role of Messiah, there are a number of highlights that we discuss in this chapter.

Furthermore, especially during the last 400 years of the preparations in Israel, there were also many significant developments in various parts of the world that were part of the providence, although they played a supporting role to the events surrounding the life of Jesus. Some of the highlights of these global developments are discussed at the end of this chapter.

The Importance of Abraham's Family

Abraham's family looms so large in providential history because it was the first family after the Fall to establish a significant foundation to restore humanity to its original, sinless state. From Abraham's family came the primary, or central, providence that emerged from Jacob's family of 12 sons who became the 12 tribes of the chosen nation of Israel. Then there was the secondary providence that emerged from Abraham's first son, Ishmael, whose 12 sons became 12 tribes of Arabs to whom the prophet Mohammed was sent many centuries later, establishing the religion of Islam. The tertiary providence was that of Lot, Abraham's nephew, from whom came the people of Moab and Ammon. All would play important roles in the providence, roles determined by the direction taken in the central providence.

Jacob's Victorious Course as Abel and Adam

Jacob was of particular importance in Abraham's family because he succeeded in reversing the pattern of Cain-type sons dominating and murdering their Abel-type younger brothers. With the help of his mother Rebekah, Jacob was able to win the birthright and blessing from his older twin Esau, who wanted to kill him in revenge for losing the blessing. Again with the help of Rebekah, Jacob then worked for Rebekah's brother Laban in Haran, overcoming his uncle's devious behavior and thereby conditionally restoring the rightful position of Adam over Lucifer, the archangel, represented by Laban.

Jacob confirmed his dominion over the angels when after serving Laban for 21 years he returned to his homeland to meet Esau. On the eve of that meeting, he defeated an angel who confronted and wrestled with him at a ford over the river Jabbok.

Based on this victory over an angel, Jacob was given the new name Israel, meaning he who prevails with God. In the Bible, from this time on Jacob and Israel are used interchangeably for him, but Israel became the name for the nation, and Israelites became the name for the descendants of Jacob.

Once he had dominated the angel, Jacob then proceeded towards the place where Esau, harboring resentment from the loss of the birthright and blessing, had led an army of 400 to attack him. Jacob had already sent ahead a large number of animals as gifts to appease his brother, and when he saw Esau he led his family in bowing before Esau with great humility. Esau was moved by the gifts and the sight of Jacob bowing low seven times as he approached:

> [Jacob] himself went on before them, bowing himself to the

ground seven times, until he came near to his brother. But Esau ran to meet him, and embraced him, and fell on his neck and kissed him, and they wept. (Genesis 33:3-4)

Thus Jacob was a victorious Abel in winning over his brother Esau—reversing Cain's murder of Abel—and a victorious Adam in winning over both his uncle Laban and the angel at Jabbok—reversing Lucifer's angelic dominion over Adam through Eve.

This was a great moment in the providence, when Esau was able to overcome his bitterness and embrace his brother, instead of repeating the sin of Cain by killing him. And it was a victory for God that finally Abel could overcome Cain through service and love. Esau himself was transformed by the experience:

> Esau said, "What do you mean by all this company which I met?" Jacob answered, "To find favor in the sight of my lord." But Esau said, "I have enough, my brother; keep what you have for yourself." Jacob said, "No, I pray you, if I have found favor in your sight, then accept my present from my hand; for truly to see your face is like seeing the face of God, with such favor have you received me." (Genesis 33:8-10)

Rebekah's Victorious Role as Eve

Jacob's mother Rebekah played a very important role in helping her Abel-type son achieve providential success. First, she was victorious in reversing Eve's failure to resist the seduction of Lucifer—when she overcame the seduction of King Abimelech (see Chapter 9). Second, she was victorious in reversing Eve's seduction of Adam by helping her husband Isaac do the right thing when he blessed Jacob rather than Esau—despite Isaac favoring Esau. Third, Rebekah was victorious in reversing Eve's failure to help Abel overcome Cain when, as Jacob's mother, she helped him to receive the blessing from Isaac, helped him avoid the wrath of Esau, and ultimately helped him win over Esau on his own, Godly terms—without using force.

Jacob was not sinless, and not the Messiah. But he established a pattern of success for the providence that foreshadowed the course for Jesus himself. Jesus, too, would have to reverse the relationship of Abel with Cain and establish the dominion of Adam over Lucifer in order to create a new Godly family and lineage.

And Mary would have to follow the example of Rebekah in enabling her son to succeed in his mission. Thus the path of Jacob and Rebekah sheds light on the path that Jesus and Mary had to tread, and can help us understand the significance of Jesus' life leading to the crucifixion, and the role Mary played in that outcome.

Establishing a Nation to Receive the Messiah

Because of the success of Jacob and Rebekah in making conditions to restore the family of Adam and Eve, Jacob's 12 sons were chosen to establish a Godly nation that could receive the Messiah. Each son would become the patriarch of his own providential tribe, and all the tribes together would create the providential nation of Israel.

This was a necessary process since without the protection of an Abel-type nation, the mission of the Messiah to save the Cain-type world of Satanic dominion would be extraordinarily difficult. The likelihood of Cain-type forces killing the Abel-type Messiah would be great without this protection. Thus the central providence from the time of Jacob to the advent of Jesus was for the chosen people of Israel to establish a nation that would serve as an Abel-type environment to receive and protect the Messiah.

400 Years of Slavery in Egypt

However, while Jacob was still alive, his whole family moved to Egypt to escape a famine, and there became enslaved. This had been foretold when Abraham had failed in making a sacrifice of birds as instructed:

> As the sun was going down, a deep sleep fell on Abram; and lo, a dread and great darkness fell upon him. Then the Lord said to Abram, "Know of a surety that your descendants will be sojourners in a land that is not theirs, and will be slaves there, and they will be oppressed for four hundred years." (Genesis 15:12-13)

Moses Struggled With a Disobedient People

After the Israelites spent four centuries in Egypt, Moses was sent as their liberator and—after receiving the Ten Commandments from God at Sinai—he took them on a trek through wilderness country to the promised land of Canaan, where they were to establish a nation for the first time. It was during this period that the chosen people received the first ever laws to govern their lives, in the form of Ten Commandments—which were later elaborated into the Mosaic Law.

However, because of the Israelites' frequent complaining and lack of faith in the Divine Providence and the leadership of Moses, what could have been a trip of a few months became a grueling 40-year odyssey. This prolongation took place after Moses sent 12 spies into Canaan to evaluate the situation there for 40 days. Only two of the spies, Joshua and Caleb, returned with a positive report:

> But Caleb quieted the people before Moses, and said, "Let us go up at once, and occupy it; for we are well able to overcome it." (Numbers 13:30)

But the other ten spies said it would be too dangerous and difficult to enter Canaan:

> Then the men who had gone up with him said, "We are not able to go up against the people; for they are stronger than we." (Numbers 13:31)

The people ignored Joshua and Caleb and heeded the dire warnings of the other ten spies, clamoring to return to Egypt:

> Then all the congregation raised a loud cry; and the people wept that night. And all the people of Israel murmured against Moses and Aaron; the whole congregation said to them, "Would that we had died in the land of Egypt! Or would that we had died in this wilderness! Why does the Lord bring us into this land, to fall by the sword? Our wives and our little ones will become a prey;

would it not be better for us to go back to Egypt?" And they said to one another, "Let us choose a captain, and go back to Egypt." (Numbers 14:1-4)

After all the signs the people had received to show them that Moses was the leader God had sent them, they still doubted him and, as at Sinai, wanted to return to the relative security of slavery in Egypt.

This susceptibility to intimidation from a Cain-type foe would prove to be the classical problem of Cain-type elements within an Abel camp, and it has oft been repeated in providential history—including during the life of Jesus. The result is prolongation of suffering by Abel and postponement of the providence. In this case, Moses and Aaron pleaded with the people to listen to Joshua and Caleb, but the people refused and threatened to stone their leaders.

The Bible describes the wrath of God at this faithlessness:

> Then the glory of the Lord appeared at the tent of meeting to all the people of Israel. And the Lord said to Moses, "How long will this people despise me? And how long will they not believe in me, in spite of all the signs which I have wrought among them? I will strike them with the pestilence and disinherit them, and I will make of you a nation greater and mightier than they." (Numbers 14:10-12)

Thus God wanted to disinherit Israel and use Moses separately from them to establish a nation to receive the Messiah. But Moses pleaded with God to spare the Israelites. They were spared immediate destruction but their suffering in the wilderness was extended to 40 years and that generation was not permitted to enter Canaan:

> Then the Lord said, "I have pardoned, according to your word; but truly, as I live, and as all the earth shall be filled with the glory of the Lord, none of the men who have seen my glory and my signs which I wrought in Egypt and in the wilderness, and yet have put me to the proof these ten times and have not hear-

> kened to my voice, shall see the land which I swore to give to their fathers; and none of those who despised me shall see it. But my servant Caleb, because he has a different spirit and has followed me fully, I will bring into the land into which he went, and his descendants shall possess it. (Numbers 14:20-24)

Thus Caleb—and Joshua, although not mentioned here—were exempted from this punishment because of their faithfulness in seeing the possibility of realizing the providence in Canaan.

Moses and Aaron were held to a higher standard of faith and obedience, and they would also be forbidden from entering Canaan when their faith was shown to be lacking. This occurred when the people were thirsty and God told Moses and Aaron to gather them before a rock in Kadesh, and to show the power of the Almighty by telling the rock to give water. But Moses was unable to contain his frustration at the faithlessness of the people, and instead of simply commanding the rock to give water, as he had been told to do, he struck it twice in anger, causing water to spring forth.

Moses and Aaron were told that this demonstration of ungodly anger would mean that they too would not be allowed to enter Canaan:

> Then Moses and Aaron went from the presence of the assembly to the door of the tent of meeting, and fell on their faces. And the glory of the LORD appeared to them, and the LORD said to Moses, "Take the rod, and assemble the congregation, you and Aaron your brother, and tell the rock before their eyes to yield its water; so you shall bring water out of the rock for them; so you shall give drink to the congregation and their cattle." And Moses took the rod from before the LORD, as he commanded him. And Moses and Aaron gathered the assembly together before the rock, and he said to them, "Hear now, you rebels; shall we bring forth water for you out of this rock?" And Moses lifted up his hand and struck the rock with his rod twice; and water came forth abundantly, and the congregation drank, and their cattle. And the Lord said to Moses and Aaron, "Because you did not believe in me, to sanctify me in the eyes of the people of Israel,

therefore you shall not bring this assembly into the land which I have given them." (Numbers 20:6-12)

And so it was. Aaron died before Moses, who was only allowed to see the promised land from Mount Nebo before he too died. Moses passed the leadership of Israel to Joshua, who would take the people across the Jordan River into Canaan.

The struggles of Moses and Aaron with the almost constant faithlessness of the Israelites would become an oft-repeated pattern in the history of Israel as, again and again, the chosen people and their leaders failed to fulfill the responsibilities required of an Abel-type population and nation qualified to receive the Messiah. Sadly, this was exactly the problem Jesus faced centuries later when he struggled to overcome the opposition of Israel to his Messianic mission.

400 Years of Judges

Canaan was the land promised to the Israelites, the place of their settlement after centuries of slavery under pagan masters and four decades of wandering in the wilderness. Here for the first time, then, the people of Israel could establish a nation to receive the Messiah.

Jacob's family had numbered 70 when it moved to Egypt at the invitation of Joseph, the second to last son of Jacob. He had risen from slave to prime minister and was able to invite them to live with him. By the time of their liberation by Moses, the number of Israelites had grown to some 600,000 men and their families. The tribe of Joseph had been split between his twin sons, Ephraim and Manasseh, making 13 tribes in all.

Since the Levites were the priestly tribe, they were not given territory in the promised land, but were granted concessions in certain cities. Thus the land was divided among 12 tribes, mainly on the west side of the Jordan River, although the tribes of Reuben and Gad, and half tribe of Manasseh, were given land on the east side of the Jordan.

Their first leader in Canaan was Joshua, who had been loyal to Moses and faithful to God during the wilderness passage. His mandate as given him through Moses was to establish the tribes in the land of Canaan. During his lifetime he conquered 31 minor kings in the territory of Canaan and oversaw the distribution of territory among the 12 tribes. Joshua was the first judge of Israel. On his death, other judges would take his place. The judges were complemented by priests and prophets who shared in the task of educating the people and keeping them pure from idolatry and intermarriage with the various Canaanite tribes.

The United Kingdom of Israel

As we discussed in the previous chapter, the United Kingdom of Israel was established by Samuel in response to the requests of the Jews for a king who could unite the tribes into a nation capable of staving off the attacks of their many enemies. From a providential point of view, creating a single nation was a necessary step in Israel's preparations to receive the Messiah.

Samuel anointed Saul the first king of the United Kingdom of Israel, but during his 40-year reign he was ineffective and embroiled Israel in many conflicts that weakened rather than strengthened the nascent nation. With Samuel's blessing, once Saul died David became king. David also ruled for 40 years, but he was a great king and warrior, and greatly expanded Israel's domains. On his death, Solomon ascended the throne. During Solomon's 40-year reign, Israel's power and wealth reached its zenith, but Solomon failed to unite the tribes around the one God when he allowed idolatry to get established in his kingdom.

This was such a serious mistake that Israel lost its qualification to become God's chosen nation. On Solomon's death, the kingdom was divided, north and south, with his servant Jeroboam becoming king over ten tribes in the north, and his son Rehoboam becoming king over two tribes (Judah and Benjamin) in the south.

Thus the foundation for the Messiah established by the United Kingdom was lost. The tribes were divided because of Solomon's failure to fulfill his providential responsibilities and the advent of the Messiah had to be postponed until a united kingdom could be established once again. This would take place only after several centuries, when Nehemiah and Ezra oversaw the rebuilding of Jerusalem and the Temple after the Babylonian exile.

The Divided Kingdoms and Babylonian Exile

The divided kingdoms era was characterized by idolatry and disobedience towards God, despite the repeated warnings of prophets such as Elijah, Isaiah and Jeremiah. The Northern Kingdom of Israel was eventually punished by the invasion of Assyrians who conquered Samaria and enslaved the Jews, permanently dispersing the ten tribes. The Southern Kingdom of Judah was conquered by the Babylonians, Jerusalem and the Temple were destroyed and the tribespeople of Judah and Benjamin taken into captivity in Babylon.

This exile was a period of remorse and repentance for the Israelites, as they realized the errors that had led to the loss of their Temple, capital city and nation. They had abandoned God to pursue false idols and the false teachings associated with them, and they had not listened to the warnings of the prophets God had sent to them.

Israel is Reconstituted

After the 70-year exile, the people were allowed to return to Jerusalem by Cyrus the Great of Persia, who had conquered Babylon. Under the leadership of the governor Nehemiah and the scribe Ezra, who had returned from Babylon, the walls of Jerusalem and the Temple were rebuilt and the people were read the law of Moses, which they committed to follow. They confessed and repented of their sins and turned back to God:

> And all the people gathered as one man into the square before the Water Gate; and they told Ezra the scribe to bring the book of the law of Moses which the Lord had given to Israel. And Ezra the priest brought the law before the assembly, both men and women and all who could hear with understanding, on the first day of the seventh month. And he read from it facing the square before the Water Gate from early morning until midday, in the presence of the men and the women and those who could

> understand; and the ears of all the people were attentive to the book of the law. (Nehemiah 8:1-3)
>
> Now on the twenty-fourth day of this month the people of Israel were assembled with fasting and in sackcloth, and with earth upon their heads. And the Israelites separated themselves from all foreigners, and stood and confessed their sins and the iniquities of their fathers. And they stood up in their place and read from the book of the law of the Lord their God for a fourth of the day; for another fourth of it they made confession and worshiped the Lord their God. (Nehemiah 9:1-3)

Israel was still only a province of the Achaemenid Empire, so the Israelites were still subjects of their Persian rulers, although they enjoyed greater freedom than their ancestors had in Egypt. Nevertheless, once more they longed for an independent nation of their own ruled by a king of their own, and therefore entered into a new covenant with God in the hope that they would be liberated from slavery once more:

> Now therefore, our God, the great and mighty and terrible God, who keepest covenant and steadfast love, let not all the hardship seem little to thee that has come upon us, upon our kings, our princes, our priests, our prophets, our fathers, and all thy people, since the time of the kings of Assyria until this day... Behold, we are slaves this day; in the land that thou gavest to our fathers to enjoy its fruit and its good gifts, behold, we are slaves. And its rich yield goes to the kings whom thou hast set over us because of our sins; they have power also over our bodies and over our cattle at their pleasure, and we are in great distress. Because of all this we make a firm covenant and write it, and our princes, our Levites, and our priests set their seal to it. (Nehemiah 9:32, 36-38)

Thus the nation chosen to receive the Messiah was reconstituted albeit with only limited independence—some 400 years before the advent of Jesus. (In John 2:20 the Jews told Jesus it had taken 46 years to rebuild the Temple. This would have been 46 years from 444 BC when Nehemiah arrived from Susa.)

The Final 400-Year Preparation of Israel for the Messiah

The final four centuries before the advent of Jesus were not a peaceful period. Beginning as a vassal state of Persia, Israel was conquered by Alexander the Great and then ruled by the descendant Ptolemaic and Seleucid kingdoms. In 170 BC the Temple was ransacked and looted by the Seleucid king Antiochus, and in 168 an altar to Zeus was set up in the Temple. This "abomination of abominations" prompted a bloody revolt by the sons of the Levitical priest Mattathias, a family known as the Maccabees. Their leader was Judas Maccabeus, whose brother Simon Thassi established the Hasmonean dynasty in Israel.

Under Hasmonean rule, from 142 BC Israel enjoyed 80 years of independence. This came to an end in 63 BC when Roman Emperor Pompey captured Jerusalem and the Hasmoneans became clients of Rome. With the support of Roman general Mark Anthony, in 37 BC Herod the Great—an Idumean (Idumea was the Roman term for Edom) whose father was an Edomite and mother a Nabatean Ishmaelite—captured Jerusalem from Antigonus II Mattathias, ending the Hasmonean dynasty. Herod and his sons continued to rule Israel as clients of Rome throughout the life of Jesus.

Herod's lineage combined descendants of the two main Cain-type figures of Abraham's family: Ishmael and Esau. Thus Herod the Great, who was in power when Jesus was born, was in the Cain position to the Abel-type lineage of Isaac, Jacob, Judah and David—whose throne Jesus was destined to ascend. This made Herod a natural enemy of Jesus, and someone who was bent on killing the new-born Christ as soon as he heard that Jesus was destined to be a ruler of Israel.

In the next chapter we will discuss details of the threat posed to Jesus by Herod as well as the other circumstances that made the early life of the Messiah extremely difficult.

The Axial Age: Worldwide Preparation for a Global Savior

Although the Bible focuses almost exclusively on the central providence through which Israel was chosen as the nation to receive the Messiah, there was a parallel movement of global enlightenment that was part of the providence preparing for a worldwide savior. This related movement was particularly notable in the rise of Asian religions and spiritual philosophies, and in the civilizational advances made in Greece and Rome. So significant was this period in world history that it was labeled the Axial Age by the German philosopher Karl Jaspers.

Building on the millennia-long foundations of Hinduism, both Buddhism and Jainism took root in India during the 6th century BC. In China, Confucianism was founded in the 6th century BC, followed by Taoism in the 4th century. Further west, Zoroastrianism was founded in Persia during the 6th century BC. (This religion would have a direct impact on the central providence of Israel when, in 538 BC, the Zoroastrian Persian emperor Cyrus the Great conquered Babylon and freed the Israelite captives, allowing them to return to their homeland and rebuild Jerusalem and the Temple.)

All these teachings brought fresh insights into truth and guided followers to live a virtuous life. More than that, they provided believers with a spiritual framework for understanding the world, and for leading lives that contribute to the Divine Providence.

While Asia was experiencing these sweeping changes, Greek thinkers were making unprecedented advances in philosophy, science and medicine. Socrates, Plato and Aristotle are considered the leading philosophers of this era, although Aristotle also contributed significantly to medicine. Pythagoras, Thales, Anaximander, Anaxagoras, Hippocrates, Eudoxus, Democritus, Theophrastus, Aristarchus, Euclid, Archimedes and Eratosthenes all made significant discoveries about the nature of the world and universe in fields ranging from botany, zoology and medicine to mathematics, astronomy and physics.

These discoveries would lead to many new inventions—including calipers, cartography, cranes, gears, plumbing, pumps, streets and winches—and would form the foundations for modern science which developed in Europe two millennia later through the twin revolutions of the Renaissance and Reformation.

Meanwhile, political leaders like Solon, Cleisthenes and Pericles pioneered early forms of democracy, while military leaders, notably Alexander the Great, helped establish a common cultural environment that included much of the known world. This facilitated the spread of enlightened thinking across political and linguistic boundaries.

This remarkable period of enlightenment in classical Greece would have a major impact on the world, earning it the moniker "Cradle of Western Civilization". Rome was the initial beneficiary of the developments in Greece and together Greece and Rome would have an enormous influence on the world, which became fully evident when two millennia later their ideas gave rise to science, democracy and capitalism.

The providence is not limited to religion, and thus religious, philosophical, scientific and all other forms of enlightenment contribute to the fulfillment of our Creator's purpose. Nevertheless, it is the Divine Providence that is the driving force of human development and the axis around which progress in all fields is able to fulfill its ultimate purpose.

PART II
THE PROVIDENCE BETRAYED IN THE CRUCIFIXION

Chapter 12

Jesus' Difficult Early Life

His Family Failed to Support Him

From his childhood, Jesus was remarkable. Quick to learn the scriptures, he developed a profound understanding of their meaning and of the Divine Providence of which he was the central player. After three decades of preparation, he launched his public ministry to share these insights with the people of Israel. His words had authority because he lived a morally perfect life, and demonstrated an intimate relationship with the Creator. However, throughout his life he suffered persecution and betrayal from the nation that had been expressly prepared to receive him as the Messiah, and his teaching was rejected by all but a small group of disciples. Thus he was an absolute yet lonely Abel let down by Cain-type individuals whose mission was to support him, and eventually captured, imprisoned, flogged and crucified by the Cain-type Israeli establishment bent on his destruction, working through the Roman governor Pontius Pilate.

Jesus Was Targeted for Murder at Birth

As we discussed in the previous chapter, the centuries leading up to the advent of Jesus were turbulent in Israel, with control of the state changing hands among powerful kingdoms and empires. At the time of Jesus' birth, Israel was ruled by King Herod the Great as a vassal state of the Roman Empire. (Many historians place Herod the Great's death in 4 BC, but this discrepancy with Biblical accounts is explained by an error of Dionysius, who made a calendar in the 6th century AD that placed the birth of Jesus a few years after it likely occurred.)

Herod earned "the Great" moniker because of the many massive construction projects he undertook, including rebuilding the walls of Jerusalem as well as the Temple and its environs on the Temple Mount. His rule over Israel was tenuous, however, since he was not a Jew, as we mentioned in the previous chapter. Thus he had good reason to be afraid of rivals to the throne rising from among the Jews, and especially anyone identified as the promised Messiah, who was expected to inherit the throne of David.

The Gospel of Matthew recounts the arrival of "wise men from the East" in Jerusalem, looking for a new-born king of the Jews they had been told of:

> Now when Jesus was born in Bethlehem of Judea in the days of Herod the king, behold, wise men from the East came to Jerusalem, saying, "Where is he who has been born king of the Jews? For we have seen his star in the East, and have come to worship him." (Matthew 2:1-2)

When Herod heard of this he was worried, and sought the advice of the religious leaders, who told him that there was a prophesy that Christ would be born in nearby Bethlehem:

> When Herod the king heard this, he was troubled, and all Jerusalem with him; and assembling all the chief priests and scribes of the people, he inquired of them where the Christ was to be born. They told him, "In Bethlehem of Judea; for so it is written by the prophet: 'And you, O Bethlehem, in the land of Judah, are by no means least among the rulers of Judah; for from you shall come a ruler who will govern my people Israel.'" (Matthew 2:3-6)

The passage they were referring to is from the Prophet Micah:

> But you, O Bethlehem Ephrathah, who are little to be among the clans of Judah, from you shall come forth for me one who

> is to be ruler in Israel, whose origin is from of old, from ancient days... And he shall stand and feed his flock in the strength of the LORD, in the majesty of the name of the LORD his God. And they shall dwell secure, for now he shall be great to the ends of the earth. (Micah 5:2, 4)

(For the providential significance of Bethlehem and the Ephrathites from the time of Boaz and Ruth, Obed, Jesse and David, see Chapter 9.)

Matthew goes on to explain how Herod tried to find out where the newborn child was, under the pretext that he wanted to worship the future king, but his visitors did not report to him. In a rage, he ordered that all the male children under the age of two in Bethlehem and the surrounding area should be put to death:

> Then Herod, when he saw that he had been tricked by the wise men, was in a furious rage, and he sent and killed all the male children in Bethlehem and in all that region who were two years old or under, according to the time which he had ascertained from the wise men. (Matthew 2:16)

An angel warned Joseph of Herod's murderous intentions, and encouraged him to escape with Mary and Jesus to Egypt:

> ...an angel of the Lord appeared to Joseph in a dream and said, "Rise, take the child and his mother, and flee to Egypt, and remain there till I tell you; for Herod is about to search for the child, to destroy him." (Matthew 2:13)

Once it was safe, the family returned to Israel and Joseph's hometown of Nazareth, where Jesus grew up helping with his father's carpentry business. Thus Jesus surviving birth in a most hostile environment was in itself miraculous, and much credit is due to Joseph and Mary for being obedient to the instructions they received from the angels who guided them to safety.

Jesus Was Treated as an Ordinary, Non-Levitical Jew

Of the four Gospels, only two, Matthew and Luke, provide descriptions of the birth and earliest years of Jesus, and they differ from each other significantly. This means there are several gaps in the Biblical account of the early years of Jesus. However, since Herod sought to kill Jesus shortly after he was born, the flight to Egypt must have occurred very soon after his birth. There is no report of this escape to Egypt in Luke, but there is a description of Joseph and Mary fulfilling their obligations as Jewish parents of a first-born male in the first weeks after Jesus' birth, which must have preceded their flight to Egypt:

> And at the end of eight days, when he was circumcised, he was called Jesus, the name given by the angel before he was conceived in the womb. And when the time came for their purification according to the law of Moses, they brought him up to Jerusalem to present him to the Lord (as it is written in the law of the Lord, "Every male that opens the womb shall be called holy to the Lord") and to offer a sacrifice according to what is said in the law of the Lord, "a pair of turtledoves, or two young pigeons." (Luke 2:21-24)

The law referred to here is this:

> The Lord said to Moses, "Say to the people of Israel, If a woman conceives, and bears a male child, then she shall be unclean seven days; as at the time of her menstruation, she shall be unclean. And on the eighth day the flesh of his foreskin shall be circumcised. Then she shall continue for thirty-three days in the blood of her purifying; she shall not touch any hallowed thing, nor come into the sanctuary, until the days of her purifying are completed." (Leviticus 12:1-4)

Thus when Jesus was eight days old he was circumcised. And, after an additional 33 days to allow for Mary to be purified, his parents took him to the Temple to consecrate him to God by providing a priest with an offering to sacrifice on behalf of the child—a Jewish ceremony known as *pidyon haben*. This tradition had originated when the Hebrews lost faith in

God while Moses was on Mount Sinai receiving the Ten Commandments. Only Moses and his fellow Levites refused to worship the Egyptian idol, a Golden Calf, that Aaron had made in response to the peoples' demands while his younger brother Moses was on the mountain. The lives of the first born of Israel had been redeemed at the cost of Egypt's first born (the final sign given to Moses to make Pharaoh release the Hebrews from bondage). This was a condition to liberate Adam and Eve's first-born son Cain from the dominion of Satan. By reverting to Egyptian idolatry, the Hebrews forfeited this redemption and had to make a condition of their own to protect their first-born from Satanic influences. This, then, was the purpose of the 40th day observance of *pidyon haben*.

So the first-born had to be consecrated to God by their parents through a Levitical priest:

> The Lord said to Moses, "Consecrate to me all the first-born; whatever is the first to open the womb among the people of Israel, both of man and of beast, is mine." (Exodus 13:1-2)

Only the Levites were exempt from this condition, since they had obeyed God and Moses at Sinai and as a tribe were therefore put in the position to inherit the redemption of the first-born Hebrews in Egypt. God told Moses:

> And you shall give the Levites to Aaron and his sons; they are wholly given to him from among the people of Israel. And you shall appoint Aaron and his sons, and they shall attend to their priesthood; but if any one else comes near, he shall be put to death." And the Lord said to Moses, "Behold, I have taken the Levites from among the people of Israel instead of every first-born that opens the womb among the people of Israel. The Levites shall be mine, for all the first-born are mine; on the day that I slew all the first-born in the land of Egypt, I consecrated for my own all the first-born in Israel, both of man and of beast; they shall be mine: I am the Lord." (Numbers 3:9-13)

Thus because of the faithfulness of Moses and the Levites, God claimed the whole tribe of Levi as redeemed in place of all the first-born of the other tribes of Israel. They would play a special role and receive special treatment as the priestly tribe of Israel from the time of Moses onwards.

Joseph and Mary had gone to Bethlehem from Nazareth in the first place because of a Roman census ordered by Caesar Augustus. Bethlehem was the birthplace of David, such that the people of Judah in David's lineage, including Joseph, were counted as belonging to Bethlehem. Only five or six miles from Bethlehem was Jerusalem and the Temple, making the consecration of Jesus at the Temple something his parents could do easily, before they returned to Nazareth.

Joseph and Mary Received Many Messages About Jesus

As we have indicated, Joseph and Mary received abundant messages and signs regarding the great providential significance of Jesus. We can enumerate at least some of them from Gospel accounts. (Some of these passages are used elsewhere in this book, but they are assembled here for emphasis.)

First, Mary was told by the angel Gabriel of the child she was to expect:

> And the angel said to her, "Do not be afraid, Mary, for you have found favor with God. And behold, you will conceive in your womb and bear a son, and you shall call his name Jesus. He will be great, and will be called the Son of the Most High; and the Lord God will give to him the throne of his father David, and he will reign over the house of Jacob for ever; and of his kingdom there will be no end." (Luke 1:30-33)

Second, Joseph was also told by an angel:

> But as he considered this, behold, an angel of the Lord appeared to him in a dream, saying, "Joseph, son of David, do not fear to take Mary your wife, for that which is conceived in her is of the Holy Spirit; she will bear a son, and you shall call his name Jesus, for he will save his people from their sins." (Matthew 1:20-21)

Third, Mary's cousin Elizabeth had testified to Jesus:

> And when Elizabeth heard the greeting of Mary, the babe leaped in her womb; and Elizabeth was filled with the Holy Spirit and she exclaimed with a loud cry, "Blessed are you among women, and blessed is the fruit of your womb! And why is this granted me, that the mother of my Lord should come to me?" (Luke 1:41-43)

Fourth, Zechariah had testified to the coming child, whom he wanted to serve "all the days of our life":

> Blessed be the Lord God of Israel, for he has visited and redeemed his people, and has raised up a horn of salvation for us in the house of his servant David, as he spoke by the mouth of his holy prophets from of old, that we should be saved from our enemies, and from the hand of all who hate us; to perform the mercy promised to our fathers, and to remember his holy covenant, the oath which he swore to our father Abraham, to grant us that we, being delivered from the hand of our enemies, might serve him without fear, in holiness and righteousness before him all the days of our life. (Luke 1:68-75)

Fifth, 'wise men' from the East testified to the great significance of Jesus:

> Now when Jesus was born in Bethlehem of Judea in the days of Herod the king, behold, wise men from the East came to Jerusalem, saying, "Where is he who has been born king of the Jews? For we have seen his star in the East, and have come to worship him." (Matthew 2:1-2)

And in Bethlehem they confirmed the importance of Jesus:

> ...and going into the house they saw the child with Mary his mother, and they fell down and worshiped him. Then, opening their treasures, they offered him gifts, gold and frankincense and myrrh. (Matthew 2:11)

Jesus' Difficult Early Life

Sixth, shepherds confirmed this testimony to the parents of the newly-born Jesus:

> And in that region there were shepherds out in the field, keeping watch over their flock by night. And an angel of the Lord appeared to them, and the glory of the Lord shone around them, and they were filled with fear. And the angel said to them, "Be not afraid; for behold, I bring you good news of a great joy which will come to all the people; for to you is born this day in the city of David a Savior, who is Christ the Lord. And this will be a sign for you: you will find a babe wrapped in swaddling cloths and lying in a manger." And suddenly there was with the angel a multitude of the heavenly host praising God and saying, "Glory to God in the highest, and on earth peace among men with whom he is pleased!" When the angels went away from them into heaven, the shepherds said to one another, "Let us go over to Bethlehem and see this thing that has happened, which the Lord has made known to us." And they went with haste, and found Mary and Joseph, and the babe lying in a manger. And when they saw it they made known the saying which had been told them concerning this child; and all who heard it wondered at what the shepherds told them. But Mary kept all these things, pondering them in her heart. (Luke 2:8-19)

Seventh, when Joseph and Mary went to consecrate Jesus in the Temple, 40 days after his birth, they met an old man, Simeon, who had been promised he would see the Christ before he died:

> And inspired by the Spirit he came into the temple; and when the parents brought in the child Jesus, to do for him according to the custom of the law, he took him up in his arms and blessed God and said, "Lord, now lettest thou thy servant depart in peace, according to thy word; for mine eyes have seen thy salvation which thou hast prepared in the presence of all peoples, a light for revelation to the Gentiles, and for glory to thy people

> Israel." And his father and his mother marveled at what was said about him. (Luke 2:27-33)

Eighth, a prophetess called Anna who was constantly at the Temple, also recognized Jesus at the same time, and testified to him:

> And coming up at that very hour she gave thanks to God, and spoke of him to all who were looking for the redemption of Jerusalem. (Luke 2:38)

Jesus' Parents Failed to Grasp His Importance

After Joseph and Mary returned from Egypt and went to their home in Nazareth, we do not see them again until they take a twelve-year-old Jesus to the Temple for the annual celebration of Passover. There they lose track of him, and are already on the way home when they realize he is missing:

> Now his parents went to Jerusalem every year at the feast of the Passover. And when he was twelve years old, they went up according to custom; and when the feast was ended, as they were returning, the boy Jesus stayed behind in Jerusalem. His parents did not know it, but supposing him to be in the company they went a day's journey, and they sought him among their kinsfolk and acquaintances; and when they did not find him, they returned to Jerusalem, seeking him. (Luke 2:41-45)

Losing a 12-year-old boy in a strange city would suggests that Joseph and Mary were not exactly focused on their son and his wellbeing. It took them three days to find him because they never thought to look in the Temple. Apparently they were unaware of his deep knowledge of the scriptures, and when he explained to them that he belonged in his heavenly Father's house, they literally did not know what he was talking about:

> After three days they found him in the temple, sitting among the teachers, listening to them and asking them questions; and all who heard him were amazed at his understanding and his answers. And when they saw him they were astonished; and his

mother said to him, "Son, why have you treated us so? Behold, your father and I have been looking for you anxiously." And he said to them, "How is it that you sought me? Did you not know that I must be in my Father's house?" (Luke 2:46-49)

This reply befuddled them:

> And they did not understand the saying which he spoke to them. And he went down with them and came to Nazareth, and was obedient to them; and his mother kept all these things in her heart. And Jesus increased in wisdom and in stature, and in favor with God and man. (Luke 2:50-51)

This was the third time the Bible tells us that Joseph and Mary were surprised to learn just how important Jesus was. The first time this occurred was when wise men and shepherds came to do homage at his birth, and Mary had to think about what this meant: "But Mary kept all these things, pondering them in her heart." (Luke 2:19). The second was when they were surprised by what Simeon said about Jesus in the Temple: "And his father and his mother marveled at what was said about him." (Luke 2:33) The third time was the occasion just cited, when they were "astonished" to find Jesus in the Temple, and Mary berated Jesus, complaining: "Son, why have you treated us so?" Instead of recognizing their lack of understanding of—and support for—Jesus and his mission, she complained about the trouble he had caused his parents by pursuing his mission. And, as if to confirm this gross misjudgment of their son, Luke states: "And they did not understand the saying which he spoke to them."

Although this appearance of Jesus and his parents in Jerusalem is very brief, it speaks volumes about the situation in their family. Joseph and Mary appear to have forgotten the miraculous circumstances of Jesus' birth and their role in it. The messages from angels about the providential importance of Jesus, and the confirmation of his status once born by wise men, prophets and simple shepherds, had all receded in their minds and hearts. For Joseph and Mary their growing family and Joseph's carpentry shop in Nazareth were of primary importance in their lives. For them, Jesus was just one of their children who worked with his step-father.

The passage also acknowledges Jesus' humility, accepting the role in his family that his parents had made for him: "And he went down with them and came to Nazareth, and was obedient to them." Nevertheless, we see that at age 12 Jesus was already knowledgeable about scriptural matters and becoming known outside his family as a remarkable young man: "And Jesus increased in wisdom and in stature, and in favor with God and man."

The Bible offers us no further insights into the relationship between Jesus and his parents until after he begins his public ministry, some two decades after the Temple incident. By this time he has four half-brothers and at least two half-sisters (the children of Joseph and Mary) and his family seems alienated from him. There is no record of them contributing to his mission.

Mary's Mission as a Good Eve and Mother

Mary had responded obediently to the message of the angel Gabriel when he told her she would conceive a special child through the intercession of the Holy Spirit. And she immediately went to the home of Zechariah to fulfill her mission. But she was in a very difficult position with her husband Joseph and with the Israelite society as a whole. She had to trust that his acceptance of her pregnancy as the will of God would hold and that he would remain loyal to her. This was critical since in the eyes of the law she had actually given birth to Jesus out of wedlock.

For the public, then, Jesus had to be known as the first child of the marriage of Joseph and Mary, and for their whole lives they had to keep secret the truth about his unorthodox birth. Furthermore, to preserve her life and position of respect in society, Mary had to continue her marriage to Joseph and submit to his authority, including in the matter of having several children with him.

Nevertheless, despite this constraint, her mission was to support Jesus as the Abel child of the family, and treat his siblings as Cain-type family members who should unite with and follow Jesus. From a providential perspective, Joseph and Mary should have devoted their lives to helping Jesus accomplish his mission. But it was Mary who was the key to the realization of this purpose. Joseph had a supporting role as the step-father, but she was the actual mother of Jesus who had been told of his importance many times by Divine representatives. Thus, above all else, Mary was to protect and nurture Jesus and help him accomplish his mission, first as a perfect Abel and second as a new sinless Adam responsible for finding a bride as a new Eve and creating with her a new, sinless lineage.

The mission of Mary was, then, to do everything possible to help Jesus, as Rebekah had helped Jacob to avoid the wrath of Isaac and the murderous intensions of Esau, sending her Abel-type son to relatives where he found the women who would become the mothers of the chosen tribes of Israel. Going further back in the providence, Mary had to restore the failure of Eve who had succumbed to the temptations of Lucifer and failed to help Abel overcome the murderous intensions of his older brother, Cain.

Only by retaining a deep understanding of her first son's historic providential mission could Mary have overcome all the difficulties of her circumstances to devote her life to serving and supporting Jesus.

Joseph's Mission as Good Archangel and Son of David

In the context of restoring the failures of the Fall, Joseph was in the position of an archangel with the mission to restore Lucifer's abuse of Eve and destruction of the first family. He was therefore supposed to protect Mary from the fallen, Cain-type world and help her raise Jesus as a perfected Abel who could then become a perfected second Adam. Joseph did this initially when he heeded the words of the angel Gabriel and married Mary, even though he knew Jesus was not his son. This was not a small matter for a husband, especially since it implied that he was not qualified to be the father of Jesus, and Joseph deserves credit for maintaining a public identity as Jesus' father.

But from the time of Jesus' birth it would seem that Joseph insisted on treating him as any other first-born of Israel. Thus, by not enjoying the Levitical privilege, Jesus had to go through the 40th day ceremony at the Temple.

Joseph went on to create a large family with Mary and focused on them and his own business, rather than attending to the needs of Jesus. There is no record at all of Joseph helping Jesus with his mission to restore the first family and its lineage, or to help his other children to accept Jesus as their Abel, and to support him.

There was another important aspect to Joseph's mission. As the genealogies of Matthew and Luke point out, he was a descendant of David, and thus Jacob, Isaac and Abraham. As such, his mission was to help Jesus fulfill both the internal, spiritual role of priest and savior as well as the external, temporal role of king of the Jews—inheriting the throne of David, as prophesized. Again, initially Joseph played his providential role well when he accepted a pregnant Mary as his wife and then took Mary and the baby Jesus to Egypt, to escape the wrath of Herod and save Jesus' life. He lacked a position of influence in Israel to help Jesus ascend the throne, but we know of nothing he even attempted to do towards this goal.

The Family Did Not Help Jesus in his Public Ministry

From everything we know, then, when Jesus at age 30 started his public ministry, his family was of little if any help to him. In fact, by that time he appeared to have very little to do with his parents or siblings, who we never see among his disciples and supporters.

For us looking back across the centuries that have shown Jesus to be a figure of unparalleled virtue and significance in history, this is hard to believe. Surely Jesus was so great, so spiritually insightful and powerful, so wise beyond his years, that he must have been easily recognized as a truly unique figure by his own family, and therefore loved and supported by them. Apparently not. Indeed, the Bible indicates the opposite, as we are demonstrating in this chapter.

At one point during his ministry, Jesus visited his hometown Nazareth, where he received little attention or support. Clearly the people there were unaware of his importance when he was growing up in their midst:

> ...and coming to his own country he taught them in their synagogue, so that they were astonished, and said, "Where did this man get this wisdom and these mighty works? Is not this the carpenter's son? Is not his mother called Mary? And are not his brothers James and Joseph and Simon and Judas? And are not all his sisters with us? Where then did this man get all this?" (Matthew 13:54-56)

In other words, Jesus' family had shown no special treatment of Jesus and among the people of Nazareth he was unknown as anyone other than the son of Joseph and Mary. Jesus explained this phenomenon to his disciples:

> And Jesus said to them, "A prophet is not without honor, except in his own country, and among his own kin, and in his own house." (Mark 6:4)

Once Jesus became prominent as a teacher and healer, his mother and brothers visited him while he was teaching. They requested a meeting with him. At that point, Jesus declined to meet them, and expressed his frustration with them:

> While he was still speaking to the people, behold, his mother and his brothers stood outside, asking to speak to him. But he replied to the man who told him, "Who is my mother, and who are my brothers?" And stretching out his hand toward his disciples, he said, "Here are my mother and my brothers! For whoever does the will of my Father in heaven is my brother, and sister, and mother." (Matthew 12:46-50)

This was clearly a rebuke to his family for failing to support him in his mission. His parents should not have been consumed with raising a large family. They should have been devoted to assisting Jesus in his providential mission. The implication is clear: his parents and other family members did not understand the importance of his mission. If they had, they would have followed the example of his disciples, who sacrificed their own lives to follow him. Without Jesus, Joseph and Mary had no significant role in the providence. As his parents, however, they had a very significant role to play, a role they seem to have largely failed to fulfill after their initial obedience to Divine instructions.

Instead of Mary and his sisters serving and supporting him and his disciples, Jesus attracted the support of several other women who played that role:

> Soon afterward he went on through cities and villages, preaching and bringing the good news of the kingdom of God. And the twelve were with him, and also some women who had been healed of evil spirits and infirmities: Mary, called Magdalene, from whom seven demons had gone out, and Joanna, the wife of Chuza, Herod's steward, and Susanna, and many others, who provided for them out of their means. (Luke 8:1-3)

When Jesus faced his final showdown with the religious and political establishment of Israel, his father, mother and siblings were missing. Only John's Gospel says Mary was present at the crucifixion, and then only to record Jesus asking him (John) to take care of Mary. (John 19:26-27). None of the Gospels record any of Jesus' family members at his tomb after the crucifixion. (There is however evidence that some of Jesus' siblings were involved with the disciples after his death. In Galatians 1:19 Paul mentions meeting James, the brother of Jesus: "But I saw none of the other apostles except James the Lord's brother.")

It was only some time after Jesus' death that Mary was elevated to the position of Mother of God and Mother of the Church by some leaders of the faith. (See Chapters 8 and 9 for an explanation of this.) And Mary continues to play a very important role in some Christian denominations to this day, especially Catholic and Orthodox churches. Since Jesus never had a bride to take the place of Eve, Mary came to be a figure who represented the motherly aspect of the parenthood of God.

Jesus came to restore the elder-son position to what it would have been in the first family if Adam and Eve had not fallen. The first son would have been the primary inheritor of the blessings of the Creator and the champion of the Divine Providence in the second generation of the family. By not fully supporting and uniting with Jesus, his parents and siblings became Cain-type figures in the providence, making his mission as a perfect Abel much more difficult.

Chapter 13

The Sermon on the Mount

Teaching the Way of Abel

Jesus Begins his Ministry

According to the Gospels, Jesus started his public ministry after he was baptized by John, the son of Zechariah and Elizabeth, who was six months his senior and who had been told from birth that he was to prepare the way for the Messiah. In Chapter 18 we will discuss in detail the role of John the Baptist and how his doubts about Jesus affected the providence, but let it suffice to say for now that by the time of his baptism Jesus clearly understood that the people of Israel, and their leadership in particular, were not ready to receive and follow him as the Messiah. For this to change, the people needed to undergo a transformation of heart and mind, a spiritual awakening and enlightenment. Neither the words of Israel's many prophets in the past, nor the teachings of John the Baptist in the present, had been able to effect such a transformation.

Thus to fulfill his mission, Jesus had first to teach the people himself so that they could understand the providence and support him in becoming a victorious second Adam. In other words, as a perfected Abel Jesus would have to educate Cain—the people of Israel—so that they could be separated from Satan and submit to Divine authority through him. Only once a minimum segment of Israel's society had accepted him as the Messiah could

Jesus fulfill his mission as savior of humankind and founding ruler of the Kingdom of Heaven on earth.

Revealing the Depth of God's Parental Heart

It was the depth of his heart that gave Jesus great wisdom and the ability to reveal the nature and purpose of the Creator so fully. As he is recorded to have said in John 14:9: "Believe me that I am in the Father and the Father in me." No one before him could make that claim.

This is why Jesus' teachings resonated with those who became his dedicated disciples, men and women who were moved by his message in their inmost beings. It is also why our original nature through our conscience responds to Jesus as the standard-bearer of a true morality, and why his words have continued to echo down through the centuries in the hearts and minds of Christians who are guided by them to live a virtuous life.

Through Jesus too, for the first time we can understand our Creator as a suffering parent. No one before Jesus had understood fully the pain caused God by the fall of Adam and Eve, the pain of parents who had lost their children to forces of evil. And no one before him had understood so fully the mission of Abel as a man to liberate the Cain-type world from evil so that a new generation of people could be united with the Creator and restore the position of sinless children that had been lost through the Fall.

Only mature children can grasp their parents' suffering, and the Old Testament lacks this depth of understanding because even the most important Abel figures were not sinless and therefore had a limited experience of God's deepest sentiments. As a sinless Abel, Jesus came to teach fallen humanity—starting with the Israelites—how to become true sons and daughters of God so that they would be able to share our Creator's heart of love and establish a new, sinless Garden of Eden: the Kingdom of Heaven on earth.

A Revolutionary Message

The truly revolutionary aspect of his message was that all people should, like him, become sinless and responsible sons and daughters of the Heavenly Father. As he said in Matthew 5:48: " You, therefore, must be perfect, as your heavenly Father is perfect." Beginning with the Jews who had been so well prepared for the Messiah, the people of the world were to learn from his teachings and advance spiritually beyond the status of obedient servants to a distant Lord in heaven to become the children of the living God, in heart and mind.

Achieving true enlightenment has always been the main challenge for education. People tend to cling to what they know, especially the belief systems that they are accustomed to and that provide an explanation for their salvation. For the Jewish people, who had long been promised the position of chosen nation in the world, resistance to Jesus' radical new teaching was to be expected, especially when he made statements like this:

> ...and do not presume to say to yourselves, 'We have Abraham as our father'; for I tell you, God is able from these stones to raise up children to Abraham. (Matthew 3:9)

However, as we have seen, Jesus came not to destroy the law that the Jews were accustomed to, but to fulfill it: "Think not that I have come to abolish the law and the prophets; I have come not to abolish them but to fulfill them." (Matthew 5:17) As a national (and worldwide) Abel, Jesus could well relate to the difficulties of earlier prophets who had struggled with the disobedience and idolatry of the chosen people. Whether it was Moses and Aaron, or the great prophets such as Elijah, Isaiah and Jeremiah, the people typically rejected God's messengers and their messages, preferring to continue in their worship of man-made deities and other ungodly practices.

To counter the practice of idolatry, the first two of the Ten Commandments specifically instruct the Israelites to worship one God only, and prohibits them from making and worshipping idols:

I   You shall have no other gods before me.

II You shall not make for yourself a graven image, or any likeness of anything that is in heaven above, or that is in the earth beneath, or that is in the water under the earth; you shall not bow down to them or serve them. (Exodus 20:3-5)

These commandments were fundamental to faith in the One God, but they were violated again and again in the history of Israel, resulting in frequent setbacks to the providence. One of the most significant examples of this was when Solomon started worshipping idols and consequently was told that his kingdom would be taken from him and given to his servant. Thus the United Kingdom of Israel was divided and the preparations for the Messiah greatly delayed:

> He had seven hundred wives, princesses, and three hundred concubines; and his wives turned away his heart. For when Solomon was old his wives turned away his heart after other gods; and his heart was not wholly true to the Lord his God, as was the heart of David his father... And the Lord was angry with Solomon, because his heart had turned away from the Lord, the God of Israel, who had appeared to him twice, and had commanded him concerning this thing, that he should not go after other gods; but he did not keep what the Lord commanded. Therefore the Lord said to Solomon, "Since this has been your mind and you have not kept my covenant and my statutes which I have commanded you, I will surely tear the kingdom from you and will give it to your servant." (I Kings 11:3-4; 9-11)

Thus the challenge for Jesus was to break this pattern of disobedience. The people of Judah had been punished through hardships and defeat at the hands of their enemies many times, and finally through their exile to Babylon. When they returned to Jerusalem they had lost much of their understanding of scriptures and had to receive instruction in the Mosaic Law from Ezra and other scribes and priests. They repented of their sins, but, as time would tell and Jesus would discover, while idolatry never returned on the scale that had led to the Babylonian exile, the general level of the Israelites' understanding of, and faith in the Divine Providence was extremely limited.

The Sermon on the Mount: Teaching the Way of Perfected Abel

Jesus appeared in Israel some four centuries after Ezra. However, his mission was much more difficult than that of Ezra, whose mission had been to restore the people's obedience to the law they had all been raised to believe in, whereas Jesus had to introduce a completely new understanding to the people. Jesus grew up in an Israel in which the people were only marginally more obedient to God and the Mosaic Law than they had been at the time of Ezra. Thus it was apparent that a recommitment to the law alone would not bring about the fundamental changes needed to replace the dominion of Satan with the dominion of God.

However—as we discuss in detail in Chapter 17—the religious establishment in Israel was not at all receptive to Jesus' teachings. Instead of learning from him, the religious leaders constantly tried to find fault with his words and actions, and eventually sought to have him killed. Thus Jesus had to teach the ordinary, largely uneducated people directly that the Way of Abel was the true path to salvation. These teachings are most fully set out in the Sermon on the Mount (Matthew 5-7), and summarized as the Beatitudes:

- Blessed are the poor in spirit, for theirs is the kingdom of heaven.
- Blessed are those who mourn, for they shall be comforted.
- Blessed are the meek, for they shall inherit the earth.
- Blessed are those who hunger and thirst for righteousness, for they shall be satisfied.
- Blessed are the merciful, for they shall obtain mercy.
- Blessed are the pure in heart, for they shall see God.
- Blessed are the peacemakers, for they shall be called sons of God.
- Blessed are those who are persecuted for righteousness' sake, for theirs is the kingdom of heaven.
- Blessed are you when men revile you and persecute you and utter all kinds of evil against you falsely on my account. Rejoice and be glad,

for your reward is great in heaven, for so men persecuted the prophets who were before you. (Matthew 5:3-12)

The first six Beatitudes encapsulate the purity and goodness to which believers should aspire, qualities essential for knowing, loving and obeying God. The last three have to do with overcoming the evils of the fallen world, the Cain-type attitudes and behaviors that inevitably face Abel as he seeks to manifest God's love and truth in the world. Jesus elaborated on Abel's path:

> You have heard that it was said, "You shall love your neighbor and hate your enemy." But I say to you, Love your enemies and pray for those who persecute you, so that you may be sons of your Father who is in heaven; for he makes his sun rise on the evil and on the good, and sends rain on the just and on the unjust. For if you love those who love you, what reward have you? Do not even the tax collectors do the same? And if you salute only your brethren, what more are you doing than others? Do not even the Gentiles do the same? (Matthew 5:43-47)

The nature of a true Abel is to love God and humankind. Abel is naturally obedient to the will and laws of the creation. Abel is faithful, prayerful, patient, forgiving and responsible. Abel shares both the joys and sorrows of the Creator. And Abel is willing to sacrifice himself to overcome evil and liberate Cain from the bondage of Satan.

Saint Paul summarized the role of a Christ-like Abel in these uplifting words, which underscore the importance of manifesting a loving heart and parental attitude towards Cain:

> If I speak in the tongues of men and of angels, but have not love, I am a noisy gong or a clanging cymbal. And if I have prophetic powers, and understand all mysteries and all knowledge, and if I have all faith, so as to remove mountains, but have not love, I am nothing. If I give away all I have, and if I deliver my body to be burned, but have not love, I gain nothing. Love is patient and kind; love is not jealous or boastful; it is not arro-

> gant or rude. Love does not insist on its own way; it is not irritable or resentful; it does not rejoice at wrong, but rejoices in the right. Love bears all things, believes all things, hopes all things, endures all things. Love never ends; as for prophecies, they will pass away; as for tongues, they will cease; as for knowledge, it will pass away. For our knowledge is imperfect and our prophecy is imperfect; but when the perfect comes, the imperfect will pass away. When I was a child, I spoke like a child, I thought like a child, I reasoned like a child; when I became a man, I gave up childish ways. For now we see in a mirror dimly, but then face to face. Now I know in part; then I shall understand fully, even as I have been fully understood. So faith, hope, love abide, these three; but the greatest of these is love. (1 Corinthians 13)

In contrast, it is the nature of Cain to be arrogant and proud of his knowledge, to be jealous and resentful of others, to blame the innocent and refuse to take personal responsibility for his own shortcomings and sins, to seek vengeance for his perceived grievances and to resort to murder to achieve his objectives.

The Teachings of Jesus Superseded the Law

The Sermon on the Mount takes our understanding of the role of Mosaic Law—and of Divine law in general—to a new level. Any person who is at one with the Creator, and practices the virtuous life prescribed in the Beatitudes, will naturally be in compliance with the law. Jesus demonstrated this in teaching that particular laws were superseded by a higher moral standard.

For example, the 7th Commandment given to Moses is this: "You shall not commit adultery." (Exodus 1:20:14) Jesus explained in Matthew 15:19 that this and other sins come from evil in the hearts of people: "For out of the heart come evil thoughts, murder, adultery, fornication, theft, false witness, slander." Therefore, to end sin one must purify one's heart:

> You have heard that it was said, "You shall not commit adultery." But I say to you that every one who looks at a woman lustfully

has already committed adultery with her in his heart. (Matthew 5:27-28)

Jesus' words about adultery are aimed at finally separating fallen humanity from the very first sin—Lucifer's ungodly lust for Eve. It was out of an attitude of jealousy and resentment for the greater blessings received from the Creator by Adam and Eve that Lucifer developed a desire for Eve that eventually led to an illicit relationship and the alienation of Adam, Eve and Lucifer from God. The first sin could have been prevented if Lucifer had been responsible and rejected the lustful desires of his own heart. Thus sin begins in the heart and mind, and then manifests as action. To end sin we have to go beyond laws and prohibitions to the realm of original motivation.

How Cain and Abel Can Be Reconciled on Abel's Terms

Jesus taught how Abel can help Cain overcome his resentment and anger so that the brothers can be reconciled peacefully, on Abel's terms. In the passage from Matthew 5:44 quoted above, Jesus says it is not good enough to love your neighbor but hate your enemy: "But I say to you, Love your enemies and pray for those who persecute you." To make the world a heavenly place we have to learn to love our enemies so that we can liberate them from evil. To be able to do this we need the Divine heart of parental love which seeks to save both Cain and Abel.

In another example of how Abel should reconcile with Cain on Abel's terms, Jesus said:

> You have heard that it was said, "An eye for an eye and a tooth for a tooth." But I say to you, Do not resist one who is evil. But if any one strikes you on the right cheek, turn to him the other also; and if any one would sue you and take your coat, let him have your cloak as well; and if any one forces you to go one mile, go with him two miles. Give to him who begs from you, and do not refuse him who would borrow from you. (Matthew 5:38-42)

Jesus' reference here is to a passage in Exodus:

> If any harm follows, then you shall give life for life, eye for eye, tooth for tooth, hand for hand, foot for foot, burn for burn, wound for wound, stripe for stripe. (Exodus 21:23-25)

This Old Testament notion of how to punish wrongdoing achieves a certain level of justice, but it does not solve the problem of Cain's enmity towards Abel and it certainly does not offer a path for the brothers to be reconciled in a way that separates both of them from Satan. Thus Jesus taught his disciples to rise above the vengeful spirit of Cain and to give Cain a way to be liberated from Satan and united with his brother. A mature Abel acts in a parental way towards others not by condoning their wrongdoing but by demonstrating a responsible way of dealing with differences and conflicts.

This does not mean that Abel should surrender to Cain! That would merely contribute to a victory for evil, through which both would suffer all the more. Abel has to set a virtuous standard and be uncompromising in his opposition to evil. To turn the other cheek is not to appease Cain, but to show him proper behavior through the resolute and relentless pursuit of goodness and justice in the cause of eliminating evil. Thus Abel must not only show Cain the proper behavior expected of a child of God, but also must prevent Cain from doing evil to others, even if this requires the use of force.

Love Was Jesus' Core Teaching

The Beatitudes teach human values of faith, humility, purity and service to others. Jesus summarized these teachings with these words:

> "Love the Lord your God with all your heart and with all your soul and with all your mind." This is the first and greatest commandment. And the second is like it: "Love your neighbor as yourself." All the Law and the Prophets hang on these two commandments. (Matthew 22:37-40)

It is from a relationship of loving oneness with our Heavenly Father that we can gain the heart and mind to be able to love others. And it is in the perfecting of these relationships (with God and with other people) that we ourselves become perfected. This is the Way of Abel that was both taught and exemplified by Jesus. It is the foundation for Christian civilization and the hope for the realization of the Kingdom of Heaven, as we shall see.

Chapter 14

Parables and Miracles to Open Minds and Hearts

A Stubborn People Rejected Jesus' Message

Jesus Faced a Proud, Close-Minded People

Most people naturally resist new ideas. Fearful of losing the security of their existing beliefs—even though those beliefs are manifestly inadequate in explaining the world and their own circumstances—they cling to what they know, or think they know. So it was with the resistance of the Jews to the teaching of Jesus. Most had been raised to believe that they were the chosen people, that God had already shown that they were special, and that from as early as the time of Abraham they were blessed among all people and all nations:

> Now the LORD said to Abram, "Go from your country and your kindred and your father's house to the land that I will show you. And I will make of you a great nation, and I will bless you, and make your name great, so that you will be a blessing. I will bless those who bless you, and him who curses you I will curse; and by you all the families of the earth shall bless themselves. (Genesis 12:1-3)

This blessing had been repeated to Isaac and Jacob, Moses and David. It was a central tenet for the people of Israel. As we have mentioned, for the Jewish people the fulfillment of these promises by God was expected in the form of a great king who would inherit the throne of David. Jesus, however, was born and raised in the home of a humble carpenter, and thus lacked the credentials expected of a king. (It should be noted that the people of Israel should have been wiser and more alert to the Messiah coming from an unexpected position in society, considering that David himself had been chosen to lead the people although he was just a shepherd boy when Samuel anointed him.)

Given the resistance of the people to his message, Jesus resorted to two methods to try and win the attention, interest and belief of the Jews: parables and miracles.

Lessons Through Parables

To get his messages across, Jesus often first presented them as parables—stories that contained providential or moral lessons. Usually, he would have to explain what his parables meant, but the parables themselves were more memorable than the truths they communicated. There are many recorded in the Gospels, but we will just take one as an example, used by Jesus to explain the love of God for humankind and the importance of our repentance for sins if we are to be reunited with God:

> So he told them this parable: "What man of you, having a hundred sheep, if he has lost one of them, does not leave the ninety-nine in the wilderness, and go after the one which is lost, until he finds it? And when he has found it, he lays it on his shoulders, rejoicing. And when he comes home, he calls together his friends and his neighbors, saying to them, 'Rejoice with me, for I have found my sheep which was lost.' Just so, I tell you, there will be more joy in heaven over one sinner who repents than over ninety-nine righteous persons who need no repentance." (Luke 15:3-7)

This parable uses an example taken from daily life in Israel, that of a shepherd who has lost one of his sheep. The concern of the shepherd for this one sheep could easily be understood by the people. But the lesson being taught was much deeper, and something they needed to hear, namely that

God's love for each human being is much greater than that of a shepherd for his sheep. The God he described for them is a Heavenly Father who loves his children with a deep, parental passion. The 'heart' of this God is behind the providence to save fallen humanity, the lost sheep of the parable. Sheep cannot sin and therefore cannot repent, but we can sin and we therefore must repent if we are to be saved.

Miraculous Healings

Jesus used miracles to demonstrate the power of God working with and through him. He cured many diseases, from blindness and deafness to leprosy and physical handicaps and deformities. He turned water into wine, walked on water and even raised people from death.

The miracles he performed most often were the result of spiritual cleansing, demonstrating God's healing spiritual power working through him. Jesus was able to recognize the evil spirits that were possessing and harming people, and then drive those spirits out. The most remarkable example of this was the case of a crazy man possessed by many evil spirits:

> Then they arrived at the country of the Gerasenes, which is opposite Galilee. And as he stepped out on land, there met him a man from the city who had demons; for a long time he had worn no clothes, and he lived not in a house but among the tombs. When he saw Jesus, he cried out and fell down before him, and said with a loud voice, "What have you to do with me, Jesus, Son of the Most High God? I beseech you, do not torment me." For he had commanded the unclean spirit to come out of the man. (For many a time it had seized him; he was kept under guard, and bound with chains and fetters, but he broke the bonds and was driven by the demon into the desert.) Jesus then asked him, "What is your name?" And he said, "Legion"; for many demons had entered him. And they begged him not to command them to depart into the abyss. Now a large herd of swine was feeding there on the hillside; and they begged him to let them enter these. So he gave them leave. Then the demons came out of

the man and entered the swine, and the herd rushed down the steep bank into the lake and were drowned. (Luke 8:26-33)

Spirit possession was the cause of many afflictions, which Jesus healed by chastising and removing the spirits responsible for the maladies. In the following case, a deaf and dumb boy—who was also the victim of spirit-induced epileptic fits—could not be cured by the healing efforts of Jesus' disciples, so Jesus was asked to intervene:

> And one of the crowd answered him, "Teacher, I brought my son to you, for he has a dumb spirit; and wherever it seizes him, it dashes him down; and he foams and grinds his teeth and becomes rigid; and I asked your disciples to cast it out, and they were not able." And he answered them, "O faithless generation, how long am I to be with you? How long am I to bear with you? Bring him to me." And they brought the boy to him; and when the spirit saw him, immediately it convulsed the boy, and he fell on the ground and rolled about, foaming at the mouth. And Jesus asked his father, "How long has he had this?" And he said, "From childhood. And it has often cast him into the fire and into the water, to destroy him; but if you can do anything, have pity on us and help us." And Jesus said to him, "If you can! All things are possible to him who believes." Immediately the father of the child cried out and said, "I believe; help my unbelief!" And when Jesus saw that a crowd came running together, he rebuked the unclean spirit, saying to it, "You dumb and deaf spirit, I command you, come out of him, and never enter him again." And after crying out and convulsing him terribly, it came out, and the boy was like a corpse; so that most of them said, "He is dead." But Jesus took him by the hand and lifted him up, and he arose. And when he had entered the house, his disciples asked him privately, "Why could we not cast it out?" And he said to them, "This kind cannot be driven out by anything but prayer." (Mark 9:17-29)

Healing Bodies; Purifying Spirits

These demonstrations of spiritual healing helped to show the people that he was indeed the representative of God on earth. They were not in themselves essential to the salvific mission of Jesus, but they did help open the hearts and minds of the Jews to his unique qualification as a healer and savior. To be rid of the possession of an evil spirit, or spirits, was to be blessed with the opportunity to be transformed from a sinful to a sinless person through Christ.

Being purified in this way was not a guarantee that you could now live free from sin, but it was a demonstration of the role of Jesus as Christ, the Messiah. Through him, sin was to be driven out of Israel and the world, and Cain was to be liberated from Satan's dominion so that he could unite with his savior, Abel.

The only condition the people had to make to receive this grace was to demonstrate their faith in God and Jesus by asking for Christ's intercession: "All things are possible to him who believes." With just this small condition of faith, the Father worked through the son to do great things for those in need, healing the bodies and liberating the spirits of those he had come to save.

However, once healed, the patient had to commit to refraining from sin. This is the responsibility that each person has to fulfill, and the Israelites were no exception. Jesus would say this to those he had cured. Here is one example:

> Afterward, Jesus found him in the temple, and said to him, "See, you are well! Sin no more, that nothing worse befall you." (John 5:14)

A Stubborn and Ungrateful People

But despite his parables and many miracles, the people of Israel remained stubbornly unmoved by his message. With bitterness and sadness, Jesus lamented their faithlessness, comparing them unfavorably with the people of Tyre and Sidon, who belonged to neighboring Cain-type cultures:

Woe to you, Chorazin! woe to you, Bethsaida! for if the mighty works done in you had been done in Tyre and Sidon, they would have repented long ago in sackcloth and ashes. (Matthew 11:21)

Chapter 15

Jesus' Mastery of the Spirit World

Cain and Abel Spirits and Angels Influence Our Lives

Cain-type and Abel-type Spirits and Angels

God is an eternal being who created us humans to enjoy an eternal heavenly companionship of life and love with our Creator. Thus when our life on earth comes to an end, our body dies but our spirit continues its eternal existence in the invisible Spirit World. We are endowed with free will so that we can fulfill our original, Divine purpose, but because of our fallen state we can also misuse our free will to rebel against God and create a life and world that stand in opposition to the providence and therefore multiply evil on earth.

The relative good or evil of our contribution to humanity and the providence can best be understood in terms of Cain- and Abel-type behavior. This applies to our life on earth as well as to our existence in the Spirit World. As a spirit, our support or opposition to the providence translates into playing either a Cain- or Abel-type role in influencing people on earth, the course of history, the current state of the world, and the future of humanity.

Also in the Spirit World there are angels who were created as spiritual servants of God and can likewise play good or bad roles in the providence, depending on whether they followed Lucifer in his rebellion against God or side with Abel-type figures, ideas and causes that contribute to the salvation of the children of God.

The Identity of Demons and Divines

The New Testament often refers to Satanic spiritual entities as demons. This term applies to both evil spirits and rebellious angels who manifest Cain-type characteristics in exploiting our fallen nature to encourage us to do evil. However, as human beings we have more in common with spirits than we do with angels, so it is evil spirits that cruelly possess the spiritually weak and vulnerable. And it was these 'unclean spirits' that Jesus drove out of the spiritually possessed when he cured them.

There are, of course, also good, Abel-type spirits who support the Divine Providence. These we are calling Divines. Two such spirits, Moses and Elijah, met with Jesus on the Mount of Transfiguration to guide and encourage him in the difficult mission he was about to face in going to his death on the cross.

And there are righteous angels who have likewise played Abel-type roles in the providence, such as Gabriel when he helped Joseph and Mary, Zechariah and Elizabeth to understand how God was working to bring about salvation through the birth of Jesus and John the Baptist. Gabriel encouraged them to trust in God and fulfill their responsibilities so that the heavenly purpose could be accomplished. Thus Abel-type spirits and angels help people to obey God and overcome the difficulties in doing so. They are the source of the invisible forces behind the miracles and good fortune seen in history and experienced in our lives.

The Conditions We Make Attract Good or Evil Spirits

Through orienting our lives to support the Divine Providence, with prayer, fasting, study of the truth and good deeds, we naturally attract Abel-type spirits and angels who can help us with our personal efforts to become ever better children of our Heavenly Parent. Experience tells us that it takes consistent commitment and work to make the conditions necessary for the Abel-type Spirit World to intervene in our lives.

The inverse is also true. In other words, if instead of making good conditions that demonstrate our Abel-type faith in God we make bad conditions that demonstrate our Cain-type lack of faith in God, we invite the intervention in our lives of evil spirits and fallen angels. This intervention encourages our fallen behavior and results in our greater alienation from God and assumption of greater—and more difficult—conditions to regain our original nature.

Good conditions made in obedience to God and in support of the providence enable the Abel-type Spirit World to assist us in being selfless and altruistic on behalf of the providence. However, bad conditions made in disobedience to God and opposition to the providence enable the Cain-type Spirit World to encourage us in being selfish and hedonistic in a way that is harmful to ourselves and to the providence.

A Failed Condition Requires a Greater Sacrifice to Restore it

The conditions we have to make represent our portion of responsibility after the Fall, before which the only condition Adam and Eve had to make to become a true son and a true daughter of God was to obey a single instruction—to not eat the fruit of the Tree of the Knowledge of Good and Evil. In their sinless state, obedience was not a matter of great effort or suffering, but a choice that proved to have cosmic significance.

After the Fall, the sinful nature of humankind made obedience to God extremely difficult, necessitating a step-by-step process through which fallen individuals chosen to develop the providence of salvation were required to make ever more demanding sacrifices. This process started with Cain and Abel:

> In the course of time Cain brought to the Lord an offering of the fruit of the ground, and Abel brought of the firstlings of his flock and of their fat portions. And the Lord had regard for Abel and his offering, but for Cain and his offering he had no regard. So Cain was very angry, and his countenance fell. The Lord said to Cain, "Why are you angry, and why has your countenance fallen? If you do well, will you not be accepted? And if you do not do well, sin is couching at the door; its desire is for you, but you must master it." (Genesis 4:3-7)

In Hebrews, we get this explanation for why Cain's offering was not accepted:

> By faith Abel offered to God a more acceptable sacrifice than Cain, through which he received approval as righteous, God bearing witness by accepting his gifts; he died, but through his faith he is still speaking. (Hebrews 11:4)

Thus the nature of an unfaithful Cain was differentiated from a faithful Abel. And when Cain was offered an opportunity to change and become good, he chose to act on his anger and resentment by killing Abel. His unrepentant faithlessness, resentment and anger became the core of the Cain archetype.

When, centuries later, Abraham made a mistake in sacrificing two birds, he was told that his descendants would have to suffer 400 years of slavery, which took place when his great-grandsons and their descendants were enslaved in Egypt. But he himself was later given a chance to make up for his mistake by sacrificing his son Isaac, as a condition to keep the central providence in his family. This was infinitely more difficult than sacrificing animals, but—unlike Cain—Abraham repented for his earlier error and faithfully prepared to carry out this gruesome task. At the last moment, his faith was rewarded and an angel interceded to let him know he would not have to kill Isaac.

This extreme condition of faith and obedience made it possible for Abraham's family to continue to play its central role in the providence, despite his prior mistake.

Hence we have to make very difficult conditions to break away from our own fallen nature and become children of God. This law of indemnification for our sins also operates for groups and nations. In these cases collective conditions are needed to pay for past sins or future blessings. If we fail in making a condition, we have to do it again, but the condition becomes more difficult the second time around.

Jesus Made Conditions for the World

Importantly, we can also make conditions for other individuals, for groups, nations and the world. Jesus himself began his public ministry to save Israel and the world after making a 40-day condition of fasting and prayer—followed by overcoming three temptations. Jesus was sinless and thus did not need to make conditions for his own salvation. He did need to make conditions, however, for the people of Israel to accept and follow him.

Jesus explained the importance of making conditions for God and the Abel-type Spirit World to assist their mission work when some of his disciples were unable to exorcise an evil spirit from a boy. According to the New King James Version of the Bible, among others, he told them:

> This kind can come out by nothing but prayer and fasting. (Mark 9:29)

In other words, there had to be strong conditions made by the person performing the exorcism for it to work. (Many other versions of the Bible, including the RSV, only mention prayer, but the lesson is the same.) Individuals can make conditions to benefit themselves and/or others; nations can make conditions to benefit themselves and/or others.

Jesus came to Israel to be its savior and king, but the Israelites had the responsibility to accept and follow him. When they refused to do so, despite all the conditions established by Abel-type leaders in their history and all the conditions made by Jesus himself, Jesus had to go the way of the cross. By making this ultimate sacrifice of his own life, Jesus established a condition for the victory of the Divine Providence over Satan and for the salvation of all humanity.

Jesus Understood and Controlled the Spirit World

Jesus' miraculous healing of those suffering illnesses brought on by spiritual possession was not only confirmation of his unity with God, but also of his mastery of the Spirit World. For Jesus, the Spirit World was not a distant, ethereal realm, but the place from where good and evil spirits and angels can exert a powerful influence over people on earth.

Evil spirits are like parasites that draw their strength and energy from the people they possess, destroying their hosts to sustain their own lives. This behavior resembles that of Lucifer when he wrongly sought a relationship with Eve for his own benefit but at the cost of the spiritual life of Adam and Eve. It also resembles the behavior of Cain when he acted on his envy of Abel by killing his brother in an effort to take by force the blessing of God.

Jesus was aware that both fallen angels like Lucifer and evil spirits were active in influencing the people of his time to oppose him and to harm those with a weak spirit, such as the man who had been possessed by a legion of spirits. More broadly, he understood that unless he could break this Satanic grip on the chosen people they would not be able to fulfill their providential mission to accept him as the Messiah.

Through his healing work, Jesus sought to rectify the damage done by evil spirits as manifest in various physical handicaps and mental disorders.[1] Thus, as we discussed in the previous chapter, many if not most of the miracles Jesus performed were the result of his driving evil spirits from those suffering from spirit possession. This aspect of his ministry was unique in Israel since the Jewish religious establishment was limited to law-giving and was incapable of either understanding or controlling the invisible Spirit World.

However, instead of acknowledging Jesus' spiritual authority the religious leaders accused him of acting on behalf of Satan:

> Then a blind and dumb demoniac was brought to him, and he healed him, so that the dumb man spoke and saw. And all the people were amazed, and said, "Can this be the Son of David?"

---

1. Emanuel Swedenborg studied the phenomena of spiritual possession and obsession as they manifest in mental illnesses. This work was referenced in a paper that summarizes some of these phenomena: The Presence of Spirits in Madness, by Wilson Van Dusen, published by the Swedenborg Foundation.

> But when the Pharisees heard it they said, "It is only by Beelzebul, the prince of demons, that this man casts out demons." (Matthew 12:22-24)

Evil Spirits Recognized Jesus

Jesus was a threat to the evil spirits and their activities. Indeed, as with the Cain people of his time, the evil spirits had to submit to the authority of Jesus. Ironically, the evil spirits themselves recognized who Jesus was while very few of the Israelites he was trying to educate recognized his true identity. For example:

> And immediately there was in their synagogue a man with an unclean spirit; and he cried out, "What have you to do with us, Jesus of Nazareth? Have you come to destroy us? I know who you are, the Holy One of God." (Mark 1:23-24)

Unlike anyone before him, Jesus understood that a person could survive a Satanic possession and become part of the providence only if the spirit was driven out completely:

> But Jesus rebuked him, saying, "Be silent, and come out of him!" And the unclean spirit, convulsing him and crying with a loud voice, came out of him. (Mark 1:25-26)

The people who witnessed this exorcism were surprised that Jesus had such great spiritual authority:

> And they were all amazed, so that they questioned among themselves, saying, "What is this? A new teaching! With authority he commands even the unclean spirits, and they obey him." (Mark 1:27)

The Responsibility of Those Cleansed by Jesus

But Jesus warned that someone liberated from a spiritual possession had to be responsible for keeping evil spirits away by not succumbing to spiritual temptations. That was the condition they had to fulfill to avoid being possessed once more with even worse consequences. This is how Jesus explained this phenomenon:

> "When the unclean spirit has gone out of a man, he passes through waterless places seeking rest, but he finds none. Then he says, 'I will return to my house from which I came.' And when he comes he finds it empty, swept, and put in order. Then he goes and brings with him seven other spirits more evil than himself, and they enter and dwell there; and the last state of that man becomes worse than the first. So shall it be also with this evil generation." (Matthew 12:43-45)

The Disciples Inherited Jesus' Spiritual Powers

So critical was spiritual healing to Jesus' ministry that when he sent out his disciples to spread the Gospel, he shared his spiritual powers with them so that they too would be able to heal those suffering from spirit possession and the diseases it caused:

> And he called to him his twelve disciples and gave them authority over unclean spirits, to cast them out, and to heal every disease and every infirmity. (Matthew 10:1)

This spiritual power of healing would continue to be used after Jesus had been crucified and his disciples had to build a following. For example, Saint Peter had great spiritual powers:

> And more than ever believers were added to the Lord, multitudes both of men and women, so that they even carried out the sick into the streets, and laid them on beds and pallets, that as Peter came by at least his shadow might fall on some of them. The people also gathered from the towns around Jerusalem, bringing the sick and those afflicted with unclean spirits, and they were all healed. (Acts 5:14-16)

Saint Paul also had these powers:

> And God did extraordinary miracles by the hands of Paul, so

> that handkerchiefs or aprons were carried away from his body to the sick, and diseases left them and the evil spirits came out of them. (Acts 19:11-12)

However, when people other than his followers tried to imitate these powers, they were not successful:

> Then some of the itinerant Jewish exorcists undertook to pronounce the name of the Lord Jesus over those who had evil spirits, saying, "I adjure you by the Jesus whom Paul preaches." Seven sons of a Jewish high priest named Sceva were doing this. But the evil spirit answered them, "Jesus I know, and Paul I know; but who are you?" And the man in whom the evil spirit was leaped on them, mastered all of them, and overpowered them, so that they fled out of that house naked and wounded. (Acts 19:13-16)

Ignorance of the Spirit World Persists

Jesus' knowledge of—and power over—the Spirit World was something truly remarkable for the people of his day, as we have indicated. Like us, they suffered from the spiritual ignorance that overcame our first ancestors when they became alienated from our Creator through the Fall. We have all inherited that dullness and therefore are rarely aware of our own spiritual nature and the influences we are subjected to by the Spirit World, influences amplified by shared lineage, associations, character traits, beliefs and interests.

In today's largely secular world we do not easily acknowledge the existence of spiritual beings that can influence our lives, whether for good or bad. However, their existence and activity is often the cause of the conflicts we experience in our own lives and see in the world around us. Evil spirits are also responsible for massive confusion in society, whether it be about fundamental issues such as the alignment of sex with gender and the importance of the traditional family unit, or the Divine origin and nature of the creation.

Acknowledging the existence of the eternal Spirit World—and that all human beings are destined to transition to it upon the death of their physical bodies—is the first step in understanding the invisible Cain and Abel influences in our life and the importance of Jesus' spiritual ministry. Through his mastery of the Spirit World, Jesus showed us the reality of the spiritual forces at play in the providence and in our lives. He also showed us that we can influence the involvement of the Spirit World in our lives, for good or bad, by making conditions that either advance or retard the Divine Providence.

Chapter 16

Persecution by Israel's Political Establishment

Herod and Pilate had Jesus Tortured and Killed

Herod's Illegitimate Dynasty

In Chapter 12 we discussed how Herod the Great was bent on killing Jesus from the moment of Christ's birth. Jesus narrowly escaped with his life when Herod ordered all the male children under the age of two who were living in the Bethlehem area to be killed. This was after he had been told by wise men visiting from the east that a great king was to be born in Bethlehem. Jesus was saved because Joseph and Mary listened to the warning of an angel and took him into hiding in Egypt. He only returned to Israel with his parents when Herod had died.

In this chapter we will explain in some detail why Herod's rule was illegitimate and why he and his sons continued to persecute Jesus and conspired with Israel's religious establishment and the Roman governor Pilate to have him killed.

It should be remembered that the Herodian animus towards Jesus was driven primarily by the Cain-type lineage of their dynasty, an ancestry that had long been in opposition to the providence. Herod's father Antipater was an Edomite and his mother Cypros a Nabatean Arab princess—descendants of Esau and Ishmael respectively. He took power in Israel in 37 BC when—with the help of Roman general Mark Anthony—he defeated the last Hasmonean ruler in Jerusalem.

Persecution by Israel's Political Establishment

The Hasmoneans, known as the Maccabees, had rebelled against the Hellenization of Israel under the influence of two of Alexander the Great's descendant kingdoms—the Ptolemies in Egypt and Seleucids in Syria—and by 164 BC they had captured Jerusalem from the Seleucids and purified the Temple of pagan Greek gods. In 142 BC the Maccabees established the first independent state of Israel since the Babylonians had destroyed Judah and taken the people into exile some five centuries earlier.

The patriarch of the Maccabees was the priest Mattathias, and it was his sons who led the fighting against the Seleucids. Thus the Hasmoneans combined the priestly functions of the Levites and Aaron with the ruling functions of Judah and David. This was the Abel-type lineage of Abraham, Isaac and Jacob which was responsible for preparing for the advent of the Messiah.

The independence of the Hasmonean kingdom had come to an end in 63 BC, when Roman Emperor Pompey conquered Judea. However, Rome would go a step further in crushing the legitimate kings of Israel when in 40 BC the Roman Senate appointed Herod to be king of Judea and then supported his conquest of Jerusalem in 37 BC, replacing the Abel-type Hasmoneans with the Cain-type Herod. In providential terms, this was enabling Cain to gain dominion over Abel, thereby making the mission of the Messiah a great deal more difficult.

The Messiah was to reclaim from the Cain-type Herodian dynasty the throne of Israel for David's Abel-type lineage, and therefore Herod had good cause to worry about Jesus when he heard that a child had been born as Israel's savior. Herod's lineage was not qualified to rule Israel, and he must have known that. His sons, too, must have known that theirs was an illegitimate dynasty.

Herod Should Have Followed Jesus

The providence advances when Abel-type figures gain ascendancy over Cain-type counterparts. Ideally this is a peaceful process in which Abel wins Cain's willing surrender to his younger brother. When Herod the Great was told by learned visitors that a future leader of Israel was to be born in Bethlehem, he should have sought out Jesus so that he could follow him. It was not Herod's mission to kill Jesus!

Later, his son Herod Antipas would hear about Jesus and his teachings and miracles, but like his father he too showed no interest in following Jesus. Instead he treated Israel's savior as a threat to the throne and conspired to have him killed, as we explain later in this chapter.

Providential history shows how difficult it is for Cain to swallow his pride and be sufficiently humble to accept the authority of Abel. Thus Esau wanted to kill Jacob, Joseph's older brothers wanted to kill him, Pharaoh wanted to kill Moses, and Saul wanted to kill David.

Jesus pursued his mission using peaceful means, seeking to persuade the Israelites of the truth he brought. There is no evidence that he had a following that could have unseated the Herodians from power and put him on the throne of David.

The Herodian Dynasty Conspired to Kill Jesus

Herod the Great would die shortly after the birth of Jesus, but the threat posed to Jesus by the Herodian dynasty would continue to hang like a dark shadow over him for the rest of his life. Thus, even after Herod had died, when Joseph received a heavenly message to return to Israel he was afraid that Herod's son Archelaus would kill Jesus:

> But when Herod died, behold, an angel of the Lord appeared in a dream to Joseph in Egypt, saying, "Rise, take the child and his mother, and go to the land of Israel, for those who sought the child's life are dead." And he rose and took the child and his mother, and went to the land of Israel. But when he heard that Archelaus reigned over Judea in place of his father Herod, he was afraid to go there, and being warned in a dream he withdrew to the district of Galilee. (Matthew 2:19-22)

By the time Jesus had reached adulthood, another son of Herod the Great had followed Archelaus into power. This was Herod Antipas, who

Persecution by Israel's Political Establishment

would demonstrate as much animus for any potential rivals as his father and brother had shown. Once Jesus started his public ministry, he became visible to the political leadership in Israel, and they plotted with Israel's religious leaders to get rid of him:

> The Pharisees went out, and immediately held counsel with the Herodians against him, how to destroy him. (Mark 3:6)

Jesus warned his disciples of these conspiracies:

> And he cautioned them, saying, "Take heed, beware of the leaven of the Pharisees and the leaven of Herod." (Mark 8:15)

On another occasion, Jesus was warned that Herod was seeking to kill him:

> At that very hour some Pharisees came, and said to him, "Get away from here, for Herod wants to kill you." And he said to them, "Go and tell that fox, 'Behold, I cast out demons and perform cures today and tomorrow, and the third day I finish my course. Nevertheless I must go on my way today and tomorrow and the day following; for it cannot be that a prophet should perish away from Jerusalem.'" (Luke 13:31-34)

It was the Cain-like Herod Antipas who executed John the Baptist at the whimsical request of his step-daughter Salome on behalf of his jealous wife Herodias, another member of Herod the Great's family. John was no threat to Herod, and had committed no violation of the law, making his execution an act of totally unjustified evil.

It was Herod Antipas, too, who went along with the Jesus-hating Jewish leaders in condemning Jesus to death by allowing the Roman governor Pontius Pilate to have Jesus crucified without cause:

> And when [Pilot] learned that [Jesus] belonged to Herod's jurisdiction, he sent him over to Herod, who was himself in Jerusalem at that time. When Herod saw Jesus, he was very glad, for he had long desired to see him, because he had heard about him, and he was hoping to see some sign done by him. So he

> questioned him at some length; but he made no answer. The chief priests and the scribes stood by, vehemently accusing him. And Herod with his soldiers treated him with contempt and mocked him; then, arraying him in gorgeous apparel, he sent him back to Pilate. (Luke 23:7-11)

Herod apparently had no awareness or appreciation of Jesus' Messianic mission, but simply thought of him as a magician who could perform entertaining tricks. He was perfectly happy to believe the accusations against Jesus made by the priests, who accused Jesus of blasphemy and seeking power.

According to Luke, Herod's mockery of Jesus brought him and Pilate together for the first time, something that would have been beneficial to Herod as king under Roman rule.

> And Herod and Pilate became friends with each other that very day, for before this they had been at enmity with each other. (Luke 23:12)

Pilate had sent Jesus to Herod looking for confirmation that he deserved the death demanded by the religious leaders. Herod had no such evidence, as Pilate would later testify:

> Pilate then called together the chief priests and the rulers and the people, and said to them, "You brought me this man as one who was perverting the people; and after examining him before you, behold, I did not find this man guilty of any of your charges against him; neither did Herod, for he sent him back to us. Behold, nothing deserving death has been done by him; I will therefore chastise him and release him." (Luke 23:13-16)

But Pilate eventually gave in to the cries for blood from the mob that had been incited by the Jewish leaders:

> Pilate addressed them once more, desiring to release Jesus; but they shouted out, "Crucify, crucify him!" A third time he said

to them, "Why, what evil has he done? I have found in him no crime deserving death; I will therefore chastise him and release him." But they were urgent, demanding with loud cries that he should be crucified. And their voices prevailed. So Pilate gave sentence that their demand should be granted. He released the man who had been thrown into prison for insurrection and murder, whom they asked for; but Jesus he delivered up to their will. (Luke 23:20-25)

Pilate's soldiers imitated the behavior of Herod and his soldiers who had dressed Jesus in finery and then mocked him as king of the Jews:

And they stripped him and put a scarlet robe upon him, and plaiting a crown of thorns they put it on his head, and put a reed in his right hand. And kneeling before him they mocked him, saying, "Hail, King of the Jews!" And they spat upon him, and took the reed and struck him on the head. And when they had mocked him, they stripped him of the robe, and put his own clothes on him, and led him away to crucify him. (Matthew 27:28-31)

Herod Antipas used the religious opposition to Jesus as an opportunity to get rid of a potential threat to his throne, however remote that appears to us now and might have appeared at the time. Instead of accepting Jesus as the awaited Messiah, he repeated his unjustified killing of John the Baptist when he allowed Pilate to execute Jesus without cause. Herod could likely have stopped the crucifixion, but his connivance with Israel's religious leaders sealed the fate of Jesus.

Chapter 17

Persecution by Israel's Religious Establishment

The Wise Men of the Temple Rejected Jesus

Israel's Ossified Religious Establishment

The religious establishment of Israel was composed of scholars and priests who dedicated their lives to understanding the Mosaic Law and interpreting it for the Jewish people. They were responsible for Israel's proper practice of rituals, sacrifices and celebrations, and for the Israelites' proper behavior within their families and society. From the time of Moses and Aaron, members of the tribe of Levi were separated from the rest of the people and tasked with serving Israel as priests. Thus the Levites had the special responsibility of learning and teaching the words of God as revealed through Moses and supplemented by other figures of religious authority in the providence.

In recognition of this special role, the Levites were not granted territory in the newly-settled land of Canaan, but they were granted special privileges, including the right to receive tithes in money and kind and, later, to collect the Temple tax. As with all ecclesiastical bureaucracies, these privileges became a major source of temptation to lassitude and corruption amid an ossification of belief and dogmatism in interpretation of the law. In these circumstances, the spirit and purpose behind the law could easily be lost in the name of legal rectitude.

This was the situation with the religious establishment in Israel at the time of Jesus, a religious establishment that became uniformly hostile to Jesus. As we know from the Sermon on the Mount and the many other occasions when he tried to educate the Israelites, Jesus introduced a radically new perspective on the truth and its meaning and implications for life—as we discussed in Chapter 13. The Jewish religious leaders were unmoved.

Jesus and His Teachings Were Rejected by the Religious Leaders

It was the religious establishment in Israel that had the primary responsibility to receive and support the Messiah, the person who would save Israel. They should have embraced Jesus and enabled the political leadership and the rest of the people to accept and follow him too. This they never did. Instead, they devoted their energies to finding fault in his teachings and behavior as a pretext to get rid of him.

Thus, instead of recognizing the great spiritual power and wisdom of Jesus, members of the religious establishment constantly tried to find Jesus in violation of the Mosaic Law, to prove him a blasphemer and heretic. Jesus always had a ready answer for them, based on his own, deeper understanding of scriptures and the providence, which made them even more frustrated and angry at him. This anger and hostility revealed their lack of humility and inability to recognize Jesus' teaching for what it was—a profound revelation of the Divine purpose, including the role the law was to play in paving the way for the Messiah.

There were two main factions within the Jewish religious hierarchy, the Pharisees and Sadducees, who differed over interpretation of the scriptures. The scribes, who were experts on the scriptures, were generally aligned with the Pharisees. None of these supposedly wise men was able to overcome their narrow-mindedness and prejudices to recognize Jesus as the Messiah and his teaching as the message God wanted them to hear and that Israel needed for its salvation. With the chief priests, members of these groups composed the Sanhedrin, the judicial body that ultimately convicted Jesus of blasphemy and violations of the law and turned him over to the Romans for execution.

Jesus Chastised the Religious Leaders for Their Failings

Members of the Jewish religious establishment tried to trip Jesus up by asking him leading questions about the Sabbath, marriage and various points of the Mosaic law. His answers inevitably pointed to their insincerity in asking and the fact that they were not actually interested in a deeper understanding of scriptures, but only looking for a way to be able to condemn him as a heretic. There are many passages in the Gospels in which he castigates the religious leaders as Cain-type hypocrites, whom he called serpents and vipers.

Most of Matthew 23 records Jesus' condemnation of the 'Scribes and Pharisees'. These passages are particularly poignant because they come from the period after Jesus met with Moses and Elijah on the Mount of Transfiguration and began to tell his disciples that he was destined to die at the hands of Israel's ruling authorities:

> The scribes and the Pharisees sit on Moses' seat; so practice and observe whatever they tell you, but not what they do; for they preach, but do not practice. They bind heavy burdens, hard to bear, and lay them on men's shoulders; but they themselves will not move them with their finger. They do all their deeds to be seen by men; for they make their phylacteries broad and their fringes long, and they love the place of honor at feasts and the best seats in the synagogues, and salutations in the market places, and being called rabbi by men. (Matthew 23:2-7)

> But woe to you, scribes and Pharisees, hypocrites! because you shut the kingdom of heaven against men; for you neither enter yourselves, nor allow those who would enter to go in. Woe to you, scribes and Pharisees, hypocrites! for you traverse sea and land to make a single proselyte, and when he becomes a proselyte, you make him twice as much a child of hell as yourselves. (Matthew 23:13-15)

> Woe to you, blind guides, who say, "If any one swears by the temple, it is nothing; but if any one swears by the gold of the

temple, he is bound by his oath." You blind fools! for which is greater, the gold or the temple that has made the gold sacred? And you say, "If any one swears by the altar, it is nothing; but if any one swears by the gift that is on the altar, he is bound by his oath." You blind men! for which is greater, the gift or the altar that makes the gift sacred? (Matthew 23:16-19)

Woe to you, scribes and Pharisees, hypocrites! for you tithe mint and dill and cumin, and have neglected the weightier matters of the law, justice and mercy and faith; these you ought to have done, without neglecting the others. You blind guides, straining out a gnat and swallowing a camel! (Matthew 23:23-24)

Woe to you, scribes and Pharisees, hypocrites! for you cleanse the outside of the cup and of the plate, but inside they are full of extortion and rapacity. You blind Pharisee! first cleanse the inside of the cup and of the plate, that the outside also may be clean. (Matthew 23:25-26)

Woe to you, scribes and Pharisees, hypocrites! for you are like whitewashed tombs, which outwardly appear beautiful, but within they are full of dead men's bones and all uncleanness. So you also outwardly appear righteous to men, but within you are full of hypocrisy and iniquity. (Matthew 23:27-28)

Jesus Identified His Persecutors as Cain-like

Why was Jesus so angry at these leaders of the people? From the perspective of the providence they were blocking the way forward. They had inherited the positions of central authority in Israel, yet instead of using their knowledge and privilege to recognize Jesus and support his mission, they only attacked him. Jesus was the fulfillment of the prophecies of Isaiah and others who anticipated the Messiah, but he was rejected by the very people he came to save.

He said that because of their faithlessness they would inherit the responsibility for the shedding of innocent blood, from Abel to Zechariah, a priest murdered in the Temple during the Divided Kingdoms era. In other words,

Jesus associated them with Cain and all the Cain-type figures of history who had shed innocent blood, for which they would become responsible. Furthermore, he called them "serpents," meaning they had the nature of the first serpent, Lucifer. Finally, he warned them that they would be responsible for his death too:

> Woe to you, scribes and Pharisees, hypocrites! for you build the tombs of the prophets and adorn the monuments of the righteous, saying, "If we had lived in the days of our fathers, we would not have taken part with them in shedding the blood of the prophets." Thus you witness against yourselves, that you are sons of those who murdered the prophets. Fill up, then, the measure of your fathers. You serpents, you brood of vipers, how are you to escape being sentenced to hell? Therefore I send you prophets and wise men and scribes, some of whom you will kill and crucify, and some you will scourge in your synagogues and persecute from town to town, that upon you may come all the righteous blood shed on earth, from the blood of innocent Abel to the blood of Zechariah the son of Barachiah, whom you murdered between the sanctuary and the altar. Truly, I say to you, all this will come upon this generation. (Matthew 23:29-36)

There was no pleasure for Jesus in castigating the religious leaders, for he knew that by rejecting and killing him they would condemn the people of Israel to immeasurable suffering. Thus he lamented over the faithlessness of the chosen people:

> O Jerusalem, Jerusalem, killing the prophets and stoning those who are sent to you! How often would I have gathered your children together as a hen gathers her brood under her wings, and you would not! Behold, your house is forsaken and desolate. (Matthew 23:37-38)

A Cain-type Lust to Kill Jesus
Cain was filled with envy of his brother Abel, whose offering had been accepted by God. Cain nurtured that resentment to the point where he was

willing to murder Abel in a fit of jealous rage. Israel's religious establishment responded to Jesus in the same way. They recognized that Jesus was superior to them in his spiritual stature and wisdom, including his knowledge of the scriptures, which was the area of their supposed expertise. But instead of humbling themselves to him, they chose the Way of Cain and worked to have him killed.

After Jesus had been preaching for just three years, the animus of the religious leaders towards him had reached a fever pitch. When they condemned Jesus and asked Pilate to execute him, the Roman governor questioned Jesus himself but soon declared that he found no reason to execute him. Even Pilate's wife told him that she had seen in a dream that Jesus was innocent, and that he should be released. Pilate then offered to execute a known criminal, Barabbas, in place of Jesus. But the chief priests were adamant that Jesus should be killed. Pilate recognized their real motivation and eventually relented:

> And [Pilate] answered them, "Do you want me to release for you the King of the Jews?" For he perceived that it was out of envy that the chief priests had delivered him up. But the chief priests stirred up the crowd to have him release for them Barabbas instead. And Pilate again said to them, "Then what shall I do with the man whom you call the King of the Jews?" And they cried out again, "Crucify him." And Pilate said to them, "Why, what evil has he done?" But they shouted all the more, "Crucify him." So Pilate, wishing to satisfy the crowd, released for them Barabbas; and having scourged Jesus, he delivered him to be crucified. (Mark 15:9-15)

The repeated cries of "Crucify him, Crucify him" that came from the mouths of the people incited by their priests, echoed the voice of a jealous Cain thirsting to shed the blood of Abel. It is the cry of evil seeking to crush good that has reverberated down through history in countless repetitions of Satan working through Cain to murder Abel.

Cain's Self-righteousness

The Way of Abel is the difficult course of self-sacrifice that Jesus lived and taught his disciples. He knew that Israel's religious leaders would never take responsibility for the suffering they inflicted on him and his disciples. He warned his close followers that they, like him, would likely be repaid for their good deeds with rejection and even death, and that the perpetrators of this wrongdoing would in their ignorance believe themselves virtuous for doing so:

> They will put you out of the synagogues; indeed, the hour is coming when whoever kills you will think he is offering service to God. And they will do this because they have not known the Father, nor me. (Matthew 16:2-3)

Here Jesus is describing attitudes and behavior typical of Cain: feeling justified and even virtuous in persecuting Abel. Thus Abel suffers because Cain does not understand the heart of the Father—he does not understand the sadness and suffering he gives the Father by persecuting Abel. In his ignorance and alienation from God, Cain believes himself justified in his resentment and refuses to take responsibility for his sins:

> Cain said to Abel his brother, "Let us go out to the field." And when they were in the field, Cain rose up against his brother Abel, and killed him. Then the LORD said to Cain, "Where is Abel your brother?" He said, "I do not know; am I my brother's keeper?" (Genesis 4:8-9)

Only Jesus Understood the Heart of the Father

Jesus was the first person to fully understand and reveal to the world the deep heart of God as our Heavenly Father. To demonstrate what he meant, Jesus pointed out just how much greater the love of God is for human beings than is our love for our own children:

> If you then, who are evil, know how to give good gifts to your

> children, how much more will your Father who is in heaven give good things to those who ask him! (Matthew 7:11)

By the same token, how much greater is our Father's grief over the suffering of human beings than is our grief over the suffering of our own children? Indeed, it is this parental heart of God that explains the Divine purpose for our creation, God's hope for Adam and Eve and immeasurable sorrow at their Fall, and the unwavering commitment of our Heavenly Father to save fallen humanity and regain Eden in the form of the Kingdom of Heaven on earth. This is the heart behind the providence, the selection of Abraham's family to lead the return to God, the raising up of Moses to lead the Israelites out of Egypt and into Canaan, and the coming of Jesus as the Messiah to save Israel and the world.

The Jewish leaders of Israel were apparently unable to grasp the significance of Jesus from God's point of view, and therefore they did not recognize the deep love God had for Jesus. They looked at Jesus superficially, through the eyes of the law rather than a heart of love. Even Jesus' family and disciples were unable to understand fully the bond of love between God and Jesus, a bond that was unprecedented in history and therefore unknown to them.

Jesus lacked the standing in society that would have encouraged Israel's religious establishment to show him respect and humility. Without their support, the task that Jesus faced as Messiah was truly monumental. How could he convince the people and political leadership to follow him without this assistance? This failure of Israel's leadership condemned Jesus to persecution, torture and death.

Chapter 18

The Doubting Mind of John the Baptist

The Crucial Mission of Elijah Went Unfulfilled

The Miraculous Birth of John the Baptist

The Bible recounts the miraculous birth of John the Baptist. It came about when his parents, the priest Zechariah and his wife Elizabeth, were advanced in years. Elizabeth had been barren all her life, but the angel Gabriel informed the couple that they were to have a providential son, to be called John. This heavenly intervention repeated a pattern of miraculous births that we first saw when Abraham and his barren wife Sarah in old age were visited by an angel who told them they would finally be able to have a son, to be called Isaac. The wife of Isaac, Rebekah, also was barren for many years before she gave birth to Jacob and Esau, and Jacob's wife Rachel was barren all her life until she was able to have two sons, Joseph and Benjamin. All of these miraculous pregnancies produced individuals who would become key figures in the providence. Here is the Biblical account:

> In the days of Herod, king of Judea, there was a priest named Zechariah, of the division of Abijah; and he had a wife of the daughters of Aaron, and her name was Elizabeth. And they were both righteous before God, walking in all the commandments and ordinances of the Lord blameless. But they had no child, because Elizabeth was barren, and both were advanced in years. Now while he was serving as priest before God when his division

was on duty, according to the custom of the priesthood, it fell to him by lot to enter the temple of the Lord and burn incense. And the whole multitude of the people were praying outside at the hour of incense. And there appeared to him an angel of the Lord standing on the right side of the altar of incense. And Zechariah was troubled when he saw him, and fear fell upon him. But the angel said to him, "Do not be afraid, Zechariah, for your prayer is heard, and your wife Elizabeth will bear you a son, and you shall call his name John. And you will have joy and gladness, and many will rejoice at his birth; for he will be great before the Lord, and he shall drink no wine nor strong drink, and he will be filled with the Holy Spirit, even from his mother's womb. And he will turn many of the sons of Israel to the Lord their God, and he will go before him in the spirit and power of Elijah, to turn the hearts of the fathers to the children, and the disobedient to the wisdom of the just, to make ready for the Lord a people prepared." (Luke 1:5-17)

Abraham and Sarah had been incredulous at the angelic news, since it flew in the face of common human experience. Zechariah also doubted Gabriel, for the same reason, but he was struck dumb for the duration of Elizabeth's pregnancy to show him that this was indeed the work of God:

> And Zechariah said to the angel, "How shall I know this? For I am an old man, and my wife is advanced in years." And the angel answered him, "I am Gabriel, who stands in the presence of God; and I was sent to speak to you, and to bring you this good news. And behold, you will be silent and unable to speak until the day that these things come to pass, because you did not believe my words, which will be fulfilled in their time." And the people were waiting for Zechariah, and they wondered at his delay in the temple. And when he came out, he could not speak to them, and they perceived that he had seen a vision in the temple; and he made signs to them and remained dumb. (Luke 1:18-22)

Thus John was conceived within the Divine Providence for a special purpose. His mission was to "make ready for the Lord a people prepared." When Elizabeth was six months pregnant with John, her cousin Mary came to their home to tell them of her own visitation from Gabriel and the news that she had been chosen to give birth to Israel's savior, Jesus. At that moment Elizabeth was "filled with the Holy Spirit" and she experienced her unborn son leap for joy in her womb, confirming to her that Mary had been chosen for a mission even greater than hers, and that John's mission would be to serve Mary's son, Jesus.

These two Levitical cousins had been chosen to accomplish the most important role of any women in history: Mary was to be the mother of the Messiah and Elizabeth the mother of the man tasked with preparing Israel to receive the Messiah. Here is the Biblical account of their providential meeting:

> In those days Mary arose and went with haste into the hill country, to a city of Judah, and she entered the house of Zechariah and greeted Elizabeth. And when Elizabeth heard the greeting of Mary, the babe leaped in her womb; and Elizabeth was filled with the Holy Spirit and she exclaimed with a loud cry, "Blessed are you among women, and blessed is the fruit of your womb! And why is this granted me, that the mother of my Lord should come to me? For behold, when the voice of your greeting came to my ears, the babe in my womb leaped for joy. And blessed is she who believed that there would be a fulfilment of what was spoken to her from the Lord." (Luke 1:39-45)

When John was born, Zechariah regained his speech and prophesized that John was destined to serve the coming Lord:

> And you, child, will be called the prophet of the Most High; for you will go before the Lord to prepare his ways, to give knowledge of salvation to his people in the forgiveness of their sins, through the tender mercy of our God, when the day shall dawn upon us from on high to give light to those who sit in darkness

and in the shadow of death, to guide our feet into the way of peace. (Luke 1:76-79)

As a priest, Zechariah was a very public figure, and inevitably his temporary loss of speech and his prophecies about his son were noticed by people, who wondered about John:

> And all these things were talked about through all the hill country of Judea; and all who heard them laid them up in their hearts, saying, "What then will this child be?" For the hand of the Lord was with him. (Luke 1:65-66)

Thus Zechariah, Elizabeth and Mary all knew that John was to serve Jesus by introducing him to the people of Israel as their savior, and many in Israel knew of John's miraculous birth and mission to prepare the way for the Messiah.

The Providential Person and Mission of John the Baptist

What then, was the role and mission of John in the providence? The answer is provided quite specifically by Gabriel within the quote from Luke above. It's worth repeating:

> And he will turn many of the sons of Israel to the Lord their God, and he will go before him in the spirit and power of Elijah, to turn the hearts of the fathers to the children, and the disobedient to the wisdom of the just, to make ready for the Lord a people prepared. (Luke 1:16-17)

Rephrasing this, John's mission was to prepare the people of Israel to receive Jesus as the Messiah by getting them to return to a life of faith based on child-like humility and obedience to God.

What do we know about John as a person? First, his father was the notable priest Zechariah who was known to have been struck dumb during Elizabeth's pregnancy. As we have discussed, the miraculous circumstances of John's birth were well known, and both Zechariah and Elizabeth had testified to receiving messages from Gabriel about the great providential importance of John. So John was raised as a member of a prominent Levitical family whose men were all expected to become priests.

Because of his sterling credentials as a Levite, over time John became well known in Israel as an ascetic and as a great teacher and prophet who spoke of the Messiah to come and who purified the Israelites through baptisms—hence we know him as John the Baptist.

Here are three passages about John at this time that show him to be a great ascetic and powerful preacher.

He lived an ascetic life:

> And the child grew and became strong in spirit, and he was in the wilderness till the day of his manifestation to Israel. (Luke 1:80)

People from far and wide flocked to hear him and be baptized by him:

> In those days came John the Baptist, preaching in the wilderness of Judea, "Repent, for the kingdom of heaven is at hand." For this is he who was spoken of by the prophet Isaiah when he said, "The voice of one crying in the wilderness: Prepare the way of the Lord, make his paths straight." Now John wore a garment of camel's hair, and a leather girdle around his waist; and his food was locusts and wild honey. Then went out to him Jerusalem and all Judea and all the region about the Jordan, and they were baptized by him in the river Jordan, confessing their sins. (Matthew 3:1-6)

Even the religious leaders of Israel sought him out:

> But when he saw many of the Pharisees and Sadducees coming for baptism, he said to them, "You brood of vipers! Who warned you to flee from the wrath to come? Bear fruit that befits repentance, and do not presume to say to yourselves, 'We have Abraham as our father'; for I tell you, God is able from these stones to raise up children to Abraham. Even now the axe is laid to the

root of the trees; every tree therefore that does not bear good fruit is cut down and thrown into the fire. (Matthew 3:7-10)

John's Mission Was Greater Than That of a Prophet

However, John was more than a prophet because he was not just someone sent to warn of the future advent of the Messiah. He had the much more important mission of showing the Israelites that his close relative Jesus—who was living in their midst—was their long-awaited savior. Not being a committed disciple of Christ, John proved reluctant to carry out this most important mission. And his uncertainty about the identity and mission of Jesus would be reflected in the confusion of the Israelites regarding John's own providential role. Some of them even wondered if John himself was the Messiah:

> As the people were in expectation, and all men questioned in their hearts concerning John, whether perhaps he were the Christ, John answered them all, "I baptize you with water; but he who is mightier than I is coming, the thong of whose sandals I am not worthy to untie; he will baptize you with the Holy Spirit and with fire. His winnowing fork is in his hand, to clear his threshing floor, and to gather the wheat into his granary, but the chaff he will burn with unquenchable fire." (Luke 3:15-17)

For his part, Jesus was very clear about the importance of John's role and mission:

> When the messengers of John had gone, [Jesus] began to speak to the crowds concerning John: "What did you go out into the wilderness to behold? A reed shaken by the wind? What then did you go out to see? A man clothed in soft clothing? Behold, those who are gorgeously appareled and live in luxury are in kings' courts. What then did you go out to see? A prophet? Yes, I tell you, and more than a prophet. This is he of whom it is written, 'Behold, I send my messenger before thy face, who shall prepare thy way before thee.' I tell you, among those born of women none is greater than John." (Luke 7:24-28)

Thus it is evident that in the eyes of the religious establishment and the public of Israel, John the Baptist was a great prophet and preacher, a Levite who set a very high standard of personal faith and dedication to God.

John and Jesus Went Down Different Paths

What was John's relationship with Jesus like? The Bible tells us nothing about the relationship between these two closely related providential figures, whether as children or as they matured into adults. We first see them together when Jesus asked John to baptize him, which probably occurred when both of them were already 30 years old and well set on their separate paths.

However, we do know that starting at an early age Jesus gained great understanding of the scriptures and how they should be understood in his time, even though his daily life was taken up with helping his father in the carpentry business. When he was just 12, Jesus' parents found Jesus talking about the meaning of scriptures with elders in the Temple, demonstrating uncommon wisdom for someone his age.

The fruit of this learning became evident when Jesus began his public ministry, and in particular when in his Sermon on the Mount (Matthew 5-7) he laid out the standard of morality and values that the people of Israel should aspire to. This teaching represents the heart of the Christian message. It is a radical departure from traditional interpretations of the Mosaic Law, as we have explained in earlier chapters. As far as we know, Jesus' teaching was very different from the education John would have received as a Levite.

Thus we also know that there was a great deal that John should have learned from Jesus if he was "to make ready for the Lord a people prepared." His parents were responsible to help John fulfill the mission the angel Gabriel had told them was his—to prepare the people of Israel to receive the Messiah. But there is no evidence that they did this for John.

In retrospect, it is very clear that without following Jesus as a disciple, and without learning the depth of Jesus' teaching, that John the Baptist would be unable to fulfill his providential mission.

Why John Was So Important for the Success of Jesus

John was a famous preacher, but Jesus was the Messiah, and it was Jesus not John who truly understood the changes that needed to take place in the faith of the Israelites if they were to be able to accept Jesus as the Messiah. However, Jesus lacked standing in society. As a carpenter's son, no one would expect him to be a preacher or prophet, let alone the Messiah. His credentials as a Levite were kept a secret by his family, who treated him as just one of the Judahite children of Joseph.

Which is why John was so important for the success of Jesus' mission. He had the credentials as a Levite and renowned preacher to create a bridge between Jesus and the people of Israel, and in particular Israel's religious leadership.

John could have solved the problem of standing that Jesus faced if he had clearly and consistently testified to Jesus as the Messiah. Making such a testimony of faith in Jesus would have required John to live his life as a humble disciple of Jesus, and to turn his own followers into disciples of Christ. In this way, the providential foundation established by John would have been inherited by Jesus, and the problem caused due to Jesus' lack of public credentials would have been solved. Unfortunately, John never showed a willingness to become the disciple of Jesus. He followed his own path and kept his disciples for himself.

This meant Jesus was put in the very difficult position of winning over Israel by himself. Ideally, the religious leaders should have been the first to recognize, welcome and follow Jesus as the Messiah. However, they were wedded to their belief in the Mosaic Law and without the help of John's intercessionary ministry it became immeasurably more difficult for Jesus to win them over to accept his teaching and support his ministry.

Why John's Association With Elijah Was So Important

One of the mysterious elements of John's miraculous birth was his identification by Gabriel as a representative of the prophet Elijah, who had lived some eight centuries earlier. According to Biblical scriptures, Elijah never died, but was caught up to heaven in a whirlwind:

> And Elijah went up by a whirlwind into heaven. And Elisha saw it and he cried, "My father, my father! the chariots of Israel and its horsemen!" And he saw him no more. (2 Kings 2:11-12)

Some four centuries after this event, the very last prophet of the Old Testament, Malachi, foretold the return of Elijah to prepare the way for the Messiah:

> Behold, I will send you Elijah the prophet before the great and terrible day of the Lord comes. And he will turn the hearts of fathers to their children and the hearts of children to their fathers, lest I come and smite the land with a curse. (Malachi 4:5-6)

This prophecy was so well known that many in Israel were looking for Elijah to return as the sign that the Messiah's advent was imminent. Thus it was very important to the success of Jesus' mission that the angel Gabriel told Zechariah that his son, John, would precede the Messiah "in the spirit and power of Elijah." It prepared the Levites and the common people to look to John to show them the Messiah.

Jesus Identified John as the Returned Elijah

It was not only Gabriel who said that John would come "in the spirit and power of Elijah." Jesus himself identified John as Elijah:

> For all the prophets and the law prophesied until John; and if you are willing to accept it, he is Elijah who is to come. He who has ears to hear, let him hear. (Matthew 11:13-15)

When three disciples accompanied Jesus on the Mount of Transfiguration, where he met Moses and Elijah in spirit, they naturally wondered how the prophecy of Elijah's return could be fulfilled if Elijah was actively working with Moses in the Spirit World. Jesus explained to them that John the Baptist had been sent to fulfill the role of Elijah in preparing the way for the Messiah:

> As they were coming down the mountain, Jesus instructed them, "Don't tell anyone what you have seen, until the Son of Man has been raised from the dead." The disciples asked him, "Why then do the teachers of the law say that Elijah must come first?" Jesus replied, "To be sure, Elijah comes and will restore all things. But I tell you, Elijah has already come, and they did not recognize him, but have done to him everything they wished. In the same way the Son of Man is going to suffer at their hands." Then the disciples understood that he was talking to them about John the Baptist. (Matthew 17:9-13)

But John Denied Being Elijah or a Prophet

Because of Malachi's prophecy, Israel's anticipation of Elijah's return was almost as great as it was for the Messiah's own advent, since the Jews believed that Elijah had to come first. So it was only natural for the religious leaders to ask John about his relationship to Elijah when he was preaching repentance in preparation for the advent of the Messiah:

> Now this was John's testimony when the Jewish leaders in Jerusalem sent priests and Levites to ask him who he was. He did not fail to confess, but confessed freely, "I am not the Messiah." They asked him, "Then who are you? Are you Elijah?" He said, "I am not." "Are you the Prophet?" He answered, "No." (John 1:19-21)

John denied being the Messiah. But he also denied being Elijah or the prophet who would prepare the way for the Messiah. In effect, John was saying that Jesus was lying when he identified John as Elijah and the most important prophet of all. This was not a gesture of humility by John, but rather a denial of the role he had been given from birth, the role that Jesus had identified as his.

If John had believed Jesus was the Messiah, he would no doubt have acknowledged that his own role was indeed that of Elijah. Apparently John either never believed he was Elijah, or as time progressed he was unable to overcome his doubts about the messiahship of Jesus.

John's Unrealistic Expectations for the Messiah

It is very likely that John's expectations for the Messiah were shaped by the prophecies of Isaiah and others who said he would come as a mighty king to inherit the throne of David. How could he square the Messiah as mighty king with the lowly status of his poor relative Jesus? When asked if he might be the Messiah, John revealed his unrealistic expectations:

> John answered them all, "I baptize you with water; but he who is mightier than I is coming, the thong of whose sandals I am not worthy to untie; he will baptize you with the Holy Spirit and with fire." (Luke 3:16)

In John's Gospel, John the Baptist makes the stunning admission that before he saw the Holy Spirit descend on Jesus on the occasion of his baptism, John had not recognized Jesus as the Messiah:

> I myself did not know him; but he who sent me to baptize with water said to me, "He on whom you see the Spirit descend and remain, this is he who baptizes with the Holy Spirit." (John 1:33)

The Meaning of John Baptizing Jesus

As we have seen, through his words and deeds John clearly rejected being in Elijah's position. No wonder, then, that while he preached repentance and performed baptisms he did not identify Jesus as the Messiah the people were expecting, nor did he encourage Israel to believe in and follow Jesus.

Because of this failure, Jesus had to take on the mission of Elijah and John himself. He had to teach the people what they needed to know to receive the Messiah and he had to build up a following of his own. Because of his lack of standing in society, he was unable to win over the religious establishment but instead had to teach uneducated but more humble non-Levitical Israelites.

This explains the unusual meeting between John and Jesus at the Jordan River. When they met, John acknowledged Jesus' superior spiritual status and requested that Jesus baptize him. Jesus declined and instead insisted that John baptize him:

> Then Jesus came from Galilee to the Jordan to John, to be baptized by him. John would have prevented him, saying, "I need to be baptized by you, and do you come to me?" But Jesus answered him, "Let it be so now; for thus it is fitting for us to fulfil all righteousness." (Matthew 3:13-15)

Unlike John, Jesus was sinless and therefore did not need the purification of baptism. So why did Jesus seek to be baptized by John? It had to do with John's role as the last prophet sent to prepare the way for the Messiah. As such, John represented the culmination of providential preparations for Israel to receive a savior. By being baptized by John, Jesus inherited the providential foundation that had been laid for Christ, and then launched his own public ministry on that foundation. Thus his baptism was a ceremony of anointing Jesus as the heir to the providence up to that moment, an anointing manifested by the blessing Jesus received from the Holy Spirit:

> And when Jesus was baptized, he went up immediately from the water, and behold, the heavens were opened and he saw the Spirit of God descending like a dove, and alighting on him; and lo, a voice from heaven, saying, "This is my beloved Son, with whom I am well pleased." (Matthew 3:16-17)

John witnessed this great confirmation of Jesus' Divinely mandated role, but he did not change direction. He continued on his separate way, and instead of dedicating himself to serving Jesus as the first disciple of Christ he continued preaching and baptizing as before, and soon become entangled in the irrelevant family matters of Herod Antipas.

Why John Didn't Follow Jesus After His Baptism

The baptism of Jesus was a crossroads for John, a moment when he had to see beyond his own limited understanding of God's providence to recognize Jesus as the Messiah. However, based on his behavior after he baptized Jesus, John never came to terms with the messiahship of Christ.

The Gospel of John describes how the day after the baptism two of John the Baptist's disciples were with him when he testified again to Jesus. But even then, John did not follow Jesus, although the two disciples did:

> The next day again John was standing with two of his disciples; and he looked at Jesus as he walked, and said, "Behold, the Lamb of God!" The two disciples heard him say this, and they followed Jesus. Jesus turned, and saw them following, and said to them, "What do you seek?" And they said to him, "Rabbi" (which means Teacher), "where are you staying?" He said to them, "Come and see." They came and saw where he was staying; and they stayed with him that day, for it was about the tenth hour. One of the two who heard John speak, and followed him, was Andrew, Simon Peter's brother. He first found his brother Simon, and said to him, "We have found the Messiah" (which means Christ). He brought him to Jesus. Jesus looked at him, and said, "So you are Simon the son of John? You shall be called Cephas" (which means Peter). (John 1:35-42)

We have no record of how many of John's disciples did follow Jesus, but it is clear that it was not all of them and that John continued to keep disciples around himself rather than offer all of them to Jesus, as would have made sense if he believed Jesus to be the Messiah. And John continued to communicate his doubts about Jesus to his disciples, causing a split between the two leaders and their followers:

> Then the disciples of John came to him, saying, "Why do we and the Pharisees fast, but your disciples do not fast?" And Jesus said to them, "Can the wedding guests mourn as long as the bridegroom is with them? The days will come, when the bride-

groom is taken away from them, and then they will fast." (Matthew 9:14-15)

Jesus was the bridegroom but John was behaving as if the bridegroom was yet to come. Jesus continued his answer by making another analogy:

> Neither is new wine put into old wineskins; if it is, the skins burst, and the wine is spilled, and the skins are destroyed; but new wine is put into fresh wineskins, and so both are preserved. (Matthew 9:17)

The old wineskins represented the world of the Jewish establishment under the Mosaic law, which John and his disciples were still bound to. The new revelation of truth from Jesus could not be reconciled with the Mosaic Law—could not be contained within the old wineskins represented by the law, in terms of Jesus' metaphor—without a new mindset and understanding of the providence on John's part. John lacked that new perspective and therefore pursued the practices dictated by the law rather than simply following the teachings of Jesus, which superseded the law.

On another occasion, when both John and Jesus were preaching and baptizing, John responded to questions from his disciples about Jesus in a way that indicated they were not on the same path:

> After this Jesus and his disciples went into the land of Judea; there he remained with them and baptized. John also was baptizing at Aenon near Salim, because there was much water there; and people came and were baptized. For John had not yet been put in prison. Now a discussion arose between John's disciples and a Jew over purifying. And they came to John, and said to him, "Rabbi, he who was with you beyond the Jordan, to whom you bore witness, here he is, baptizing, and all are going to him." John answered, "No one can receive anything except what is given him from heaven. You yourselves bear me witness, that I said, I am not the Christ, but I have been sent before him. He who has the bride is the bridegroom; the friend of the bridegroom, who stands and hears him, rejoices greatly at the bride-

> groom's voice; therefore this joy of mine is now full. He must increase, but I must decrease." (John 3:22-30)

On its face, this may seem a statement of humility by John—claiming that his joy was complete now that Jesus was carrying out his messianic mission. But if John really believed Jesus to be the Christ, why did John continue to go his own way and preach about a future coming of the Messiah?

Furthermore, if John had accepted his role as Elijah, and followed Jesus, he would have increased mightily in providential importance, not decreased. Of all those preparing for Christ, John had the most important position and therefore the most important mission. That mission was not just to prepare for Jesus but to help Jesus complete the mission of the Messiah. John's statement was an expression of a Cain-type envy that would prove his downfall.

Indeed, John was unable to make a commitment of faith to follow Jesus. He continued on his own path, which not only proved irrelevant to the mission of Jesus, but led to a dungeon in the palace of Herod Antipas.

Jesus Rebuked John for His Lack of Faith

John's doubting mind was revealed a final time when he was in prison and sent his disciples to ask Jesus if he was indeed the expected Messiah:

> Now when John heard in prison about the deeds of the Christ, he sent word by his disciples and said to him, "Are you he who is to come, or shall we look for another?" (Matthew 11:2-3)

When Jesus heard this question from John's disciples, he was deeply disappointed in John, who above all others should have known who Jesus really was:

> And Jesus answered them, "Go and tell John what you hear and see: the blind receive their sight and the lame walk, lepers are cleansed and the deaf hear, and the dead are raised up, and the

poor have good news preached to them. And blessed is he who takes no offense at me." (Matthew 11:4-6)

After John's disciples had left to return to their master, Jesus explained to his own disciples just how important John's mission was, but also how terrible were the consequences of John's failure to follow the Messiah:

> Truly, I say to you, among those born of women there has risen no one greater than John the Baptist; yet he who is least in the kingdom of heaven is greater than he. From the days of John the Baptist until now the kingdom of heaven has suffered violence, and men of violence take it by force. For all the prophets and the law prophesied until John; and if you are willing to accept it, he is Elijah who is to come. (Matthew 11:11-13)

This was a grim indictment of John for his failure to fulfill the mission of Elijah, and a warning of the terrible consequences that would result for God's people and the providence in general. It marked the end of John's opportunity to play the great role he was destined to.

John had been born the most important person in the providence before Jesus, but his failure meant his destiny would be tragic. This wretched destiny was realized when John was beheaded by Herod, not on behalf of the providence but in order to satisfy the whim of the king's jealous and selfish wife, Herodias.

Furthermore, because of his failure, the providence for a peaceful victory of Abel over Cain that Jesus was working to achieve would be replaced with a providence of violent conflict between Cain and Abel in the age-old struggle of good to overcome evil and establish God's kingdom on earth.

In the next chapter we look at some of the catastrophic repercussions John's loss of faith incurred for the mission of Jesus and for the providence over all.

Chapter 19

The Catastrophic Consequences of John's Failure

Moses and Elijah Confirm a Change in Jesus' Mission

A History of Small Mistakes with Huge Consequences

Providential history is filled with accounts of how even small errors by central figures can result in great suffering and huge delays in the realization of the Divine Providence. For example, when Abraham was called to make a sacrifice of animals which he was to cut in two—representing the separation of good from evil, Abel from Cain—he cut the heifer, ram and she goat in half but failed to halve the two birds. He was consequently told that his descendants would suffer 400 years of slavery for this mistake:

> [God] said to him, "Bring me a heifer three years old, a she-goat three years old, a ram three years old, a turtledove, and a young pigeon." And he brought him all these, cut them in two, and laid each half over against the other; but he did not cut the birds in two. And when birds of prey came down upon the carcasses, Abram drove them away. As the sun was going down, a deep sleep fell on Abram; and lo, a dread and great darkness fell upon him. Then the Lord said to Abram, "Know of a surety that your descendants will be sojourners in a land that is not theirs, and will be slaves there, and they will be oppressed for four hundred years. (Genesis 15:9-13)

The birds of prey devouring the sacrifice represented Satan attacking the offering which had not been properly purified through the symbolic separating of good from evil parts.

Abraham was later called to make amends for this mistake by making a much greater sacrifice—that of Isaac, his only son by his wife Sarah. Abraham obeyed and this time he was rewarded with the trust of God and the promise of blessings for his lineage:

> By myself I have sworn, says the Lord, because you have done this, and have not withheld your son, your only son, I will indeed bless you, and I will multiply your descendants as the stars of heaven and as the sand which is on the seashore. And your descendants shall possess the gate of their enemies, and by your descendants shall all the nations of the earth bless themselves, because you have obeyed my voice. (Genesis 22:16-18)

In another example, when Ham was ashamed to see his father Noah naked and drunk after the Ark had landed on Mount Ararat, he was punished for not showing faith in his father despite the undeniable demonstration of trust God had placed in Noah by saving his family from the flood:

> Noah was the first tiller of the soil. He planted a vineyard; and he drank of the wine, and became drunk, and lay uncovered in his tent. And Ham, the father of Canaan, saw the nakedness of his father, and told his two brothers outside. Then Shem and Japheth took a garment, laid it upon both their shoulders, and walked backward and covered the nakedness of their father; their faces were turned away, and they did not see their father's nakedness. When Noah awoke from his wine and knew what his youngest son had done to him, he said, "Cursed be Canaan; a slave of slaves shall he be to his brothers." He also said, "Blessed by the Lord my God be Shem; and let Canaan be his slave. God enlarge Japheth, and let him dwell in the tents of Shem; and let Canaan be his slave." (Genesis 9:20-27)

After the pattern of Adam's family, Shem, Ham and Japheth represented Cain, Abel and Seth, respectively. When Ham showed that he lacked faith in his father by assuming he was doing something shameful, Noah became angry and cursed Ham's son Canaan, saying he would have to serve Shem and Japheth. This implied that Satan had claimed Ham and his lineage, even though Ham was part of the central lineage that had recently been separated from the rest of the fallen world through the 40-day flood. As a consequence, Ham lost his position as Abel and God was able to claim Shem in place of Ham. It was out of Shem's lineage that Abraham was later chosen to establish a new central family in the providence.

Thus the mistakes of Abraham and Ham may seem trivial to us, but in the context of their providential significance, their consequences were dramatic and long-lasting.

John's Mistakes Had Catastrophic Consequences for Jesus

So it was with John the Baptist. Despite the many messages his family had received about Jesus and John's specific mission to serve him, and despite the encouragement Jesus offered him, John could not overcome his reservations about Jesus. He denied that he was in the position of Elijah and refused to submit to Jesus' authority by becoming his disciple. These may seem like relatively small mistakes on John's part, but because of the importance of his mission as the representative of Elijah, a member of the Levitical religious establishment, and the last prophet before Christ, his mistakes took on monumental proportions.

It is clear from what Jesus said that his primary mission was to save the people of Israel, since these were the people prepared to receive him. Thus when a non-Israelite woman asked him to heal her daughter, he initially refused:

> And Jesus went away from there and withdrew to the district of Tyre and Sidon. And behold, a Canaanite woman from that region came out and cried, "Have mercy on me, O Lord, Son of David; my daughter is severely possessed by a demon." But he did not answer her a word. And his disciples came and begged him, saying, "Send her away, for she is crying after us." He

answered, "I was sent only to the lost sheep of the house of Israel." But she came and knelt before him, saying, "Lord, help me." And he answered, "It is not fair to take the children's bread and throw it to the dogs." She said, "Yes, Lord, yet even the dogs eat the crumbs that fall from their masters' table." Then Jesus answered her, "O woman, great is your faith! Be it done for you as you desire." And her daughter was healed instantly. (Matthew 15:21-24)

But how was Jesus to win over the Jewish people when their leadership was so opposed to him, as we have described? As John's Gospel put it:

He came to his own, and those who were his own did not receive him. (John 1:11)

This is why a core purpose of John's mission was to create a bridge between Jesus and the religious establishment in Israel. John's unresolved doubts about Jesus meant that he was unwilling to play this role, forcing Jesus to take on teaching the religious leaders and the common people himself.

Jesus Had to Redo John's Foundation

To indemnify John's failure and lay a foundation for his own ministry, Jesus took the drastic step of fasting in the desert for 40 days. (This echoed the two 40-day fasts Moses went through on Sinai as a condition to receive the Ten Commandments and to establish the law, the priesthood and the Tabernacle, all in preparation for the creation of a chosen nation in the promised land of Canaan.)

At the end of his fast Jesus was in a greatly weakened state. But he had to overcome three temptations from Satan as a condition to fulfill his mission of reclaiming the chosen nation of Israel from the Satanic dominion it was under. (This echoed Moses' purification of the people after his first fast, when he destroyed the Golden Calf and made the people repent.)

In each of the temptations, Satan tried to get Jesus to abandon his faith in exchange for getting what he must have needed and wanted in the moment: first food, then the magical intervention of God to end his suffering, and finally the power to dominate the world. If Jesus had succumbed to any of these temptations, he would have surrendered his position as God's representative and Israel's savior, and his messianic mission would have been completely nullified.

The First Temptation

Jesus was tempted to turn stones into bread, so that he could end his hunger:

> And the tempter came and said to him, "If you are the Son of God, command these stones to become loaves of bread." (Matthew 4:3)

Jesus replied:

> It is written, "Man shall not live by bread alone, but by every word that proceeds from the mouth of God." (Matthew 4:4)

The temptation was to make the needs of the body superior to those of the spirit, which is exactly what had happened in the Fall.

The Second Temptation

Jesus was taken in spirit to the high point on the Temple in Jerusalem, where Satan tempted him to leap to the ground in the knowledge that angels would prevent him from being killed in this way:

> If you are the Son of God, throw yourself down; for it is written, "He will give his angels charge of you," and "On their hands they will bear you up, lest you strike your foot against a stone." (Matthew 4:6)

Jesus replied:

> Again it is written, "You shall not tempt the Lord your God." (Matthew 4:7)

In the Fall, Adam, Eve and Lucifer had all tested the word of God by going against Divine instructions in the hope of getting what they wanted. Furthermore, through the Fall the angelic world gained dominion over the human world when Eve was seduced by Lucifer, who is Satan. Lucifer's nature is the root of Cain's nature, which must be subjugated by the goodness of Abel. This cannot be done through the magical intervention of angels or God the Father. This would be born out when Jesus had to accept the way of the cross, undergoing immense suffering. He could not look to God or the angels to save him from a sacrifice that the providence required him to make.

The Third Temptation

Finally, Jesus was taken in spirit to a high mountain, and offered dominion of the world if he would just bow down to Satan:

> Again, the devil took him to a very high mountain, and showed him all the kingdoms of the world and the glory of them; and he said to him, "All these I will give you, if you will fall down and worship me." (Matthew 4:8-10)

Jesus replied:

> Begone, Satan! for it is written, "You shall worship the Lord your God and him only shall you serve." (Matthew 4:10-11)

This was a final rejection of Satan's dominion over the world, which had been established through the Fall. Ever since, Satan has ruled the world through Cain. The whole point of Jesus' mission was to end this dominion and restore a true dominion of God over the world.

Because of his steadfast faith, Jesus was victorious over these temptations, making a spiritual foundation through which he replaced John as the precursor of the Messiah. Like Abraham having to make the much greater sacrifice of Isaac to make up for failing to offer two birds correctly, Jesus had to take on the much greater condition of suffering death on the cross, not because of any mistake he had made, but because John had failed to fulfill his mission to prepare for Jesus' coming as the Messiah.

Upon his victory over Satan, Jesus was immediately rewarded by good angels, who came to help him at this moment of need:

> Then the devil left him, and behold, angels came and ministered to him. (Matthew 4:11)

And so it always is with temptations that are based on Satan's lies and seductions. What appears to be a sacrifice in rejecting the temptation always turns out to be the right decision. After fulfilling the responsibility of rejecting Satan, the victorious individual (or group for that matter) receives the blessing of God.

Jesus Had to Do The Work of John

Jesus now began his own public ministry. He had to do the work that John should have done—teaching the people of Israel about the coming Messiah and purifying them through baptism in preparation to receive him. He began to gather his own disciples and to teach large groups of people.

After John's failure, Jesus was no longer focused on winning over the religious leadership. Instead, he took his message to the ordinary people who were less attached to the letter of the Mosaic Law and more open to the working of God in the form of the Holy Spirit. Nevertheless, his primary mission—to save Israel—had not changed, and he used parables and miracles to open the minds and hearts of ordinary people to the truth—teaching them with parables, healing them of infirmities and driving out demons, as we discussed in detail in Chapters 14 and 15.

Instead of Jesus recruiting disciples from among the Levites—as he would have done if John had followed him—he inspired members of humble trades, such as Galilean fishermen. Their humility enabled them to appreciate the goodness and virtue of Jesus, and gave them the faith to follow Jesus wherever he led. Jesus was able to raise a core group of 12 disciples to the point where they could go out and preach the essentials of Jesus' message. He instructed them to focus their efforts on fellow Israelites:

> These twelve Jesus sent out after instructing them: "Do not go in

the way of the Gentiles, and do not enter any city of the Samaritans; but rather go to the lost sheep of the house of Israel." (Matthew 10:5-6)

But there were other than Israelites drawn to Jesus. In one notable case, a Roman centurion showed complete faith in Jesus, prompting Christ to compare him favorably with the faithless religious leaders of Israel:

> When Jesus had entered Capernaum, a centurion came to him, asking for help. "Lord," he said, "my servant lies at home paralyzed, suffering terribly." Jesus said to him, "Shall I come and heal him?" The centurion replied, "Lord, I do not deserve to have you come under my roof. But just say the word, and my servant will be healed. For I myself am a man under authority, with soldiers under me. I tell this one, 'Go,' and he goes; and that one, 'Come,' and he comes. I say to my servant, 'Do this,' and he does it." When Jesus heard this, he was amazed and said to those following him, "Truly I tell you, I have not found anyone in Israel with such great faith." (Matthew 8:5-10)

Nevertheless, those who followed Jesus with faith and dedication were a tiny minority of Israel's population, and Jesus lamented the faithlessness of the people:

> Jerusalem, Jerusalem, you who kill the prophets and stone those sent to you, how often I have longed to gather your children together, as a hen gathers her chicks under her wings, and you were not willing. (Matthew 23:37)

Jesus' Path Now Led to the Cross

Without the help of John the Baptist, and faced with rejection by the leadership of Israel, Jesus lacked the foundation to complete the messianic mission. He began to tell his disciples that he would have to go a path of suffering leading to death:

> From that time Jesus began to show his disciples that He must go to Jerusalem, and suffer many things from the elders and

> chief priests and scribes, and be killed, and be raised up on the third day. (Matthew 16:21)

He took his three closest disciples, Peter, James and John, and went up a mountain to pray for guidance. Once there, the disciples were amazed to see Jesus transfigured before their eyes:

> His face shone like the sun and his clothes became as white as light. (Matthew 17:2)

Their surprise only increased when Moses and Elijah appeared in spirit and spoke with Jesus. And then the disciples heard the voice of God:

> This is my Son, whom I love; with him I am well pleased. Listen to him! (Matthew 17:5)

Moses and Elijah represented the foundation established for the Messiah by Israel. Moses had been the central providential figure in transforming the people of Israel from stateless slaves in Egypt to a people settled in a land of their own, where they were to make a nation to receive the Messiah. Elijah was a great prophet who had purified the people of Israel in the Divided Kingdoms era, preparing them to receive the Messiah. Thus both of them knew what the original mission of the Messiah was and just how damaging to the providence John's failure was. Their sad task was to inform Jesus of the path he would now have to take, a path that would lead to great suffering and death on the cross.

Jesus was 30 when baptized by John. He would only have three short years of public ministry before he was betrayed by Judas, accused and convicted of blasphemy by the Sanhedrin, and sentenced to the cruel death of crucifixion by Pontius Pilate.

His fast had enabled him to have even this short ministry, but it could not change the ultimate destiny that was a consequence of John's failure. If Jesus had not been able to have this period for his public ministry, we would not have the Gospels with their record of Jesus's life and teachings.

The history of the world after Jesus would have been completely different, and very much darker.

A Providential Perspective: The Kingdom Delayed

The ultimate purpose of Jesus was to restore the position of Adam before the Fall. To prepare for this, Israel had to be purified so that it would recognize and follow Jesus. John the Baptist was the Abel figure chosen for this preparatory mission. In other words he had to win over the nation of Israel to recognize and follow Jesus as the Messiah. (Israel ruled by Herod and the religious establishment was in the Cain position to John the Baptist so long as he represented Jesus.)

If John had united with Jesus and succeeded in winning over Israel, a condition would have been established for Jesus to be accepted as a second Adam, fulfilling the mission of Messiah. As Saint Paul wrote:

> For as by a man came death, by a man has come also the resurrection of the dead. For as in Adam all die, so also in Christ shall all be made alive. (I Corinthians 21-22)

John's failure meant that Jesus had to take on John's mission as Abel to Israel's Cain. Jesus was never able to be the second Adam, to establish a sinless family and build the Kingdom of Heaven on earth. Jesus did achieve a spiritual victory on the cross, which established a condition for the eventual restoration of Adam and Eve and the Garden of Eden, but that would now be a very long time coming.

Chapter 20

Betrayal By His Disciples

Satan Invaded the Inner Circle of Jesus

Satan's Murderous Agenda

Try to imagine Jesus from the point of view of Satan. Jesus was the embodiment of everything Satan hates, especially because of Christ's profound love for and loyalty to the Creator. Thus Jesus as an absolute Abel represented the ultimate threat to Satan and his dominion over the world. As we have shown, God advances the providence by supporting Abel against Cain. Naturally, then, Satan advances his agenda by encouraging and supporting Cain-type individuals, families, societies and nations.

From the first manifestations of Satan's nature in Cain's murder of Abel, Satan's animus against Abel-types in history has been infused with bitter resentment and accusation, deception and selfishness, violence and murder. Thus the history of Cain-type activity is littered with cruelty and suffering, anguish and tears, bloodshed and murder. True to this history, upon the advent of Jesus as the first absolute Abel, Satan's whole focus became using Cain-type figures and institutions in Israel to destroy him.

Satan Always Uses Those Closest to His Target

We have already explained how the religious and political establishments of Israel were readily used by Satan for this purpose. Herod tried to kill Jesus right after his birth, and his sons continued the persecution of Jesus and his followers, while the religious leaders harassed and persecuted Jesus all his life, eventually convicting him of blasphemy and handing him to the Romans to be killed.

But this national-level persecution had its roots much closer to home, for Satan knows that anyone is most vulnerable to attack from those closest to him or her. Thus when Joseph and Mary were focused on protecting the infant Jesus from Herod, they were guided by an angel to escape with him to Egypt, thus saving his life. However, when they later became distracted by the work of raising their many other children, they drifted away from their providential mission and exposed Jesus to attacks from Cain-type actors, such as the Jewish establishment.

So it was with Jesus' disciples. After his family, they were the people closest to him, and indeed when his mother and brothers visited him, Jesus rebuked them for failing to follow and support him. The passage describing this event we have used elsewhere, but it bears repeating here:

> While he was still speaking to the people, behold, his mother and his brothers stood outside, asking to speak to him. But he replied to the man who told him, "Who is my mother, and who are my brothers?" And stretching out his hand toward his disciples, he said, "Here are my mother and my brothers! For whoever does the will of my Father in heaven is my brother, and sister, and mother." (Matthew 12:46-50)

Jesus was informing both his family and his disciples that his family had let him down and that the disciples now took their place as the people with the closest relationship to him.

After John Failed, Jesus Chose 12 Disciples

As we discussed in detail in the previous two chapters, John the Baptist should have become the first and most important disciple of Jesus. But Satan planted seeds of doubt in his mind and heart, to the point where he could not humble himself to follow Jesus, instead becoming a Cain-type figure in the providence. He went his own way, relinquishing the protection of the providence, and soon was killed by Herod Antipas. Through this disastrous failure John was lost forever as a disciple and his whole foundation of credibility with the religious establishment was lost to Jesus and God's providence.

After John's failure, Jesus established a group of 12 close disciples to represent the 12 sons of Jacob who had become the 12 tribes of Israel. As he would later tell them:

> You are those who have continued with me in my trials; as my Father appointed a kingdom for me, so do I appoint for you that you may eat and drink at my table in my kingdom, and sit on thrones judging the twelve tribes of Israel. (Luke 22:28-30)

The mission of the 12 disciples was to share in the work of the providence through obedience to Jesus and by extending his teaching and healing to an ever wider audience in Israel. To fulfill this core role, Jesus taught them a deeper understanding of the truth, often explaining to them what the public was unable to understand:

> And when he was alone, those who were about him with the twelve asked him concerning the parables. And he said to them, "To you has been given the secret of the kingdom of God, but for those outside everything is in parables; so that they may indeed see but not perceive, and may indeed hear but not understand; lest they should turn again, and be forgiven." (Mark 4:10-12)

And he instructed them on how they were to follow his example as Abel-type figures in Israel, to be humble and, by implication, to avoid the spiritual and providential arrogance that had proved to be John's downfall:

> A dispute also arose among them, which of them was to be regarded as the greatest. And he said to them, "The kings of the Gentiles exercise lordship over them; and those in authority over them are called benefactors. But not so with you; rather let the greatest among you become as the youngest, and the leader as one who serves. For which is the greater, one who sits

at table, or one who serves? Is it not the one who sits at table? But I am among you as one who serves." (Luke 22:24-27)

Judas Became Satan's Tool

The circle of 12 disciples was expanded to 72 as the mission advanced. But even Jesus' closest disciples were vulnerable to the influence of Satan, and Satan soon found the weakest among the 12 in Judas Iscariot, who apparently harbored resentment towards Jesus. Whatever the cause of his problem with Jesus, it made Judas susceptible to the schemes of the religious leaders who were plotting to have Jesus killed during the Passover celebrations when they expected Jesus to be in Jerusalem, along with all other practicing Jews:

> Then the chief priests and the elders of the people gathered in the palace of the high priest, who was called Caiaphas, and took counsel together in order to arrest Jesus by stealth and kill him. But they said, "Not during the feast, lest there be a tumult among the people." (Matthew 26:3-5)

How pleased these religious leaders must have been when one of Jesus' closest disciples gave them the opportunity they needed to carry out their plans:

> Then Satan entered into Judas called Iscariot, who was of the number of the twelve; he went away and conferred with the chief priests and officers how he might betray him to them. And they were glad, and engaged to give him money. So he agreed, and sought an opportunity to betray him to them in the absence of the multitude. (Luke 22:3-6)

Why did Judas betray Jesus? Matthew 26:15 states: "And they paid him thirty pieces of silver." (So well known is this transaction that "thirty silver pieces" has become synonymous with the price of betrayal.) But there was likely more than greed behind Judas' betrayal of Jesus. After all, if his betrayal was successful, Jesus would be killed and the disciples likely disbanded, putting an end to the opportunities Judas had to steal from the money box he was in charge of.

According to John's Gospel, Judas was responsible for the money Jesus and his disciples shared, and had a history of stealing from the common purse. When Jesus had visited the home of Lazarus and his two sisters, Mary and Martha, Mary had used an expensive ointment on Jesus' feet, prompting a complaint from Judas:

> But Judas Iscariot, one of his disciples (he who was to betray him), said, "Why was this ointment not sold for three hundred denarii and given to the poor?" This he said, not that he cared for the poor but because he was a thief, and as he had the money box he used to take what was put into it. (John 12:4-6)

Whatever Cain-type motivation drove Judas to betrayal—whether simple greed or some deeper well of envy and resentment—Jesus recognized his disciple's spiritual problem, although the other disciples missed it. At the Last Supper, Jesus told them that one of their number would betray him that night. When they asked him who it was, he indicated it was Judas, albeit indirectly:

> Jesus answered, "It is he to whom I shall give this morsel when I have dipped it." So when he had dipped the morsel, he gave it to Judas, the son of Simon Iscariot. Then after the morsel, Satan entered into him. Jesus said to him, "What you are going to do, do quickly." (John 13:26-27)

Guided by Satan, Judas fulfilled his bargain with Caiaphas and the other religious leaders. During the night he led a mob to arrest Jesus in Gethsemane, telling them that they would recognize Jesus as the one he would kiss:

> While he was still speaking, Judas came, one of the twelve, and with him a great crowd with swords and clubs, from the chief priests and the elders of the people. Now the betrayer had given

> them a sign, saying, "The one I shall kiss is the man; seize him." And he came up to Jesus at once and said, "Hail, Master!" And he kissed him. Jesus said to him, "Friend, why are you here?" Then they came up and laid hands on Jesus and seized him. (Matthew 26:47-50)

Once a tool of Satan completes his master's work, Satan leaves him to pay the price of sin, which is spiritual death—and likely physical suffering and/or death as well. Thus when Judas saw that his actions had led to Jesus being convicted by the Sanhedrin who then handed him over to Pilate for execution, he repented bitterly, returning the money and hanging himself in remorse:

> When Judas, his betrayer, saw that [Jesus] was condemned, he repented and brought back the thirty pieces of silver to the chief priests and the elders, saying, "I have sinned in betraying innocent blood." They said, "What is that to us? See to it yourself." And throwing down the pieces of silver in the temple, he departed; and he went and hanged himself. (Matthew 27:3-5)

It was too late. The damage had been done, and Jesus was now in the hands of those bent on killing him.

Jesus' Last Line of Defense: Peter, James and John

After Judas had been won over by Satan, and had left the Passover meal to betray Jesus, there was still one final line of defense for Jesus, namely his three closest disciples: Peter, James and John, who represented the three sons that formed the core of providential families—Cain, Abel and Seth in Adam's family; Shem, Ham and Japheth in Noah's family. These three had been with him when he had met Moses and Elijah in spirit, and they were chosen by him to remain awake and alert while he made a final prayer in which he pleaded with God to find a way for him to avoid the impending destruction of his mission through the crucifixion:

> Then Jesus went with them to a place called Gethsemane, and he said to his disciples, "Sit here, while I go yonder and pray." And taking with him Peter and the two sons of Zebedee, he began to be sorrowful and troubled. Then he said to them, "My soul is very sorrowful, even to death; remain here, and watch with me." And going a little farther he fell on his face and prayed, "My Father, if it be possible, let this cup pass from me; nevertheless, not as I will, but as thou wilt." And he came to the disciples and found them sleeping; and he said to Peter, "So, could you not watch with me one hour? Watch and pray that you may not enter into temptation; the spirit indeed is willing, but the flesh is weak." (Matthew 26:36-41)

When Jesus was arrested, the disciples were faced with a final opportunity to remain loyal to Jesus. But they all fled in fear:

> And they all forsook him, and fled. (Mark 14:50)

Only Peter Followed Jesus

Out of the 11, only Peter tried to follow Jesus after his arrest, perhaps hoping against hope that he could somehow save Christ from impending death.

But the night before, at the Last Supper, Jesus had already warned Peter that he would succumb to Satan and betray Christ:

> "Simon, Simon, behold, Satan demanded to have you, that he might sift you like wheat, but I have prayed for you that your faith may not fail; and when you have turned again, strengthen your brethren." And he said to him, "Lord, I am ready to go with you to prison and to death." He said, "I tell you, Peter, the cock will not crow this day, until you three times deny that you know me." (Luke 22:31-34)

Jesus recognized that even his closest disciple had been claimed by Satan, due to the lost conditions of all those who should have accepted Jesus and followed him, and in particular John the Baptist, whose position as leading disciple Peter had taken.

Jesus' prophecy about Peter would soon be fulfilled:

> Then they seized him and led him away, bringing him into the high priest's house. Peter followed at a distance; and when they had kindled a fire in the middle of the courtyard and sat down together, Peter sat among them. Then a maid, seeing him as he sat in the light and gazing at him, said, "This man also was with him." But he denied it, saying, "Woman, I do not know him." And a little later some one else saw him and said, "You also are one of them." But Peter said, "Man, I am not." And after an interval of about an hour still another insisted, saying, "Certainly this man also was with him; for he is a Galilean." But Peter said, "Man, I do not know what you are saying." And immediately, while he was still speaking, the cock crowed. (Luke 22:54-60)

This moment marked the culmination of the problem created by John the Baptist: there was not a single person in Israel who was willing to sacrifice their life for the living Messiah. Jesus was totally alone. Imagine his expression when he turned to Peter:

> And the Lord turned and looked at Peter. And Peter remembered the word of the Lord, how he had said to him, "Before the cock crows today, you will deny me three times." And he went out and wept bitterly. (Luke 22:61-62)

Jesus had already anticipated Peter's betrayal, and had prayed that he might recover his faith, which he was later able to do. But at that moment, when Jesus' life hung in the balance, the Messiah was alone and would soon be executed, not for any crime or sin he committed, but because the people of Israel had finally and completely rejected him.

Satan's Victory

Satan had won. Cain had murdered Abel once more. The Serpent had penetrated all the levels of protection God had established for Jesus, finally reaching and corrupting Peter, the person on earth closest to Jesus.

The only defense Jesus had against Satan was the unity between himself as the Messiah and the people chosen to receive him. After all, it had taken millennia for the providence to get this far in preparing a foundation for his mission, a foundation for the people to understand and follow Jesus as the Messiah. To Jesus the Israelites were Cain. In order for him to be protected from Satan, Jesus needed them to surrender to him willingly and fully. Likewise, for the people of Israel to be protected from Satan, they needed to surrender to him willingly and fully. In the end, not even Peter was able to fulfill that condition.

The crucifixion of Jesus was now inevitable, as was the destruction of Israel itself.

Chapter 21

The Tragic Death of Jesus on the Cross

Cain-type Forces Conspired to Kill Christ

More Than a Lack of Understanding

As we have explained in preceding chapters, the crucifixion of Jesus marked a victory for Satan, who worked through Cain-type individuals and institutions in Israel to kill Jesus. It is only by grasping this fact that it is possible to understand the position of Jesus in the history of the Divine Providence.

Jesus' remarkable life of teaching, healing and forgiving the sinful people of Israel is unparalleled in history, and his greatness in the providence has been borne out through the spread of Christianity to every corner of the earth and the immeasurable rewards of living as a Christian experienced by hundreds of millions of the faithful.

The success of Christianity as a religion should not, however, be allowed to disguise the monumental human failures at the time of Jesus. These failures prevented Jesus from fulfilling the prophesized mission of the Messiah who was to sit upon the throne of David—to rule Israel and show the world the way to the Kingdom of Heaven.

Saint Paul would later write what seems obvious in hindsight, namely that for those who understand the providential role of Jesus his importance is clear, and he should never have been opposed and killed by the religious and political leaders of his time:

> Yet among the mature we do impart wisdom, although it is not a wisdom of this age or of the rulers of this age, who are doomed to pass away. But we impart a secret and hidden wisdom of God, which God decreed before the ages for our glorification. None of the rulers of this age understood this; for if they had, they would not have crucified the Lord of glory. (1 Corinthians 2:6-8)

However, this statement assumes that if the leaders of Israel had known that Jesus was the Messiah, they would not have killed him but followed him. Our contention is that all the key players in the life and death of Jesus were aware of his providential importance, either through messages delivered by angels, wise men from the east, humble shepherds guided to his birthplace, Simeon in the Temple, John the Baptist and others, or through the wisdom of his words and the countless miracles and dramatic healings he performed. The problem was not that the leaders didn't understand who Jesus was; the problem was that they refused to heed and act on the many messages they received about his messiahship.

For Israel's establishment, the evidence of the messiahship of Jesus represented a threat to the status quo—for the Herodians Jesus was seen as a rival to the throne; and for the religious leaders he was seen as a threat to them as the official teachers and arbiters of the Mosaic Law. Thus all the leaders of Israel were interested only in destroying Jesus. If they had been humble and open to the truth, Saint Paul's statement would most certainly have been true. As it was, not only were they resistant to the truth, they actively conspired to have Jesus killed.

The Cain-Like Conspiracy to Kill Jesus

We have already detailed the opposition to Jesus that culminated in his death. It is now time to examine in some detail the active conspiracy of the chief priest Caiaphas and the Sanhedrin, abetted by the faithlessness of those closest to Jesus who failed to prevent his tragic death. We are calling the first group witting conspirators, and the latter group unwitting conspirators.

Satan is perfectly able to work through all levels of Cain-type attitudes and behaviors, and used both the witting and unwitting individuals and groups to achieve the rejection and crucifixion of Jesus. However, they bear differing degrees of responsibility for the final outcome. We begin with the unwitting group.

The Unwitting Conspirators

These were not people who actively sought to destroy Jesus, but rather contributed to his death on the cross by nurturing doubts, wavering in the face of opposition and—when push came to shove—ultimately abandoning Jesus. Theirs can be considered sins of omission. To paraphrase the words of John Stuart Mill: "All it takes for the triumph of evil is for good men to do nothing." In this group are his parents and family, John the Baptist and his disciples, and Jesus' own disciples who could not stay awake in Gethsemane and fled when Jesus was arrested.

If their sins were of omission, it is legitimate to ask what these people should have done to help Jesus, but didn't.

<u>Joseph and Mary</u>

Joseph and Mary should have devoted themselves to the wellbeing and education of Jesus, so that he could fulfill his mission as the Messiah, a second Adam. They should have worked to make sure that John the Baptist fulfilled his own responsibility in preparing the way for Jesus, they should have helped Jesus find a suitable spouse to take the place of Eve to his Adam, and they should have supported him by encouraging his siblings to become his disciples and to serve him and his other disciples and followers. Finally, they should have supported him in his time of greatest need, when he faced a bogus trial by the Sanhedrin, the mockery of Herod and Pilate, a cruel beating by the Roman soldiers and, finally, an excruciating crucifixion.

There is no evidence they did any of these things. Instead, they were preoccupied with their other six children and failed to support Jesus, even during his excruciating final days of life.

Zechariah and Elizabeth

Zechariah was a senior member of the Israelite clergy and served as the high priest at the time John was conceived by Elizabeth. Both Zechariah and Elizabeth received revelations delivered by Gabriel about the importance of Jesus and the role John was to play in assisting him. However, there is no evidence that John grew up learning from Jesus, which implies that he was not educated to do so by his parents. As we have seen, John was not aware that he was to represent Elijah, as Zechariah had prophesied, and—according to John's Gospel—he did not know how important Jesus was until he baptized him in the Jordan River and witnessed the Holy Spirit descend on him.

There is no evidence they did anything to help John to fulfill his vital role as Elijah tasked with preparing the way for Jesus. Indeed, there is no mention in the Gospels at all of Zechariah and Elizabeth after the birth of John and Zechariah's prophecy about the greatness of John's mission as Elijah.

John the Baptist

According to Jesus, John was the most important prophet of all because he had the mission to prepare the way for Jesus to be accepted by his contemporaries in Israel, and in particular by the religious establishment of which he was a part. When John baptized Jesus he recognized the Divine mandate for his younger relative, and at that point should have devoted his life to serving Jesus, in effect putting his own foundation of recognition in Israel at the service of Jesus. John had disciples whom he could have transferred to Jesus, and John had access to the religious establishment (he had baptized some of its leaders) that he should have used to enable Jesus to begin his mission with a significant base of followers and allies.

John didn't oppose Jesus but he doubted him. These doubts led to his estrangement from Jesus. After the baptism of Jesus, John kept his disciples and continued his own preaching and baptisms. This made little sense since he was preaching that the Messiah would come, not that Jesus was the

Messiah. And if he believed the Messiah was so much greater than he was, wouldn't he want his own followers to receive the baptism of Jesus instead of his own?

That he made a huge providential mistake by failing to follow Jesus soon became evident when John became embroiled in a family matter of King Herod Antipas, and was consequently executed by the king.

<u>Eleven Disciples</u>
Judas betrayed Jesus to the religious leaders seeking to kill him, but the other 11 disciples should have remained loyal to Jesus and remained close to him throughout his ordeal. Their core mission was to protect Jesus from Satan but at the Last Supper Jesus told them that they would all lose faith that night:

> Then Jesus said to them, "You will all fall away because of me this night; for it is written, 'I will strike the shepherd, and the sheep of the flock will be scattered.'" (Matthew 26:31)

A minimum condition of loyalty was for them to remain awake and in prayer in the Garden of Gethsemane while Jesus was desperately praying that a way for him to continue his mission could be found. We cannot know what difference it would have made if the disciples had remained awake, but we can speculate that such a condition of loyalty might have enabled Jesus to avoid arrest, conviction and crucifixion.

When Jesus was arrested, only Peter among his disciples followed him. But when questioned Peter would deny that he was a disciple of Jesus.

The Witting Conspirators

For the others responsible for Jesus' rejection and crucifixion, the sin was one of commission, not omission. They all had their own reasons for wanting Jesus dead, and this shared Satanic motivation was exploited by Israel's religious leaders who organized a conspiracy to arrest, try, convict and execute Jesus.

The Religious Establishment

The religious leaders of Israel inherited centuries of Divine revelations, the teachings of the Mosaic Law, and the prophesies about a savior Messiah to liberate Israel from oppression and establish a kingdom under God. When Jesus came, there were many signs pointing to his providential importance, beginning with the miraculous conception and birth of both John and Jesus, and the many messages from angels and others as to his messiahship. Then there was the great wisdom of Jesus, demonstrated from as early as when he talked with elders in the Temple at age 12. Finally, there were the miracles of healing and other manifestations of Jesus' spiritual authority and importance.

The ability of Jesus to interpret the scriptures in a profound way should in itself have been sufficient to persuade them of his mission. But instead of humbling themselves to learn, the Scribes, Pharisees and Sadducees used their knowledge and positions to try and trip him up and discredit him. And they accused him of performing his miracles on behalf of Satan; for example in Matthew 12:24: "But when the Pharisees heard it they said, 'It is only by Beelzebul, the prince of demons, that this man casts out demons.'"

The religious leaders should have all become the disciples of Jesus. They should have learned from him the deeper meanings of the scriptures. They should have become teachers of the messages Jesus was preaching. They should have helped Jesus reclaim the throne of David from the Herodian dynasty. And they should have helped Jesus spread his message to the rest of the world.

They did none of these things. Instead, under the leadership of the chief priest Caiaphas, they recruited Judas to betray Jesus' whereabouts at the time of the Passover—when he was in Jerusalem with his disciples. They paid Judas 30 pieces of silver for this betrayal. Once Judas had done his dirty work and Jesus had been captured, they interrogated Jesus to try and make him blaspheme the law. Once they had condemned him through this extrajudicial process, they riled up the crowds to demand his death from Pilate. When Pilate demurred they pressed harder. And when Pilate sought the advise of Herod Antipas, they pushed Herod hard to reject clemency and endorse a sentence of death.

The Political Establishment
King Herod the Great had taken the crown of Israel from the Hasmoneans, a dynasty whose members came from the Levite priest Mattathias and his descendants, the Maccabees. Coming from a Cain lineage that combined Ishmaelite and Edomite lines, Herod and his descendants should have submitted to Jesus as the Abel figure of the providence. When he was informed of the birth of Christ by the wise men from the East, Herod should have protected Jesus and made him heir to the throne. His sons likewise should have protected Jesus until he came of age and was able to assume David's throne.

However, from the moment of Jesus' birth, Herod the Great was propelled by Cain-type instincts of envy and conspired to kill him, fearful that an authentic Jewish king would put an end to his illicit rule. This hostility to Jesus was continued by his sons who succeeded him on the throne. It was one of them, Herod Antipas, who had John the Baptist beheaded and who later mocked Jesus and collaborated with the religious leaders in having Pilate put Jesus to death.

Judas Iscariot
Judas should never have succumbed to the temptation to betray Jesus, regardless of the cause for his jealousy and animosity towards his leader, let alone the offer of financial compensation for his betrayal. Even after he had accepted the money, he should have repented of his error and reported the plot to kill his master to Jesus. He was in a position to thwart the plot and help unite the disciples in defense of Jesus.

When Judas saw what his betrayal had wrought, and he realized Jesus was to be killed, he repented and repaid the money to Caiaphas. But it was too late, and in bitterness and remorse he killed himself.

The Significance of Jesus' Prayer in Gethsemane
By the time of the Last Supper, Satan's scheme to kill Jesus by using the

Cain-type motivations of Israel's establishment was in full swing and the conspiracy of the Sanhedrin was on the eve of completing its evil implementation. Jesus must have been fully cognizant of this, and it was with the enormous weight of his providential mission now pressing with unbearable weight on his soul that he made one final plea for God to intervene to avert the crucifixion that was now awaiting him:

> Then Jesus went with them to a place called Gethsemane, and he said to his disciples, "Sit here, while I go yonder and pray." And taking with him Peter and the two sons of Zebedee, he began to be sorrowful and troubled. Then he said to them, "My soul is very sorrowful, even to death; remain here, and watch with me." And going a little farther he fell on his face and prayed, "My Father, if it be possible, let this cup pass from me; nevertheless, not as I will, but as thou wilt." (Matthew 26:36-39)

It is sometimes said that Jesus' prayer in Gethsemane proves that he was indeed a man who could experience suffering, and like all people wanted to avoid it if possible. This is not good enough. The agony of Jesus as he prayed desperately for "this cup to pass" was caused by far more than a personal concern for himself, or desire to avoid pain. Going the way of the cross meant a victory for Satan and a prolongation of the providence, meaning an immeasurable multiplication of suffering for God the Father and for all God's children, the whole of humanity.

Never losing his own heart of love for God and the people, Jesus on the cross would intervene on behalf of all those who had failed him and conspired to have him killed:

> And Jesus said, "Father, forgive them; for they know not what they do." (Luke 23:34)

The Profound Agony of Jesus

No one can really understand the depths of Jesus' suffering on the cross because no one knows just how great a providential tragedy it was. Jesus came as a Second Adam to drive Satan and evil from Israel and to create a sinless family that would take the place of Adam and Eve, in a new Eden. Fulfilling this internal mission would have enabled him to fulfill the external mission of assuming the throne of David and guiding Israel to accomplish its purpose as a nation chosen to lead the world.

The crucifixion meant not only that the great effort and suffering of those sent to prepare the way for the Messiah did not bear the intended fruit but that Israel itself would lose its privileged status as the chosen nation. It also meant that the individuals, institutions and nations who would inherit the providential mantle from Israel would inevitably undergo great suffering as they worked to repair the damage done by the Satanic murder of Jesus.

The sorrow of Christ in anticipation of all these tragic outcomes was the great sorrow of his Heavenly Father too, the sorrow of a parent who had labored so long and hard to save the children of the Creator's Divine love.

Evidence That the Cross Was Not God's Will

The only reasonable conclusion to be drawn from this account of what happened in the life of Jesus is that the crucifixion was not God's will but rather a victory for Satan, who had successfully exploited the jealousy, resentment and murderous instincts of key figures in Israel to arrange the death of Jesus. God does not advance the Divine Providence through the efforts of Cain to kill Abel, but rather through the efforts of Abel to liberate Cain from evil at the cost of his life. Thus the crucifixion was in no way the will of God. It was the work of Satan.

However, because of Jesus' unwavering faith and loyalty to his Father throughout this unbearable ordeal, God was able to claim a spiritual victory for the providence, a victory recognizable in the resurrection of Jesus three days after his death. It is that spiritual victory that is the foundation upon which Christianity was established and has flourished. And it is that victory that made possible the salvation of fallen people who repent of their sins and follow Jesus in a life of faith and service.

That the crucifixion was not God's will but rather the work of Satan through various Cain-type figures at the time of Jesus is evidenced by what happened to them. John the Baptist was beheaded. Judas committed suicide. With the exception of John, the disciples were all executed after Jesus' death. And, in 70 AD, some 40 years after the death of Jesus, Rome destroyed Jerusalem and the Second Temple, dismembering the religious and political establishments of Israel and setting in motion the Great Diaspora, which saw the Jews scattered across much of the known world, where theirs would become a tragic history of persecution and suffering. The nation of Israel would not be reconstituted until 1948.

The Crucifixion Ended the Temple's Providential Purpose

A consequence of the crucifixion that adds to this evidence was the demise of the Temple's role in the providence. This was demonstrated at the moment of Jesus' death when the curtain separating the Holy from the Most Holy sections was torn in two, symbolizing the death of the Temple as the representative of the Divine presence on earth:

> And behold, the curtain of the temple was torn in two, from top to bottom; and the earth shook, and the rocks were split. (Matthew 27:51)

The wrongful crucifixion of Jesus marked the culmination of Israel's failure to receive him as the Messiah. The people of Israel had been raised to prepare for the Messiah by being faithful to the Mosaic Law, the Tabernacle and the Temple, which were the pillars of their religion given to them by God. Their rejection of Jesus demonstrated, however, that their religious beliefs and practices were below the standard required of the chosen people.

Thus when the leaders of Israel had Jesus put to death, Israel and its people lost their chosen status and the Law and the Temple lost their importance in the Divine Providence. In the new providence that was ushered in by Jesus' victory of faith on the cross, the Mosaic Law was replaced by the teachings of Jesus, and the Temple of stone and wood was replaced by the living Christ.

Consequences for Followers of Christ

For Christians, the history of their faith is one of persecution and suffering in imitation of the persecution and suffering of Jesus himself. From the disciples onward, those who have striven to follow in the path of Christ, the absolute Abel, have had to suffer in a world that continues to be dominated by Cain. Going the way of the cross will continue to be the path that faithful Christians must follow until a final victory over Satan by God's side will be realized in the establishment of the Kingdom of Heaven on earth.

In the next chapters we will discuss the consequences of the crucifixion for the providence in more detail, including the compensatory victory that God was able to claim from the crucifixion because of the faith and sacrificial life of Jesus. The Kingdom of Heaven was not created on earth at the time of Jesus, but his spirit has guided the efforts of his followers and spiritual descendants for the two millennia since his death, laying a foundation for a renewed providence to complete the original mission of the Messiah.

Jesus in the Divine Providence

PART III

CHRISTIANS INHERIT A PROVIDENTIAL MISSION FROM JESUS

Chapter 22

Consequences of the Crucifixion

The Creation of an Otherworldly Kingdom

Repercussions from Jesus' Death on the Cross

As we have explained, the death of Jesus on the Cross was not the will of God, but the result of Satan's manipulation of Cain-type actors in Israel to secure the death of Jesus. That was 2,000 years ago, and so we have an expansive historical record of what has taken place on earth since. In the next few chapters we will look at this history from a providential perspective to examine the consequences of the crucifixion as it impacted the original purpose of the Messiah, and what this meant for Christianity.

To begin with, in this chapter we examine the immediate providence that unfolded through the disciples of Jesus. Their faith and work shaped Christianity as the religion which inherited from the people of Israel the central position in the providence.

A Spiritual Victory and Outpouring

Despite the constant persecution he had suffered and the terrible torture he was forced to undergo on the cross, Jesus never wavered from his mission. Against all the odds stacked against him, Jesus achieved a spiritual victory as Abel over the Cain-type people of Israel and the Roman Empire.

The first beneficiaries of Jesus' spiritual victory were the Abel-type spirits—whom we have called Divines—who had contributed to the providence by helping prepare the way for the Messiah. Jesus opened up a new spiritual realm which allowed them to work with him in the new providence. Thus at the moment of his death, when the Temple curtain was torn signifying the end of an era in the providence, the spirits of many saintly people appeared in Jerusalem:

> And behold, the curtain of the temple was torn in two, from top to bottom; and the earth shook, and the rocks were split; the tombs also were opened, and many bodies of the saints who had fallen asleep were raised, and coming out of the tombs after his resurrection they went into the holy city and appeared to many. (Matthew 27:51-53)

These were not physical bodies, of course, but the spirit bodies of saints who had not been able to receive the Messiah in their lifetimes, but who had been true to the providence. Much as Moses and Elijah had appeared to Jesus and his three closest disciples on the Mount of Transfiguration, and as Jesus himself had appeared to his disciples at given times after the crucifixion, so too these spirits appeared to those at one with Christ to encourage them in their discipleship.

The Spiritual Power Unleashed at Pentecost

The power of Jesus' victory soon became evident in the miraculous manifestations of God's Holy Spirit among the disciples, inspiring them to great feats of devotion and service. Several of them received the gifts of healing, driving out spirits and even raising the dead, much as Jesus himself had done.

At Pentecost, 50 days after the death of Jesus, the Holy Spirit descended on the core disciples with a great outpouring of spiritual power. Filled with the spirit, the disciples were able to speak in the various languages of people in Jerusalem:

> When the day of Pentecost had come, they were all together in one place. And suddenly a sound came from heaven like the rush of a mighty wind, and it filled all the house where they were sitting. And there appeared to them tongues as of fire,

> distributed and resting on each one of them. And they were all filled with the Holy Spirit and began to speak in other tongues, as the Spirit gave them utterance. (Acts 2:1-4)

Thousands were converted to the new faith on that day, marking the beginning of a new religion:

> Now when they heard this they were cut to the heart, and said to Peter and the rest of the apostles, "Brethren, what shall we do?" And Peter said to them, "Repent, and be baptized every one of you in the name of Jesus Christ for the forgiveness of your sins; and you shall receive the gift of the Holy Spirit. For the promise is to you and to your children and to all that are far off, every one whom the Lord our God calls to him." And he testified with many other words and exhorted them, saying, "Save yourselves from this crooked generation." So those who received his word were baptized, and there were added that day about three thousand souls. And they devoted themselves to the apostles' teaching and fellowship, to the breaking of bread and the prayers. (Acts 2:37-42)

The new converts were so inspired by the spiritual manifestations surrounding the preaching of the disciples that they went through a radical transformation, offering all their possessions to the nascent community, no doubt seeking to hasten the return of Christ and the imminent advent of the promised Kingdom of Heaven:

> And fear came upon every soul; and many wonders and signs were done through the apostles. And all who believed were together and had all things in common; and they sold their possessions and goods and distributed them to all, as any had need. And day by day, attending the temple together and breaking bread in their homes, they partook of food with glad and generous hearts, praising God and having favor with all the people. And the Lord added to their number day by day those who were being saved. (Acts 2:43-47)

Consequences of the Crucifixion

Although this practice of communal living was not sustained for very long by most believers, it would later take root in monastic orders and other religious communities as a sacrificial way of life intended to put the teachings of Jesus into daily practice. And many of the good deeds done by Christians over the centuries were carried out by these and similarly dedicated communal believers.

For the disciples, the spiritual phenomena that began to manifest at Pentecost were the Divine confirmation they needed to have the courage to speak out boldly in public about Jesus and his mission, despite the continuous opposition of the religious establishment:

> And as they were speaking to the people, the priests and the captain of the temple and the Sadducees came upon them, annoyed because they were teaching the people and proclaiming in Jesus the resurrection from the dead. And they arrested them and put them in custody until the morrow, for it was already evening. But many of those who heard the word believed; and the number of the men came to about five thousand. On the morrow their rulers and elders and scribes were gathered together in Jerusalem, with Annas the high priest and Caiaphas and John and Alexander, and all who were of the high-priestly family. And when they had set them in the midst, they inquired, "By what power or by what name did you do this?" Then Peter, filled with the Holy Spirit, said to them, "Rulers of the people and elders, if we are being examined today concerning a good deed done to a cripple, by what means this man has been healed, be it known to you all, and to all the people of Israel, that by the name of Jesus Christ of Nazareth, whom you crucified, whom God raised from the dead, by him this man is standing before you well. This is the stone which was rejected by you builders, but which has become the head of the corner. And there is salvation in no one else, for there is no other name under heaven given among men by which we must be saved." (Acts 4:1-12)

From this time, then, the new religion began to grow rapidly, and it is now the largest religion on earth, with some 2.4 billion adherents. With this immense presence throughout the world, Christianity is now in the position to be the vehicle that God uses to once more send Christ to complete the unfinished work of Jesus and Christianity. Thus the life of Jesus did not mark the fulfillment of providential history, but rather its most significant milestone.

An Otherworldly Kingdom

How best to practice Christianity is an ongoing issue, especially given that its founder's life was cut short before he could establish a family and sinless lineage. At the heart of this issue is the nature of the Kingdom of Heaven and what we have to do to become part of it. For the tribes of Israel, the goal was always concrete: creating a kingdom to which the Messiah would come as savior and king. This meant enlightening and purifying the people so that they could receive the Messiah, which was the mission undertaken by Moses and Aaron and then pursued by the Levitical priests and the prophets, supported by several good kings, notably David. It was also the purpose behind the work of Ezra and Nehemiah when they reestablished Jerusalem and the Temple after the Babylonian exile.

When Jesus realized that because of Israel's faithlessness and rejection he would not be able to fulfill the providence to inherit the throne of David, he told Pilate that his kingdom was not of this earth:

> Pilate entered the praetorium again and called Jesus, and said to him, "Are you the King of the Jews?" Jesus answered, "Do you say this of your own accord, or did others say it to you about me?" Pilate answered, "Am I a Jew? Your own nation and the chief priests have handed you over to me; what have you done?" Jesus answered, "My kingship is not of this world; if my kingship were of this world, my servants would fight, that I might not be handed over to the Jews; but my kingship is not from the world." Pilate said to him, "So you are a king?" Jesus answered, "You say that I am a king. For this I was born, and for this I have come into

the world, to bear witness to the truth. Every one who is of the
truth hears my voice." (John 18:33-37)

The New King James Version adds a couple of clarifying words to this report of what Jesus told Pilate. In verse 37, Jesus says: "You say rightly that I am a king. For this cause I was born…" In other words, Jesus confirmed that he was born to be king. Second, in verse 36, Jesus tells Pilate: "If My kingdom were of this world, My servants would fight, so that I should not be delivered to the Jews; but now My kingdom is not from here." The implication is that Jesus had come to terms with the reality presented him while in prayer in Gethsemane: his destiny was to go the way of the cross. The kingdom he had been destined to establish could no longer be temporal, it could only be spiritual.

Thus when Peter cut off the ear of one of those sent to arrest Jesus it was too late for the disciples to use force to save the heir to David's throne:

> Then Simon Peter, having a sword, drew it and struck the high priest's servant, and cut off his right ear. The servant's name was Malchus. So Jesus said to Peter, "Put your sword into the sheath. Shall I not drink the cup which My Father has given Me?" (John 18:10-11)

Remember, Jesus had taught his disciples to pray for his kingdom to come on earth:

> Our Father in heaven, Hallowed be Your name. Your kingdom come. Your will be done on earth as it is in heaven. (Matthew 6:9-10)

A Christian Heaven

All Christians continue to pray for heaven to be established on earth. However, in the meantime, Christians understand heaven to be the realm created by Jesus for those who fulfill their God-given responsibilities and are saved from their sins by Christ, through the sacrifice he made on the cross.

We should not forget, then, the words of Jesus to Pilate we have quoted above, in which he states that for now his kingship is not of this earth. The implication is that eventually his kingship must be of this earth. We can understand this because Jesus came to restore Adam, a person born on earth to live with Eve in a heavenly Garden of Eden. In other words, the physical body remains essential to fulfillment of our original purpose as 'children of our heavenly Father'.

As we discuss in the final chapter of this book, the return of Christ in the Second Coming must be realized in the physical realm of our existence. The importance of this lies in the fact that the test of faith that Israel failed has yet to be met by human beings on earth. Thus the Kingdom of Heaven that some expect to miraculously appear at the Second Coming will actually have to be created on earth by men and women of faith dedicated to serving God and the Divine Providence, and led by the returned Christ. Our salvation is a grace from heaven, but that does not mean that we can receive it if we have not accomplished our own portion of responsibility.

Thus the 'otherworldliness' of Christianity should not be misused by Christians to excuse them from fulfilling their responsibilities in the belief that they can be saved in a magical way by Christ. As history has shown, it is this very unrealistic expectation that has made Christianity vulnerable to accusations from materialists who offer false, man-made Utopias, such as Communism, as attractive alternatives to otherworldly Christianity.

The Way of Abel for Christians

Jesus did not establish a Kingdom of Heaven or even a nation that was dedicated to following his teachings, but he did show the way, in word and deed, that his followers should take to fulfill their responsibilities before God. His teachings were far from otherworldly. They laid out instructions for living the virtuous life of a true Abel, as we have shown in previous chapters.

Not knowing details of the providential future of humanity, our task is to do our best to follow the teachings of Christ so that we can create an environment conducive to the second coming of Christ and the creation of a substantial Kingdom of Heaven. This is a very difficult course, the Way of

Absolute Abel. It requires constant dedication and spiritual renewal as we strive to overcome our own Cain-like nature and tendencies.

We have to learn to behave in the here and now in the way that we expect those saved by Christ to live in a substantial Kingdom of Heaven on earth.

Immeasurable Suffering Since Jesus

People inspired by the life and words of Jesus have done great good in the world. They have ministered to the needy, they have healed those with physical and spiritual diseases. They have provided education and helped create a more prosperous world. And they have developed fine legal systems and democratic governments, as well as great cultures that feature wonderful music and art.

Yet the world is still riven with conflicts and peace seems forever elusive. Christians should recognize, then, that the world is not yet what it should be, and that the development of Godly societies is still far from where it must ultimately be if God's kingdom is to be established on earth.

Indeed, in some ways, human suffering has increased dramatically since the time of Jesus, especially as science and technology have advanced, enabling Cain-type people, groups and nations to inflict death and destruction at unprecedented levels. Consider, for example, how many people have suffered persecution and torture, or have lost their lives in wars, over the intervening centuries.

What if Jesus Had Not Been Killed?

How different the history of the last two millennia would have been if Jesus had been accepted by Israel, made its king, and transformed the chosen nation into the Kingdom of Heaven on earth! That nation would indeed have been a light to the world, a light of good behavior and wise government that would have spread to every corner of the earth.

While still on earth, Jesus was clearly frustrated with the difficulty his disciples had in understanding him, and consequently his need to explain continuously his meanings to them. He told them that the truth would have to be revealed more fully in the future when they were better able to understand it:

> I have yet many things to say to you, but you cannot bear them now. When the Spirit of truth comes, he will guide you into all the truth; for he will not speak on his own authority, but whatever he hears he will speak, and he will declare to you the things that are to come. (John 16:12-13)

Because most Christians have long believed that Jesus had to shed his blood on the cross for their salvation from sin, they have assumed that the crucifixion represented the will of God. We have pointed out that this is an erroneous belief. It conflates the fact of Jesus' gift of salvation through offering himself up to die on the cross with the providential will of God. In other words, the fact of Jesus' death on the cross does not mean it was the path originally intended by God. Rather, it was the path imposed on Jesus by the faithlessness of Israel. (Otherwise, why is there a need for a Second Coming of Christ?)

As we discuss in the next chapter, we are not ultimately saved by the blood Jesus shed when he sacrificed his life on the cross, but through being united with the living Christ so that we can become one with the Father, as Jesus is.

It is perfectly reasonable, then, to speculate about what might have happened if those prepared to receive and follow the Messiah had done so, rather than conspiring to kill him. As we discussed in the previous chapter, none of the key people or institutions in the life of Jesus fulfilled their responsibilities. If they had, Jesus would have been able to complete the establishment of a family and lineage in place of Adam and Eve and their fallen lineage, and would have shown the way to the creation of a just and equitable world.

At the time of Jesus, the Roman Empire was the most powerful in the world, and it was linked to the remote province of Palestine through its control of the Herodian dynasty. Jesus was destined to replace that dynasty and lead Israel in winning over Rome to the providence. If Rome had accepted Jesus, it would have become an Abel-type empire that would have exerted a powerful force for good on the rest of the world.

Christianity would later follow this providential path, going from persecuted sect to official religion of the Roman Empire in four centuries. And through the Catholic Church, Rome would become a major force in spreading Christianity worldwide.

A history like this would have fulfilled all the promises and covenants God had established with the Jews, beginning with Abraham, as here repeated to Isaac:

> ... for to you and to your descendants I will give all these lands, and I will fulfill the oath that I swore to your father Abraham. I will make your offspring as numerous as the stars of heaven, and will give to your offspring all these lands; and all the nations of the earth shall gain blessing for themselves through your offspring, because Abraham obeyed my voice and kept my charge, my commandments, my statutes, and my laws. (Genesis 26:3-5)

Chapter 23

The Meaning of Salvation Through the Cross

Why the Kingdom of Heaven Remains Elusive

Salvation is a Process, Not an Event

The term "salvation" is typically used without a clear understanding of what it means. As a general religious concept it means being separated from Satan and evil and being assured of a destiny in heaven rather than hell. For Christians, the only way to be saved is through the intercession of Christ, a sinless person capable of forgiving sins and assuring us of our place with God in the Kingdom of Heaven. We need this intercession because Christ is uniquely free from the original sin. After all, we all suffer from our alienation from God, a state of being that we are unable to resolve because of our own fallen nature.

Christians have different views as to how salvation is achieved, but we hold that salvation is a process, not an event. At the same time, we recognize that many Christians have had powerful spiritual experiences with Christ, experiences that have transformed their lives. These events are not ends in themselves, but they are important heavenly intercessions that open hearts and minds to the workings of Divine Providence. They should motivate people of faith to bring their lives ever closer to the example set by Jesus.

That salvation is a process is clearly demonstrated by the millennia-long history of the Divine Providence, which in turn points to the necessary ingredient for salvation—the fulfillment of human responsibility. Christ is needed for human separation from Satan. However, as we have shown, it took thousands of years for chosen people to fulfill the necessary conditions of responsibility before the advent of Jesus as the Messiah. Furthermore, Christians have been waiting for the return of Christ for two full millennia. Surely if Christ could appear to save humankind from evil without there being certain preparations, he would have returned long since.

The Original Mind Seeks Salvation

The desire for salvation is deeply rooted in men and women who suffer from the legacy of the Fall. Reason tells us that if the original human beings were created in the image of a good God, we ourselves must be possessed of an original nature that is also good. This logic is supported by our intrinsic idealism as human beings—even the most cynical people can recognize and appreciate goodness, truth and beauty, even if only begrudgingly.

The more enlightened and mature we are, the more we seek a state of being that is totally free from the fallen nature that encumbers us, a nature that limits our ability to achieve our full potential and experience the full blessings of life as children of God. We want to be in the Garden of Eden before the Fall, and we recognize that we can achieve that sinless state only through the intercession of a sinless savior who establishes the Kingdom of Heaven on earth, and offers us a path to dwell therein.

Importantly, the individuals we admire in the Bible, whether from before, during or after Jesus lived on earth, all recognized the existence of good and evil tendencies in their lives, tendencies at war with each other. And all recognized the need for forgiveness of sin if they were to be saved. However, although Christians—including saints like Peter and Paul—have continued to struggle with their fallen nature despite the blessings of salvation they have received from Jesus on the cross, there is an important difference between the fallen state of humanity before and after Jesus.

Forgiveness of Sin and Salvation in the Old Testament

In Psalm 51, David describes his personal struggle between good and evil within himself, and his longing for purity:

> Have mercy on me, O God, according to thy steadfast love; according to thy abundant mercy blot out my transgressions. Wash me thoroughly from my iniquity, and cleanse me from my sin! For I know my transgressions, and my sin is ever before me. Against thee, thee only, have I sinned, and done that which is evil in thy sight, so that thou art justified in thy sentence and blameless in thy judgment.
>
> Behold, I was brought forth in iniquity, and in sin did my mother conceive me. Behold, thou desirest truth in the inward being; therefore teach me wisdom in my secret heart. Purge me with hyssop, and I shall be clean; wash me, and I shall be whiter than snow. Fill me with joy and gladness; let the bones which thou hast broken rejoice.
>
> Hide thy face from my sins, and blot out all my iniquities. Create in me a clean heart, O God, and put a new and right spirit within me. Cast me not away from thy presence, and take not thy holy Spirit from me. Restore to me the joy of thy salvation, and uphold me with a willing spirit. (Psalm 51:1-12)

These heartfelt words of David were written a millennium before the advent of Jesus. David longed for a purity which required that his sins be forgiven. Only in this way could he be saved from sin, and "dwell in the house of the Lord for ever," as he said in Psalm 23.6.

David believed that his responsibility was to obey the Mosaic Law as perfectly as possible, and that his obedience would be rewarded with salvation. In Psalm 119, for example, David repeatedly says his desire is to follow the law perfectly:

> Teach me, O LORD, the way of thy statutes; and I will keep it to the end. Give me understanding, that I may keep thy law and observe it with my whole heart. Lead me in the path of thy commandments, for I delight in it. (Psalm 119:33-35)
>
> ...for I find my delight in thy commandments, which I love. I

> revere thy commandments, which I love, and I will meditate on thy statutes. (Psalm 119:47-48)
>
> Let thy steadfast love be ready to comfort me according to thy promise to thy servant. Let thy mercy come to me, that I may live; for thy law is my delight. (Psalm 119:76-77)
>
> My soul longs for your salvation; I hope in your word. (Psalm 119:81)

The great prophet Isaiah received a revelation that God could forgive sins so that they would not continue to remain a burden for the Creator:

> I, I am He who blots out your transgressions for my own sake, and I will not remember your sins. (Isaiah 43:25)

And Jeremiah looked forward to a time when God would be one with human beings once their sins had been forgiven:

> Behold, the days are coming, says the Lord, when I will make a new covenant with the house of Israel and the house of Judah, not like the covenant which I made with their fathers when I took them by the hand to bring them out of the land of Egypt, my covenant which they broke, though I was their husband, says the Lord. But this is the covenant which I will make with the house of Israel after those days, says the Lord: I will put my law within them, and I will write it upon their hearts; and I will be their God, and they shall be my people. And no longer shall each man teach his neighbor and each his brother, saying, "Know the Lord," for they shall all know me, from the least of them to the greatest, says the Lord; for I will forgive their iniquity, and I will remember their sin no more. (Jeremiah 31:31-34)

Jeremiah was anticipating the time when people would no longer need the law to guide their behavior because their consciousness would be so developed that they would naturally do what is right. People would know God through Christ whose sinless nature enabled him to enjoy perfect union with the Creator. In that state of purity they too would know God and be one with God, separated from the inheritance of original sin. This was the substance of Jesus' teaching about the Kingdom of Heaven—it would be a world of goodness created through individuals fulfilling their responsibilities and thereby becoming perfected human beings at one with their Creator and Heavenly Father. As he said:

> You, therefore, must be perfect, as your heavenly Father is perfect. (Matthew 5:48)

Forgiveness of Sin and Salvation in the New Testament

Christians experience salvation through their faith in Christ. In other words, they experience what Jeremiah foretold, a purification and enlightenment that elevates their relationship with God and empowers them to do good and resist evil. Thus if they fulfill the teachings of Jesus in his Sermon on the Mount, they no longer need to study the law as the source of their morality. Rather, by fulfilling their responsibilities to the Father as taught by Jesus they automatically live a life that is free from the sins proscribed by the Mosaic Law.

Forgiving the sins of the Cain-type people of Israel was an essential part of Jesus mission as an Absolute Abel, and something he did throughout his ministry. At one point he was criticized by the religious leaders for this, but he chastised them:

> And getting into a boat he crossed over and came to his own city. And behold, they brought to him a paralytic, lying on his bed; and when Jesus saw their faith he said to the paralytic, "Take heart, my son; your sins are forgiven." And behold, some of the scribes said to themselves, "This man is blaspheming." But Jesus, knowing their thoughts, said, "Why do you think evil in your hearts? For which is easier, to say, 'Your sins are forgiven,' or to say, 'Rise and walk'? But that you may know that the Son of man has authority on earth to forgive sins"—he then said to the paralytic—"Rise, take up your bed and go home." And he rose and went home. (Matthew 9:1-7)

The Meaning of Salvation Through the Cross

The way Jesus viewed God was fundamentally different from the perspective of Old Testament patriarchs and prophets. They saw God as a Master and Lawgiver, but Jesus saw God as a loving Father. This view is reflected in John's Gospel when he describes God's own perspective on Jesus:

> For God so loved the world that he gave his only Son, that whoever believes in him should not perish but have eternal life. For God sent the Son into the world, not to condemn the world, but that the world might be saved through him. (John 3:16-17)

Jesus encouraged his disciples to believe that they were children of God, and that their salvation was attainable if they followed the way of Christ:

> Jesus said to him, "I am the way, and the truth, and the life; no one comes to the Father, but by me." (John 14:6)

Jesus himself became the gateway to the Kingdom of Heaven such that those seeking salvation had to live by the standard Jesus set on behalf of God:

> Not every one who says to me, "Lord, Lord," shall enter the kingdom of heaven, but he who does the will of my Father who is in heaven. (Matthew 7:21)

And Jesus warned that following him was not easy:

> And he called to him the multitude with his disciples, and said to them, "If any man would come after me, let him deny himself and take up his cross and follow me. For whoever would save his life will lose it; and whoever loses his life for my sake and the gospel's will save it." (Mark 8:34-35)

Jesus spoke about forgiveness of sins as a responsibility of Abel—something Abel should do not only to save Cain from his sinful nature but also so that Abel's own sins can be forgiven by God and Abel can get ever closer to his heavenly Father:

> For if you forgive men their trespasses, your heavenly Father also will forgive you; but if you do not forgive men their trespasses, neither will your Father forgive your trespasses. (Matthew 6:14-15)

And Jesus emphasized that forgiveness has no limits:

> Then Peter came to Jesus and asked, "Lord, how many times shall I forgive my brother or sister who sins against me? Up to seven times?" Jesus answered, "I tell you, not seven times, but seventy-seven times." (Matthew 18:21)

From these passages it is clear that forgiving those who sin against you is critical to your purification and thus your salvation. Cain has enormous difficulties in forgiving others, because of his arrogance and judgmentalism. Thus the only way people in conflict can be reconciled on Abel's terms is if Abel takes on the responsibility of forgiving Cain. This is the path for Abel to become Christlike and to be welcomed into the Kingdom of Heaven.

Jesus was Abel to the people of Israel, and therefore his forgiveness of their sins despite their rejection and persecution of him was the condition he made for their salvation. Thus he prayed on the cross:

> Father, forgive them; for they know not what they do. (Luke 23:34)

The salvation we can receive through Christ, then, is due to Jesus' forgiveness of Cain's sins, including our own. But we ourselves must follow in the footsteps of Jesus by forgiving others if we are to receive the blessing of salvation. We must make the way of Abel our own.

After the crucifixion, Jesus' disciples inherited Abel's mission on earth from Jesus, and indeed Christians as a whole have inherited that mission and carry it to this day. Jesus had already granted his disciples the power to drive out evil spirits and heal the sick. Now he specifically anointed them with the power to forgive the sins of others:

And when he had said this, he breathed on them, and said to them, "Receive the Holy Spirit. If you forgive the sins of any, they are forgiven; if you retain the sins of any, they are retained." (John 20:22-23)

From Old Testament Servants to Adopted Children of God

So what is the status of Christians who have accepted Jesus as their savior and who strive to follow Christ by exemplifying the Way of Abel? We know that we are unable to free ourselves from sin completely, but we are nevertheless no longer bound by the law.

Saint Paul would emphasize that those who follow Christ are no longer the slaves or servants of a master God, but rather sons and daughters of a parental God, and thus able to enjoy a much more intimate relationship with their Creator:

> For all who are led by the Spirit of God are sons of God. For you did not receive the spirit of slavery to fall back into fear, but you have received the spirit of sonship. When we cry, "Abba! Father!" it is the Spirit himself bearing witness with our spirit that we are children of God, and if children, then heirs, heirs of God and fellow heirs with Christ, provided we suffer with him in order that we may also be glorified with him. (Romans 8:14-17)

Because we are still descendants of the fallen lineage of Adam and Eve, and therefore continue to possess a sinful nature, we are not yet able to achieve the perfection of Christ. Thus Paul qualified our status as sons and daughters by describing us as adopted children of God. As such we are nevertheless heirs of Christ:

> But when the time had fully come, God sent forth his Son, born of woman, born under the law, to redeem those who were under the law, so that we might receive adoption as sons. And because you are sons, God has sent the Spirit of his Son into our hearts, crying, "Abba! Father!" So through God you are no longer a slave but a son, and if a son then an heir. (Galatians 4:4-7)

Looked at a bit differently, the goal of salvation is for fallen humanity to be restored to the full sonship/daughterhood enjoyed by Adam and Eve before the Fall, by inheriting sinless nature from sinless parents. Jesus came to establish a new sinless family in place of Adam, but was unable to marry a sinless Eve and create a sinless lineage before he was put to death by the authorities in Israel. The victory of Jesus on the cross, however, enabled him to establish a spiritual parenthood with the Holy Spirit in the place of Eve, manifesting the feminine aspect of our Creator.

For now, we can be born again as adopted sons and daughters of Christ by practicing the Way of Abel in imitation of Christ. This rebirth can be a powerful experience of the Holy Spirit and an opening up of our minds and hearts to the love and truth of God. Jesus described the attitude of humility we need to achieve this transformation:

> Truly, truly, I say to you, unless one is born anew, he cannot see the Kingdom of God. (John 3:3)

The Limits of Salvation Through the Cross

Since the Fall took place when Adam and Eve were on earth, its full reversal must also take place on earth. Thus until there is a new, sinless lineage established by a new and sinless man and woman in place of Adam and Eve, salvation will not be complete. Thus we find in one of John's letters, a description of our continued struggle with our own fallen nature:

> This is the message we have heard from him and proclaim to you, that God is light and in him is no darkness at all. If we say we have fellowship with him while we walk in darkness, we lie and do not live according to the truth; but if we walk in the light, as he is in the light, we have fellowship with one another, and the blood of Jesus his Son cleanses us from all sin. If we say we have no sin, we deceive ourselves, and the truth is not in us. If we confess our sins, he is faithful and just, and will forgive our sins and cleanse us from all unrighteousness. If we say we have not sinned, we make him a liar, and his word is not in us. (1 John 1:5-10)

The Meaning of Salvation Through the Cross

The message here is that it is undeniable that we do sin, but if we confess to our sins and seek forgiveness we can be forgiven by Jesus. Receiving forgiveness is essential for salvation, but it is a precondition for full salvation not its realization. Salvation will be complete only when we become, like Christ, sinless men and women. Even the great Saint Paul recognized this truth about himself:

> So I find it to be a law that when I want to do right, evil lies close at hand. For I delight in the law of God, in my inmost self, but I see in my members another law at war with the law of my mind and making me captive to the law of sin which dwells in my members. Wretched man that I am! Who will deliver me from this body of death? Thanks be to God through Jesus Christ our Lord! So then, I of myself serve the law of God with my mind, but with my flesh I serve the law of sin. (Romans 7:21-25)

Although sins are thoughts—or acts that result from thoughts—that violate the Divine order and purpose, speaking of them as being located in the body rather than the spirit is meaningful insofar as Jesus himself suffered the attacks of Satan on his physical body. Thus Satan could claim the death of Jesus on the cross as a victory over Christ in the physical earthly realm, but through the resurrection God could claim a victory over Satan in the spiritual realm.

When Jesus appeared in spirit to his disciples after the crucifixion, it demonstrated that Jesus had gained a victory over the forces of Satan that had worked to have him killed. However, that victory was spiritual only, which explains why even the most holy Christians cannot free themselves of the inheritance of sin we all suffer from. Thus salvation from sin through the cross was only partial, and the world continues to wait for it to be completed. Full salvation must be achieved on earth first, reversing the Fall that also occurred on earth:

> I will give you the keys of the kingdom of heaven, and whatever

> you bind on earth shall be bound in heaven, and whatever you loose on earth shall be loosed in heaven. (Matthew 16:19)

This explains why the providence of salvation has extended for two millennia since Christ lived on earth. Believers in him, the Christians, have multiplied greatly in this time, reaching every corner of the earth as prophesized, but evil has not been eradicated from individuals, families, tribes, nations or any part or aspect of the world. Everyone who seeks sincerely to be good, will sooner or later come to the realization of the truth that Paul wrote about, the truth that our salvation is not as yet complete because evil continues to reside in us.

Satan's dominion of the world—which is manifest in Cain-type behavior—will not come to an end until we are fully separated from Satan, in spirit and body.

Was Jesus Shedding Blood Important to Salvation?

Many Christians believe that they are saved by the blood of Christ. In other words, that by his death on the cross Jesus was making himself a sacrificial offering in place of the animals offered as sacrifices in the Old Testament. For example, in Hebrews we find this:

> But when Christ came as high priest of the good things that are now already here, he went through the greater and more perfect tabernacle that is not made with human hands, that is to say, is not a part of this creation. He did not enter by means of the blood of goats and calves; but he entered the Most Holy Place once for all by his own blood, thus obtaining eternal redemption. (Hebrews 9:11-12)

And this:

> In fact, the law requires that nearly everything be cleansed with blood, and without the shedding of blood there is no forgiveness. (Hebrews 9:22)

And from a letter of John:

> But if we walk in the light, as he is in the light, we have fellowship with one another, and the blood of Jesus, his Son, purifies us from all sin. (1 John 1:7)

These passages need context to be understood. It is of course true that from the time of Cain and Abel men and women were called to make sacrifices of animals and food to prove their faith in God. And it is true that sacrifices were the first way that human beings could demonstrate their faith in and obedience to the Divine. Abraham had to sacrifice three animals and two birds, and a mistake he made in this sacrifice meant he was told he had to sacrifice Isaac, his only son by Sarah. When the Mosaic Law was instituted, the Jews were required to make a variety of regular sacrifices to satisfy their God.

But David recognized that it was faith that God wanted to see among men and women, and that sacrifices of their livestock and crops was only symbolic of the real sacrifices that we must make to separate ourselves from Satan:

> For thou hast no delight in sacrifice; were I to give a burnt offering, thou wouldst not be pleased. The sacrifice acceptable to God is a broken spirit; a broken and contrite heart, O God, thou wilt not despise. (Psalm 51:16-17)

And Jesus never taught the need to make these sacrifices. Rather, he encouraged his disciples to sacrifice themselves through living a very humble life of giving and service to others, imitating his own lifestyle.

Thus it was not the blood that Jesus shed on the cross that gives us salvation, but the heart behind that sacrifice, the offering of his life to carry out his providential mission. Indeed, it is Abel's willingness to offer himself at the cost of his life to defeat evil and liberate Cain from Satan's dominion that God can use to liberate humanity from Satan.

Shedding Blood Does Not Remove Sin

And forgiveness of sin is not predicated on shedding blood, except in a metaphorical sense of developing a contrite heart and making sacrificial efforts for God. We find, for example, that God forgave the Israelites after Moses interceded on their behalf, although that forgiveness was not without cost to those forgiven:

> "Pardon the iniquity of this people, I pray thee, according to the greatness of thy steadfast love, and according as thou hast forgiven this people, from Egypt even until now." Then the Lord said, "I have pardoned, according to your word; but truly, as I live, and as all the earth shall be filled with the glory of the Lord, none of the men who have seen my glory and my signs which I wrought in Egypt and in the wilderness, and yet have put me to the proof these ten times and have not hearkened to my voice, shall see the land which I swore to give to their fathers; and none of those who despised me shall see it." (Numbers 14:19-23)

And in the Psalms:

> He does not deal with us according to our sins, nor requite us according to our iniquities. For as the heavens are high above the earth, so great is his steadfast love toward those who fear him; as far as the east is from the west, so far does he remove our transgressions from us. As a father pities his children, so the Lord pities those who fear him. For he knows our frame; he remembers that we are dust. (Psalm 103:10-14)

Was the Crucifixion Pre-Ordained?

One problem with believing salvation comes through the shedding of blood by Jesus is that it leads to the logical conclusion that the crucifixion was therefore foreordained and the will of God. In other words, that without his death on the cross there would be no salvation. This is wrong. How could a victory by Satan be part of the Divine plan for salvation?

A clear distinction must be made: the death of Jesus on the cross was the work of Satan through Cain-type figures in Israel. However, the unbroken faith of Jesus on the cross was used by God to advance the providence of salvation.

Perhaps the best exposition of the meaning of Christ's sacrifice on the cross can be found in the prophetic words of Isaiah:

> For he grew up before him like a young plant, and like a root out of dry ground; he had no form or comeliness that we should look at him, and no beauty that we should desire him. He was despised and rejected by men; a man of sorrows, and acquainted with grief; and as one from whom men hide their faces he was despised, and we esteemed him not.
>
> Surely he has borne our griefs and carried our sorrows; yet we esteemed him stricken, smitten by God, and afflicted. But he was wounded for our transgressions, he was bruised for our iniquities; upon him was the chastisement that made us whole, and with his stripes we are healed.
>
> All we like sheep have gone astray; we have turned every one to his own way; and the Lord has laid on him the iniquity of us all. He was oppressed, and he was afflicted, yet he opened not his mouth; like a lamb that is led to the slaughter, and like a sheep that before its shearers is dumb, so he opened not his mouth... he poured out his soul to death, and was numbered with the transgressors; yet he bore the sin of many, and made intercession for the transgressors. (Isaiah 53:2-7, 12)

Jesus died on the cross not for his sins, but for ours. It was not the will of God that he die, but that he live, that he establish a family and the Kingdom of Heaven on earth. His death was the result of faithlessness, not righteousness; of disobedience to God's will, not obedience to it.

Thus it was only because of Jesus' faith and humility in the face of the terrible injustice of his death on the cross that God could claim a spiritual victory from the crucifixion and that we are able to experience salvation through Christ.

Chapter 24

Inheriting the Mission of Jesus

The Path to Becoming One with Christ

The moral force of Jesus lies in his purity and goodness, which are characteristics derived from his sinlessness. This sinlessness was a gift at birth, a gift made possible by centuries of effort by Abel-type people chosen to establish a foundation for God to be able to send a man in the place of Adam before he fell under the dominion of Lucifer, the angel who became Satan.

As we have seen, this endowment of sinlessness brought with it enormous challenges and responsibilities, and the life of Jesus was one of suffering and rejection, leading to the cross. Jesus was tempted by Satan to give up the struggle against evil and become a mighty ruler, so long as he would just submit to Satan. But he stayed the course, doing his utmost to fulfill his Father's mandate for the Messiah, eventually having to sacrifice his life at the young age of 33.

From our point of view as people who are unable to get rid of our fallen nature, Jesus stands as a unique and inimitable figure in history. He is so far above us in virtue that we can only worship at his feet and hope and pray that he will save us from our sins. Our contention here is that Christians are called to do more than worship Jesus, and that Jesus himself made this clear in the instructions he gave to his disciples. As Christians, we are called to share the burden that Jesus has carried for two millennia. Only by doing so will the goal of salvation dear to all Christians become attainable.

Today there are some 2.4 billion Christians around the world who do believe in Jesus, albeit with widely varying degrees of sincerity and commitment. Many Christians believe that simply having faith in Jesus or being 'born again' fulfills what is required of them to receive salvation. Yet heaven is still elusive and evil still rampant in the world. Isn't it likely, then, that we are not doing enough to support the providence that leads to salvation? And isn't it likely that we are falling far short of becoming the Christ-like men and women that Jesus needs to create the Kingdom of Heaven on earth?

The Imitation of Christ

There are some Christians, of course, who have gone much further than most in seeking to imitate Christ, sacrificing the comforts of life to worship Jesus and serve humanity as exemplars of a saintly existence. The Catholic Church has bestowed the title of Saint upon many of these, and thus Christian history has been illuminated by the bright lights of Saint Peter, Saint Paul, Saint Augustine, Saint Benedict, Saint Dominic, Saint Francis, and many, many more. Today there are more than 10,000 Catholic saints in all. The church has a system for approving men and women as saints, based on criteria such as their lives of faith, the miracles associated with them, or their martyrdom.

The Orthodox Church also has a large number of saints, who are often honored with icons in churches, or have specific churches named after them. Some of these saints are shared with the Catholic Church. In both Catholic and Orthodox traditions, certain saints are believed to have special intercessionary powers (for health, safety, etc.), and are honored and prayed to on that basis.

The Protestant churches do not have official saints, although many protestant leaders and missionaries have been great role models of a Christian's imitation of Christ, and some have been martyred for their faith, including those tortured and killed by the church for heresy, such as John Huss and victims of the Inquisition, and those among all the Christians persecuted for their faith under Communism in the Soviet Union, China and elsewhere.

Inheriting the Mission of Jesus

The important thing to recognize, however, is that imitating the life of Christ is the fundamental obligation of every Christian, not just a relatively small group of saintly individuals. This is the message of the Sermon on the Mount, and in particular of these words of Jesus in Matthew 5:48, which we have often referred to: "You, therefore, must be perfect, as your heavenly Father is perfect." This was, and is, a message to every person who would follow Christ.

Saint Paul would call all those who became Christians "saints", as can be seen in his letter to members of the church in Ephesus:

> Paul, an apostle of Christ Jesus by the will of God, To the saints who are also faithful in Christ Jesus: Grace to you and peace from God our Father and the Lord Jesus Christ. (Ephesians 1:1-2)

The way to imitate Christ is to continue the work for our Heavenly Father that Jesus undertook on earth and now advances from the Spirit World. As Jesus himself said:

> Then Jesus told his disciples, "If any man would come after me, let him deny himself and take up his cross and follow me. For whoever would save his life will lose it, and whoever loses his life for my sake will find it. For what will it profit a man, if he gains the whole world and forfeits his life? Or what shall a man give in return for his life? For the Son of man is to come with his angels in the glory of his Father, and then he will repay every man for what he has done." (Matthew 16:24-27)

That Jesus needs us to carry on his work on earth is evidenced in the instructions he gave his disciples regarding what they should do after his crucifixion, as well as the powers he vested in them so that they could fulfill this mission. The point is that his disciples were not just to believe in him as the Messiah, but to take up the work that he was doing to save humankind.

Thus whether making conditions of prayer and fasting, whether teaching the words of Jesus, whether serving others through healing or other ministrations, or whether making the ultimate sacrifice of martyrdom, our lives should follow in the footsteps of Jesus. This is the only way to grow into a Christ-like person. Indeed, this is the true meaning of being a Christian. All Christians lack the sinlessness of Jesus, but all Christians have been shown the way to follow Christ and eventually fulfill their God-given responsibilities and thus become Christ-like.

The Gifts of Christ For The Christian Providence

In addition to the truths he imparted through his teachings, and the example he set in his life, Jesus gave several important powers to his disciples to enable them to carry on his work. In particular these were the powers to forgive, to heal and to drive out evil spirits. In addition, he gave them the authority to offer two sacraments through which they could act on his behalf in bringing new souls into the Abel sphere that was under his dominion: baptism and the Eucharist. Through these blessings his disciples were empowered to represent Jesus on earth and do the work he expected of them. And throughout Christian history, these sacraments have empowered Christians to share in Christ's work of salvation.

To fulfill his mission, a Christian must become an Abel-type person, someone who is attuned to the spirit and truth of God, and who is able to forgive Cain and liberate him from the dominion of Satan. In practicing the Way of Abel, a Christian grows closer to Christ and becomes ever more fully a child of our Heavenly Father. (In Chapter 26 we elaborate on the role Christians have had to play over the past 2,000 years as members of an Abel-type religion.)

Purification And Empowerment Through Baptism

Baptism is a ceremony through which someone is conditionally purified of their sinful nature. It was used by John the Baptist as a means of purifying the people of Israel in preparation for the Messiah. Why then did the sinless Jesus insist on receiving the baptism of John? What purpose did his baptism have? At the moment of Jesus' baptism, John witnessed the Holy Spirit descending on Jesus in the form of a dove:

> And when Jesus was baptized, he went up immediately from the water, and behold, the heavens were opened and he [John] saw the Spirit of God descending like a dove, and alighting on him. (Matthew 3:16)

This baptism served a providential purpose. It enabled Jesus to inherit from John the foundation for the providence for the Messiah that had been laid in the Old Testament era. As John had told those whom he baptized:

> I baptize you with water for repentance, but he who is coming after me is mightier than I, whose sandals I am not worthy to carry; he will baptize you with the Holy Spirit and with fire. (Matthew 3:11)

The fire here means the word, or the truth. Through Jesus, then, baptism came to have a much greater significance than John's baptism. It was an event that marked God's Holy Spirit engaging directly in the providence on earth, igniting the hearts and minds of Abel to love Cain, teach the truth and defeat Satan. From this time onward the baptism of the Holy Spirit would be the deeper purpose behind the baptism with water.

Jesus sought the baptism of John only after John had failed to prepare for Jesus to succeed as the Messiah. Thus John's baptism of Jesus marked the transition of responsibility for preparing the way for the Messiah from John to Jesus. The appearance of the Holy Spirit over Jesus signaled that Jesus was now blessed with the support of Heaven in preparing Israel, support that John appears to have lost. From this time, then, Jesus also began to baptize the people of Israel to prepare them to receive the word and salvation of the Messiah:

> After this Jesus and his disciples went into the land of Judea; there he remained with them and baptized. (John 3:22)

The Importance of Baptism with the Holy Spirit

The line between the Old Testament Era and New Testament Era can be drawn at John's baptism of Jesus. It is encapsulated in the difference between baptism with water and baptism with the Holy Spirit. John provided the former; Jesus introduced the latter. For the disciples of Jesus after his death on the cross, it was baptism by the Holy Spirit—not with water—that brought about spiritual rebirth and renewal, enabling conversion to the new faith.

What does baptism by the Holy Spirit mean? It means the inflooding of our spirit with the love and truth of our Creator. As such, it is profoundly transformative. It creates a conversion experience, a spiritual awakening to the reality of Divine love and the principles by which it manifests, it empowers us to reorient our lives to serving God and the Divine Providence—to love others and teach the truth with the passion that our Heavenly Father wants to express to his children. To be blessed with this experience requires an attitude of humility and the making of Abel-type conditions of faith and service that prepare you to receive the awakening and empowering of the Holy Spirit.

That the disciples spoke in tongues at the Pentecost does not mean that baptism by the Holy Spirit necessarily means gaining that spiritual facility. After all, salvation is not achieved through the acquisition of spiritual gifts, but through the hearts and minds of men and women being liberated from the dominion of Satan so that they can become the true children of God.

The Disciples Were Empowered to Baptize

After his crucifixion, when Jesus met his disciples in spirit, one of the key powers he transferred to them was that of baptism:

> Now the eleven disciples went to Galilee, to the mountain to which Jesus had directed them. And when they saw him they worshiped him; but some doubted. And Jesus came and said

to them, "All authority in heaven and on earth has been given to me. Go therefore and make disciples of all nations, baptizing them in the name of the Father and of the Son and of the Holy Spirit, teaching them to observe all that I have commanded you; and lo, I am with you always, to the close of the age." (Matthew 28:16-20)

From the time of Pentecost, then, the disciples were empowered not only to baptize members of the 12 tribes of Israel, but also the Gentiles. This was demonstrated to Peter in a dramatic way. Cornelius, a Roman centurion in Caesaria, was inspired in a dream to seek the wisdom of Peter. And Peter himself was shown in a dream that he should respond to this request, even though Cornelius was not a Jew. On arriving at the home of Cornelius, Peter found a whole group of Gentiles eager to hear him speak. When Cornelius explained that he had been guided in a dream to seek out Peter, the disciple said:

> And Peter opened his mouth and said: "Truly I perceive that God shows no partiality, but in every nation any one who fears him and does what is right is acceptable to him. You know the word which he sent to Israel, preaching good news of peace by Jesus Christ (he is Lord of all), the word which was proclaimed throughout all Judea, beginning from Galilee after the baptism which John preached: how God anointed Jesus of Nazareth with the Holy Spirit and with power; how he went about doing good and healing all that were oppressed by the devil, for God was with him. And we are witnesses to all that he did both in the country of the Jews and in Jerusalem. (Acts 10:34-39)

Peter explained that the baptism of Jesus by the Holy Spirit—when John baptized him with water—marked the beginning of Jesus' public ministry. And Peter explained that Jesus had commissioned the disciples to share his mission:

> And he commanded us to preach to the people, and to testify that he is the one ordained by God to be judge of the living

and the dead. To him all the prophets bear witness that every one who believes in him receives forgiveness of sins through his name. (Acts 10:42-43)

In the same way that Jesus' public ministry had been launched by the visitation of the Holy Spirit, the disciples began their post-crucifixion ministry after receiving the baptism of the Holy Spirit at Pentecost, 50 days after Jesus passed into the Spirit World:

When the day of Pentecost had come, they were all together in one place. And suddenly a sound came from heaven like the rush of a mighty wind, and it filled all the house where they were sitting. And there appeared to them tongues as of fire, distributed and resting on each one of them. And they were all filled with the Holy Spirit and began to speak in other tongues, as the Spirit gave them utterance. (Acts 2:2-4)

The hallmark of a true baptism in Christ was, then, the Holy Spirit transforming an individual into a disciple of Christ. For Cornelius and his family and friends, the moment of conversion came when the Holy Spirit descended on them:

While Peter was still saying this, the Holy Spirit fell on all who heard the word. And the believers from among the circumcised who came with Peter were amazed, because the gift of the Holy Spirit had been poured out even on the Gentiles. For they heard them speaking in tongues and extolling God. Then Peter declared, "Can any one forbid water for baptizing these people who have received the Holy Spirit just as we have?" And he commanded them to be baptized in the name of Jesus Christ. (Acts 10:44-48)

As we have seen throughout the life of Jesus, the intervention of the Holy Spirit in someone's life was no guarantee that that person would remain committed to serving the Divine Providence. Nevertheless, the power of the Holy Spirit could indeed change lives for good, as the disciples themselves demonstrated. Having been simple fishermen and the like, through Jesus empowering them with the authority to baptize with the Holy Spirit, to forgive the sins of others, to heal the sick and drive out evil spirits, they were transformed into saintly people who were able to perform miracles for God's providence and establish the most successful religion in human history.

Infant Baptism Replaced Circumcision

One of the main issues dividing Christians is whether or not children should be baptized while still innocent infants, or whether baptism should be reserved for adults who are capable of making a conscious decision to seek purification through this sacrament, and who are therefore able to take responsibility for it. The Eastern Orthodox Churches, the Catholic Church and several protestant churches, including Lutherans, Anglicans, Episcopalians, Methodists and Presbyterians, all practice child baptism. (There are several ways in which the various churches practice baptism, from full immersion in water to sprinkling or pouring water on the head.)

The tradition of child baptism likely has its origin in the early history of the Church, probably during the first or second century after the crucifixion, when baptism into a life of faith in Christ became a substitute for the Jewish rite of circumcision.

Saint Paul explained that the value of circumcision as a ritual of purification was no longer meaningful for Christians, and was replaced by baptism:

> In him also you were circumcised with a circumcision made without hands, by putting off the body of flesh in the circumcision of Christ; and you were buried with him in baptism, in which you were also raised with him through faith in the working of God, who raised him from the dead. And you, who were dead in trespasses and the uncircumcision of your flesh, God made alive together with him, having forgiven us all our trespasses, having canceled the bond which stood against us with its legal

demands; this he set aside, nailing it to the cross. (Colossians 2:11-14)

For the Jews, all eight-day-old males had their foreskin cut off as a condition of purification for the sexual sin of the Fall. This rite was first established when Abraham (in Genesis 17) was told by God to circumcise every male in his household who was at least eight days old—including his slaves. Thus while circumcision for infants at eight days was practiced by his descendants from that time, circumcision for male adults was also practiced as a ritual to symbolically separate them from the fallen world so that they could become grafted into the lineage of Abraham.

As we demonstrated in the section above, the Christian providence from its outset included both Jews and Gentiles, the circumcised and uncircumcised. Baptism was a Christian ceremony that bound those baptized to Christ in spirit, enabling them to participate in Jesus' victory over Satan. Again, Paul referred to circumcision as internal and spiritual, not physical:

> For he is not a real Jew who is one outwardly, nor is true circumcision something external and physical. He is a Jew who is one inwardly, and real circumcision is a matter of the heart, spiritual and not literal. (Romans 2:28-29)

In the Orthodox Churches to this day, infants are baptized at eight days, in recognition of the ceremony's replacement of the ritual of circumcision. Some Catholic churches also follow this tradition, although the general practice is to baptize children within the first few weeks of life. As a ceremony of spiritual rebirth through removal of the original sin, the baptism of infants is conducted to secure their salvation. This was particularly important in previous times when child mortality was very common. The church was worried that unbaptized infants could not be saved from sin.

The Importance of Adult Baptism

The obvious limitation of infant baptism—as well as circumcision—is that those baptized do not exercise their free till to participate in the ceremony. They are too young. Furthermore, as they grow to adulthood they do not exhibit sinlessness. Like all fallen people, they have to struggle with a fallen nature that makes a life of faith in God and service to humanity difficult. No one is free from the Original Sin inherited from our first ancestors.

Furthermore, the Gospels do not provide evidence that Jesus or his disciples baptized infants in particular, although Saint Peter likely baptized children when he baptized the whole household of Cornelius, as indicated in Acts 10, referenced above. (This baptism echoed Abraham circumcising his whole household.) Indeed, the scriptures indicate that the disciples were engaged primarily in baptizing adults into the new faith, and it was the presence of the Holy Spirit on these occasions that confirmed new conversions.

These adult baptisms were based on men and women responding to the movement of the Holy Spirit in their hearts and minds, leading to a transformation into Christians, regardless of background. The one condition they had to make was to accept this baptism and the life of faith it entailed out of their own volition.

It was the need for the baptized to choose baptism as a free will commitment that caused the Anabaptists to break from the Catholic Church and the Lutheran Protestants in the Radical Reformation (described in the next chapter) and to insist that baptism be for adults only. For an adult, baptism represents a commitment of faith, a determination to follow Christ in fulfillment of our God-given responsibility to go the Way of Abel in the imitation of Christ. Thus for an adult baptism is the sacrament through which they enter into the discipleship of Christ—they become a Christian.

The adult commitment to follow Christ that is implied in adult baptism is an important step beyond the conditional purification of infant baptism. Neither infant nor adult baptism is a magical removal of sinful nature, but an empowerment to become an Abel-type person. The conscious commitment to follow Christ that can only be made by an adult is ultimately essential for a Christian. It represents the recognition of our personal responsibility to follow Christ as our absolute Abel, so that we too can fulfill the role in our salvation that is ours alone, and thereby also contribute to the realization of the Divine Providence.

Becoming Christ-like Through the Eucharist

By the time Jesus met with his disciples for the final time, at the Last Supper, he knew that he would have to go the way of the cross. Thus he instituted a tradition in which the disciples could become one with him in spirit and purpose by eating bread that represented his body, and drinking wine that represented his blood, the source of his life:

> And as they were eating, he took bread, and blessed, and broke it, and gave it to them, and said, "Take; this is my body." And he took a cup, and when he had given thanks he gave it to them, and they all drank of it. And he said to them, "This is my blood of the covenant, which is poured out for many." (Mark 14:24)

This ceremony can be understood as Jesus adopting the disciples into his sinless lineage. If he had been able to establish a family with a second Eve, their descendants would have been the first members of a new, sinless lineage. The next best thing was for Jesus' disciples to symbolically become his children.

Saint Paul would write about the importance of this ceremony:

> For I received from the Lord what I also delivered to you, that the Lord Jesus on the night when he was betrayed took bread, and when he had given thanks, he broke it, and said, "This is my body which is for you. Do this in remembrance of me." In the same way also the cup, after supper, saying, "This cup is the new covenant in my blood. Do this, as often as you drink it, in remembrance of me." For as often as you eat this bread and drink the cup, you proclaim the Lord's death until he comes. Whoever, therefore, eats the bread or drinks the cup of the Lord in an unworthy manner will be guilty of profaning the body and blood of the Lord. (1 Corinthians 11:23-27)

What Jesus did at the Last Supper became a Christian sacrament, called the Eucharist or Communion. Churches practice it in various ways, but in general it represents the blessing of Christ for those who have confessed their sins and asked for forgiveness. Once purified, Christians can become one with Christ conditionally through ingesting bread and wine that represent his body and blood. Thus the Eucharist represents another blessing that Jesus gave to his disciples to make them an extension of his own being, and thus empowered to fulfill the mission that they inherited from him.

Blessings Come With Responsibilities

Jesus made it clear to his disciples that being baptized by him came with a burden of huge responsibilities. When two of them asked to sit on either side of him in his glory, he warned them of the costs of such discipleship:

> And he said to them, "What do you want me to do for you?" And they said to him, "Grant us to sit, one at your right hand and one at your left, in your glory." But Jesus said to them, "You do not know what you are asking. Are you able to drink the cup that I drink, or to be baptized with the baptism with which I am baptized?" And they said to him, "We are able." And Jesus said to them, "The cup that I drink you will drink; and with the baptism with which I am baptized, you will be baptized; but to sit at my right hand or at my left is not mine to grant, but it is for those for whom it has been prepared." (Mark 10:36-40)

In other words, his disciples could inherit the blessings of Heaven but only on condition that they were willing to undergo the suffering that Jesus himself faced and had to overcome. This is the real meaning of the sacraments of baptism and the Eucharist for all Christians—they are blessings that come at the high price of living a sacrificial life for God's providence.

The conclusion is that to inherit the blessings of Heaven we must inherit the responsibilities that come with the mission work of Jesus. Furthermore, it is by advancing this Christ-like work that we can become Christlike people.

Chapter 25

Inheriting the Mission of Israel

Christians Must Learn from the Israelites' Mistakes

The Birth of a New Religion

Because of Jesus' absolute faith and loyalty to God, his death became a sacrificial offering that opened the way to salvation for those who believe in him. His sacrificial life was also used by God to establish a new religion that was vested with the responsibility to carry forward the salvific work of Christ, who had passed to his followers the authority and powers needed for this purpose, as we discussed in the previous chapter.

For the people of Israel, the centuries-long providence preparing for the Messiah was over. The Messiah had come and been rejected by the chosen nation, whose religious leaders chose to cling to the Mosaic Law rather than accepting and following the perfect embodiment of the law in the person of Jesus. It was inevitable, then, that a division would take place among the people of Israel—between the old and the new, between those attached to the Mosaic Law and those who chose to follow Jesus. This latter group would become known as Christians and their religion as Christianity.

On the surface, Christians have been united in a shared belief that Jesus was the Messiah and is the savior of fallen humanity. However, from the time of the earliest Christians to the present day there have always been differences in beliefs regarding the nature of Jesus and how best to implement his teachings. Combined with disputes over the time and manner of the return of Christ, these differences have been responsible for the continuous process of division and subdivision of Christian churches into many sects and denominations. Institutional and ecclesiastical divisions have played a major role in the history of Christianity.

But what is the significance of these divisions, and how are they related to the transition from a religion based on laws that regulated the practice of the faith, to one based on following Jesus as the Messiah? The answer to that question is critical to understanding the providential purpose of Christianity and the inner meanings of events that have unfolded since the crucifixion of Jesus.

The Providential Mission of Christianity

Many of the divisions within Christianity can be seen to have a purpose if looked at from the perspective of the Divine Providence. As we have shown, Jesus was the most important figure in the providence, but he was not the first and necessarily not the last. His crucifixion ended his life on earth and launched his spiritual mission as ruler of the Spirit World, but his work on earth was inherited by his followers and advanced under his spiritual guidance. This explains why he bound his disciples to himself through the Eucharist and endowed them with many of the spiritual powers he himself had employed on earth. These included the ability to discern good from evil and to exercise the authority to drive out evil spirits and heal the sick, to grant forgiveness, to baptize Jews and Gentiles alike, and to celebrate the Eucharist as representatives of Christ.

The purpose of the providence—restoring fallen humanity to a state of sinlessness—is unchanging and was therefore unchanged by the death of Jesus on the cross. The Divine Providence precedes and therefore transcends all human divisions, whether based on religion, race, ethnicity, class, or any other category. Thus considerations about the relative value or virtue of one theological position or religious practice compared with others can best be weighed based on providential criteria—how successful or unsuccessful are they in advancing God's providence of salvation for the world?

This is a meaningful basis for measuring the significance and consequences of divisions within Christianity, but also for measuring the providential efficacy of Christianity within the wider world of various religions and cultures. In other words, it is through the lens of the providence that we can best determine the extent to which Christianity has fulfilled its mission as an Abel-type religion capable of leading the rest of the world towards fulfillment of our Creator's original purpose.

The difficulty faced by Christians in this respect is due to the lack of a scriptural basis to guide them across the centuries since Jesus lived on earth. The Old Testament scriptures trace providential history from the first family to Malachi, the last prophet before Jesus, while the New Testament scriptures only recount a small part of the words and deeds of Jesus and his disciples, and take us less than a century into the new providence centered on Christianity. How, then, can we understand providential history and Christianity's role since then? That is the question we are answering in this and the remaining chapters of this book.

A New Iteration of Israel's Mission

Most fundamentally, the mission of Christianity should be seen as an extension, and new iteration, of the mission of Israel, which was to prepare the way for Christ to establish the Kingdom of Heaven on earth. A key difference is that Christianity is centered on the living figure of Jesus and his teaching, whereas Judaism was—and is—centered on the words of the providential figures of the Old Testament and the Mosaic Law.

This difference is very significant. First of all, Christians have a perfect role model in Jesus as a man perfected in the image of God, a man who lived his own teachings to the full. The Israelites only had—and the Jews since Jesus have only had—the imperfect role models of their patriarchs, prophets, priests and kings, none of whom were sinless or without error.

Second, the missions of the two groups of believers differ. The mission of Christianity is to serve as a global Abel responsible for the salvation of the world; the mission of Israel was to become a nation comprised of

Jacob's descendants that could receive the Messiah. (See Chapter 27 for a full discussion of Christianity as global Abel.)

Nevertheless, despite the much broader scope of Christianity's mission, and the dearth of scriptures to guide the faithful through the providence for the Christian era, the teachings of Jesus give Christians the depth of understanding they need to become the people capable of fulfilling that providence. The challenge to Christians, then, is to understand the providence and how they can best fulfill their responsibilities in seeing to its realization.

Christians Can Expect to Suffer Like Jesus

It is important to remember that Christianity's mission is constrained by the limitations imposed on its founder. Putting this another way, following Jesus does not lead to a victorious establishment of the Kingdom of Heaven on earth, but rather to a life of suffering for your faith, and the possibility that you may have to sacrifice your life for the providence. This suffering is inevitable because Satan's dominion of the world through Cain was not ended in the lifetime of Jesus and has not been ended since.

The reality of Christian history is that the men and women who have dedicated their lives to Christ have always faced persecution—the more complete their imitation of Christ, the greater the persecution, even to death. Thus the history of Christianity is filled with accounts of suffering and martyrdom, beginning with the tragic death of Stephen, who was killed by a mob incited by the religious leaders of Israel. All of Jesus' 12 disciples, except John, met violent deaths at the hands of enemies of the new faith.

Many of the early Christians were used by the Romans as entertainment in the Colosseum, where they were torn to pieces by wild animals or slaughtered by gladiators. Saint Paul was also killed by his enemies in Rome, and at one point during his ministry he described the many ways he had been persecuted throughout his life as a disciple of Christ:

> But whatever any one dares to boast of—I am speaking as a fool—I also dare to boast of that. Are they Hebrews? So am I. Are they Israelites? So am I. Are they descendants of Abraham?

> So am I. Are they servants of Christ? I am a better one—I am talking like a madman—with far greater labors, far more imprisonments, with countless beatings, and often near death. Five times I have received at the hands of the Jews the forty lashes less one. Three times I have been beaten with rods; once I was stoned. Three times I have been shipwrecked; a night and a day I have been adrift at sea; on frequent journeys, in danger from rivers, danger from robbers, danger from my own people, danger from Gentiles, danger in the city, danger in the wilderness, danger at sea, danger from false brethren; in toil and hardship, through many a sleepless night, in hunger and thirst, often without food, in cold and exposure. (2 Corinthians 11:21-27)

Today Christians continue to suffer persecution at the hands of their enemies, especially in countries ruled by authoritarian rulers and outright dictators. This has occurred for centuries in Muslim lands, and in the last century Christian suffering became particularly widespread in Socialist and Communist states where they were routinely tortured and killed by atheistic totalitarians. Christians continue to suffer in Communist China and North Korea to this day.

Christians Must Not Repeat Israel's Mistakes

The Divine Providence is always broader and more subtle than individual religious leaders and religious teachings can anticipate. Thus most of the Jews raised on the Mosaic Law were unable to adjust their beliefs to recognize Jesus as the Messiah. It was out of this error of judgment that they opposed Jesus and had him killed. Only those who were able to reconcile their expectations for the Messiah with the reality of Jesus in their midst were able to change the direction of their lives to follow Jesus.

When Stephen was condemned to death by the Council of the Sanhedrin and killed in the presence of Saul of Tarsus (later Paul, who at the time was a strict Pharisee and leading persecutor of the new faith), he challenged the religious leaders for their murder of Jesus. According to Acts 6:15, Stephen was an angelic figure who spoke with great spiritual fervor: "And gazing at him, all who sat in the council saw that his face was like the face of an angel." Aflame with the love of God, Stephen spoke about Israel's history of disobedience to God, concluding with:

> You stiff-necked people, uncircumcised in heart and ears, you always resist the Holy Spirit. As your fathers did, so do you. Which of the prophets did not your fathers persecute? And they killed those who announced beforehand the coming of the Righteous One, whom you have now betrayed and murdered, you who received the law as delivered by angels and did not keep it. (Acts 7:51-55)

The Council was unmoved. Stephen was immediately condemned to die, taken outside and stoned to death by a furious mob. Despite the miraculous events that surrounded the death of Jesus, and the many signs the leaders were given regarding the Messiahship of Jesus, their reaction was to do all in their power to crush the new religion. It did not have to be that way. If they had allowed the truth of what they had witnessed in Jesus and his followers to change their hearts and minds, they could have repented of their earlier error in killing Jesus and become his disciples.

As it was, they stubbornly continued their persecution of Jesus' followers and just 40 years after his death Israel and the Temple were destroyed by the Romans, and the Jews scattered.

This is a cautionary tale for Christians, and especially those alive at the end times. Like the Israelites at the time of Jesus, Christians still live in a world under the dominion of Satan, a world that will reject Christ in the second coming. We do not know how God will work in the last days to achieve the fulfillment of the providence. Indeed, we should expect the providence centered on a second coming of Christ to surprise us, and we should make sure that we do not repeat the mistakes of the Israelites when they rejected Jesus out of ignorance, narrow-mindedness and envy. As Jesus warned:

But of that day and hour no one knows, not even the angels of heaven, nor the Son, but the Father only. (Matthew 24:36)

Chapter 26

The Providence Unfolds Through Christianity

Preparing for the Second Coming of Christ

We have seen that Israel's mission was inherited by Christianity, with the great difference that Christians have the living example of Jesus to follow, and therefore should avoid the mistakes of the Israelites when they rejected and killed the Messiah they were to welcome and follow. In this chapter we begin by discussing the 'ground rules' that Christians should follow if they are to accomplish their providential mission. We then trace the path that Christianity has pursued over the past two millennia as Christians have labored to prepare a welcoming environment for the second coming of Christ.

Christian Discipleship Requires Faith and Works

One of the points of theological contention among Christians has to do with the nature of salvation, and whether this grace is granted by Christ based solely on faith in him, or whether it requires work on the part of the believer. The answer to this question has already been suggested in this book, but it bears elaboration for this chapter.

To be a true Christian can be understood as having two parts: the first is to believe in Christ as the Messiah and savior, to study his teachings and learn to apply them to your life; the second—more difficult—is to 'pick up your cross' and follow Jesus by sharing in the work of the providence that he undertook while on earth and now continues from the Spirit World. The first part establishes an individual as a candidate to be an authentic disciple of Christ, but the second part is essential to actually become an authentic disciple of Christ. Thus it is through faith and works that a true disciple can contribute to the providence and help prepare for the second advent of Christ. This point is made clear in the second letter of James:

> What does it profit, my brethren, if a man says he has faith but has not works? Can his faith save him? If a brother or sister is ill-clad and in lack of daily food, and one of you says to them, "Go in peace, be warmed and filled," without giving them the things needed for the body, what does it profit? So faith by itself, if it has no works, is dead. (James 2:14-17)

What Then is Predestination?

For some Christians the issue of faith versus works is superseded by a belief in predestination, namely that our destiny is predetermined by God. This belief is based on a misunderstanding of the providence. Predestination is the absolute will of God to save us, a Parent's determination to rescue their children from evil. This is revealed in Isaiah:

> I have spoken, and I will bring it to pass; I have purposed, and I will do it. (Isaiah 14:11)

Thus while God's purpose for humanity is predestined, the destiny of particular individuals, groups and nations is determined by how they respond to the providence. In other words, whether or not they exercise their free will responsibly.

If this were not the case, we would all be part of a predetermined plan for humanity, a plan that could not be affected by our choices in life. Believing in such a plan can lead to an irresponsible and therefore dangerous fatalism.

As we have shown, there have been many individuals, groups and nations chosen to play a leading role in the providence, from Abraham and Moses to the nation of Israel and Jesus himself. They were chosen based on circumstances, such as conditions they had made or had been made for them by their parents or ancestors. But there was never a guarantee that being chosen for a providential role would result in the successful completion of their mission.

Indeed, the results of failures by major providential figures or nations were catastrophic. For example, when Abraham failed to sacrifice two birds according to God's instructions, he was told his descendants would suffer four centuries of slavery, and later he was instructed to sacrifice his son Isaac in place of the birds; when Moses in anger violated God's instructions by striking the rock at Kadesh to get water for the people, he was told that he and Aaron would not be able to enter Canaan; when Solomon turned to idolatry, his great kingdom was divided and eventually destroyed by the Assyrians and Babylonians; and when Israel rejected and killed Jesus, the chosen nation was destroyed and the Jewish people scattered, delaying the providence for two millennia.

This history shows that while the ultimate success of the providence is predestined, the specific individuals, groups or nations chosen to carry out particular providential missions are not predestined to succeed. This does not mean their predestination was not important for their success. After all, being chosen for a special mission means that you are of particular interest to God the Father, and therefore enjoy the support of heaven. But it also means that you are a prime target of Satan's efforts to thwart the Divine Providence, and can therefore expect exceptional difficulty in fulfilling your responsibilities.

Predestination for Christians

The following passage authored by Paul is the source of some confusion about the role of predestination in our lives since it has been interpreted as fatalistic by some believers:

> We know that in everything God works for good with those who love him, who are called according to his purpose. For those whom he foreknew he also predestined to be conformed to the

> image of his Son, in order that he might be the first-born among many brethren. And those whom he predestined he also called; and those whom he called he also justified; and those whom he justified he also glorified. (Romans 8:28-30)

Given the explanation of predestination above, how can we understand these words of Paul? For Christians, the predestination Paul spoke of is their inheritance of Israel's central position in the providence.

What does this mean in practice? Because of the sacrificial life Jesus lived as the Messiah, Christians who unite with Christ and live in accordance with his teachings and example are a new chosen people. Like the people of Israel before them, however, if Christians are to reap the blessings of this privileged position, they must fulfill the responsibilities incumbent upon disciples of Christ.

Purification Through Cain-Abel Divisions

As we have seen earlier in this book, evil must first be separated from good before it can be recognized and defeated. This division enables Abel-type people to separate from the world dominated by Cain so that they can pursue a life of service to God. For Christianity, this process occurred through reformist sects emerging from the established churches, which often had become spiritually ossified and even Cain-like in their teachings and behavior. The specific causes for these divisions differed, but from the point of view of the providence they were part of an ongoing process of purification of the faith. The end goal was the creation of an environment that would welcome the return of Christ.

There were some practices of the church that were clearly contrary to the teachings of Jesus and could never be reconciled with the virtuous life of Jesus himself. These Cain-type behaviors included the persecution, torture and murder of those considered heretics by the church; the attacks on members of other faiths, such as during the Crusades when Jews, Orthodox Christians and Muslims were all attacked by Catholic armies; the practice of indulgences; the involvement with slavery; and the several wars between Protestant and Catholic armies seeking power in Europe.

If one accepts that the church as an institution is an imperfect embodiment of the teaching and example of Jesus, a process of constant purification is essential for the advance of the Divine Providence. The Abel-type response to ideas and movements that unsettle the status quo in favor of a better understanding of Biblical scriptures and the mission of Christianity is to learn from the new insights and become more Christ-like accordingly. The Cain-type response is to resist the new and better ideas and practices and persecute their advocates as heretics.

This does not mean that the new is always Abel and the old always Cain. Deciding whether to follow the old or the new, one church or another, is the personal responsibility of each Christian. The decision should be based on discerning which side is Abel and which is Cain based on the degree of its alignment with the providential mission of Christianity. That is the criterion that counts. Nevertheless, the history of change in the church has, by and large, been one of newly enlightened groups breaking away from corrupt church institutions. After all, entrenched ecclesiastical bureaucracies naturally seek to preserve themselves, making any changes from within a church very difficult for reformers to achieve.

The Great Schism and Protestant Reformation

The process of renewal and change through separation of one church from another got underway in a global context when, in 1054, the Great Schism saw the Roman Catholic Church separate from the Orthodox Churches of the East. There were theological differences at the heart of this division, but the more important cause was the dispute over the extent of the authority of Rome. The patriarchs of the eastern churches, or sees—Constantinople, Antioch, Alexandria and Jerusalem—did not accept the primacy of Rome.

Time would show that this division would lead to a process of necessary reform that would unfold over centuries, reform that would take place almost exclusively in the world of the Roman Catholic Church. The first major schism within the Western church was the Protestant Reformation.

From Wycliffe to Luther

The Reformation was a movement for the purification of a corrupt church administration and for the Gospel message to become available to the masses. It got underway in the 14th century when the English priest and scholar John Wycliffe (1330-1384) questioned many of the dogmas of the church and criticized the privileged status and authority of the Papacy and clergy, as well as the corruption of members of both ecclesiastical and monastic institutions. He led the translation of the Bible from Latin into Middle English, making it available to people outside the priesthood and monastic orders. After his death he was labeled a heretic at the Council of Constance (1414 to 1418). His works were burned and his body disinterred from a Catholic cemetery, burned and the ashes cast in a river. Many of his followers were excommunicated and some were burnt at the stake.

But Wycliffe's work gave voice to a growing dissatisfaction with the church among many thoughtful Christians, and it would trigger a series of developments in continental Europe that resulted in a full-blown rift between the church and dissident groups.

The first of these dissidents was the Czech theologian and priest John Hus, or Jon Huss, (1370-1415), who looked up to Wycliffe and sought to follow him. He shared most of Wycliffe's criticisms of the church, including the practice of indulgences and the Papacy-led Crusades, and he translated the Bible into Czech. His followers were persecuted by the church, and some beheaded. Afraid of his growing popularity in Bohemia, the church invited him to the Council of Constance (the 16th Ecumenical Council), where he was imprisoned, declared a heretic, defrocked and sentenced to burn at the stake. As with the remains of Wycliffe, his ashes were thrown into a river (the Rhine) so that his body could not be venerated.

Most of the Czechs of Bohemia supported Hus at this point. They were so angry at his execution that their opposition to the church only got stronger. The Papacy reacted by declaring a crusade against them. The Hussites defeated the crusade, as well as three others that followed. In 1436 the church gave up its military opposition and allowed the Hussites to practice Christianity as they wished.

The Protestant Reformation got fully underway when another priest, Martin Luther (1483-1546), in 1517 nailed his 95 Theses criticizing the church practice of indulgences to the door of the Castle Church in Wittenberg, Germany. Indulgences were a Catholic scheme through which Christians could pay with money for forgiveness of their sins. Luther greatly admired Hus, including his willingness to die for what he believed. He would declare: "We are all Hussites." In 1520 Luther was excommunicated by the church. By this time, however, opposition to the church was so widespread that the Protestant movement was unstoppable, and grew rapidly.

The Radical Reformation

Other leading figures in the Reformation movement around the time of Luther were the Swiss Huldrych, or Ulrich, Zwingli (1484-1531), the Frenchman John Calvin (1509-1564), and the Scotsman John Knox (1514-1572). But the changes wrought by Luther and these men were not radical enough for some devout Christians, known as the Anabaptists, who as early as the 16th century split off from the mainstream of Protestantism. They differed from both Catholics and other Protestants in opposing child baptism, believing that only baptism of adults was meaningful because it required a free will commitment to follow Christ. Leaders of the Radical Reformation also criticized Catholics and members of the churches of Luther and his followers for failing to embrace fully the radical lifestyle of Jesus. They admired the simplicity and communalism of the first Christians in Jerusalem:

> And all who believed were together and had all things in common; and they sold their possessions and goods and distributed them to all, as any had need. (Acts 2:44-45)

Thus members of these groups, such as the Hutterites, Mennonites, Brethren and Amish, held property in common and lived together in Christian communities, or adopted other practices that set them apart from other mainstream churches. They remain distinctive to this day.

The Protestant Work Ethic

One of the main contributions of Protestantism to the evolution of Christianity and the advancement of the providence was what Max Weber would—centuries after Luther—call the Protestant work ethic. Behind this concept lies the notion that salvation is not only a gift that Christians can receive through the mediation of Jesus, facilitated by the church, but something that requires the effort of human beings.

This attitude of personal responsibility is entirely consistent with the principle of spiritual growth and salvation that we have presented in this book. It addresses the failure of Adam and Eve who took their blessings for granted. It also addresses the fundamental fallacy and deception behind Papal indulgences, namely that you can purchase your salvation with money.

Thus Protestantism fostered personal responsibility, discipline and hard work. It recognized that the Kingdom of Heaven would not just descend from the clouds but would come about through Divine grace if men and women were conscientious in doing the work God had made them to do. This principle is fundamental to the development of humanity, and lies at the heart of not only the Reformation but also the Renaissance and the development of science and technology, which have transformed the world we live in.

The Counter-Reformation

As we have seen, the response of the Catholic Church to its critics was initially to condemn them as heretics, excommunicate them, and punish them and their followers. However, as the Protestant movement grew stronger, the church began to look inward and, at the Council of Trent (1545-1563), undertook some significant reforms itself. Several of the key figures behind this Catholic response to the Reformation were Spaniards who founded the

Jesuit order and helped spread the faith around the world: Ignatius Loyola (1491-1556) and Francis Xavier (1506-1552). Providing Catholicism with a strong spiritual core were mystics such as Teresa of Avila (1515-1582), a nun, and the priest and friar John of the Cross (1542-1591).

This 'Counter-Reformation' in the Catholic Church, and the Protestant Reformation that inspired it, were both influenced by a movement of Christian humanism, which saw the beauty and goodness in the creation as revelatory of these qualities in the Creator. This movement would become known as the Renaissance because it sought to renew in European culture the role of art and literature that had flourished in the glory days of Greece and Rome.

The founder of this movement of renaissance was the Italian contemporary of Wycliffe, Francesco Petrarch (1304-1374). It was advanced by the Dutchman Erasmus (d. 1536), who influenced Luther and Zwingli, among many other reformers, both within the Catholic Church and in the Protestant movement. These Christian humanists would pave the way for the development of science, as we discuss in Chapter 32.

The Pilgrims and America's Great Awakening

In England, some of the Protestants who wanted greater freedom to worship as they saw fit, first went to Holland, which was largely welcoming, but then decided to sail across the Atlantic to America, to establish themselves in the New World. Arriving in what is now Massachusetts in 1620, they established a colony at Plymouth that eventually thrived, and became the first foothold of a movement of European Christians seeking freedom from religious controls or outright suppression. They settled along the Atlantic coast and, over time, moved westward into the interior.

One of these movements was founded in England by George Fox (1624-1691), who objected to the privileged treatment of royalty and the aristocracy, insisting that all are equal under God. His followers, the Quakers, would themselves be granted a territory in the New World, which they called Pennsylvania, after their leader, William Penn (1644-1718). Maryland was established as a colony primarily for Catholics.

In the 18th century the Christians in America were caught up in a great Christian revival movement, known as the Great Awakening. Great preachers like John Wesley (1703-1791), who founded the Methodist Church, George Whitfield (1740-1770) and Jonathan Edwards (1703-1758) inspired believers to live their lives according to the teachings of Jesus. This movement would influence the outstanding individuals who became known as the Founding Fathers of the United States. It inspired them to establish a new nation 'under God'.

Thus the United States was established on the principle that our rights as human beings are granted by God, and not by any human ruler or government institution. From the Declaration of Independence:

> We hold these truths to be self-evident, that all men are created equal, that they are endowed by their Creator with certain unalienable Rights, that among these are Life, Liberty and the pursuit of Happiness. That to secure these rights, Governments are instituted among Men, deriving their just powers from the consent of the governed.[1]

This was truly revolutionary. Finally, for the first time since God's nation Israel had been destroyed by the Romans after the crucifixion of Jesus, a new nation had been established under the authority of God and governed according to the principles of goodness and justice that Jesus had taught. This made America unique in the world and a central player in the Divine Providence, as the Founders recognized in the Declaration:

> And for the support of this Declaration, with a firm reliance on the protection of divine Providence, we mutually pledge to each other our Lives, our Fortunes and our sacred Honor.

Several decades later, when America was engaged in a civil war and

---

1. July 4, 1776. The Declaration of Independence.

the country as founded was in great jeopardy, President Abraham Lincoln reminded the country of its unique founding and transcendent purpose as he honored those who had sacrificed their lives to save the Union at the battle of Gettysburg:

> It is rather for us to be here dedicated to the great task remaining before us—that from these honored dead we take increased devotion to that cause for which they gave the last full measure of devotion—that we here highly resolve that these dead shall not have died in vain—that this nation, under God, shall have a new birth of freedom—and that government of the people, by the people, for the people, shall not perish from the earth.[2]

With the protections of its republican constitution, America became a model for countries around the world to create democracies of their own. And the guarantees of religious, political and economic freedoms under the US Constitution would enable America to play a leading role in the providence as it advanced towards its goal of preparing the world for the second coming of Christ.

Preparing for a Second Coming of Christ

As we have discussed, once Jesus realized that he would have to go the way of the cross, he began speaking about the need for a second coming of Christ. Some of his followers undoubtedly expected this to be imminent, especially after Jesus foretold the end times in these words:

> Immediately after the tribulation of those days the sun will be darkened, and the moon will not give its light, and the stars will fall from heaven, and the powers of the heavens will be shaken; then will appear the sign of the Son of man in heaven, and then all the tribes of the earth will mourn, and they will see the Son of man coming on the clouds of heaven with power and great glory; and he will send out his angels with a loud trumpet call,

---

2. Abraham Lincoln. November 19, 1863. The Gettysburg Address.

> and they will gather his elect from the four winds, from one end of heaven to the other. From the fig tree learn its lesson: as soon as its branch becomes tender and puts forth its leaves, you know that summer is near. So also, when you see all these things, you know that he is near, at the very gates. Truly, I say to you, this generation will not pass away till all these things take place. (Matthew 24:30-34)

As the centuries have passed since Jesus lived on earth, predicting a time for the second coming has proved to be impossible. Perhaps the most important lesson here is that there is no set time for the second advent. Rather, that time will be determined by the readiness of the world to receive Christ a second time, without repeating the mistakes that Israel made. Thus instead of speculating on the time, place and manner of Christ's return, it is more useful to remain focused on creating an environment that will assure the success of the second advent. That is something we can influence.

One of the conditions that Jesus set for the second coming is that his teachings must first be preached in every nation:

> But take heed to yourselves; for they will deliver you up to councils; and you will be beaten in synagogues; and you will stand before governors and kings for my sake, to bear testimony before them. And the gospel must first be preached to all nations. (Mark 13:9-10)

And again:

> And this gospel of the kingdom will be preached throughout the whole world, as a testimony to all nations; and then the end will come. (Matthew 24:14)

This has already been fulfilled. However, it is not merely the universal expansion of Christianity that is a necessary condition for a return of Christ. If a repeat of the rejection of Jesus when he walked the earth is to be avoided, the level of Christian faith must be deep. This is the challenge that faces Christianity. The world has changed dramatically over the past two millennia, and the foundation for Christ is not just national but worldwide. Those chosen to lead the providence can come from any corner of the earth. Thus Christians must expect to be challenged in their assumptions about the return of Christ.

Chapter 27

Christianity as Global Abel

The Challenge to Save a Cain-Dominated World

The Blessings and Responsibilities of Abel

Because Christianity is the religion based on the life and teachings of Jesus, the absolute Abel, its purpose is to represent Jesus to the world as an Abel-type force for good that can liberate Cain from the dominion of Satan. This mission has broad implications in all fields, from religion to science and politics.

The role of Abel is never easy, and providential history shows that those chosen to fulfill it all too often fail, allowing Cain to march on with his program of world dominion. The Old Testament history includes many of these failures and their disastrous consequences, such as the repeated failure of the kings of Judah to maintain the Mosaic Law in the face of idolatry which eventually resulted in the destruction of Jerusalem and the Temple by Nebuchadnezzar II and the exile of the Jews to Babylon.

The most serious failing of the Old Testament era was, however, that of the chosen nation of Israel, which lost its position as global Abel by rejecting and murdering Jesus. The burden of Abel's responsibility was therefore passed to Christianity, which was tasked with creating a new nation to take the place of Israel.

Being a global Abel is a huge responsibility for Christianity, but it is commensurate with the blessings Christians receive from the enlightenment and salvation they are granted by following Jesus. Christians cannot simply use these blessings for their own, personal salvation, but must share them with the rest of the world through serving others as Abel. The challenge they face is to grow in heart and in their love for the rest of humanity, in imitation of the parental heart of Jesus who loved all people on behalf of his Heavenly Father.

Following are some of the dimensions of Christianity's mission as global Abel. The main areas that Christianity should focus on are elaborated in subsequent chapters. However, below is an overview of these challenges and guidance as to how Christians can overcome them.

Christians and Fellow Christians

In a global community of some 2.4 billion Christians, divided among hundreds if not thousands of sects and denominations, the object of intra-Christian relations should be to achieve a unity of heart and mind that is at one with the spirit and truth of Jesus and therefore transcends dogma and historical disputes. Very often members of one denomination hold members of a rival group—often another denomination with only very slight differences in belief—as the enemy that must be hated and spurned. This is truly Cain-like!

Christianity as a religion cannot succeed in its mission as global Abel if it is divided. Thus Abel-type individuals and groups within Christianity must take the lead in uniting Christians in support of the providence by serving others with Christ-like understanding and love. In this respect, it must be remembered that Christians themselves are not, and cannot be, monolithic in their faith—each has his or her own particular set of beliefs, and there are degrees of Cain- and Abel-type characteristics found in all Christians, as there are in all people.

Christians and Members of Other Religions

Religious beliefs are often the most powerful force in the lives of the faithful. Thus it is particularly difficult to advance a new stage in the providence without incurring hostility from believers who are entrenched in their own beliefs and traditions. Nevertheless, it is people of faith who have a foundation of knowledge and experience that should enable them to comprehend and respond to the providence. Thus it is the people of all faiths who should be in the vanguard of efforts to coalesce humanity around a shared providential purpose. The implication for Christians is that they should take the lead in catalyzing and mobilizing this providential movement.

Religion should never be propagated by force, which is the way of Cain. Rather, Christians must emulate the parental heart and virtuous life of Jesus in winning over those of other faiths to the common providential cause. Furthermore, if Abel is to win the heart of others he must seek to understand them within a religious context that recognizes there is a place in the providence for all people of faith. Thus Christians need to learn how to create bridges of faith and commonly shared values with members of other religions, recognizing that those with different beliefs may well be morally equal or superior. From a providential standpoint, it is particularly important for Christians initially to build these bridges with members of the other Abrahamic faiths: Judaism and Islam.

Christian Abels Must Give Light to the Whole World

Israel's rejection of Jesus holds a special significance for Christians because it resulted in the transfer of the central providence from the Jewish people to followers of Jesus. And while the focus of Jesus' mission was on members of the 12 tribes chosen to establish a nation to receive the Messiah, his ultimate mission was to bring salvation to the whole world.

This global providential purpose was established with Abraham when he first received God's blessing:

> Now the LORD said to Abram, "Go from your country and your kindred and your father's house to the land that I will show you. And I will make of you a great nation, and I will bless you, and make your name great, so that you will be a blessing. I will bless those who bless you, and him who curses you I will curse; and by

you all the families of the earth shall bless themselves." (Genesis 12:1-3)

Later, Isaiah received a revelation from God that confirmed the global mission of Abraham's lineage through Isaac and Jacob:

> It is too light a thing that you should be my servant to raise up the tribes of Jacob and to restore the preserved of Israel; I will give you as a light to the nations, that my salvation may reach to the end of the earth. (Isaiah 49:6)

Jesus confirmed that he had inherited 'the light for all nations' from Abraham and Israel:

> Again Jesus spoke to them, saying, "I am the light of the world; he who follows me will not walk in darkness, but will have the light of life." (John 8:12)

And Jesus taught his disciples that they too were to share this light with the world:

> You are the light of the world. A city set on a hill cannot be hid. Nor do men light a lamp and put it under a bushel, but on a stand, and it gives light to all in the house. Let your light so shine before men, that they may see your good works and give glory to your Father who is in heaven. (Matthew 5:14-16)

And Jesus made it clear that to receive the blessing of this mission did not guarantee you could keep it if you failed to fulfill the responsibilities it entailed:

> But when he saw many of the Pharisees and Sadducees coming for baptism, he said to them, "You brood of vipers! Who warned you to flee from the wrath to come? Bear fruit that befits repentance, and do not presume to say to yourselves, 'We have Abraham as our father'; for I tell you, God is able from these stones to raise up children to Abraham." (Matthew 3:7-9)

The special preparation of Israel to receive the Messiah was so that they could inherit the light of salvation from Jesus and share it with the rest of the world. Their failure to believe in Jesus meant that those who did follow Jesus inherited from the Jews as a people the mission to share the light of salvation with all humankind.

In his final instruction to his disciples, Jesus made their mission explicit:

> And Jesus came and said to them, "All authority in heaven and on earth has been given to me. Go therefore and make disciples of all nations, baptizing them in the name of the Father and of the Son and of the Holy Spirit, teaching them to observe all that I have commanded you; and lo, I am with you always, to the close of the age." (Matthew 28:18-20)

For the disciples of Jesus who had grown up in Israel with its centuries of scriptures and traditions that reinforced the belief that their nation was chosen by God, it was a major shift in thinking to concern themselves with the Gentiles as well as the Jews. Initially there was discussion among them about this, but both Peter and Paul received signs showing them that they must include the Gentiles in their work. (A Gentile was any non-Jew.)

Peter had a vision in which he saw that not only Jews were qualified to receive a baptism and become members of the new faith. This awakening came at the very time when a Roman centurion of Caesaria called Cornelius sent messengers to ask Peter to visit his household. Because of his vision, Peter agreed to go to the home of Cornelius, where he found a group of Gentile family members and friends who were inspired by God and eager to hear his words:

> And Peter opened his mouth and said: "Truly I perceive that God shows no partiality, but in every nation any one who fears him and does what is right is acceptable to him." (Acts 10:34-35)

Immediately, the Holy Spirit descended on Cornelius and his family and friends, who began speaking in tongues, just as the disciples had done at Pentecost. Peter realized that they should receive the baptism with water since they had already received the baptism of the Holy Spirit:

> While Peter was still saying this, the Holy Spirit fell on all who heard the word. And the believers from among the circumcised who came with Peter were amazed, because the gift of the Holy Spirit had been poured out even on the Gentiles. For they heard them speaking in tongues and extolling God. Then Peter declared, "Can any one forbid water for baptizing these people who have received the Holy Spirit just as we have?" And he commanded them to be baptized in the name of Jesus Christ. (Acts 10:44-48)

Christianity's greatest early evangelist, Paul, and his companion Barnabas, were called specifically to evangelize the Gentiles:

> For so the Lord has commanded us, saying, "I have set you to be a light for the Gentiles, that you may bring salvation to the uttermost parts of the earth." (Acts 13:47)

Later, Paul would repeat that the Gentiles were now fellow heirs of the providence:

> When you read this you can perceive my insight into the mystery of Christ, which was not made known to the sons of men in other generations as it has now been revealed to his holy apostles and prophets by the Spirit; that is, how the Gentiles are fellow heirs, members of the same body, and partakers of the promise in Christ Jesus through the gospel. (Ephesians 3:4-6)

Thus all those who receive the light of salvation through Jesus are called to serve the providence as Abel-type Christians. For every Christian this means cultivating the Christ-like heart of a parent towards all people of the world, regardless of their race, nationality and beliefs, and whether they are religious or not.

Christians Together Must Create a New, Abel-type Israel

Christians individually must cultivate an Abel-type character to save their brethren around the world, and they must also work together to create an Abel-type nation that can take the place of Israel in the providence. What does it mean to be an Abel-type Christian nation? It means providing moral leadership to other nations, elevating them through education and service, and protecting them from the predations of Cain.

Israel was to have been the first Abel-type nation blessed by God as a model of goodness for the world to imitate. When the providence for Israel as the chosen nation ended with the crucifixion of Jesus, the role of a chosen people was left unfulfilled, pending qualification for this position from among those nations most closely embodying the Christian ideal.

In the centuries following the death of Jesus, there were step-by-step developments towards the creation of a just and Godly society. This evolution occurred through the purification of Christianity and the development of democracy leading to the establishment of the United States on the principle of God-given natural rights and a government "of the people, by the people, for the people," as Abraham Lincoln would later put it. This made America a providential nation with a mission to serve the world on behalf of the providence.

All Religion is Personal

If you reflect for a moment, you will realize that your set of beliefs is unique to you. In other words, there is nobody on earth with a perfectly identical set of beliefs. This is the case because each one of us is a particular manifestation of the Divine, a specific and unique part of the image of God. Thus it is that we must respect all fellow Christians and all people of other faiths, at least to the extent that they are sincere in their faith and not contravening moral norms that are universally upheld by authentic religions. The responsibility of Abel is not to force himself and his beliefs on Cain, but rather to help Cain elevate his personal religion so that he can himself become Abel-like and contribute to the providence.

To fulfill the mission of Abel, Christians must seek Abel-type individuals and institutions within other faiths, based on a belief that God works through all individuals who, as children of Divine purpose and love, seek to understand and fulfill their providential purpose. Extending brotherly—and ultimately parental—love to those seeking and serving the Divine is the basis upon which inter-faith harmony can contribute to the fulfillment of the Divine Providence. Thus the hope for humanity is not that all people come to share the same belief but that all people fulfill their potential as children of God and thereby are able to share the Divine love for others that is exemplified by Christ.

The Kingdom of Heaven Has No Religions

Salvation is not provided by religious institutions but granted as a grace of Heaven to individuals who fulfill their God-given responsibilities. The purpose of religious institutions is, then, to help individuals accomplish their responsibilities. This is important to keep in mind since history shows that all institutions created by fallen human beings are susceptible to corruption. This susceptibility is in direct proportion to the power of the institution. As Lord Acton famously said: "Power tends to corrupt, and absolute power corrupts absolutely."

Religious institutions are no exception. As they grow in members and resources they become more and more taken with administration and finances and increasingly less likely to help their members experience the living God and grow to spiritual maturity. (Which is why Christianity has had to go through countless rounds of reformation and renewal to remain aligned with the Divine Providence.)

This nature of religious institutions also underscores our earlier point that members of one faith should not seek to convert members of another. This type of proselytizing can manifest as a kind of religious aggression that leads to resentment and conflict between the diverse denominations and religions. By the same token, religions should not place walls of obedience and allegiance around their members, stifling personal quests for understanding and spiritual growth that can transform people of faith into sons and daughters of God.

The Kingdom of Heaven will not be populated with a myriad temples, churches and mosques, each catering to a different shade of religious belief. Rather, the Kingdom of Heaven will be the home of individuals and families who have realized their true purpose as children of God. Revelation, the last book in the New Testament, offers a beautiful image of this. It describes Heaven as the place where God and God's children live together in joy and peace:

> Then I saw a new heaven and a new earth; for the first heaven and the first earth had passed away, and the sea was no more. And I saw the holy city, new Jerusalem, coming down out of heaven from God, prepared as a bride adorned for her husband; and I heard a loud voice from the throne saying, "Behold, the dwelling of God is with men. He will dwell with them, and they shall be his people, and God himself will be with them; he will wipe away every tear from their eyes, and death shall be no more, neither shall there be mourning nor crying nor pain any more, for the former things have passed away." (Revelation 21:1-4)

And in this Heaven there will be no temples:

> And I saw no temple in the city, for its temple is the Lord God the Almighty and the Lamb. And the city has no need of sun or moon to shine upon it, for the glory of God is its light, and its lamp is the Lamb. By its light shall the nations walk; and the kings of the earth shall bring their glory into it, and its gates shall never be shut by day—and there shall be no night there; they shall bring into it the glory and the honor of the nations. But nothing unclean shall enter it, nor any one who practices abomination or falsehood, but only those who are written in the Lamb's book of life. (Revelation 21:22-27)

The New Jerusalem will have twelve gates to allow entry for those who have made their way to the kingdom from all directions of the compass, meaning from all the different spiritual paths. There are three gates facing each main direction—east, north, south and west—representing the totality of humanity, all races and religions:

> It had a great, high wall, with twelve gates, and at the gates twelve angels, and on the gates the names of the twelve tribes of the sons of Israel were inscribed; on the east three gates, on the north three gates, on the south three gates, and on the west three gates. (Revelation 21:12-13)

The 12 gates represent the 12 disciples who represented the 12 tribes of Israel, who were to represent the whole world.

Christians and Materialism

Jesus said in his Sermon on the Mount that one must choose between God and mammon, that is between love for God and lust for material things:

> No one can serve two masters; for either he will hate the one and love the other, or he will be devoted to the one and despise the other. You cannot serve God and mammon. (Matthew 6:24)

All of us exist with a physical body that has needs that must be met if we are to survive on this earth. There is nothing wrong with the body; it was created by God with a Godly purpose, namely to facilitate growth of the spirit to maturity and the multiplication of human beings. Therefore it needs care and nourishment. However, from the time of the Fall the needs and desires of the body have been given precedence over those of the spirit, in effect reversing the original order intended by the Creator.

This is the source of the problem of mammon that Jesus warned about. Thus the goal of religion has been to strengthen the spirit and mind so that they can control the body for the sake of God's providence and so that we can fulfill our original purpose as human beings. In terms of the Cain-Abel paradigm, the spirit and mind are Abel and the body is Cain. Thus to grow spiritually and fulfill our purpose we must train our mind to be in control of our body.

Thus the religious life has traditionally been one of denial of material things, of prioritizing mind over body. This self-denial is needed in immaturity, but in maturity the person who has control over his or her body can exert a rightful dominion, or stewardship, over the physical world, as we humans were created to do. This means that truly mature people are able to use wisely the material world to support the Divine Providence, and can serve as Abel in the Cain-dominated world around them.

Christians and Materialist Ideologies

Materialism that manifests as greed is harmful to the providence, but worse still is ideological materialism based on the belief that there is no God and therefore no providential purpose for life. Among these theories Marxism and Neo-Marxism (the Frankfurt School and Postmodernism in particular) are the most pernicious and destructive ideologies in the world today. They have already been responsible for tens of millions of deaths and immeasurable suffering for tens of millions more, especially in the last century. They are also responsible for promoting anti-religion and anti-family ideologies.

Christians has a leading role to fulfill in countering this world of Cain-type ideologies and the evil practices they have spawned. There can be no marriage between Christianity and materialist ideologies: one is good, the other evil, such that any compromise between them inevitably opens the door for evil to corrupt any good purpose they might mutually espouse.

As Abel, Christianity must clearly explain the Cain nature of materialist ideologies, expose their use in the world, and work to defeat them for the sake of liberating those in their thrall—the victims of Cain's program to gain power and extend the dominion of Satan over humankind.

Christians, Science and Technology

In Chapter 32 we elaborate on the role of science and technology in the providence. At this point, however, it is worth pointing out that science and technology have a huge potential to either benefit or harm society and the world. In themselves they are neutral, neither good or evil. Thus the mission of Christians is to make sure that science and technology fulfill an Abel-type role in the world, in line with the providence, and prevent their use for Cain-type purposes.

Christians and Politics

Here, too, the purpose of Christians is to guide the world of politics to fulfill an Abel-type purpose. Regimes that deceive and oppress people with Cain-type ideologies, policies and programs must be resisted and replaced with regimes that embrace Abel-type ideologies, policies and programs. In essence, all political systems should exist to help individuals to fulfill their God-given purposes.

Christians and Economic Systems

Economic systems that crush the individual rights of citizens through unjust ownership structures or business practices must be opposed and replaced with just systems of economic activity. As with good political systems, Abel-type economic systems respect individual rights, including the right to own property and produce wealth so long as this is not at the expense of other people. Thus it is the mission of Christians to advocate for free market capitalist systems.

Chapter 28

The Role of Christianity in Conflict and War

The Importance of Discerning Cain from Abel

The Christian Dilemma Over Use of Force

Most Christians are rightly concerned with what is appropriate behavior for them in situations of conflict and war. In other words, how can they be sure that they are doing the right thing when they involve themselves in situations where two sides are engaged in a struggle that may or may not involve violence and bloodshed? When viewed through the lens of the Divine Providence, all such disputes can be seen to contain elements of the contest between Cain and Abel, evil and good. Using this lens it is crystal clear that everything that supports and advances the Divine Providence is good, and everything that works to stymie and destroy it is evil.

Given their Abel role in the world, Christians must be able to discern between Cain and Abel and lead the forces of good in opposing and defeating all evil so that the world of God's original purpose can be realized.

How then can Christians understand these words of Jesus from his Sermon on the Mount?

> You have heard that it was said, "An eye for an eye and a tooth for a tooth." But I say to you, Do not resist one who is evil. But if any one strikes you on the right cheek, turn to him the other also. (Matthew 5:38-39)

Can these words of Jesus be reconciled with a mission to free the world from Evil?

Most Christians believe they are justified in using physical force to contain and destroy evil, including the use of lethal force if need be. Others take these words of Jesus literally and hold that no use of physical force is justified, regardless of the danger posed by evil. These pacifists are a small minority of Christians and are found primarily within the Anabaptist churches of the Radical Reformation we have previously referred to. Typically they refuse to fight for their country in war, and are willing to go to jail for their convictions. (There are other 'branches' of pacifism that are based on non-violent principles in other faiths, or on principles of humanism and justice, but this book is concerned primarily with pacifism based on Christian beliefs.)

Which position is consistent with supporting the Divine Providence? Is the use of force justified for Christians, or not?

In the Old Testament there are numerous stories of how God encouraged his chosen people to enter into battle against the forces arrayed against them, beginning with the many conflicts against enemies during their 40 years traveling from Egypt to Canaan under the leadership of Moses. Subsequently, God supported Israel's leaders like Joshua and David in their conquests on behalf of establishing a chosen nation.

In the New Testament, Jesus at one point instructed his disciples to arm themselves with swords: "And let him who has no sword sell his mantle and buy one." (Luke 22:36) This implies that the most useful possession for a Christian was a sword. But Jesus never stood at the head of an army, or an armed group of any sort. As we have shown, this was because he never had an opportunity to become Israel's king, the position the Messiah was to inherit from David. Instead he was killed by Israel's leaders, the very people who should have put him on the throne.

In the two millennia since the crucifixion of Jesus, Christians have often been threatened by murderous forces bent on their destruction. A merely pacifist response has meant annihilation and setbacks for the providence.

This has been demonstrated most graphically through the rise of ruthless, atheistic Socialist and Communist revolutions and dictatorial regimes, which have sought to crush all religion and destroy all Christian churches. The death toll of Christians at the hands of Marxist regimes is in the tens of millions.

Furthermore, the predatory nature of Marxists has manifest in the Communist strategy to exploit pacifism in rival cultures and nations to weaken its enemies. For example, the Soviet Union used the World Peace Council and manipulated the leadership of the World Council of Churches to promote anti-war and anti-nuclear weapons movements to weaken NATO and the West in general. No such movements have ever been permitted to flourish within Communist countries, except for propaganda purposes.

All Marxist regimes, whether Socialist or Communist in name, have been based on the premise that violent revolutions and a 'dictatorship of the Proletariat' are the only means for the world to advance towards a Communist Utopia. And they believe that this end justifies all and any means, including the perpetration of the worst violence and atrocities ever witnessed in history.

Who has been able to stop the spread of Marxism and its evil program to destroy religion? It has not been pacifists but nations rooted in Christian values of goodness and justice whose leaders have recognized the dangers of Communism and have been determined to defeat it. Critical to their success, the good people of these nations have been willing to sacrifice their lives in fighting to defeat Marxist revolutions and regimes in order to liberate those suffering from Communist oppression.

The more capable and resolute these nations and their leaders have been, the more successful have their endeavors been. For example, in WWII victorious Allied armies defeated fascism in Germany, Italy and Japan, and in the Cold War, a powerful military in the predominantly Christian West—and in America in particular—brought about the demise of the Soviet empire. It was the resolute opposition to Communism of the Reagan administration, combined with the West's possession of the economic and military strength necessary to defeat the Soviet Union and its allies that brought about the collapse of the Soviet regime and its satellites without a shot being fired.

The Cain-Abel Paradigm and Conflict Resolution

What does this history of conflicts and their resolution tell Christians about how they should deal with evil? The answer lies in the Cain-Abel paradigm, which provides a solution to the dilemma of conscience regarding an appropriate Christian response to evil by showing the way for the conflicts between Cain and Abel to be resolved on Abel's terms, thus defeating evil and advancing the Divine Providence.

To begin with, this paradigm explains why Cain and Abel were put in positions of relative evil and relative good in the first place. From a superficial standpoint, this separation into two very different positions could be judged unfair. But it is not. On the contrary, it is only by evil being separated from good that it can be exposed for what it is and then overcome by the forces of good. In other words, without this separation, neither Cain nor Abel are able to overcome the fallen nature they both inherited and suffer from.

Secondly, the paradigm underscores the importance of Abel being a person who becomes ever closer to the Creator through a life of faith, devotion and commitment. For Abel to overcome Cain with love, he must be very strong and resolute in his faith and action, and he must be willing to use force if that is necessary to prevent Cain from doing evil.

Discerning Two Types of Cain

As the heirs of Jesus' Abel-type work on earth, Christians must become strong and effective representatives of Jesus and his teachings. And they must be able to discern the difference between two types of Cain in the world because Christian success as an Abel-type religion depends on relating to the two types differently.

The first type is a Cain who is part of the providence and therefore must be embraced and supported as such. This applies, for example, to all the descendants of Abraham, including members of the Jewish and Muslim faiths. It also applies to all people of faith who sincerely seek to live according to Divine principles of goodness. For Jesus, these 'providential Cains' were the Israelites in general, but more specifically his own family and disciples who were lacking in faith and commitment. Jesus showed them love and forgiveness, despite their failings.

The second Cain-type are those who seek to damage or destroy the providence. These include the enemies of Abraham's lineage who warred against his descendants. For Jesus, they were the members of Israel's establishment who actively sought to prevent him from fulfilling his mission as Messiah and employed all their energies towards having him killed. Jesus criticized them resolutely in his words, and suggested that under other circumstances he would have led his disciples in a war to defeat them. As Israelites, they had the opportunity to be part of the providence, but through their actions they lost the privilege of this inheritance and instead became enemies of the providence. They should have died, not Jesus.

Cains Who Are Part of the Providence

The original Cain was part of the same providence as Abel but was unable by himself to complete his responsibility as a child of God. Abel's task was to serve his older brother and help him overcome his shortcomings, so that both of them could be blessed by God within the providence. Cain represented the fallen nature of his parents Adam and Eve more fully than did Abel, thus if he had surrendered to his younger brother and followed him in faith the two of them would have established a condition to reverse the Fall of their parents, who surrendered to the influence of Lucifer. This would have been the first step towards reversing the results of the Fall and would have meant that both Cain and Abel could have been blessed by God.

The prototypical dynamic between Cain and Abel has been repeated throughout history, and continues to be repeated today. As we have shown, it shaped the problematic relationship between Ishmael and Isaac as well as Esau and Jacob, between the 11 tribes who lost faith at Sinai and the Levites who were faithful to Moses, between the Northern Kingdom of Israel and the Southern Kingdom of Judah, and between the leaders of Israel and Jesus.

Providential history shows how difficult this Cain-Abel relationship usually is. It requires of Abel a parental heart that embraces Cain with patience and love, despite Cain's resentment, accusation and even vengeful violence directed at Abel. Cain is burdened by a fallen nature that resists the influence of Abel, and he must struggle against this nature in order to submit to the greater wisdom and goodness of Abel. Use of force is the last resort of Abel in his relationship with a providential Cain, but in extremis the survival and success of Abel may depend on the use of force to contain Cain and prevent a repeat of the murder of Abel, who cannot complete his mission if he is dead.

Abel cannot behave like Cain, whose fallen instincts impel him to accuse and avenge himself on Abel with violent behavior that can lead to murder. This is what Christians did when the Crusades were initiated to recover the Holy Land from the Muslims. Christian knights attacked Jewish communities they encountered on the way to the Holy Land, ransacked Constantinople and the main Orthodox church, Saint Sophia, and slaughtered Muslims who stood in their way.

This was not the way to fulfill Christianity's mission as the Abel faith among the Abrahamic peoples. Abel cannot behave like Cain without becoming Cain, and the church would suffer great harm as a consequence of the Crusades, becoming increasingly materialistic and militaristic without good cause. This led to its division and purification through the Protestant Reformation.

Typically, if 'providential Cains' fail to submit to Abel and follow him, they are removed from the central providence and have to find their own way in the world. Thus Cain was banished from Eden after he killed Abel; Ishmael was banished from Abraham's family and its lineage through Isaac after Sarah insisted that he be sent away; and the ten tribes of the Northern Kingdom of Israel were permanently scattered when they failed to repent of their idolatry, listen to the prophets and unite with the Southern Kingdom of Judah.

Most significantly for the providence, despite the extraordinary efforts of Jesus to win over the many Cains of Israel, that nation refused to submit to his authority and killed him. As a result, Israel lost its central position in the providence and was destroyed as a nation. Forty years after the crucifixion of Jesus, the Roman Empire sacked Jerusalem and demolished the Second Temple, and the Jews were scattered around the world in the Great Diaspora.

When Cain rejects Abel, the mission of Abel is postponed, not canceled. But there are always harmful consequences for those representing both Cain and Abel. Suffering is increased as the providence is postponed. Ultimately, providential Cain-Abel relationships must be resolved on Abel's terms for the resentment between the brothers to be overcome and lasting reconciliation between them achieved.

There are not many examples of these providential successes in the Bible, but their impact is clear. Thus when Jacob won over his resentful brother Esau with love his family was blessed to become the chosen people and nation of Israel; and when Joseph showed forgiveness and love to his ten brothers who had sold him into slavery in Egypt, they were able to share in his good fortune and the 12 sons of Jacob were confirmed as 12 tribes who would become the chosen nation of Israel.

Cains Bent on Destroying the Providence

In the same way that God works through the providence to raise up Abel-type figures to prepare the way for the Messiah, so too Satan works to raise up Cain-type figures whose purpose is to destroy preparations for the Messiah and the Messiah himself. Thus there are Cain-type individuals, families, communities, ideologies, movements and nations that are bent on destroying Abel and the providence. These bad actors have no place in the providence and must be deterred and ultimately defeated.

The Old Testament describes an array of such evil actors who were determined to destroy the providence. For example, these 'enemies of Abel' appear in the form of the kings who kidnapped Lot, the tribes that attacked the Israelites under Moses in the desert, the 31 Canaanite kings that Joshua had to defeat to establish Israel, the many enemies David fought to secure Israel, the Assyrians and Babylonians who destroyed the kingdoms of Israel and Judah, and so on. Resistance to these enemies of Israel required taking up arms to defeat the armies seeking to destroy the chosen nation.

In many of the Psalms, David expresses his need for the help of God in defeating his enemies on behalf of Israel. For example, in Psalm 144 David thanks God for training him to succeed in wars that are providential:

> Blessed be the Lord, my rock, who trains my hands for war, and my fingers for battle; my rock and my fortress, my stronghold and my deliverer, my shield and he in whom I take refuge, who subdues the peoples under him. (Psalm 144:1-2)

Victory was usually achieved when the Israelites were faithful and obedient to God, thereby attracting Divine support for their cause. However, when the Israelites succumbed to idolatry, engaged in intermarriage with people of other tribes, or were disobedient in some other way, they lost Divine support and suffered great defeats and losses.

Moses Purified Israel by Killing Internal Enemies

The Divine mandate to destroy Israel's enemies was granted by God after Moses freed the Israelites from slavery in Egypt, and then spent 40 years leading them to a new life in a nation of their own established in Canaan. But Israel's enemies were not limited to non-Israelites. Enemies within Israel were ultimately more dangerous because they prevented Israel from becoming a truly Abel-type nation. At the time of Moses, this purification was necessary because the people had been raised in an idolatrous Egypt, and their relationship with God was tenuous.

Thus from the time of Moses the destruction of various kingdoms and tribes by the Israelites was often preceded by an internal purification of the Israelites themselves.

Almost immediately after they escaped from Egypt many of the Israelites reverted to idolatry. While Moses was on Mount Sinai receiving the Ten Commandments on two tablets, they complained about their difficult situation and longed for the comforts they had left behind in Egypt. This Cain-like complaining led to them persuading Aaron, Moses' older brother, to build an Egyptian idol shaped like a calf from the gold they had brought with them. Aaron complied and the people then indulged in a wild celebration honoring this pagan god, believing that they could trust it to protect them.

When Moses saw this on his return from the mountain, he was filled with anger. He ground the golden calf into dust, which he threw into water which he then made the people drink. He called for those among the people with faith in him to stand with him. The only people who responded were members of his own tribe, the Levites, including Aaron. To enable the Levites to separate themselves from the idolatry that had infected the tribes, Moses ordered his loyal fellow-tribesmen to kill their brothers, friends and neighbors who had participated in the idolatry. In this way, the Levites loyal to Moses and at one with the providence were purified and could be used as the priestly tribe of Israel:

> And when Moses saw that the people had broken loose (for Aaron had let them break loose, to their shame among their enemies), then Moses stood in the gate of the camp, and said, "Who is on the Lord's side? Come to me." And all the sons of Levi gathered themselves together to him. And he said to them, "Thus says the Lord God of Israel, 'Put every man his sword on his side, and go to and fro from gate to gate throughout the camp, and slay every man his brother, and every man his companion, and every man his neighbor.'" And the sons of Levi did according to the word of Moses; and there fell of the people that day about three thousand men. And Moses said, "Today

> you have ordained yourselves for the service of the Lord, each one at the cost of his son and of his brother, that he may bestow a blessing upon you this day." (Exodus 32:25-29)

Moses then returned to Mount Sinai to repeat the 40-day fast and to intercede with God on behalf of the people, offering his own life for their forgiveness:

> On the morrow Moses said to the people, "You have sinned a great sin. And now I will go up to the Lord; perhaps I can make atonement for your sin." So Moses returned to the Lord and said, "Alas, this people have sinned a great sin; they have made for themselves gods of gold. But now, if thou wilt forgive their sin—and if not, blot me, I pray thee, out of thy book which thou hast written." But the Lord said to Moses, "Whoever has sinned against me, him will I blot out of my book. But now go, lead the people to the place of which I have spoken to you; behold, my angel shall go before you. Nevertheless, in the day when I visit, I will visit their sin upon them." (Exodus 32:30-34)

With Aaron at their head, the purified Levites would indeed become the priesthood of Israel. To enable them to avoid materialism as much as possible, the Levites would not be included in the distribution of land among the tribes when they settled in the Promised Land. But they were granted certain privileges in specific cities and were sustained by tithes and fees from the people in exchange for the priestly services they provided. (The total number of tribes that divided up the land was 12 because Joseph's tribe became two tribes through his twin sons, Ephraim and Manasseh. This took place when Joseph's sons inherited the blessing originally intended for the oldest of Jacob's sons, Reuben, who had lost the blessing when he angered God by sleeping with one of Jacob's concubines, Bilhah, the servant of Rachel whom she had given to Jacob when she was unable to conceive. Bilhah was the mother of Dan and Naphtali.)

The role of the Levites was to study and disseminate the law. Before

Moses, the Israelites inherited a legacy of instructions given to the family of Abraham by God, but they lacked a set of Divinely-mandated laws to guide their lives of faith and the society they were to establish as a chosen people. Thus through Moses for the first time the people had Godly rules to follow as the basis for the society and nation they were to establish in the Promised Land.

However, despite all the signs and revelations from God, the people kept losing faith. When Moses sent 12 spies to see what they could expect in Canaan, only two of them, Joshua and Caleb, came back with an encouraging report that was in line with the providential plan for the Israelites to settle there. However, the people chose to believe the 10 spies who came back warning of the risk of proceeding, and counseling that they return to Egypt. This failure to unite with Moses and the Abel-type spies resulted in the period of their transit from Egypt to Canaan being extended to 40 years.

Moses Instructed the Israelites to Destroy Their Enemies

When they did finally begin to settle on the east bank of the Jordan and in Canaan, through Moses God instructed the Israelites not to intermarry with people who did not belong to the 12 tribes. This prohibition on intermarriage, as well as the instruction to drive existing peoples from Canaan by destroying them outright, seems contrary to what most Christians understand to be moral behavior. But these measures underscored the seriousness of preserving the chosen people to receive a sinless Messiah by keeping their own lineage pure. And if Moses could tell his fellow Levites to kill their brothers to purify the tribe so that it could fulfill its Abel-type mission, he could certainly tell the Israelites to destroy their enemies altogether in the cause of creating a chosen nation.

Several times Moses gave instructions for the Israelites to defeat their enemies and kill everyone. In a final time before Moses died, he was told by God that all the Midianites who had previously betrayed the Israelites had to be destroyed:

> They warred against Midian, as the LORD commanded Moses,

and slew every male. They slew the kings of Midian with the rest of their slain, Evi, Rekem, Zur, Hur, and Reba, the five kings of Midian; and they also slew Balaam the son of Beor with the sword. And the people of Israel took captive the women of Midian and their little ones; and they took as booty all their cattle, their flocks, and all their goods. All their cities in the places where they dwelt, and all their encampments, they burned with fire, and took all the spoil and all the booty, both of man and of beast. Then they brought the captives and the booty and the spoil to Moses, and to Eleazar the priest, and to the congregation of the people of Israel, at the camp on the plains of Moab by the Jordan at Jericho. (Numbers 31:7-12)

But Moses was not satisfied, since they had spared the women and children:

Moses, and Eleazar the priest, and all the leaders of the congregation, went forth to meet them outside the camp. And Moses was angry with the officers of the army, the commanders of thousands and the commanders of hundreds, who had come from service in the war. Moses said to them, "Have you let all the women live? Behold, these caused the people of Israel, by the counsel of Balaam, to act treacherously against the Lord in the matter of Peor, and so the plague came among the congregation of the Lord. Now therefore, kill every male among the little ones, and kill every woman who has known man by lying with him. But all the young girls who have not known man by lying with him, keep alive for yourselves." (Numbers 31:13-18)

A similarly radical instruction was given to the people when they entered the promised land. They were told to destroy all the people living there:

But in the cities of these peoples that the Lord your God gives you for an inheritance, you shall save alive nothing that breathes, but you shall utterly destroy them, the Hittites and the Amorites, the Canaanites and the Perizzites, the Hivites and the Jebusites, as the Lord your God has commanded; that they may not teach you to do according to all their abominable practices which they have done in the service of their gods, and so to sin against the Lord your God. (Deuteronomy 20:16-18)

The killing of 3,000 Israelites by the Levites was to purify Abel. The killing by the Israelites of other tribal groups was to prevent Cain from reinfecting the Israelites with idolatry. Joshua and the judges who followed him; the kings Saul, David, Solomon and their successors; and finally the Maccabees in the lead-up to the advent of Jesus, all carried on this tradition of destroying the enemies of Israel in the name of the purification of the people in service to the providence. The history of Israel shows that it was when the people failed to spurn idolatry and when they married with people from other than the Jewish tribes (often leading to adoption of idolatry), the whole nation would be punished.

So it was that after the destruction of Israel and Judah, and the exile in Babylon, Israel was reconstituted in preparation for the Messiah by Ezra and Nehemiah making the Jews who had returned to Jerusalem from exile to disavow idolatry and commit to the Mosaic Law, and to put away non-Jewish spouses.

Jesus Was in No Position to Use Force

When Jesus faced betrayal among those destined to support him and his mission, he appeared to consider taking up arms to protect the providence from Israel's rulers:

> And he said to them, "When I sent you out with no purse or bag or sandals, did you lack anything?" They said, "Nothing." He said to them, "But now, let him who has a purse take it, and likewise a bag. And let him who has no sword sell his mantle and buy one. For I tell you that this scripture must be fulfilled in me, 'And he was reckoned with transgressors'; for what is written about me has its fulfilment." And they said, "Look, Lord, here are two swords." And he said to them, "It is enough." (Luke 22:35-38)

Later that night, his disciple Peter would use a sword to cut off the ear of one of the men sent by the high priest to arrest him. But clearly this was not a time to take up weapons to defend Abel and the providence, since the circumstances precluded the possibility of self defense:

> While he was still speaking, there came a crowd, and the man called Judas, one of the twelve, was leading them. He drew near to Jesus to kiss him; but Jesus said to him, "Judas, would you betray the Son of man with a kiss?" And when those who were about him saw what would follow, they said, "Lord, shall we strike with the sword?" And one of them struck the slave of the high priest and cut off his right ear. But Jesus said, "No more of this!" And he touched his ear and healed him. Then Jesus said to the chief priests and officers of the temple and elders, who had come out against him, "Have you come out as against a robber, with swords and clubs? When I was with you day after day in the temple, you did not lay hands on me. But this is your hour, and the power of darkness." (Luke 22:47-53)

As we have discussed, even Jesus' disciples were scared off by the mob sent by the chief priest, and dispersed when their leader and savior was arrested, rather than staying with him. Jesus must have recognized that he lacked a foundation to resist the onslaught of the Cain forces in Israel. His best option was to make himself an offering for the salvation of Israel and the world. In this way, Jesus was able to secure a victory over Satan, albeit on the spiritual plane. Jesus was filled with grief because this meant that those who followed him would now be limited to spiritual salvation while Israel itself would lose its position as the chosen nation, this time permanently.

Jesus as Abel Sacrificed His Life to Save Cain

It was Jesus' willingness to sacrifice his life for the sinful world of Cain that confirmed his position in history as a unique and absolute Abel. All the other Abel figures who preceded him in the providence—including Noah, Shem, Abraham, Isaac, Jacob, Joseph, Moses and the prophets—had been permitted to die naturally. But none of them had the unique status of Jesus and none of them was able to effect a transformation of the world that compared with the impact of Jesus.

As we have noted, Jesus was sinless so that his sacrifice on the cross was not for his own salvation or benefit, but purely for the sake of saving the world of Cain from evil. The fact that he lacked the support to defend himself or to take the throne of David by force, should not distract from the fact that he did absolutely everything in his power to fulfill the mission of global Abel. As we have shown, in his words to his disciples he implied that if the situation had been different, there would have been cause to use swords to protect and advance the providence.

Christians Should Follow Jesus When Using Force

Christians who inherit the mission of global Abel from Jesus do indeed have a mandate to defend themselves and the providence from aggression. After all, as we have seen, if Cain wins, everybody loses, including Cain. Thus for the providence centered on Jesus to advance, it is imperative that Abel wins. Hence, if there is a clear-cut, anti-providential Cain-type force at work in the world, it is the Christian duty to oppose and defeat that force, using whatever weapons necessary. It is always better to avoid bloodshed if possible, but it is most important that Abel win over Cain. If Abel wins, everybody wins, including Cain.

Thus although Nazi Germany and Soviet Russia were countries with majority Christian populations, it was absolutely right for Abel-type Christians to form alliances that defeated them. After all, if the forces of Cain had triumphed over the Allies the damage to the providence and the world that they would have likely inflicted would have been immeasurably greater than it already had been before they were defeated. As it was, they were already responsible for tens of millions of deaths and the suffering of many millions more.

Christians Cannot Compromise with Evil

It should also be recognized that it is a mistake to think that anti-providential Cain is really willing to compromise. This was the mistake of Britain's

Prime Minister Neville Chamberlain who believed that by compromising with Hitler he could avoid a war. And, more recently, western powers were in error when they were reluctant to stand up to Vladimir Putin's wholly unjustified annexation of parts of Georgia and Ukraine's Crimea. Chamberlain's appeasement of Hitler only emboldened him in his expansionist Nazi ambitions. And the West's weakness in the face of Putin's predatory annexations only encouraged him to try and capture the whole of Ukraine as part of the expansion of Russia's empire.

In all the wars since World War II, when Nazi Germany, imperial Japan and fascist Italy were forced into unconditional surrender by the Allies, led by the United States, the Abel-type side has stopped short of total victory and the surrender of the enemy. The result has been that anti-providential Cain-type regimes have lived to renew their aggression once again. This is evident in the examples of wars that have been fought against the Communist regimes in China, Korea, Vietnam and Cambodia, and the Islamist regimes and movements in Iraq, Iran and Afghanistan. Without a conclusive victory for Abel, the Cain side recovers and starts its aggressive behavior once more.

In the case of Ukraine, for example, there is a very clear Cain-Abel contest underway. Tens of thousands of Ukrainians have lost their lives to Russian aggression, and millions have been made refugees. The suffering of the people is immense. The Christian conscience is outraged by this unjust violence against innocents, and thus the West (the US, EU, NATO and others) is rightly supporting Ukraine. However, it is most important that Russia is driven completely out of Ukraine before any negotiations for peace are entered into. Otherwise, if Russia is allowed to keep any part of Ukraine, Putin will calculate that he has succeeded, and he will seek future opportunities to continue his aggression.

Communist China is a similar threat. Foolish investors from Western and other nations have given China the wherewithal to develop its military, oppress its religious and ethnic minorities, and threaten the rest of the world, starting with Taiwan. It is up to Christian nations to stand with

Taiwan, Hong Kong and Tibet and other victims of this aggression. China must not be allowed to succeed.

Christian Discernment of Cain and Abel

A true measure of maturity in Christians is their ability to discern the differences between Cain and Abel, in their own lives as well as in national and international affairs. This is never easy because Cain always wraps his destructive agenda in virtuous language, a deception that has worked again and again. However, Jesus gave us a tool to use in recognizing the difference between those forces working for the providence and those working to destroy it:

> Beware of false prophets, who come to you in sheep's clothing but inwardly are ravenous wolves. You will know them by their fruits. Are grapes gathered from thorns, or figs from thistles? So, every sound tree bears good fruit, but the bad tree bears evil fruit. A sound tree cannot bear evil fruit, nor can a bad tree bear good fruit. Every tree that does not bear good fruit is cut down and thrown into the fire. Thus you will know them by their fruits. (Matthew 7:15-20)

As fallen men and women we all experience the forces of Cain and Abel operating within our own beings and in our relationships with others. And we certainly harvest the fruits of these forces as the bad or good outcomes from our thoughts and actions. After all, we live in a world of Cain and Abel individuals, ideas, movements, political parties, government policies and good and bad actors on the world stage. In all cases, the 'fruits' reveal the relative good or evil of the 'tree'. Christians should be the most discerning people in recognizing Cain and Abel, whether in themselves or within the world around them. Simply put, Abel is on the side of the providence while Cain is bent on destroying the providence.

Christians should also be able to recognize the difference between Cains within the providence and those bent on its destruction. Thus the Christian response to someone like Hitler, Stalin, the Chinese Communist Party and

Putin, should be different than its response to people of other faiths, and in particular members of other Christian sects and the two other monotheistic religions, Judaism and Islam.

In the next chapters we will provide a framework for making these distinctions. This is critical to the success of Christianity as the global Abel of the past two millennia and in the world today.

Chapter 29

Christianity and Judaism

Becoming An Abel-Type Younger Brother

The Crucifixion Resulted in the Destruction of Israel

As we have discussed, the Jewish establishment did not accept Jesus as the promised Messiah, despite the wisdom of his teachings and the remarkable spiritual power he exhibited when he drove out evil spirits to heal the sick. Israel's leaders saw him and his followers as a threat to the established faith and ecclesiastic hierarchy, and they actively sought to trip him up on points of law and its practice, so as to discredit him in the eyes of the people. Eventually they conspired with Judas to capture him while in the Garden of Gethsemane, tried him for blasphemy, and then persuaded Herod Antipas and Pilate to have him put to death.

Israel's leaders could not have foreseen the catastrophic consequences of these actions. In 70 AD the Roman emperor Titus destroyed Jerusalem and the Second Temple, much as the Babylonian King Nebuchadnezzar II had done six centuries earlier when he destroyed Jerusalem and the First Temple, built by Solomon.

On that previous occasion, the destruction of Jerusalem led to the exile of the Jews to Babylon. After 70 years in captivity, Cyrus the Great of Persia conquered Babylon and allowed the Jews to return to their homeland, which they did in stages. After the crucifixion of Jesus, however, the destruction of

Jerusalem and the Temple was accompanied by a two-millennia exile of the people of Israel from their homeland, in what is called the Great Diaspora.

During that long period, the Jews were scattered in foreign lands and Jerusalem became a place of memory and longing, a place of pilgrimage for the fortunate. Every year at the Passover Seder and Yom Kippur Jews express their longing for the homeland they lost with these words: "Next year in Jerusalem." Only after a modern Israel was established in 1948 were the Jews once more able to live freely in Jerusalem and worship at the ruins of the Second Temple.

Thus although traditional Jews do not accept that Jesus was the Messiah, his life would prove a turning point for their faith. Their rejection of Jesus meant that the 12 tribes were no longer central to the providence. Nevertheless, the Jews belong to a providential lineage and carry with them a unique legacy of blessings. Hence, even though they have suffered greatly over the many centuries of their Christian-era exile from their homeland, they have continued to make great contributions to the providence. These are manifest in what they have contributed to our legal systems, literature, art and science, all of which have been vital to the development of the Western civilization we enjoy today and to the preparations for the second advent of Christ.

The post-70 AD faith of the Jews has been shaped not by their status as the chosen people preparing for the Messiah, but rather by the need to preserve their scriptures and traditions in the face of persecution from many of the governments and populations where they have settled over the centuries.

Of particular note in this respect was the development of the 24-chapter Masoretic Text of the Hebrew Bible, or Tanakh. This work was the product of Jewish scholarship in the first several centuries after Jesus. Based on Hebrew and Aramaic documents, it is considered the most dependable record of the Divine Providence in what Christians call the Old Testament era. It served as the basis for the King James Version of the Bible, first published in 1611, and has been used thereafter for most of the translations used by Protestants, as well as Catholic texts to some extent.

Jewish Messianism Lives On

Perhaps the most important Jewish scholar of this exile period was the 12th century codifier of Torah law and Jewish philosophy, Rabbi Moshe ben Maimon (1138-1204), known as The Rambam or Maimonides. Born in Cordoba, Spain, he spent much of his life in Morocco and Egypt.

In the introduction to Chapter 10 (Perek Helek) of his *Mishnah Tractate Sanhedrin*, one of 14 books within the *Mishneh Torah* that Maimonides compiled between 1170 and 1180 AD as a summary of the oral law of the Jews, he sets out *Shloshah Asar Ikkarim*, that is the "Thirteen Fundamental Principles" of the Jewish faith:

1. Belief in the existence of a Creator and of providence
2. Belief in His unity
3. Belief in His incorporeality
4. Belief in His eternity
5. Belief that worship is due to Him alone
6. Belief that God communicates with man through prophecy
7. Belief that Moses was the greatest of all the prophets
8. Belief in the revelation of the Torah to Moses at Sinai
9. Belief in the unchangeable nature of the revealed Law
10. Belief that God is omniscient
11. Belief in divine reward & retribution in this world and the hereafter
12. Belief in the coming of the Messiah
13. Belief in the resurrection of the dead

Another translation of the 12th principle of this creed reads: "The belief in the arrival of the Messiah and the messianic era." In the introduction, Maimonides looks forward to the advent of the Messiah and the return of the Jews to Israel:

> The "days of the Messiah" refers to a time in which sovereignty will revert to Israel and the Jewish people will return to the land of Israel. Their king will be a very great one,

with his royal palace in Zion. His name and his reputation will extend throughout all the nations, with even greater measure than did King Solomon's. All nations will make peace with him, and all countries will serve him out of respect for his great righteousness and the wonders which occur through him. All those who rise against him will be destroyed and delivered into his hands by God. All the verses of the Bible testify to his triumph and our triumph with him. However, except for the fact that sovereignty will revert to Israel, nothing will be essentially different from what it is now.[1]

This anticipation for the Messiah is almost identical to that of the Jews before Jesus lived among them. Inevitably, then, in the centuries since the time of Jesus there have been many Jews who were called Messiah by their followers, or who claimed to be the Messiah. Some were obscure, such as the 12th Century Yemeni Messiah written about by Maimonides. Others were quite famous, such as 17th Century Sabbatai Zevi, who was born in Smyrna, claimed to be the Messiah, and eventually converted to Islam. He has followers to this day.

Perhaps the most important was the last Rebbe of the Lubavitcher Hasidic dynasty, Menachem Mendel Schneerson, who lived in the 20th Century (1902-1994) and was believed by many of his followers to be the Messiah. Some of them believe that he did not actually die in 1994 and will reveal himself to be the Messiah. The Chabad movement he led has grown greatly, establishing over 3,600 synagogues and centers which provide religious, social and educational services around the world. His teachings fill 200 volumes and his followers number in the hundreds of thousands.

A Bitter Relationship With Christianity

It is not difficult to understand why most Jews rejected Jesus as the Messiah

---

[1]. Rabbi Moshe ben Maimon. 1180 AD. Introduction to Chapter 10 (Perek Helek) of *Mishnah Tractate Sanhedrin*, one of 14 books within the *Mishneh Torah*. Maimonides Heritage Center.

when he was in their midst. After all, even the parents of Jesus—as well as the parents of his family member John the Baptist—clearly found it difficult to reconcile the reality of Jesus as the unknown son of a poor carpenter with the common expectation in Israel that the Messiah would be a mighty king who would inherit the throne of King David, as foretold by Isaiah and other prophetic figures of the Old Testament. To overcome this natural doubt, all Jesus' key relatives had received messages confirming Jesus as the chosen one expected by Israel. But they apparently never truly believed the messages they had received.

Maimonides and other Jewish scholars of the Christian era have not helped the Jewish people understand Jesus. They have simply reinforced the error of the Jews at the time of Jesus by continuing in the belief that Jesus was not the Messiah, and that the Messiah was yet to come as a great king at some time in the future. This total ignoring of Jesus as a Jew of immense historical and providential importance has, of course, not gone down well with Christians, who are frustrated that the Jews continue to deny the messiahship of Jesus.

This frustration has often boiled over into outright hatred and persecution of the Jews by Christians, who have blamed the Jews for the death of Jesus. This attitude of blame and accusation of the Jews is inconsistent with the mission of Christians, who should view Jews as their elder brothers who therefore deserve respect and love. Thus the history of Christian-Jewish relations is littered with pogroms and even genocide.

For example, some of the Crusades targeted Jewish diaspora communities on their way to and from the Holy Land, where their object was to liberate the holy sites from Muslim control. In Spain, a large Jewish diaspora community faced frequent persecution from its Catholic rulers. Some of these Jews converted to Christianity to avoid this persecution, but this community of 'Converso' ex-Jews was suspected of faking its newly-professed faith and its members became prime targets of the Inquisition of the Catholic Church when it was launched in 1478.

In 1492 the Catholic monarchs of Spain issued the Alhambra Decree that expelled all the Jews from Spain. Many fled to the Ottoman Empire, thanks to the welcome extended to them by Sultan Bayezid II, but others settled in Jewish 'ghettos' in various European countries.

The greatest of all attacks on the Jews came from Hitler's Nazi Germany, which relentlessly pursued Jewish communities in all the lands it conquered, from Europe and Russia to North Africa. The death of some six million Jews at the hands of the Nazis represents an unprecedented religio-ethnic genocide.

Today there are some 15 million Jews in the world, with most living in Israel and the United States. These Jews are both descendants of the 12 tribes as well as converts to the faith. Their relatively small number compared with other major faith communities is compensated for by their outsize role in academia, science, medicine, education, finance and media.

Christianity's Elder Brother in the Providence

What should Christianity's relationship to the Jews be? As we suggested above, as heirs and participants in the salvific mission of Jesus, Christians should remember the words of Jesus to the Jews on the cross: "Father, forgive them; for they know not what they do." (Luke 23:34). Jesus did not end his life by indulging a bitter hatred for those who had rejected him and sent him to his death. That would have been the response of Cain. Rather, he adopted an Abel-type attitude towards his enemies, embracing them with a fatherly spirit of forgiveness and reconciliation which became the basis for their future salvation. Christians should emulate this Abel-type attitude towards the Jews, their elder brothers and sisters in the providence.

Thus, as always, Abel's role is to help his elder brother Cain become free from evil influences, so that both brothers together can be united in serving the Divine Providence. It is Cain who resorts to evil and murder to get his way; Abel, by contrast, has to work sacrificially to defeat evil and liberate Cain.

This is not to excuse the crucifixion of Jesus, but rather to limit its harmful impact on the providence by finding the best way to mend the damage done by that great sin. Practically speaking, it is the forgiving heart of Abel that is most likely to be accepted by Cain, who must be encouraged to recognize his failings and make amends for them. In this way, Cain and Abel can be reconciled as children of God.

Chapter 30

Christianity and Islam

Becoming An Abel-Type Older Brother

Christianity emerged from Judaism and therefore Christians know about the millennia of providential preparation for Jesus through Jewish scriptures contained within what Christians call the Old Testament of the Bible. This providential history is all about the protracted process through which God established a nation chosen to receive the Messiah, a history in which the descendants of Jacob played a central role. Hence even though the leaders of Israel rejected and killed Jesus, the Jewish people will always have a special place in the Divine Providence, a place that Christians can and should recognize and honor. As we suggested in the previous chapter, Christians can best view the Jewish people as older brothers and sisters deserving of respect and love.

Islam is another matter. It appeared in the Arabian Peninsula some six centuries after the death of Jesus. It is a religion based on a series of revelations received from Gabriel by a prophet called Mohammed, who was born and raised in Mecca but who would establish the first independent Muslim community in Medina, some 211 miles north of Mecca. These revelations are assembled in the 114 chapters, or suras, of the Quran (can be pronounced Koran). Many of the Old Testament figures appear in these scriptures, but the suras are organized by size (largest to smallest) and the chronology found in the Bible is missing in the Quran.

What are Christians to make of this younger faith? In this chapter we will discuss that issue by looking at Islam as a religion with a providential purpose that originated in the family of Abraham, making it the youngest of the Abrahamic faiths. We will suggest that this providential history that Muslims share with the Jews and Christians must be recognized by Christians if they are to fulfill their role as Abel-type older brothers and sisters to Muslims and work with Muslims for the providential preparations for the second coming of Christ.

The Root of Conflicts Among the Abrahamic Faiths

Christians have plenty of reasons to hold resentments against Muslims, from a history of persecution of Christians by Muslim-majority states to the more recent murderous predations of Islamic terrorists against innocent Christians, based on nothing more than their religion. The Jews have a similar history of persecution by Muslims, a history that has poisoned Muslim-Jewish relations.

But then Muslims will rightly point out that religious persecution has not been in just one direction. From the time of the Crusades, Muslims have experienced the sharp edge of Christian vengeance and they have legitimate claims to being treated badly in some Christian-majority countries and Israel.

The solution to conflicts is not to apportion blame, but to understand the causes of conflicts as the basis for taking remedial action to resolve them. In no arena is this more important than in matters of faith, and in no matters of inter-religious conflict is this more important than in the relationships among Jews, Christians and Muslims.

It is our contention that for the members of these three monotheistic faiths the key to understanding the roots of their conflicts lies in understanding the family of Abraham. Furthermore, we believe that the teachings of Jesus provide Christians with a framework for understanding and resolving the conflicts that originated in the family of Abraham.

Of particular importance for this chapter is to understand the root of

Muslim resentment and antipathy towards Jews and Christians as a basis for understanding what Christians can do to resolve these historical hatreds and conflicts.

The Bitter Experience of Hagar and Ishmael

For Christians, the story of Abraham explains the providential history that originated with his family, and led, via his son Isaac and grandson Jacob to the establishment of Israel as the nation chosen to receive the Messiah. But there is another history that emerged from Abraham's family that is little known but which lies at the heart of the conflicts among Jews, Christians and Muslims.

When Sarah had reached her late 70s and had not yet been able to conceive, she offered her Egyptian maid, Hagar, to Abraham as a wife, so that his lineage would be preserved. When Hagar was pregnant she unwisely mocked Sarah for being barren, making her mistress regret having ever given her to Abraham. Sarah insisted that Abraham send Hagar away, which he did. But an angel met Hagar and persuaded her to return to Abraham's home and submit to Sarah:

> The angel of the Lord said to her, "Return to your mistress, and submit to her." The angel of the Lord also said to her, "I will so greatly multiply your descendants that they cannot be numbered for multitude." And the angel of the Lord said to her, "Behold, you are with child, and shall bear a son; you shall call his name Ishmael; because the Lord has given heed to your affliction." (Genesis 16:9-11)

However, 13 years later Abraham was told that Sarah would miraculously be able to conceive and have a child of her own:

> And God said to Abraham, "As for Sarai your wife, you shall not call her name Sarai, but Sarah shall be her name. I will bless her, and moreover I will give you a son by her; I will bless her, and she shall be a mother of nations; kings of peoples shall come from her." (Genesis 17:15-16)

Abraham was initially incredulous, and began to laugh at what seemed impossible:

> Then Abraham fell on his face and laughed, and said to himself, "Shall a child be born to a man who is a hundred years old? Shall Sarah, who is ninety years old, bear a child?" And Abraham said to God, "O that Ishmael might live in thy sight!" (Genesis 17:17-18)

In response, God confirmed that it was Isaac who would receive the main providential blessing, but that Ishmael would nevertheless be blessed as well:

> God said, "No, but Sarah your wife shall bear you a son, and you shall call his name Isaac. I will establish my covenant with him as an everlasting covenant for his descendants after him. As for Ishmael, I have heard you; behold, I will bless him and make him fruitful and multiply him exceedingly; he shall be the father of twelve princes, and I will make him a great nation. But I will establish my covenant with Isaac, whom Sarah shall bear to you at this season next year." (Genesis 17:19-21)

As the second son of Abraham, Isaac was in the Abel position to Ishmael. From a providential point of view, Abraham and Sarah should have done whatever they could to raise Ishmael and Isaac as loving brothers who could both contribute to the providence. And since Isaac had received the greater blessing, it was he who on becoming mature should have initiated a loving relationship with his older brother.

But this did not happen. The Bible recounts the boys playing together, but this only aroused resentment in Sarah, who was determined that Ishmael not share in the blessings promised to Isaac. She insisted that Hagar and Ishmael be sent away. Abraham was told to accept this, and comforted by the promise that Ishmael too would be blessed:

> But Sarah saw the son of Hagar the Egyptian, whom she had borne to Abraham, playing with her son Isaac. So she said to

> Abraham, "Cast out this slave woman with her son; for the son of this slave woman shall not be heir with my son Isaac." And the thing was very displeasing to Abraham on account of his son. But God said to Abraham, "Be not displeased because of the lad and because of your slave woman; whatever Sarah says to you, do as she tells you, for through Isaac shall your descendants be named. And I will make a nation of the son of the slave woman also, because he is your offspring." (Genesis 21:9-13)

Hagar understandably had feelings of resentment towards Sarah over this rejection of Ishmael and their banishment, since it was Sarah who had suggested to Abraham that he have a child with Hagar in the first place. When Sarah had her sent away the first time, Hagar was obedient to the angel and returned to submit to Sarah. But now Sarah was having her sent away again.

After the second expulsion of Hagar from Abraham's home, mother and son wandered in the wilderness, unable to find water. Ishmael was on the verge of death when his cries were heard by God who sent an angel to comfort Hagar and show her where to find water:

> When the water in the skin was gone, she cast the child under one of the bushes. Then she went, and sat down over against him a good way off, about the distance of a bowshot; for she said, "Let me not look upon the death of the child." And as she sat over against him, the child lifted up his voice and wept. And God heard the voice of the lad; and the angel of God called to Hagar from heaven, and said to her, "What troubles you, Hagar? Fear not; for God has heard the voice of the lad where he is. Arise, lift up the lad, and hold him fast with your hand; for I will make him a great nation." Then God opened her eyes, and she saw a well of water; and she went, and filled the skin with water, and gave the lad a drink. (Genesis 21:15-19)

Hagar's resentment and bitterness towards Sarah was sharpened by her child's close encounter with death as a result of Sarah's rejection, and these hostile sentiments were naturally inherited by her son Ishmael, despite the blessings that he would receive later on. They are the root cause of the antipathy of Ishmaelites towards the people of Israel and of Muslims towards both Jews and Christians.

The Resentment of Hagar and Ishmael Burns in Muslims

There is a natural feeling of resentment that burns in the heart and mind of someone who loses a position of privilege, especially if that person is not responsible for the loss. In the providence, this bitterness is experienced by a person who loses the benefits and blessings that come with the position of elder son.

This is what happened to Hagar and Ishmael, who lost their privileged position at the center of the providence to Sarah and Isaac. Ishmael was relegated to the position of Cain in relation to Isaac, and subjected to all the challenges Cain had faced as the son most burdened with fallen nature. Ishmael had to submit to Isaac to reverse Cain's murder of Abel, but because of Sarah's hostility towards him and his mother this became extremely difficult to do.

In the family of Abraham, then, it was the deep antipathy of Hagar towards Sarah and Isaac that became the root of the bitter feelings harbored by Ishmael and his descendants towards the Jews.

A similar Cain-Abel split also occurred between the twin grandsons of Abraham, Esau and Jacob. As the younger, Jacob was blessed and his 12 sons became the 12 tribes of the chosen nation of Israel. Jacob did win over Esau with love, but inevitably Esau harbored resentments towards Jacob over his loss of the birthright and blessing. (Only an absolute Abel can completely resolve the resentments of Cain.)

There is nothing in the history of Israel that indicates the Jews ever made the effort to embrace their Abrahamic brethren on the Cain side of the family—the Ishmaelites and Edomites. Hence it was one aspect of the Messiah's mission to address and resolve this inherited resentment once and for all.

There is also no evidence that upon the death of Jesus—when Christianity inherited the central mission of Judaism in the providence—that members of the new faith had any awareness of the ingrained resentment of the Ishmaelites and Edomites towards the Jews that they now had to deal with themselves.

And when Islam arose in Arabia several centuries later to fulfill God's promise to Hagar that her son would be blessed, Christians had no awareness of its hostile roots, let alone of their responsibility to find a providential solution to a centuries-old history of Cain-type resentment and bitterness.

Christians Are Tasked With Saving All People

There are no passages in the Gospels that anticipate a new religion emerging after Jesus. For the Jews to whom Jesus addressed his teachings, the world was divided into two groups of people: the Jews (the chosen of God) and all other people, the Gentiles. When—after his crucifixion—Jesus appeared to his disciples in spirit, he instructed them to include all people in their evangelical work, thereby breaking down this division:

> And Jesus came and said to them, "All authority in heaven and on earth has been given to me. Go therefore and make disciples of all nations, baptizing them in the name of the Father and of the Son and of the Holy Spirit, teaching them to observe all that I have commanded you; and lo, I am with you always, to the close of the age." (Matthew 28:18-20)

This instruction of Jesus to his disciples confirmed the expansion of the providence from its initial focus on members of the 12 tribes of Israel, to include people of all faiths, and no faith! As we have shown, both Peter and Paul were given signs to confirm that the followers of Christ should minister to Gentiles as well as Jews. As Paul made clear:

> Now before faith came, we were confined under the law, kept under restraint until faith should be revealed. So that the law was our custodian until Christ came, that we might be justified by faith. But now that faith has come, we are no longer under

> a custodian; for in Christ Jesus you are all sons of God, through faith. For as many of you as were baptized into Christ have put on Christ. There is neither Jew nor Greek, there is neither slave nor free, there is neither male nor female; for you are all one in Christ Jesus. And if you are Christ's, then you are Abraham's offspring, heirs according to promise. (Galatians 3:23-29)

The inclusion of Gentiles among those to be evangelized was in itself a hugely challenging matter for Jesus' disciples, which required the resolute leadership of Peter and Paul to be carried out successfully. Even so, there were inevitably tensions between Jewish and Gentile converts to the new faith. For one, Jews were distinguished from Gentiles through circumcision, and many early Jewish followers of Christ considered circumcision a necessary condition for membership in the new faith. Paul made it clear that this was not the case:

> For in Christ Jesus neither circumcision nor uncircumcision is of any avail, but faith working through love. (Galatians 5:6)

Christianity Inherited the Mission to Love Ishmael and Esau

As Christianity spread through Asia, Africa and Europe, the novelty of non-Jews being full participants in the new faith wore off as Jews became an ever-shrinking minority of the believers. This was the status of the faith when, in 380 AD, Eastern Roman Emperor Theodosius I made Christianity the state religion of the empire, replacing paganism.

This was in partial fulfillment of the original purpose of the Messiah, who was to have led Israel in winning over the Roman Empire for the Divine Providence. By adopting the Christian faith, Rome compensated for its role in killing Jesus, and by helping spread the new religion worldwide in subsequent centuries it fulfilled its original purpose as a champion of Christ.

If Jesus had been accepted as the Messiah by the chosen people of Israel, his first outreach beyond the 12 tribes would naturally have been to the Cain side of Abraham's family, the descendants of Ishmael and Esau. As we have pointed out, these were both represented in the Herodian dynasty. Through his love and care for them, the resentment of Hagar and Ishmael for being cast out of Abraham's family, and of Esau for having had the birthright and blessing taken from him by Jacob, could have been resolved, once and for all.

Thus for Jesus as global Abel, winning over the Herodians was the first step beyond his mission to the Jews. Through the Herodians he would then have worked to win over Rome, and through Rome the rest of the world. None of this was possible, of course, because Jesus was stopped at the first level by the Jewish leadership.

By inheriting the mission of Jesus, Christianity also inherited the responsibility of first winning over the Israelites to the new providence, and then to do the same for the Ishmaelites and Edomites. Christianity did make some inroads among the tribes descended from Ishmael and Esau, including the Arabs, but after four centuries most of these tribespeople were still pagans who practiced idolatry. The time had come for God to fulfill his original promise to Hagar and Ishmael.

The Unexpected Advent of Islam

As we noted above, there were no scriptures to help Christians respond to the advent of Islam as a major new monotheistic religion that emerged from Arabia in the 7th century AD. Thus to this day Christians have generally held Islam in low esteem, judging it to be an inauthentic religion based on scriptures that distort the Biblical record.

This out-of-hand rejection of the beliefs of some 1.9 billion Muslims is perhaps understandable if you believe that Islam itself will simply disappear from the face of the earth when Christ returns, but it is hardly the appropriate attitude for members of the religion tasked with serving as global Abel. On the contrary, the mission of Christianity makes it incumbent upon its members to understand Islam and Muslims, and to find a way to work with them to prepare the world for the second coming of Christ, and to oppose and defeat the forces that stand in the way of that providence, especially the atheistic ideologies of Marxism and its offshoots.

A Brief History of Mohammed and Islam

A brief overview of the prophet Mohammed and the birth of Islam is in order here. Mohammed was born in Mecca, in 570 AD. In 610 he began receiving revelations from the angel Gabriel regarding the evils of the paganism of Mecca, and he began a ministry to teach the Meccans about the one true God, whom he called Allah.

His was a radical message and he was not welcomed by the people of Mecca, who made him and his early followers the target of persecution. After some 12 years of facing opposition in Mecca, Mohammed accepted an invitation from the tribes of the nearby city of Yathrib (later renamed Medina) to become their leader, and moved to that town with his most loyal disciples in what is called the *hijra*, or migration. Thus 622 AD marks the first year of the Islamic era, which follows a Lunar calendar.

In the city of Medina (meaning city), Mohammed and his followers left behind their Meccan status as a persecuted minority and became the rulers of a largely pagan Arab town that was also home to three Jewish tribes. It was in Medina, then, that the new religion began to take shape as a ruling belief system that governed the day-to-day behavior and religious practices of the Muslims. It was during this period that Mohammed received many revelations regarding the proper practice of the faith, as well as the proper behavior for men and women in establishing families and in behaving appropriately in the wider society, in matters of ownership and inheritance, and in matters of conflict within the community and in dealing with enemies.

The word Islam means "submission to God" and a Muslim therefore is someone who submits to the authority and will of God. The new faith was based on 'five pillars of Islam', namely: 1. Belief in the One God and God's messenger, Mohammed; 2. Saying prayers five times a day; 3. Fasting for the Lunar month of Ramadan; 4. Performing a pilgrimage to Mecca once in your life; and 5. Tithing one fortieth of your wealth in support of the needy. These essential practices of Islam became the spiritual foundation for life in Medina and have remained the basic elements of Muslim faith ever since.

The Muslims of Medina would be challenged three times by the fighting men of the Meccan tribes, and prevailed in all three battles. After these successes, the Muslims attacked and subdued Mecca itself, in 630 AD. The new religion would go on to dominate the tribespeople of Arabia, and from Arabia it would spread rapidly to the north and east into the territories of the Byzantine Empire and Persia, and west to Egypt and the rest of North Africa, eventually reaching Spain.

However, Mohammed himself would die in 632, and the leadership of the Muslims would pass first to his disciple Abu Bakr, and then to three other so-called Orthodox Caliphs: Umar, Uthman and Ali. The term caliph means successor to Mohammed as leader of all Muslims, as well as vice-regent of God on earth.

Not surprisingly, the Caliphate was a contested position. After the four original caliphs succeeded Mohammed, the Caliphate moved from Medina to Damascus and then to Baghdad and Cairo. Its last move was from Cairo to Constantinople (later Istanbul) in 1517, where it helped to sustain the Ottoman Empire. In 1923 the secular Turkish Republic was established by Ataturk, and in 1924 the Caliphate was abolished. (In recent times, the Islamic State has claimed that it has reestablished the Caliphate, although it represents only a tiny percentage of the world's Muslims.)

It was under the third caliph, Uthman, that the teachings of Mohammed were first organized into a single book of scriptures, the Quran. The Arabic originals of these texts are the absolute authority accepted by all Muslims. Another set of texts, called the *hadith*, include accounts of things Mohammed said and did that provide guidance for Muslims. These records of the prophet's life and words, or *sunnah*, do not enjoy the standing of the Quran because they are subject to invention. Essentially, they were compiled from oral accounts passed from one to another in what is called an *isnad*. The most widely accepted collection of *hadith* is that of Bukhari, who is quoted widely by *imams* and other religious leaders seeking to explain a Muslim's life of faith based on the words Mohammed spoke to his disciples and the religious traditions that he established.

Despite the universal acceptance of the Quran as the ultimate authority for their faith, there was a division that developed early among Muslims regarding the rightful heir of Mohammed, a division that has lasted to the present day. A faction believed that Ali, the fourth Orthodox Caliph and a son-in-law of Mohammed, was the true heir of Mohammed, and that he lost that inheritance wrongfully when he was assassinated in 661 by supporters of the faction that would establish the Umayyad Caliphate upon his death.

Ali's followers would recognize him as the first imam of Shia Islam, a minority sect that broke away from the majority Sunni Islam of the Umayyads. (Sunnis take their name from the *sunnah* of Mohammed.) Today Shia Islam is still a minority sect, accounting for 10-13 percent of all Muslims. Shia Muslims are concentrated in Iran and found in proportionately large numbers in Bahrain, Iraq, Lebanon and Yemen.

Islam and the Bible

Importantly, the Quran recognizes the authenticity of the Bible and therefore describes Jews and Christians as "people of the Book", meaning fellow believers in God. (In several passages, however, the Quran complains that Jews and Christians changed the original texts of the Bible.) Jesus himself is described in the Quran as a prophet, and his name appears more often than any of the Old Testament prophets. The Quran rejects any association of Jesus with God, considering the association of any person with God to be blasphemous.

It also holds that it was not Jesus who was crucified, but someone with his likeness. It uses the Arabic word for Messiah, *messih*, to describe him, although he is considered another prophet, not a unique savior of humanity from original sin. (Islam does not believe we inherit original sin.) The recognition of Jesus as a man of great providential importance is found in passages like this:

> And We sent, following in their footsteps, Jesus son of Mary, confirming the Torah before him, and We gave to him the Gospel, wherein is guidance and light and confirming the Torah before it, as a guidance and admonition unto the Godfearing. (Quran 5:46)

Since Mohammed lived six centuries after Jesus, Muslims generally hold that their faith contains the latest revelations from God and therefore is superior. The point we are making in this book is that the relationship among the various faiths should not be seen as competitive, but rather as related to their varied roles within the Divine Providence.

The Abrahamic Faiths Must Unite as Abel to the World

As we have shown, the central providence developed through the children of Abraham. These children now follow three major divisions within the monotheistic tradition: Judaism, Christianity and Islam. These three share a common purpose, the purpose of all religions, but also a particular providential destiny to lead the world as Abel-type exemplars of Divine purpose.

Jesus is in many ways the meeting and dividing point among them, as each has a view as to who he was and what his purpose was. For example, Jews believe that Jesus was not the Messiah they long awaited, whereas Christians believe he was. Muslims use the term *messih* for Jesus, but they do not share the belief of Judaism and Christianity that a savior Messiah is needed to liberate us from our sinfulness. Muslims and Christians both believe that Mary's conception of Jesus was miraculous. Jews do not acknowledge this or any other providential marker for Jesus. Muslims and Jews believe the Messiah to be a man, not God. Many Christians believe that Jesus was God.

These and many other differences in belief are not insignificant, but they should not be allowed to stand in the way of building an authentic brotherhood among the three faiths. And although Jews and Muslims do not accept the messianic identity of Jesus, his teachings clearly give Christians guidance as to the loving parental heart they need to embrace their sibling faiths without Jews and Muslims having first to accept Jesus as their savior.

After all, it is not that members of the Abrahamic faiths must agree on a common theology—which anyway is not possible, given the unique nature of individuals and individual faith—but rather that they must learn to respect one another as members of the family of Abraham who share a common heritage, destiny and purpose. They must reject voices of division and incitement to conflict and learn to overcome the mutual resentments and hostilities that have been bred over the centuries of bad faith and conflict that their religious ancestors indulged in by not knowing any better.

It is from this perspective that we can recognize the damage caused by Cain-type people and ideas in the past, especially in the ways they have stirred up conflicts among people of different faiths. We must avoid these mistakes if we are to fulfill our providential purpose as members of the Abrahamic faiths.

In other words, to build harmony among the three great monotheistic religions we must recognize and reject the resentment, accusation and murderous behavior of Cain. Instead, we must learn to practice the patient, forgiving and self-sacrificing way of Abel. This is the challenge facing Christianity in its relationship with its younger brother Islam, as it is in its relationship with its older brother Judaism.

The Shared Responsibility of the Abrahamic Faiths

The obligation of Christians naturally implies a related obligation for Jews and Muslims, who must overcome their own limitations to embrace Christians. After all, the Abrahamic faiths share a collective responsibility to use the blessings they have received to serve as Abel to the rest of the world, including people of other faiths.

The providential will is unchanging. It was established through a Divine covenant made with Abraham for all his descendants. It therefore embraces all the members of the Abrahamic faiths for all time. As the great prophet Isaiah said of God's determination to see the providence through to the end:

> The Lord of hosts has sworn: "As I have planned, so shall it be, and as I have purposed, so shall it stand… This is the purpose that is purposed concerning the whole earth; and this is the hand that is stretched out over all the nations." For the Lord of hosts has purposed, and who will annul it? His hand is stretched out, and who will turn it back? (Isaiah 14:24, 26-27)

God is absolute and therefore the Divine purpose is absolute. However, it is the responsibility of each one of us as individuals to understand that unchanging purpose and unite with it if we are to be included in the blessings of the providence. And it is the mission of Christianity as global Abel to lead its sibling Abrahamic faiths in educating all believers in how to fulfill the providential responsibility that is incumbent upon all who would share in the blessings promised by God in this covenant made with Abraham:

> When Abram was ninety-nine years old the Lord appeared to Abram, and said to him, "I am God Almighty; walk before me, and be blameless. And I will make my covenant between me and you, and will multiply you exceedingly." Then Abram fell on his face; and God said to him, "Behold, my covenant is with you, and you shall be the father of a multitude of nations. No longer shall your name be Abram, but your name shall be Abraham; for I have made you the father of a multitude of nations. I will make you exceedingly fruitful; and I will make nations of you, and kings shall come forth from you. And I will establish my covenant between me and you and your descendants after you throughout their generations for an everlasting covenant, to be God to you and to your descendants after you." (Genesis 17:1-7)

Chapter 31

Christianity and Marxism

Becoming a Resolute Abel to Defeat Cain

The Importance of Understanding Marxism

Despite the inspiring teaching of Jesus, his matchless life of devotion to God and his sacrificial service to humanity, Christianity has not succeeded in creating an environment conducive to the return of Christ and the establishment of the promised Kingdom of Heaven on earth. Indeed, while much good has been done in societies where Christianity is the prevailing faith, a large number of people living in these societies around the world continue to suffer from social and economic inequities. This is not due to a lack of foundational values, but rather to the inability of Christians to live up to their own highest ideals.

This disparity between the words and deeds of Christians inevitably opened the door not only to rival religious ideas and movements, as in the rise of Islam discussed earlier. But, most importantly, it opened the door to the outright rejection of religion itself and the rise of materialism and atheistic movements.

The most significant of the atheistic, anti-religion movements is Marxism, the ideology which grew out of the personal distaste for religion of Karl Marx, a German philosopher of the 19th century. He was born of Jewish ancestry but grew up in the household of a father who had converted to Protestantism to be able to advance his career as a lawyer. Marx would team up with another German disenchanted with religion, Friedrich Engels, and together they devoted their lives to the destruction of religion and the society it had produced.

In this chapter we will examine some of the salient features of Marxism that make it a mortal enemy to all people of faith. And we will explain why Christians should play a leading role in combating Marxism. Unlike Islam, which requires of Christians an Abel-type approach to a fellow Abrahamic faith, Marxism embodies the evils of an unrepentant Cain who is bent on destroying Abel. Christians must not allow Marxism to succeed. They must expose, confront and defeat it.

Marxism is the perfection of Cain-type ideology, meaning it is the ultimate tool of Satan in his campaign to destroy the providence. As such it is based on falsehood upon falsehood and therefore very difficult to comprehend and laborious to study. Hence the reader may well find the material in this chapter unpleasant because it deals directly with the evil of Marxism.

The Bloody French Revolution

The French Revolution began in 1789 and shook France to its roots over a decade of violent conflict. It unleashed the destructive forces of a Cain-type animus for the church and ruling elites. The leading protagonists of this violence were the Jacobins, led by Maximilien Robespierre. Their campaign against the French establishment reached its climax in the Reign of Terror, which saw thousands guillotined and many thousands thrown into prison.

The monarchy and aristocracy were abolished. King Louis XVI and his wife Marie-Antoinette were executed, as were many members of France's nobility and clergy. Even Robespierre himself would eventually be executed.

With its blood-lust and brutality, the French Revolution would foreshadow Fascist, Socialist and Communist regimes that sprang up in the 20th century. But it lacked a truly revolutionary ideology to unify and focus its diverse participants, although Jean-Jacques Rousseau's theory of a General Will and all-powerful state was a major influence on Robespierre. The revolution came to an end when Napoleon took power in 1799 and redirected the revolution's energy towards building up the power and prestige of France.

Marxism Destroys Religion and Throttles Faith

If you were to take the central precepts of most religious teachings—and certainly those of the Abrahamic traditions—and invert them, you would come up with Marxist doctrines. The materialist theories of Marx and Engels about human nature and the evolution of the natural world and human society are diametrically opposite to those provided by religion.

The root of Christian belief is that the world was made in the image of a loving Creator, who at the dawn of human existence blessed the first man and woman to enjoy a life of love and joy in an idyllic world:

> And God blessed them, and God said to them, "Be fruitful and multiply, and fill the earth and subdue it; and have dominion over the fish of the sea and over the birds of the air and over every living thing that moves upon the earth." (Genesis 1:28)

These three blessings can be understood to mean becoming fruitful, or mature, through a relationship with the Creator, practicing God's love in the human relationships of family and society; and exercising wise and loving stewardship over nature.

Marx believed this religious worldview to be a myth that was the product of minds looking for an explanation for human existence that would explain away the unpleasant realities of the world and free them from the need to address social ills. Marx expressed his disdain for religion in these famous words:

> Religion is the sigh of the oppressed creature, the heart of a heartless world, and the soul of soulless conditions. It is the opium of the people.[1]

---

1. Marx, Karl. [1843] 1970. "Introduction." A Contribution to the Critique of Hegel's Philosophy of Right, translated by A. Jolin and J. O'Malley, edited by J.

And in the *Manifesto of the Communist Party*, Marx and Engels scoffed at the criticism of their theories from a religious or philosophical standpoint, declaring that their own views were above reproach:

> The charges against Communism made from a religious, a philosophical, and, generally, from an ideological standpoint are not deserving of serious examination.[2]

Vladimir Lenin added his own sharp criticism of religion:

> Religion is the opium of the people: this saying of Marx is the cornerstone of the entire ideology of Marxism about religion. All modern religions and churches, all and every kind of religious organizations are always considered by Marxism as the organs of bourgeois reaction, used for the protection of the exploitation and the stupefaction of the working class.[3]

Thus the Marxist world is without a Creator and source of absolute, unchanging principles and values, and therefore without any moral absolutes. Marx and Engels believed that human beings are governed by mutable natural laws that are shaped by the means of production through which their societies are structured. Changes in these economic arrangements necessitate changes in socio-political structures and values. (This is the core concept of their economic determinism.)

Marxism is the Perfection of Anti-Christ Ideology

Jesus warned his disciples not to be deceived by antichrists:

> Children, it is the last hour; and as you have heard that antichrist is coming, so now many antichrists have come; therefore we know that it is the last hour. (1 John 2:18)

O'Malley. Cambridge University Press. - via Marxists.org.

2. Karl Marx and Friedrich Engels. 1848. The Manifesto of the Communist Party.

3. V.I. Lenin. 1973. The Attitude of the Workers' Party to Religion, Lenin Collected Works, Progress Publishers, Vol. 15, pp402-413.

Antichrist is all that opposes Christ, and antichrists are those who deny God and Christ:

> Who is the liar but he who denies that Jesus is the Christ? This is the antichrist, he who denies the Father and the Son. (1 John 2:22)

Marxism and Neo-Marxism both deny "the Father and the Son." Indeed, they see religions and the institutions built on faith as the enemies of the atheistic revolutions they espouse, as we explained in the previous section.

The Marxist promises to create a Utopian world that will be just and equitable are nothing more than lies, as was Lucifer's lie when he seduced Eve into disobeying God by telling her she would become God-like if she ate the fruit of the Tree of the Knowledge of Good and Evil. As with all Cain-type deceptions that precede the appearance of Abel-type people and movements, the Marxist promises can never be fulfilled because they are based on falsehoods.

The role of Marxism is, however, especially dangerous. It embodies Cain-type thinking with its hatred for God more fully than any other theory or movement. It has arisen to offer a false alternative to the Kingdom of Heaven that is the end point of the Divine Providence. As such, it represents the perfection of anti-God and anti-Christ thinking and action.

We can recognize Marxism's Cain-type nature when we consider that the lustful, deceptive and spiritually lethal behavior of Lucifer was passed through Adam and Eve to Cain, who inherited an envious, resentful and murderous character. Thus Cain-type people and entities have spread evil throughout the world from the dawn of our existence. The special contribution of Marx and his followers has been to translate their own Cain-type thinking and resentments into an atheistic ideology that perfectly embodies the deceptive and murderous nature of Satan.

History has provided ample proof of the Marxist lie. Whenever the theory has been practiced, religious and social institutions, especially traditional families, have been destroyed through false accusation, subversion and violence, and bloody revolutions have produced tyrannies. In other words, the Marxists and Neo-Marxists have always created Satanic imitations of heaven in the form of hellish movements and totalitarian regimes.

Marxism is Anti-Science

When Darwin's *The Origin of Species* was published 1859, a decade after the *Manifesto*, Marx and Engels believed that Darwin's theory of what Herbert Spencer would call "survival of the fittest" provided scientific confirmation for their theory of dialectical materialism. In a 1860 letter to Engels, Marx wrote that Darwin's book proves "the basis in natural history for our view."[4] And in an 1860 letter to activist Ferdinand Lassalle, he elaborated: "Darwin's work is most important and suits my purpose in that it provides a basis in natural science for the historical class struggle."[5]

Marx and Engels knew the importance of science in the modern world, and made every effort to give a scientific veneer to their work, calling their theories 'scientific socialism'. However, neither was an actual scientist who conducted field research or allowed rigorous scientific analysis of their work. As Paul Johnson points out in his excellent book *Intellectuals*:

> [Marx] was not interested in finding the truth but in proclaiming it... there was nothing scientific about him; indeed, in all that matters he was an anti-scientist.[6]
>
> The kind of facts which did not interest Marx were the facts to be discovered by examining the world and the people who live in it with his own eyes and ears. He was totally

---

4. Karl Marx and Friedrich Engels. 1975. Selected Correspondence 1846-1895, International Publishers, in Marx-Engels Collected Works (MECW) vol. 41, p232.

5. Ibid. MECW, vol. 41, pp246-47.

6. Paul Johnson. 2008. Intellectuals: From Marx and Tolstoy to Sartre and Chomsky, HarperCollins Publishers, p54.

and incorrigibly deskbound. Nothing on earth would get him out of the library and the study.[7]

Marx hoped that by praising Darwin's work he would create the impression that he too was a scientist worthy of acclaim. However, although Darwin was an atheist like Marx, he was a real scientist who traveled to remote parts of the earth to gather evidence for his theories.

Marx was not entirely happy with Darwinism, in particular because it failed to identify cases of rapid transformation in nature that dialectical materialism suggested should be evident. Darwin's theory of evolution was that nature developed higher forms of life very gradually over centuries and millennia if not millions of years. And since human beings are nothing more than a product of this gradual development it followed that they and their societies had also evolved very slowly over eons of time. (For his part, Darwin was not impressed with the writings of Marx. When he received a copy of *Das Kapital* as a gift from Marx, he never bothered to read it.)

The whole point of Marxism was to find a scientific basis for justifying violent revolutions that would overturn capitalist societies. Marx had identified capitalism as the fruit of a dialectic process of violent revolutions in history through which underclasses continuously rebelled against their oppressive masters. He said that human societies had advanced through natural laws different from those that governed nature. Thus hunters and gathers were dispossessed by agriculturists seeking their land. These farmers then competed with one another for land, which led to the rise of feudalism. And the revolt against feudal lords by individual farmers and craftsmen led to the development of capitalism.

According to this theory of historical materialism, Marx thought that the next step was the inevitable revolution of workers against owners, of the proletariat against the bourgeoisie. The dialectical struggle of this revolution would produce Socialism, a synthesis of capitalism (the existing order, or thesis) and proletarian power (the antithesis). Out of Socialism

---

7. Ibid. p60.

would emerge the Utopian system of Communism. (Mysteriously, Socialism would evolve into Communism gradually, under the wise leadership of a dictatorship of the proletariat.) As we have noted above, Marx believed that the revolutions that brought a change in power had to be violent, as he and Engels had stated in their *Manifesto*.

Marxism Destroys the Family

This view of social formation was applied by Marx and Engels to the traditional, nuclear family. They viewed families based on Judeo-Christian values as products of capitalism, not a divinely-mandated order through which individuals can learn to perfect love and become children of God. In their *Manifesto*, Marx and Engels declared that traditional families should be abolished:

> Abolition of the Family! Even the most radical flare up at this infamous proposal of the Communists. On what foundation is the present family, the bourgeois family, based? On capital, on private gain. In its completely developed form this family exists only among the bourgeoisie.[8]

It is worth noting here that the Marxist belief that traditional families are the product of capitalism is at the heart of Neo-Marxism, in particular the Frankfurt School's critical theory which advocates for a sexual revolution and the Postmodernist critical theories of gender that fly in the face of biology and are destroying our families and social order today.

Both Marxism and Neo-Marxism make families the target of their burning hostility, thereby advocating for the destruction of the most sacred social institution created by God. The family is the place where we can fulfill the second blessing granted to Adam and Eve, that is to practice love in multiplying and filling the earth.

Marxism Demonizes Private Property

Marx and Engels believed that private property is the root of all evil because

---

8. Karl Marx and Friedrich Engels. 1848. The Manifesto of the Communist Party.

it is the foundation of capitalism, the economic system they were bent on destroying. In their *Manifesto*, they made this point crystal clear:

> ... the theory of the Communists may be summed up in the single sentence: Abolition of private property.[9]

This represents a clear attack on the third blessing granted to Adam and Eve, which gave them the right and responsibility to take dominion over the creation.

As the history of Socialist and Communist regimes has amply demonstrated, it is when the state confiscates property from individuals that a plethora of problems arise because the collective management of capital—and resources in general—can never be effected wisely, efficiently and fairly by an institution that lacks direct responsibility for its actions. By its nature, the state always seeks to accumulate power for itself rather than addressing the needs and aspirations of individuals, families and communities.

The history of capitalism has shown that the most efficient way to manage capital and other resources is to place them under the authority of individuals (whether persons or companies) who know best how to use resources beneficially for themselves and others. Marx and Engels saw injustices in the industries of Europe, but they lacked the vision to see how ownership of private property would propel the world to levels of prosperity and reduction of poverty that were unimaginable in their time.

Given this fact, Marxists and Neo-Marxists today have no excuse for continuing to advocate for state ownership of all property. Which proves that the real objective of Socialists and Communists is not the betterment of all people (or the working class proletariat that Marx and Engels claimed was their concern), but the accumulation of power in the hands of those who believe they know what's best for 'the people' and never cease to hunger for more and more power.

---

9. Ibid.

Marxism Offers False Utopias

Although Marx likely never stepped inside a factory and was supported throughout his life by the capitalist efforts of his family and friends, and especially Engels, who came from an industrialist family, he constantly railed against capitalism in general and the ownership class, or the bourgeoisie, in particular.

Marx and Engels ostensibly wrote their *Manifesto* to explain their theory of classes and to justify violent revolution by the workers whom they expected to overthrow the bourgeoisie:

> The history of all hitherto existing societies is the history of class struggles. Freeman and slave, patrician and plebeian, lord and serf, guild-master and journeyman, in a word, oppressor and oppressed, stood in constant opposition to one another, carried on an uninterrupted, now hidden, now open fight, a fight that each time ended, either in a revolutionary re-constitution of society at large, or in the common ruin of the contending classes.[10]

In Marxism, the oppressed are the proletariat, or workers. The *Manifesto* calls on them to take up arms and take power from the bourgeoisie. It ends with this call to action:

> The Communists disdain to conceal their views and aims. They openly declare that their ends can be attained only by the forcible overthrow of all existing social conditions. Let the ruling classes tremble at a Communistic revolution. The proletarians have nothing to lose but their chains. They have a world to win.
>
> WORKING MEN OF ALL COUNTRIES, UNITE![11]

Although Marx and Engels wrote as if the workers in Britain—where

---

10. Ibid.
11. Ibid.

the two of them lived—as well as elsewhere in the industrializing world were the wretched of the earth, the conditions for workers in the 19th century and into the 20th steadily improved as new laws provided protections and child labor was largely ended. Ironically, perhaps, this trend of ever improving conditions for workers in the industrialized nations of the world has continued, and most workers today enjoy fine working circumstances. Most earn good wages and some participate in the ownership of their own companies, or other companies.

The same cannot be said of workers in non-industrialized economies, or in countries at an early stage of industrialization. And it certainly cannot be said of workers in Socialist and Communist states, who have had to suffer wretched conditions and a life of poverty. This was realized by some of the starry-eyed European followers of Marx in the 1920s and 30s when they visited the Soviet Union, which they believed was becoming a paradise on earth under Stalin. (Some of the best accounts of this awakening to the reality of Communism are recorded by Arthur Koestler and André Gide in the book, *The God That Failed*.)

The truth is that wherever Socialist or Communist systems have been established, the ordinary citizens have suffered deprivation and oppression from their elitist rulers. These *nomenklatura* spout lies about their concern for the underclasses while exercising total control over the nation's resources which they exploit to benefit themselves and other elite members of the ruling party.

Marxism's Utopian Seduction is Based on a Lie

In the Garden of Eden, Lucifer seduced Eve into engaging in an illicit relationship by telling her that she did not need to heed God's warning that eating the fruit of the Tree of the Knowledge of Good and Evil would lead to her death. Lucifer claimed that the real reason for this prohibition was that a jealous God did not want Adam and Eve gaining God-like wisdom. He lied to Eve:

> For God knows that when you eat of it your eyes will be opened, and you will be like God, knowing good and evil. (Genesis 3:5)

This was the first lie. When she believed it, Eve lost her relationship with God and destroyed the possibility of creating a Godly family with Adam, whom she also persuaded to disobey God's prohibition. Since then, the descendants of Adam and Eve have lived in spiritual darkness with the promise of a return to Eden as it was before the Fall an enduring vision to hope for. For Christians, that promise has meant the realization of a Kingdom of Heaven on earth or in the afterlife.

Marx and Engels were raised in Christian societies and so were very familiar with Christianity's promise of heaven. However, as the tone of the *Manifesto* shows, they ridiculed religion and what it offered, instead promoting their own materialist Utopian alternative. Engels stated this directly in his work, *On the History of Early Christianity*:

> Both Christianity and the workers' socialism preach forthcoming salvation from bondage and misery: Christianity places this salvation in a life beyond, after death, in heaven; socialism places it in this world, in a transformation of society.[12]

To be generous, Marx and Engels might have believed in the Utopian ideal they were selling. However, there has never been a shred of proof that what they offered was anything other than a huge deception, a massive lie. Unfortunately, many good people, including Christians and members of other faiths, have been fooled by this lie. They have believed that a Marxist revolution would pave the way to Utopia. Without exception they have been proved wrong. The Communist promise that each citizen of their state will give according to his or her ability and receive according to their need is demonstrably false.

---

12. Friedrich Engels. 1894. On the History of Early Christianity, published in Die Neue Zeit.

Marxism Perfects the Ideology of Satan and Cain

Marx and Engels recognized the shortcomings of the French revolutionaries, and the theories they developed were intended—in part at least—to offer a scientific basis for sustaining violent revolution until it could overthrow the existing government and usher in a new regime that would give the revolutionaries permanent power.

From a providential perspective, Marx and Engels were engaged in developing a theory that embodied the resentment, jealousy, accusation and murderous intent of Lucifer when he seduced Eve and destroyed the family of Adam and Eve. Marxism is based on the lie that it will lead to an earthly Utopia, much as Lucifer's seduction was based on the lie that Eve would become God-like if she would disobey God.

Lucifer's spiritual murder of Adam and Eve became the heart of evil that infected Cain with a Satanic nature. Cain acted on his Luciferian feelings of anger towards God and resentment towards Abel, which he had inherited from his parents, by murdering Abel.

Marxism is based on exploiting jealousies and resentments in people to get them to attack the objects of their bitterness with the promise that this will lead to a better life for them and a better world for humanity as a whole. History has shown that this is never the case, but the promise of success deceives the naïve and gullible again and again. It also attracts the cynical who don't believe in the Marxist Utopia but see the theory as a way to take and keep power.

The Satanic nature of Marxism and its offshoots in Neo-Marxism is always evident in the results of these theories being practiced. But by that time, it is often too late to reverse a slide into a dystopian future. Our interest is to expose the truth about Marxism so that people of faith and good will can be clear and robust in opposing it, and society as a whole can reject it. This is of particular importance to Christians, who bear the greatest responsibility for defeating Marxism and liberating those suffering under Marxist oppression.

Marxism is the perfection of Satanic, Cain-type ideology. Therefore it represents the greatest threat to the providence as it reaches its culmination in these times. Only a better ideology espoused by committed believers in our Creator and the Divine purpose can expose it for the evil it is, and show the world to a better, Godly alternative. This is a core mission of Christianity that will take education and focus to accomplish.

How Marxists Are Born

Marxism as a belief system was created by a Cain-type person who was filled with bitterness and resentment towards Christian-based society and capitalism. His nature was exploited by Satan to formulate atheistic Marxist ideology.

All people inherit fallen nature and therefore have both Cain- and Abel-type characteristics within them. Marxism as a Cain-type theory animates an individual's Cain-type nature. If the individual has a developed Abel-type nature, he or she might well be attracted to the promises of Marxism, but they will have the spiritual maturity to be able to recognize Marxism as the evil it is and the spiritual fortitude to reject it. In this way, Abel overcomes Cain.

However, for someone whose Abel-type nature is undeveloped, Marxist seductions will likely appeal to them, animating their Cain-type nature to the point where it dominates the Abel side of their nature. Thus a true Marxist is born. Free from the reins of conscience, his mind and heart burn with unrequited resentment and bitterness and, shorn of a moral compass, he is willing to employ any and all means in the name of achieving Utopian ends. Marxists can therefore lie, cheat, steal and kill with a sense of righteous indignation.

For the masses, Marxism justifies their resentment towards those better off than themselves. They are therefore easily manipulated by the promises of Marxist leaders. For the arrogant and intellectually vain—who may or may not believe in the ideology—Marxism provides a path to power and wealth that would never be available to them otherwise.

But there is no good end for either the Marxist intellectual or those who justify their wrongdoing in the name of Marxism's false promises. Resentment and bitterness can only be overcome through the healing power of Divine love expressed with compassion and understanding by Abel. Thus for Christians to fulfill their providential mission as Abel, they must clearly recognize the evil origins and nature of Marxism and work to debunk it and drive it from all its entrenched positions in society.

The Bitter Truth About Socialism and Communism

The truth is that no Socialist or Communist regime has been successful in providing for its people. Not only that, all of them have been authoritarian and fascist in practice, denying citizens their natural rights to worship, assemble, speak their minds and create their own livelihoods. Only the ruling elites have been able to enjoy any of the freedoms and comforts that are almost universally available in free market democracies. This is the bitter truth that those who have believed in Socialism and Communism have had to face.

Ironically, although Marx and Engels believed that violent revolutions to overthrow capitalism were inevitable, their theories were not put into practice for some decades after publication of the *Manifesto*. It took the Russian Communist leader Vladimir Lenin to add the concepts of imperialism as the final stage of capitalism, the need for a leading revolutionary party and the need for a revolutionary putsch for Marxist theory to be translated into revolutions that brought Communists to power.

Thus it was not Marxism alone, but Marxism-Leninism that sparked the Russian Revolution of 1917 and assured its eventual success in taking power over Russia and neighboring states. Lenin's Bolshevik revolutionaries were barbarians who tortured and murdered their enemies mercilessly, shedding blood at will. They were responsible for as many as 12 million deaths as the Red Russians defeated the White Russians loyal to the deposed Tsar and consolidated power as the Union of Soviet Socialist Republics, which was established at the end of 1922.

The Bolsheviks denied citizens their individual rights, turned Christian churches into warehouses and did whatever they could to eliminate Christian beliefs and traditions from their society. No dissent was tolerated. Neighboring states lost their independence and were forced to join the USSR. The Communists dreamed of controlling the world and worked to take over other countries through subversion, blackmail and military conquest.

The Russian Revolution would prove to be just the first in a series of totalitarian advances in the 20th century in the name of Socialism and Communism, advances that would result in tens of millions losing their lives and many millions more suffering loss of family members, dispossession of their properties and untold personal and economic hardships.

With the defeat of Nazi Germany in WWII, and the collapse of the Soviet Union in 1991, two of the biggest perpetrators of Satanic socialist ideology and totalitarian dictatorship ended. But Marxism in a Leninist-Maoist variant continues to be the ruling ideology of Communist China and similar Communist regimes continue in power in a handful of Socialist/Communist states like North Korea and Cuba. In all of them, individuals and families suffer under state oppression and failed economies. (In recent decades China has used capitalist policies and the investments of naïve international corporations to stave off starvation and build up the wealth it needs to appease its population while continuing its oppression of religious and ethnic minorities at home and provocation and subversion abroad.)

Neo-Marxism Spreads The Cancer of Marxism

Despite the overwhelming evidence against Marxism that was revealed in the horrors of the 20th century, this Cain-type ideology has not been purged from the world of academic study, political activism and totalitarian government. It remains the ruling ideology of Communist China, North Korea and Cuba, and continues to influence Leftist regimes in Vietnam, Laos, Venezuela, Nicaragua and other countries. At the same time, its cultural influence is only expanding.

To make these cultural advances, Marxism as a poisonous theory has metastasized into Neo-Marxist Critical Theories, first developed by the Frankfurt School—with authors like Herbert Marcuse and Wilhelm Reich—and then expanded into other areas of life and social organization by Postmodernist authors like Michel Foucault and Jacques Derrida.

Critical Theories use the dialectical materialism of Marxism to deconstruct traditional values and social institutions and apply this paradigm of conflict to human sexuality, family structures, post-colonialism, race, gender and any other facet of life that the Left can find a way to attack and destroy. Marxism focused on class conflicts, the Frankfurt School on sexual repression (marrying Marx with Freud), and the Postmodernists on the foundational beliefs and institutions of Western Civilization in general.

As with Marxism, Neo-Marxism is always dressed up in the language of virtue, of human liberation from oppression, of social justice and equity. However, like Marxism the application of Neo-Marxist theories to life produces endless conflicts, violent riots in the street, attacks on religion and the family and cancel culture.

Incredibly, many of the dominant institutions in the West have been profoundly corrupted by Critical Theories. Instead of promoting the values of faith and family, they promote sexual deviance and transgenderism; instead of promoting a color-blind society, they encourage the races to look at each other with suspicion and envy; instead of promoting equality of opportunity, they promote equality of outcomes, destroying the most basic rule of our existence, the need for every person to be responsible for their own life.

Michel Foucault is the most referenced author in the social sciences today. It would be one thing if his ideas were just discussed ad nauseam in academic papers that were sent to die in basement storage, but they have now spread throughout higher education and are moving increasingly to younger and younger students in high school, middle school and even elementary school and kindergarten, where innocent children are being taught to treat as normal the behavior of a small minority of deviant individuals in society.

History itself is being rewritten in textbooks like Howard Zinn's popular *A People's History of the United States*, which is riddled with outright lies and deceptions, all on behalf of promoting a Marxist view of America. Instead of respecting their divinely-inspired founders and the great good done by America in the world, students are taught to despise the founders as evil white slaveowners, and to hate America itself as an evil imperial power. They are taught that America is responsible for perpetrating massive crimes against humanity in its treatment of the native Americans who lived here before colonization by Europeans, and in its treatment of black and brown people around the world.

This highly damaging corruption of education is producing university graduates who are hired by corporations to oversee 'diversity programs', all of which are based on looking at employees and the world through the lens of racial and sexual identity, classes of victimhood and other categories that lend themselves to stirring up resentments and conflicts.

Meanwhile, the mainstream media has increasingly become infected with Critical Theory thinking. No longer can they be trusted to dig up and pass along facts. Now they see themselves as crusaders for causes which they can advance by omitting some information, distorting other information, and ultimately interpreting the world through their ingrained biases. These biases have also infected the entertainment industry.

In the political arena, Critical Theories influence the way parties pursue voters, in particular through identity politics which separates the electorate into groups which are then targeted with messaging designed to appeal to their separateness and victim status vis-a-vis all other voters. Worse still, Marxists are so obsessed with seizing and keeping political power that they readily indulge in hate campaigns, character assassination, voter intimidation, lies and the outright theft of elections in violation of the most sacred right of citizenship in a democracy.

The Importance of Choosing God Over Mammon

As with Islam, there is no anticipation of Marxism in Biblical scriptures.

Because of this, many Christians have been deceived by the Utopian seductions of Marxists. These include those who have drawn parallels between the ideas of Marx and the teachings of Jesus. For example, it has been claimed that when Marx called for the abolition of private property he was echoing these words of Jesus in the Sermon on the Mount:

> No one can serve two masters; for either he will hate the one and love the other, or he will be devoted to the one and despise the other. You cannot serve God and mammon. (Matthew 6:24)

Mammon is making the accumulation of material possessions the primary purpose of life. This pursuit of wealth inevitably takes you away from devoting your life to God, as Jesus pointed out. Marxism is an ideological embodiment of mammon that is antithetical to Christianity. Rejecting the worship of mammon and worshipping God instead creates a person of faith who is willing to serve the providence by serving humanity. This was the message of Jesus, who instructed his disciples to live lives of humility and sacrifice, but never preached the need for communal living.

We have noted that some early Christians contributed their possessions to the nascent community of believers, and that this practice has been continued by some monastic and other Christian communal groups to the present day. However, members of these Christian groups were, and are, united by faith in God and a religious ideal that has nothing to do with Marxist theory or practice. Thus the notion of compatibility between Christian communalism and Marxist Communism conflates two very different things.

Christianity seeks the Kingdom of Heaven; Marxism the accumulation of all capital by an all-powerful state. The Christian ideal is a world under the authority of God working through Christ; The Marxist ideal is a world under the authority of the state, which is governed by the atheistic laws of dialectical materialism. The Christian ideal is to achieve a world that resembles the sinless Garden of Eden before the Fall. The Marxist ideal is a totalitarian state that crushes the creativity and goodness of individuals, and prevents them from achieving their God-given potential.

The Fallacy of Christian Socialism

Some on the Left have used the teachings and example of Jesus to argue that he himself was a socialist. This is the basis for Christian Socialism which was developed in Europe in the 19th century as a way to make Christianity more relevant in addressing social inequities in capitalist societies.

One of its leading figures was Christoph Blumhardt (1842-1919), a theologian and preacher who in 1899 became active in Germany's Social Democratic Party, the SDP, which espoused Marxism from the mid-1870s until 1959. Other prominent Christian Socialists from this era were Hermann Kutter (1863-1931) and Leonhard Ragaz (1868-1945), both theologians based in Switzerland.

This theory that seeks to marry Christianity with Socialism has continued to draw adherents as diverse as the Anabaptist groups (Hutterite, Mennonite and Bruderhof communities, for example), Desmond Tutu of South Africa, Liberation Theology advocates in Latin America and Pope Francis.

Christian Socialism grew out of the frustration of Christians seeing injustices being perpetrated in their societies over decades and centuries, and the temptation to believe that state-controlled economies would assure more just distribution of wealth than can be achieved under capitalism. The fallacy of this view is that it wrongly conflates the voluntary pooling of resources by conscientious Christians for the sake of heaven with the forced concentration of capital in government hands for the sake of Socialist and Communist dictatorships.

A Christian Socialist may well contribute to the development of socialism, but a Marxist or Neo-Marxist will never contribute to Christianity and its true mission of creating a Kingdom of Heaven on earth. Remember, Jesus never preached socialism, in any form. He taught people the moral lessons they needed to fulfill their God-given responsibilities. Jesus warned his followers to be alert to such dangers as those posed by the seductions of the Left:

> Behold, I send you out as sheep in the midst of wolves; so be wise as serpents and innocent as doves. (Matthew 10:16)

The Fallacy That Capitalism is Evil

One of the common themes running through Marxism and its offshoots is that capitalism is evil and must be destroyed. This belief resonates with Christian Socialists who associate capitalism with mammon and greed. This anti-capitalism has its roots in Marxism, as we have noted above. However, anti-capitalism leads to Socialism and Communism, two systems that are infinitely worse than capitalism.

In 1776 Adam Smith published his groundbreaking work, *The Wealth of Nations*, in which he explained that the success of capitalism lies in its operation as a system of voluntary exchange of goods and services. He said that an 'invisible hand' operated to bring buyers and sellers together based on a shared interest to exchange goods and/or services in a way that would benefit both of them: The seller would get money which he valued more than the goods he owned, and the buyer would get the goods that he valued more than the money he had. In other words, capitalism is the economic system most closely associated with the personal freedom of individuals and the organizations they establish to create wealth.

Free market capitalism, working in tandem with the freedoms enjoyed by individuals under democratic systems of government, has transformed the world for good, producing ever better standards of living for an ever greater percentage of people on earth. Poverty everywhere has been declining for decades as capitalism has spread worldwide. Marx and Engels never imagined that capitalism would produce these good results.

At the same time, the Marxist economic prescription, Socialism, has had the opposite track record. Wherever Socialism has been tried, the result has been disastrous—think of the Soviet Union, Cuba, Venezuela and North Korea. China became an exception to this rule only because it adopted capitalism within the political structure of a Communist state. (The two cannot coexist indefinitely—China must either revert to Socialism, in which case it will go the way of the Soviet Union, or it must become a truly free economy with a democratic government.)

All economies require capital. However, history has shown that capital is best managed by individuals who operate in a free market. In the hands of individual property owners it is used most efficiently and brings the best return on investment. Bureaucracies are always inefficient and wasteful, in part because bureaucrats do not take ownership for their decisions. And for this reason too, bureaucracies always suffer from corruption.

Capitalism is compatible with Christianity because it places the responsibility for decisions made about private property squarely on the shoulders of the individual, who is responsible to God, his family and society.

A Christian embrace of Socialism has real dangers. For one, it can produce ecclesiastical structures that are rigid and too easily corrupted by administrators who are seduced by the power they wield. It can also lend undeserved moral credibility to an immoral program of radical social transformation carried out in the name of progress but implemented at the cost of God-given individual liberties. This is the danger faced by Christians who embrace the Marxist and Neo-Marxist agendas of the social justice movement.

The Fallacy of Supporting Social Justice Agendas

Not a few churches promote the causes that come right out of the destructive programs fostered by Critical Theories, very often under the banner of social justice. These programs are always promoted by the Left—meaning those ideas and organizations that are based on Marxist, Neo-Marxist or similar materialist ideologies—under the cover of widely-held values that derive from the Judeo-Christian roots of Western Civilization. This is the deception that traps Christians into supporting organizations and agendas that are inimical to Christian beliefs and goals.

For example, in recent times many churches have actively supported Black Lives Matter, a Marxist/Neo-Marxist group that hides behind the virtuous cause of racial equality to sow resentment and violence and promote the gay and transgender agendas. BLM has raised tens of millions of dollars from individuals, churches, corporations and governments that are afraid of being called racist. There is no evidence that BLM has reduced racism at all. On the contrary, it has fanned the flames of racism with irresponsible rhetoric and advocacy of violence. In the meantime, its founders have become rich through using for themselves money donated to support the cause.

The BLM phenomenon is part of a wider failure by churches that support the anti-traditional family agenda of the LGBTQ movement by flying its rainbow flag, raising banners intended to disguise its destruction of Christian values with slogans like 'Love is Love', conducting same-sex marriages, and accepting openly gay members as clergy.

These churches may argue that they are simply being inclusive, as all good Christians should be, but if you fly a movement's colors or promote it on banners draped on your building or on the walls of your sanctuary, it sends the message that you do support the agenda espoused by those organizations. Thus these churches are foolishly promoting the anti-family values of the gay pride and transgender movements. In the case of transgenderism, this means supporting the ghoulish hormone treatments and sex-change surgeries that are destroying the lives of so many children today.

It is fair to ask apologists for this behavior just what they are contributing to the advance of the providence. Furthermore, what basis is there for these movements in the Bible? Both the Old and New Testaments are emphatically clear in condemning other than heterosexual relations. As for transgenderism and other Critical Gender theories, they are so novel and inhuman that they are not even imagined in the Bible.

The Righteous Christian Response to Marxism

Cain-type character comes in all shades of darkness, from innocent sins of omission to the purely evil intentional inflicting of pain and suffering on others. The response of Abel to the behavior of Cain should vary accordingly. Thus, for example, in its role as an Abel religion, Christianity should reach out to Abel-type elements in other religions so that they can work together to serve the providence.

In the case of Marxism, however, its intention is to destroy Christianity and other faiths as well as the societies based on these religious beliefs and values. For Christians, then, there can be no collaboration with atheistic and materialistic ideologies and movements, any more than there can be collaboration with Satan himself. Indeed, to collaborate with Marxists based on vaguely similar goals is to encourage the forces of evil and undermine the forces of good.

Marxism and Neo-Marxism are based on creating divisions that will lead to conflict among people, groups and nations. Their strategy is straightforward: identify 'victim' groups that can be made to believe that their grievances justify blaming others and, if need be, mounting a violent revolution to destroy those others. These divisions are not intrinsic to the natural order, but are fabricated by the Left to justify confrontation and conflict. They are the work of Satan and Cain who thrive on conflict.

Christians need to point out that the real differences among people are not related to race, ethnicity, nationality, religion, sex, class or any other such category, but only to the roles they play as Cain- or Abel-type figures in the providence.

Christianity's Responsibility as Abel

Which brings us back to Christianity's inheritance of the mission of Jesus as global Abel. Jesus did not have to deal with Marxists, and did not anticipate the rise of Marxism, but we can learn from his words and actions how we can best relate to them. On the one hand Jesus taught his disciples to love all others; on the other he made it clear that there could be no compromise with those who opposed him:

> He who is not with me is against me, and he who does not gather with me scatters. (Matthew 12:30)

And he chastised the Pharisees for their lack of faith in him, identifying them with Satan:

> You brood of vipers! how can you speak good, when you are evil? For out of the abundance of the heart the mouth speaks. (Matthew 12:34)

The brood of vipers are the children of Satan, with whom Jesus could never compromise. Likewise, Christians can never compromise with Marxism and its offshoots. Rather, Christians must expose the fallacies and dangers of Marxist and Neo-Marxist ideologies and practices. The mission of Christianity as global Abel is to expose and defeat evil and liberate Cain from the bondage of Satan. Marxists are also victims of their own false ideology but unless they abandon it for a Godly worldview they will never be able to attain the better world they say they believe in.

Thus the contest between Marxism and Godly ideology is the culmination of the conflict between Cain and Abel, a conflict that Christians must win for the providence.

Note: For an in-depth analysis of Marxism and Neo-Marxism as the perfection of Cain-type ideology and the nemesis of the Divine Providence, see my book: The Triumph of Good: Divine Providence, The Cain-Abel Paradigm, And the End of Marxism.

Chapter 32

Christianity and Science

Humanism Spurs Both Reformation and Renaissance

Science and Technology Have Transformed the World

The world of God's creation has been transformed by the development of science and a wide range of technologies that have had a radical impact on the way we live, work and look at the universe. So important has science become that for many it has taken the place of religion as the primary source of truth upon which we base an understanding of our existence.

Many scientific discoveries and technological advances serve an obvious purpose by addressing well-recognized problems, such as disease, hunger and poverty, or the need to travel great distances in short periods of time. But science cannot answer the biggest question of all: What is the purpose of our existence? Science observes the created world but is unable to observe the invisible Creator of that world, the cause behind the effect.

It is religion that 'sees' the Creator and understands the importance of the Creator in shaping the creation and in providing a moral framework for the existence of creation. Thus science divorced from religion is unable to provide a moral compass for the use of the technology it gives rise to, and is unable to guide us in the realization of our original purpose and the creation of the ideal world of God's intention.

There is no doubt that science and technology are enormously important for our health and comfort. Just consider how primitive medicine was so often wrong, resulting in increased suffering and death. For example, for many centuries doctors bled patients in the belief that this would remove harmful impurities from the body, risking the life of their patients. As recently as 1799, George Washington had 40 percent of his blood removed over an eight-hour period to cure a fever and throat infection. He died a day later and this huge loss of blood probably killed him.

But Science Cannot Quench Our Thirst for Truth and Love

But science alone cannot satisfy our thirst for understanding of the truth as well as spiritual and mental fulfillment. Our intellect seeks the answers provided by science to explain our universe, and our body seeks the aid and comfort provided by technology. But our spirit seeks the deeper truths of our purpose for existence, which are revealed to us through revelations from our Creator. And our spirit seeks the love of God, which comes to us directly as the Holy Spirit and indirectly through the love of other people and the goodness and beauty of nature.

Our contention in this book is that the missing piece in our scientific understanding of the universe is precisely the role of our Creator and the purpose for the creation that is revealed in the Divine Providence. Without this understanding, science can be misused to harm the providence. Consider, for example, the horrific misuse of medicine in the practice of 'gender affirming' hormone therapies and surgeries that are inflicting irreversible damage on patients, and increasing dramatically the incidence of suicide among children. Without a moral compass to guide them, the medical practitioners behind this evil industry continue to destroy the lives of innocents.[1]

Christians have the benefit of Jesus' teaching about the Divine Providence and what it means to each of us as children of our Creator. This understanding of the nature and purpose of our invisible Creator is the foundation for the Christian faith. It is also the basis for understanding how science and technology should be used to contribute to the providence. Everything

---

1. See for example: Russell B. Toomey, Amy K. Syvertsen, Maura Shramko. Transgender Adolescent Suicide Behavior, Pediatrics, September 11, 2018.

created is intrinsically good, but it can serve either good or evil, depending on how it is used. Hence the need for the moral compass that Christianity should provide.

We have already explained that the responsibility of Christians as members of the Abel faith should spur them to treat as siblings the members of other Abrahamic religions, Judaism and Islam, and to bring into this holy alliance members of other faiths. And we have explained that this responsibility means Christians must reject Marxism and its offshoots for their atheistic threat to the providence. In the case of science, however, Christians should both embrace new discoveries that contribute to improving our life on earth and play a leading role in seeing that science and technology are used to support the providence.

The Providential Advent of Modern Science

In Chapter 26 we traced the evolutionary developments in Christianity that led through the Great Schism and the Protestant Reformation to the Pilgrims crossing the Atlantic to America where, after the Great Awakening, a nation was established under God. The American system of republican democracy, and the religious values it was based on, set an example of representative government that has been imitated throughout the world. It provided protection for individuals to exercise their rights—to worship as they wished, to speak their minds without fear and to participate in free markets.

The rise of democracy was boosted when, in the 14th century, an almost totally new field of human endeavor would emerge from the Christian humanism of the Renaissance—science and its offshoot technology. Indeed, the Reformation and Renaissance were two sides of a providential force that in a few centuries would transform the world. It is the Renaissance-based side of the providence that we will discuss in this chapter.

As with Islam and Marxism, there were no Biblical scriptures to help Christians respond to the rise of science. Always protective of its privileged access to knowledge through Greek and Latin, the church initially reacted to science by treating it as a dangerous threat to its monopoly on the truth.

After all, the work of the Greeks who explored the universe through observation several centuries before Jesus was considered by the church to be paganistic since their ideas were inextricably linked to the pantheism of the Greeks at that time. Thus early scientists of the Christian era, such as Nicolaus Copernicus (1473-1543) and Galileo Galilei (1564-1642) were treated as heretics by the church.

However, the dynamics of change within the established churches, and especially within the Roman Catholic Church, were always fed by the desire of conscientious Christians to find an ever more perfect expression of their faith, even at the cost of persecution as heretics.

As we have noted, one of the major figures in this movement was John Wycliffe (d. 1384), who translated the Bible into English from Latin. He had a strong influence on the Czech martyr John Hus, who in turn influenced the most important Protestant reformer of all, Martin Luther. These men questioned everything in the church, and were influenced by a new movement that would sweep through Europe, Christian humanism.

The Christian Humanism of Petrarch And Erasmus

A contemporary of Wycliffe was Italian Francesco Petrarch (1304-1374) who was a life-long Christian but also a scholar and poet who admired the classics and believed that Christianity would benefit from the appreciation for the arts that was evident in the classical age. He did not see the Christian faith as contradicting appreciation for nature and human beings in particular. Instead, he considered the beauty of creation a reflection of the goodness of the Creator, and therefore appreciation of the creation a natural part of appreciation for its Creator.

Petrarch's Christian humanism laid the groundwork for expanding human intellectual horizons beyond theology and into exploring the realm of nature and the universe. His influence would prove decisive in a movement of intellectual awakening that would lead to a broad-based Renaissance of classical learning and, ultimately, the birth of modern science. Thus Petrarch is considered the father of the Renaissance.

An article on Petrarch by John Humphreys Whitfield in the Encyclopedia Britannica sums up his pivotal role between the past and future, religion and science:

> The hallmark of Petrarch's thought was a deep consciousness of the past as the nutriment of the present. His abiding achievement was to recognize that, if there is a Providence that guides the world, then it has set man at the center. Petrarch provided a theoretical basis for the enrichment of man's life. But, even more important, the humanist attitudes of the Italian 15th century that led into the Renaissance would not have been possible without him.[2]

Petrarch was followed on this path by the Dutch theologian Erasmus (1466-1536), another Christian humanist who influenced contemporaries Ulrich Zwingli (1484-1531), Martin Luther (1483-1546) and other leaders of the burgeoning Protestant Reformation. A life-long Catholic, Erasmus would not follow Luther in breaking with the church, but he did influence the Catholic Counter-Reformation, the movement of reform within the church that was largely inspired by the Protestant Reformation.

The Intertwined History of the Reformation and Renaissance

Christian humanism not only gave birth to the Protestant Reformation, it also played an essential role in the Renaissance. Luther and other reformers were influenced by the early humanists, but so too was Luther's contemporary, Nicolaus Copernicus, a brilliant Polish polymath. Like Petrarch and Erasmus, he was a life-long Catholic. Humanism spurred him to explore the universe of God's creation. He conducted a number of experiments to test the heliocentric theory of the solar system first suggested by Aristarchus of Samos some two millennia earlier. He agreed with Aristarchus and provided evidence to prove the theory.

---

2. Francesco Petrarch quoted in J.H. Plum's 1961 The Italian Renaissance, Part Two, Chapter XI, p167. (This chapter was written by Morris Bishop.) Horizon, New World City.

The work of Copernicus was initially welcomed by Pope Clement VII, but the great scholar was apparently reluctant to publish his theory out of fear of repercussions from the church. It was only upon his death in 1543 that his sole student, Georg Rheticus, who had been sent to study with him by an associate of Luther, was able to have his seminal work, *De revolutionibus orbium coeletium* (On the Revolutions of the Celestial Spheres), published in Germany.

The impact of his work was enormous. The Copernican theory was revolutionary. It demonstrated the importance of human inquiry, observation and logic in place of blind faith, superstition and irrationality. And it proved that the dogma of the church in the matter of the design and function of the universe was without any foundation in reality.

Modern science was born.

As in the case of Wycliff, Hus and other early Christian reformers, the church would soon move to crush the new and revolutionary ideas of Copernicus. In 1616, the Roman Inquisition condemned heliocentrism as heresy. Its primary target at the time was the great Italian polymath Galileo, who had agreed with Copernicus but under threat of torture and death would recant his belief in heliocentrism. Nevertheless, as in the case of Protestantism, the changes in human thinking initiated by Copernicus could not be stopped.

Clearly the Reformation and Renaissance influenced each other in a positive way and their combined impact on the world has benefited the advance of the Divine Providence greatly. The Reformation spurred an internal transformation of the church, making it a better expression of the teachings of Jesus. The Renaissance spurred a transformation in human thinking about the nature and function of the universe, leading to the advent of modern science and countless innovations that have improved our lives greatly.

The year 1517, when Luther nailed his 95 Theses to a church door in Wittenberg, is taken as the beginning of the Protestant Reformation. In many respects it was also the moment when modern science was born, being the very time when Copernicus was completing his groundbreaking theory of the universe. In our view, this moment marked the beginning of a 400-year period of both internal (religious renewal) and external (scientific development) preparation for the second advent of Christ. It served to restore a similar period two millennia earlier when four centuries before the advent of Jesus Israel was renewed through the rebuilding of the Temple, the world underwent renewal through the Axial Age, and science was invented by the Greeks.

Freed From Church Dogma, Science Took Wing

Beginning in the 17th century, science began to advance at an ever accelerating pace as part of the Enlightenment that saw a growing number of intelligent men and women pursue knowledge without any reference to theology. Notable figures of this movement were Descartes, Locke, Newton, Adam Smith, Goethe, Voltaire and many others. Under their influence, reason and science would become more trusted than faith. Ultimately, it would be used to reject faith, as we have seen, for example, in 19th century Marxism, which claimed to be "scientific socialism."

Today, science has virtually replaced God in secular societies. However, without a moral anchor, science is always susceptible to exploitation by those who use it to advance their own anti-providential agendas. Thus we see a Godless Left advancing a range of anti-scientific theories in the name of a "scientific consensus", theories that pose a threat to our civilization. These include alarmist theories of global warming, the bogus theory that biological sex and natural gender are different, the theory that white people are intrinsically racist, and so on.

Which leads us back to our topic here: What is the role of Christianity vis a vis science? There are two considerations in answering this question. First, it should be recognized that science is nothing more than a tool for humanity to understand the creation so that we can fulfill our purpose as children of God and exercise our God-given right of stewardship more perfectly. Second, it should be recognized that science as it is generally practiced is devoid of a moral compass, a compass that should be provided by religious wisdom and faith. Thus Christianity has a leading role to play in providing direction and purpose for science.

The Compatibility of Science and Religion

When we speak of the history of science here, we are not concerned with the discoveries made in ancient Egypt and Mesopotamia, or even those made in Greece much later on. Those contributed to the life of the ancients, but they were not part of a sustained movement of enlightenment. Our interest here is the modern movement that has in just a few centuries made science the dominant source of knowledge that is responsible for the technology that has transformed the way we think and live.

It is this modern science that we want to understand within a Christian worldview. This need not be difficult, since, as we have pointed out, the science of today largely grew out of the intellectual labors of devout Christians who were responsible for the Renaissance and, later, the Enlightenment. What interests us is the way that Christianity can constructively view and influence science.

One might say that there are the rudiments of appreciation for the work of science in these words of Saint Paul about the relationship between the Creator and creation:

> Ever since the creation of the world his invisible nature, namely, his eternal power and deity, has been clearly perceived in the things that have been made. (Romans 1:20)

A good starting point is, then, to recognize that all avenues of human endeavor to understand the universe should ultimately be compatible and complementary because they are merely different ways of looking at a single reality: the creation. Religion is best suited to understand the invisible Creator and the purpose for the creation, while science is best suited to understand the laws and visible structures of the creation that embody the dual nature of the Creator.

Thus, for example, ultimately there cannot be two narratives about the creation that are contradictory but also both true. For example, some Christians who believe in the literal truth of every word in the Bible hold that the earth has existed for only 6,000 years. Scientists, however, say our planet is 4.5 billion years old. These two radically different time periods cannot both be accurate or even close to accurate. But the facts related to this issue are not a matter for religion; they are a matter for science. Therefore the scientific view is the one to trust.

But what about the religious belief that humans are composed of both invisible spiritual and visible physical elements that embody the inner and outer characteristics of our invisible Creator? Science cannot verify or prove false this belief, but it can find evidence of existence for both visible entities and invisible forces that move them. Science should therefore remain open to the possibility that religion possesses a wisdom that it lacks.

Contradictions and conflicts between science and religion do not arise because truth itself is self-contradictory—if it were, nothing could exist. Rather, these differences are the result of different perceptions of the truth that flow from different points of view—like the blind men who conclude different things about the shape of an elephant based on the bits they are touching.

The most important scientist of the 20th century, Albert Einstein, wrote about the benefits of looking at reality from both the spiritual and physical perspectives:

> Now, even though the realms of religion and science in themselves are clearly marked off from each other, nevertheless there exist between the two strong reciprocal relationships and dependencies. Though religion may be that which determines the goal, it has, nevertheless, learned from science, in the broadest sense, what means will contribute to the attainment of the goals it has set up. But science can only be created by those who are thoroughly imbued with the aspiration towards truth and understanding. This source

of feeling, however, springs from the sphere of religion. To this there also belongs the faith in the possibility that the regulations valid for the world of existence are rational, that is, comprehensible to reason. I cannot conceive of a genuine scientist without that profound faith. The situation may be expressed by an image: Science without religion is lame, religion without science is blind.[3]

Another way to make this point is that neither religion nor science is equipped to provide a comprehensive description of the reality that is the Creator and the creation. The purpose of religion is to understand the internal, invisible nature of the universe, while the purpose of science is to understand the external, measurable nature of the universe. In reality, they describe different but interrelated and complementary parts of a single, indivisible realty. They should respect each other and learn from each other.

The men and women who are versed in both religion and science are the best equipped to live well, to serve humanity well, and to fulfill the purpose for their existence.

The Moral Compass of Nature

There is yet another way to look at the role of Christianity, as well as other religions, in the world of science. Christian values, and those of religious belief and faith more generally, are fully compatible with those of nature as a whole, as science continues to discover.

It is often wrongly assumed that the natural world is without moral values. This is technically correct, insofar as only human beings are endowed with the ability to differentiate between good and evil, and to exercise free will in choosing between them. However, nature itself is endowed with the equivalent of a moral compass that plays an essential role in the order and behavior of the whole universe. The logical basis for this notion is rooted

---

3. Albert Einstein quoted by H.G. Kessler. 1971. in Diary of a Cosmopolitan, Weidenfeld and Nicolson, p157.

in the fact that all creation, human and otherwise, has originated from the same, moral Creator.

So what is the basis for 'morality' in nature? Essentially, it is a bias in favor of cooperation rather than conflict. One scientist who developed a theory of what he called Unified Science, Edward Haskell, showed this principle in operation across all scientific disciplines. He assembled a group of leading scientists from various fields to contribute their insights into this phenomenon. He set out these findings in his book: *Full Circle: The Moral Force of Unified Science*.[4]

Haskell mapped the various interactions of nature on Cartesian coordinates, with a circle added to show net positive or negative outcomes from interactions between X and Y. Using this method, he was able, for example, to plot the elements of the Periodic Table that showed Carbon to be the most combinative element (collaborative in human terms). The inert elements are the opposite (lifeless in human terms).

In biology this principle comes alive through its application to types of interaction among organisms. The behavior of Carbon he characterized as symbiosis (mutual give and take), while the inert elements demonstrate synnecrosis (mutual destruction). Between these opposite behaviors are predation (exploitation of the weaker by the stronger) and parasitism (subversion of the stronger by the weaker).

As we have suggested, human relationships can also be mapped in this way. To wit: symbiotic relationships are characterized by cooperation for mutual benefit among individuals, groups and nations; synnecrosis is seen in conflicts between individuals, groups and nations that lead to mutual destruction; predation is the unjustified aggression and exploitation of the weakness of others by an individual, group or nation; and parasitism is the subversion of the stronger by the weaker at the cost of the stronger. These four different social, political and economic behaviors reflect the different

---

4. Edward Haskell. 1972. Full Circle: The Moral Force of Unified Science. (Out of print.)

human personality types: cooperative and constructive, destructive and murderous, exploitative and oppressive, covetous and treacherous, respectively.

Thus science itself can recognize human-like values and behaviors in the structures and behaviors of nature as a whole. This means science should honor and respect religion, which champions human symbiosis, and criticize and oppose Marxism, which champions human parasitism, predation and synnecrosis.

Christianity Should Harness Science for the Providence

Which leads us once more to the importance of Christianity in providing a moral compass for science. As global Abel, Christianity is responsible for guiding science to contribute to the welfare of humanity and the fulfillment of the providence. Christianity should lead the world towards mutual respect and love (symbiosis) and away from mutual hatred and destruction (synnecrosis).

This advocacy represents the responsible exercise of human emotion, intellect and will in human relationships as well as in the human exercise of wise stewardship over the creation. In other words, Christianity should harness the power of science in support of the providence.

If the development and uses of science and technology are guided by this moral compass, they will not only contribute to the benefit of everyone, they will be weaned from their harmful uses. For example, artificial intelligence will be used to improve the lives of people everywhere, rather than as a tool for authoritarian governments to exercise unbridled and invasive control over the lives of their citizens. To put this in Biblical terms:

> He shall judge between the nations, and shall decide for many peoples; and they shall beat their swords into plowshares, and their spears into pruning hooks; nation shall not lift up sword against nation, neither shall they learn war any more. (Isaiah 2:4)

Thus it is for Christianity to assure that science and technology make the enormous contributions to building the Kingdom of Heaven on earth that they are capable of.

Chapter 33

Thy Kingdom Come on Earth

Culmination of the Divine Providence

Heaven Must Be Established on Earth

The Divine Providence is the unchanging purpose of our Creator driving humanity towards the recreation of the Garden of Eden as the Kingdom of Heaven on earth. In obedience to the instructions of Jesus, every Christian prays:

> Our Father who art in heaven, hallowed be thy name. Thy kingdom come, Thy will be done, on earth as it is in heaven. (Matthew 6:9-10)

Our original mind yearns for Eden before the Fall, for a world under the dominion of our Creator, free from sin and evil. We instinctively recognize that the work of salvation is not done until this kingdom becomes a reality. It is not enough for God to rule in a spiritual realm only; this must happen on earth too. Otherwise, the dominion of Satan on earth will not be ended and the children of God will continue to suffer under Cain-type individuals and governments.

Adam and Eve were each created with a spirit and body which needed each other for the first man and woman to grow into mature adults qualified to produce sinless children whom they could successfully raise to be true sons and daughters of the Creator. When they failed and lost their relationship with God, the purpose of the providence shifted to finding a new, sinless Adam who with a new, sinless Eve could establish a sinless lineage in a restored Garden of Eden.

The original failure of Adam and Eve was their refusal to heed the warning of their Creator, as we have explained. Because of their disobedience their children were claimed by Satan and all humanity has been infected by fallen nature. There was no one qualified to regain Eden through establishing a Kingdom of Heaven on earth until Jesus came as a sinless man.

The fact that it took millennia for the descendants of Adam and Eve to fulfill the necessary conditions for the Messiah to appear in the person of Jesus, proves that the providence is bound by the need for men and women to fulfill their God-given responsibilities, as were Adam and Eve. It also explains why despite the sinlessness of Jesus, his rejection and murder by the people prepared to receive him meant that the Kingdom of Heaven on earth could not be established at his time, causing him the great anguish he exhibited at Gethsemane and on the cross.

Through his sacrifice, Jesus did open a new spiritual realm for those who followed him, but he had to remind his disciples that the Kingdom of Heaven was attainable only through fulfillment of their responsibilities on earth:

> I will give you the keys of the kingdom of heaven, and whatever you bind on earth shall be bound in heaven, and whatever you loose on earth shall be loosed in heaven. (Matthew 16:19)

Two Millennia of Christian Evolution

The principle of human responsibility was not changed by the life and death of Jesus. As we have noted, some words Jesus spoke caused many of his followers to believe that his return to establish the Kingdom of Heaven on earth was imminent. It was of course not so. Rather, Christianity has undergone stages of purification as it has spread throughout the world, bringing enlightenment to fallen humanity over two millennia.

Thus it is abundantly clear that the kingdom will not appear magically, but will have to be created by men and women on earth who follow Christ in accepting and fulfilling their responsibilities before God. In effect, Christians are responsible for recreating Eden as the dwelling of God by reversing the disobedience of Adam and Eve through obedience to Christ.

We have traced the providential process of purification and the acceptance of greater responsibility by Christians over the last two millennia, as well as the related rise of science and improvement in political and economic systems over this period. Seen from a providential perspective, all these advances contribute to the preparations for a second coming of Christ and the final realization of the Kingdom of Heaven on earth.

Meanwhile, Satan has never rested. He has fomented conflicts that have drenched the earth in blood and caused untold suffering around the world. He has nurtured ideologies that have enabled Cain-type leaders to justify their murder of innocents, culminating in the death of tens of millions in the 20th century.

Thus while today we enjoy the fruits of Christian-based civilization, we also continue to suffer from the deadly regimes of evil dictators like Xi Jinping and Vladimir Putin, the Castros of Cuba and Kims of North Korea. And hundreds of millions still live in poverty. What will it take for God's Kingdom of Heaven to finally be established on earth?

The Futility of Just Waiting for Christ

Some Christians believe that if they love, obey and follow Jesus they will be saved by Divine grace and assured a place in a future heaven. This is the promise of the 'born again' movement in Christianity. But this expectation raises some serious problems when viewed from a providential point of view.

First, wasn't it this attitude of dependence on the advent of a kingly, almost magical messianic savior that caused the people of Israel to reject Jesus? Even though Jesus performed many miracles, his central message was that the Kingdom of Heaven could only be attained by fulfillment of personal responsibility. This was the gist of the Sermon on the Mount, summarized in these words:

> You, therefore, must be perfect, as your heavenly Father is perfect. (Matthew 5:48)

Thus Christians should not repeat the mistake of the Jews at the time of Jesus; they need to understand that the promise of salvation requires their full participation in the providence.

Second, what will heaven be like if it is populated with Christians who have been 'born again' but continue to carry with them the baggage of fallen nature? As C.S. Lewis pointed out in his book *The Great Divorce*, good and evil cannot coexist, and therefore nothing of evil and Hell can exist in Heaven:

> Evil can be undone, but it cannot 'develop' into good. Time does not heal it. The spell must be unwound, bit by bit, 'with backward mutters of dissevering power'-or else not. It is still 'either -or'. If we insist on keeping Hell (or even earth) we shall not see Heaven: if we accept Heaven we shall not be a able to retain even the smallest and most intimate souvenirs of Hell.[1]

This is a terrifying truth insofar as the only person qualified to be in Heaven by this standard is Jesus himself. But it is perfectly logical, and our original minds tell us that it is absolutely true.

Third, providence does not bear out the virtue of waiting for God to destroy evil, whether in individuals or in the world as a whole. Divine intervention is always associated with the fulfillment of human responsibility. After all, if the providence could advance without human beings doing their part, why did God wait millennia before sending Jesus, and why have we already had to wait 2,000 years for the second coming?

Salvation of fallen humanity can only be achieved through human

---

1. C.S. Lewis. 1946. The Great Divorce, HarperCollins, p1.

beings fulfilling their God-given responsibilities. This never changes and never will change because it is essential for us if we are to become co-creators with God. Thus we cannot remain passive in the face of evil, but must dedicate ourselves to identifying, exposing and defeating all that is of Satan. The spirit of righteousness needed is captured in William Blake's poem Jerusalem:

> Bring me my bow of burning gold:
> Bring me my arrows of desire:
> Bring me my spear: O clouds unfold!
> Bring me my chariot of fire.
>
> I will not cease from mental fight,
> Nor shall my sword sleep in my hand
> Till we have built Jerusalem
> In England's green and pleasant land.

Use the Cain-Abel Paradigm to Recognize and Defeat Evil

How do Christians fulfill their God-given responsibilities? When Lewis says, "the spell must be unwound, bit by bit," he means the dominion of Satan over fallen humanity must be broken and individuals must, step by step, become free from it by moving towards the Divine embrace of their Creator.

This process is achieved through the reversal of Cain's subjugation of Abel. In other words, the way the providence advances is through good and evil first being separated into Cain- and Abel-type representatives, and then Abel winning over Cain to God's side. Abel's position is not guaranteed, it must be earned through a life of faith and service. Once thus qualified, Abel's mission is to educate and love Cain, while preventing him from repeating the sins of aggression and murder.

This process starts in the individual. Everyone suffers from a nature divided between their Abel-type original nature in the image of God, and their Cain-type nature inherited from the Fall. Thus the first step is for individuals to strengthen their Abel-type nature through study of scriptures, prayer and a lifestyle in imitation of Christ, and to diminish the influence of their Cain-type nature.

Armed with an understanding of Cain and Abel, and strengthened by a life of virtue, individuals can then effectively identify and confront Cain-type ideas, individuals and groups, and provide Abel-type alternatives. It is at this point that God works through the Holy Spirit to bring about transformation of the world, step by step.

True Christian Discipleship

How, then, do Christians become Abel-type disciples of Christ? It begins with recognizing Jesus as the Messiah and then dedicating oneself to following him, at the risk of your life. This commitment to follow Jesus even to death reverses the mistakes made in the Garden of Eden when Adam and Eve risked their lives by following Satan, ignoring the warning that they would die if they ate the fruit of the Tree of the Knowledge of Good and Evil.

Fully uniting with Jesus also means taking a step beyond believing in him as the savior by joining him in the work of salvation. Jesus gave instructions to his disciples to do exactly that, promising that if they followed his example they would also be blessed with the powers of healing that he enjoyed. During his life on earth, this meant focusing on saving the Jewish people:

> These twelve Jesus sent out with the following instructions: "Do not go among the Gentiles or enter any town of the Samaritans. Go rather to the lost sheep of Israel. As you go, proclaim this message: 'The kingdom of heaven has come near.' Heal the sick, raise the dead, cleanse those who have leprosy, drive out demons. Freely you have received; freely give." (Matthew 10:5-8)

Thus being converted to a belief in Jesus, or being renewed in this faith through being 'born again', is only the first step of true discipleship. The second step is to fulfill the responsibility of liberating Cain from evil, starting with your own fallen nature and then also confronting and overcoming the fallen behavior of Cain-type individuals, groups, organizations and ideologies.

The preferred path in confronting Cain is to use words and persuasion. This is definitely the right way to engage with other Christians and members of other faiths who are likewise part of the providence. It is also the right way to engage with anti-providence Cain-type individuals and groups who are willing to accept Abel's viewpoint and change their behavior accordingly. The model for this transformation was demonstrated by the thief who was crucified to the right of Jesus, but who on the cross repented of his sins and was thereby saved.

However, if Cain is bent on destroying Abel and the providence it may be necessary to use force to prevent Cain's success. This was a conclusion that the Protestant theologian Dietrich Bonhoeffer came to when he suspended his pacifism to join a plot to kill Hitler. By killing Hitler, Bonhoeffer rightly believed that he could limit the harm perpetrated by Hitler on the world.

Cain must not be allowed to destroy Abel. When this has happened in the central providence, the providence has been delayed and the suffering of humanity greatly increased. The first demonstration of this was when Cain killed Abel and the sinful nature of Adam and Eve became fully implanted in their descendants, prolonging for millennia the establishment of God's ideal. When Noah's son Ham was invaded by Satan, the benefits of the flood were lost and the providence delayed until Abraham appeared, four centuries later. When Abraham failed in the sacrifice of birds, his descendants were destined to suffer four centuries of slavery in Egypt. When Judah was destroyed by Babylon the providence was delayed until Jerusalem and the Temple were rebuilt after their exile. And when Jesus was killed by the establishment in Israel the providence was delayed until today.

Following Jesus is never easy. For Jesus and eleven of his disciples it led to martyrdom, because Satan continued to rule through Cain-type people in Israel, the Roman Empire and the rest of the world. For many other Christians, such as those in Communist countries for example, going the way of the cross has meant great suffering and sometimes death.

In his final words to his disciples after his resurrection, Jesus passed to them his power to drive out evil spirits, heal the sick and even raise people from death. Significantly, no longer were they to limit their work to members of the 12 tribes, who had now lost their privileged position in the providence, but they were to serve all people, Jew and non-Jew alike:

> And Jesus came and said to them, "All authority in heaven and on earth has been given to me. Go therefore and make disciples of all nations, baptizing them in the name of the Father and of the Son and of the Holy Spirit, teaching them to observe all that I have commanded you; and lo, I am with you always, to the close of the age." (Matthew 28:18-20)

Beginning at Pentecost, the disciples experienced the outpouring of the Holy Spirit and the miraculous powers they had been granted by Jesus. They had truly become his representatives on earth, practicing true discipleship.

What does this mean for Christians today? It means that we cannot simply enjoy the fruits of Jesus' sacrifice on the cross, from which we have reaped so many spiritual benefits and the blessings of salvation. We have to recognize that the life of Jesus was cut short by the faithlessness of the people of Israel, and that his original mission was not to die a martyr on the cross but to be the heavenly leader of the nation of Israel, showing the way to salvation for the world. As Christians, our mission is, then, to shoulder the work of Jesus, to become as close as possible to the standard of an absolute Abel and contribute whatever we can to preparations for the second coming.

Christianity's Mission as Abel is to Prepare for Christ's Return

Abel himself suffered from the inheritance of fallen nature from his parents, and Christians likewise suffer from the inheritance of a fallen nature from their parents and ancestors. Hence a world with 2.4 billion Christians continues to suffer from all manner of evil. Simply, salvation through the cross is not complete and therefore the earth remains under Satan's dominion.

As we have shown, the pattern of the providence is that if an Abel figure fails in their mission, the Cain-side advances, the providence is delayed, and human suffering is increased as new conditions must be set to enable a replacement Abel to appear. At the time of Jesus, John the Baptist was sent as Elijah, to prepare the way for the Messiah. This was the mission of Abel-to prepare Israel (in the position of Cain) to receive Jesus as a sinless Second Adam. When John doubted Jesus and declined the role of chief disciple, Jesus himself had to take on the mission of Abel to prepare the way for his own true mission as the Messiah, a new sinless Adam.

When Israel rejected and killed Jesus, the providence of Abel and the Second Adam was lost. Jesus had to sacrifice his own life on the cross, his disciples had to face a similar end, and Israel and the Temple were destroyed. The whole history of Christianity that unfolded became one of suffering and sacrifice. But not without a providential purpose.

Christianity has inherited and has to restore the mission of John the Baptist. This time, then, Christians have to make sure that the second coming of Christ is not a repeat of the first coming in the sense that it must not lead to rejection of the second coming of Christ by the Christian establishment, which is now in the Cain position to Christ. This time, too, Christians must recognize that the providence is global, meaning that it embraces all people, not just a chosen few—as was the case when Jesus came to save the chosen people of Israel before any others. It is for this reason that Christianity has spread throughout the world in preparation for the second coming of Christ.

The Real Meaning of the End Times

Thus the meaning of the end times is not the realization of the apocalyptic events described in Revelation, the final chapter of the Bible. Rather, it is the final contest between good and evil, Abel and Cain, for the Creator to achieve a rightful dominion over the earth. This destiny, or telos, of the providence will be reached only once Christians fulfill their responsibilities as Abel.

The Book of Revelation features angelic messages to seven churches in Asia Minor. These places were never important in providential history so the messages have to be taken as lessons for all. Furthermore, the messages are two millennia old, so inevitably they lack a modern context. It is up to us to determine what this ancient revelation about the end times means for us today.

We are certainly living in what could well be the end times. We see that evil has reached a pinnacle of power in the form of destructive ideologies and cruel regimes. But we also see a world in which there is abundant potential for good, which can be triumphant if Christians show the way to all humanity by emulating the lifestyle of Christ. They must embrace people of other faiths, and especially Judaism and Islam, and reject the purveyors of atheistic materialism and oppose resolutely the regimes built on Marxist ideologies.

What Can We Know About the Time and Place?

Many Christians are waiting for Jesus to return in glory, to destroy evil and establish the Kingdom of Heaven on earth. But there have always been disputes and disagreements as to when and where this might take place. And predictions so far have all proved wrong. As Jesus himself said:

> But about that day or hour no one knows, not even the angels in heaven, nor the Son, but only the Father. Take heed, watch; for you do not know when the time will come. (Mark 13:32-33)

We should ask, then: "What should we watch for?" And: "What are God and Jesus waiting for?" Surely the answer is that they are waiting and working for the time when the world is ready to receive Christ once more. This time the environment must be prepared so that the people unite with Christ and provide the support he needs to complete his mission. The people creating that environment must be humble before God but also enlightened regarding the providence and its enemies. As Saint Paul wrote:

> For our knowledge is imperfect and our prophecy is imperfect; but when the perfect comes, the imperfect will pass away. When I was a child, I spoke like a child, I thought like a child, I reasoned like a child; when I became a man, I gave up childish ways. For now we see in a mirror dimly, but then face to face. Now I know in part; then I shall understand fully, even as I have been fully understood. (I Corinthians 13:9-12)

The time for the second coming of Christ, then, is when there is a sufficient foundation of goodness and wisdom among those prepared to receive him. This is the purpose behind the evolution of Christianity that we have described taking place over centuries. This providential movement took Christianity through the Great Schism and the Protestant Reformation to the creation of America as a nation founded on the principle that our rights derive from God, not man or government. From America, these ideas have spread worldwide.

That is not to say that the founding of America as a providential nation was without blemish. As with all events in the providence, a Cain-type facsimile of the Divine plan—inspired by Satan—appears first, seeking to dominate Abel. In the case of America, Cain was represented by the commercially-motivated settlers in Virginia who arrived in Jamestown in 1607. They enslaved natives and, in 1619, introduced slavery of Africans to America. Thus they were a Cain-type counterpart to the Abel-type settlers who arrived on the Mayflower in 1620. These pilgrims made peace with the Indians and celebrated their first harvest with the dominant tribe of their area. (It would take a bloody civil war some 240 years later to settle once and for all that America was to be an Abel-type nation. This was accomplished when the states which continued to embrace slavery were defeated by those that had abolished this evil practice.)

The founders of the United States were inspired by the same spirit that gave the Pilgrims the courage to brave the Atlantic Ocean in a small boat, at the risk of their lives. Only 40 of the 102 men, women and children who set sail from Plymouth, England would survive the first winter in the New World, but they would become the seeds of a revolutionary people who would establish a government under God for the first time since Israel was destroyed. Their zealous commitment to God was strengthened by Christian revivalists such as George Fox, John Wesley, George Whitfield and Jonathan Edwards, who inspired America's Great Awakening in the 18th century, which in turn inspired the revolution of 1776.

This means that the founders were indeed under God's guidance when they declared independence from Britain, "with a firm reliance on the protection of Divine Providence," as it says in the Declaration of Independence. They may not have all understood it at the time, but that providence and the blessings it brought to America and its people were not for America alone, but for the whole world.

We assert, then, that since its founding America has played a central role in the Divine Providence.

Contributing to the fulfillment of this purpose, America has long been a refuge for people from around the world, for people of all races and religions—many to escape religious and/or political oppression in their own countries. Thus America has been a beacon to the world for Christian values expressed in democratic governments and free markets, and a bulwark against Cain-type tyranny and totalitarianism. America has frequently come to the assistance of countries and peoples suffering oppression, such as those forced to live under Nazism and Communism.

Not since Nehemiah and Ezra worked to restore Israel to its providential role by renewing the people's commitment to the Mosaic Law and rebuilding Jerusalem and the Temple after the Babylonian exile—some four centuries before Jesus appeared and two millennia before America was founded—has there been a nation established with such a clear and promising role to play in the providence.

This does not mean that the providence will culminate in America, but it does imply that America has had, and continues to have, a very significant role in the providence. Christians should recognize this and work to keep America oriented to its providential purpose, keeping in mind that the second advent will take place when the preparations for it are complete.

Building the Kingdom of Heaven on Earth

Christianity as global Abel must lay the foundations for the kingdom by creating an environment on earth that is conducive to the realization of the Divine Providence, a new Garden of Eden to receive a new Adam and Eve. This kingdom that we pray will descend from heaven, will actually be established by the people who fulfill their responsibilities and are bound forever to our loving Creator by an unbreakable love.

The Kingdom of Heaven is not home to temples, churches or mosques; it is the realm in which perfected men and women live at one with their Creator. It is described poetically in Revelation:

> Then I saw "a new heaven and a new earth," for the first heaven and the first earth had passed away, and there was no longer any sea. I saw the Holy City, the new Jerusalem, coming down out of heaven from God, prepared as a bride beautifully dressed for her husband. And I heard a loud voice from the throne saying, "Look! God's dwelling place is now among the people, and he will dwell with them. They will be his people, and God himself will be with them and be their God. 'He will wipe every tear from their eyes. There will be no more death' or mourning or crying or pain, for the old order of things has passed away." (Revelation 21:1-4)

In the final analysis, then, only sinless men and women can create and dwell in the Kingdom of Heaven, and it is only a sinless Christ who can lead them to that kingdom.

Acknowledgments

My first real encounter with Jesus came when I was 13. I can't remember the circumstances exactly, but I was in nature when I experienced an overwhelming spiritual embrace that was both comforting and challenging. The comforting part was to feel absolutely certain of the existence of a Divine acknowledgment of my existence; the challenging part was the companion realization that this was a call for me to dedicate my life to serving God and humanity. That call has continued to echo in my heart and mind ever since.

At the time I was living with my family in a Bruderhof community on an estate outside London that had been converted to accommodate dozens of families. We lived together without owning a thing as individuals or families. All property was held in common in imitation of the way the very first Christians pooled their resources (see Acts 2:44). As children we attended school on the premises, and as adults we worked together in communal businesses.

The Bruderhof was established as a Christian community in Germany in 1920. It was intended to offer a radical alternative to a world of conflicts that was still recovering from the First World War. Growing up I had few theological notions beyond a concept of Jesus as a savior who was somehow one with God, the Creator. In retrospect, the Bruderhof was somewhat

Quaker-like in emphasizing listening to the voice of conscience as the basis for practicing a virtuous life.

Beyond reading from the Bible, the Bruderhof looked in particular to the writings of its founder, a German by the name of Eberhard Arnold, as well as several Anabaptist authors, notably Jakob Hutter and Peter Riedemann, the founders of the Hutterite communities that were transplanted from Europe to North America in the 1870s, where they thrive to this day. Some of the other sources were Christian Socialists, including the Swiss theologians Jakob Kutter and Leonhard Ragaz as well as Christoph Blumhardt, a German theologian who was active in the Marxism-based Social Democratic Party of Germany (SPD) at the end of the 19th century.

An overarching belief of the Bruderhof is that the Sermon on the Mount should be the basis for a Christian life that can best be practiced in communal living. As a result members are held to a very high moral standard, on par with life in a monastic order. As with all human institutions, fallen nature can damage or even destroy the best intentions, but for me the Bruderhof has continued to represent a noble effort to translate the ideals of Christianity into a life of dedication to Jesus.

I thought the Bruderhof would be my own destiny, but when I moved away to study I encountered some equally devout Christians who were members of various denominations I knew nothing about. I began what would become a life-long practice of listening to people of faith in an effort to understand the basis for their beliefs and practices, and studying their scriptures to the same end. This started within the world of Christian sects and denominations, but later included Muslims, Jews and believers in Asian spiritual traditions.

The most important modern Christian for me was C.S. Lewis. What attracted me to his writing was his ability to take Christian ideals and translate them into the real world of our experience. In his books like *The Screwtape Letters* and *The Great Divorce*, Lewis brought the contest between good and evil alive. His theology was embedded in his storytelling, but also elaborated in his apologetic works, such as *Mere Christianity*.

This learning process stimulated questions. Above all, I wanted to know what the best way would be for me to fulfill my teenage commitment to serve Jesus and God. The moral imperatives of the Sermon on the Mount were clear, but what was I supposed to do with my life? How could I best invest my time and energy to fulfill my purpose as a Christian? I found no answer in the writings of Lewis or any other source that I explored.

Like most Anabaptists, Bruderhof members are pacifists, and I thought anti-war activism might be my calling. On reflection, however, I realized that wars are the product of conflicts within people, and thus there could be no end to conflicts without resolving their root cause in fallen human nature.

The Bruderhof tried to address this dilemma by withdrawing from secular society. But this was no longer a solution that appealed to me. I wanted to know God's purpose for all people, regardless of their religion or race. And I wanted to know God's plan for the world after Jesus was crucified and in the present moment. In other words, I wanted to understand the Divine Providence for the world and how I could be part of it.

The answer would come through a former member of the Bruderhof who invited me to visit a group she was living with called the Unified Family. The members were followers of a Korean religious leader called Sun M. Moon. I found their teaching challenging but intriguing. The ideas they shared shed a whole new light on what I had learned from the Bible, and provided a clear set of answers to many of my questions.

That was more than 50 years ago. Over the intervening decades, I have had the chance to encounter a very wide variety of religious beliefs and practices in various parts of the world, from Orthodox monks on Mount Athos to Sufis performing *dhikr* on a public street in Omdurman beneath the sweltering Sudanese sun and Orthodox Jews celebrating a traditional wedding in Israel. I have learned that while no two people share completely identical beliefs—and therefore religions will never achieve perfect agreement on theological matters—all people of faith and good will who become

Acknowledgments

mature in their thinking and faith can learn to live in harmony with one another.

Furthermore, I have learned that the purpose of our Creator as manifest in the Divine Providence embraces all people, irrespective of any differences imposed by race, religion or nationality. I believe that all good people must band together to confront and defeat the forces that would do away with all religion and destroy the very fabric of moral societies everywhere, societies that are built by loving families working together to create virtuous communities. The common enemy of all people of faith and good will are those who deny the existence of God and intrinsic human goodness, and seek to impose a materialist alternative to the Kingdom of Heaven on earth.

Where does Jesus fit in this picture? He continues to be the most consequential person in history. Because of his purity and great intimacy with our heavenly Father, he established the way we must go to fulfill God's providence. If we look beyond our personal interest in being saved from our sinful nature by Christ, we will come to understand his pivotal role in history and what we need to do to help him hasten the final fulfillment of the Divine Providence.

I hope this book helps with that understanding. Its contents represent my personal thinking and perspective alone, informed by the influences mentioned above. Its final form has benefitted significantly from the input of a long-time friend and collaborator, David James.

Thomas Cromwell
Washington, DC
December 2022

Table of Contents in Detail

Preface ix

Introduction xiii
    Jesus Seen From a Providential Perspective   xiii
    The Three Parts of This Book   xiv
    The Need to Complete the Biblical Narrative   xv

PART I
Providential Preparations For The Messiah

1 The Mission of the Messiah 1
Replacing Adam as God's Sinless Son
    Adam and Eve and the Need for a Messiah   1
    Divine Providence and Human Responsibility   2
    The Nature and Mission of the Messiah in the Divine Providence   3
    Ending the Dominion of Evil and Sin   4
    The Mission of Israel   5
    The Christian Notion of Salvation Through the Messiah   7
    Messianic Expectations and Jesus   9

2 The Cain-Abel Paradigm 11
The Key to Understanding Providential History
    The First Family   11
    Cain and Abel Inherited Fallen Nature   13
    The Cain-Abel Paradigm   13
    Cain's Falsehoods Precede Abel's Truths in the Providence   14
    Cain Can and Should Become Abel   15
    The Importance of Personal Responsibility   16
    Jesus' Mission as Absolute Abel   17

Table of Contents in Detail

3 Jesus: God or Man? 18
Addressing Christological Confusion

An Age-Old Question Divides Christians	18
The Holy Trinity	19
How Can We Resolve This Confusion?	21
A Providential Perspective	21
Jesus In the Words of God	22
Jesus In the Words of Satan	23
Jesus In the Words of Angels	24
Jesus In the Words of Old Testament Prophets	24
Jesus In the Words of his Disciples	25
Jesus In his Own Words	27
Jesus Had to be a Man	29

4 Did Jesus Pre-Exist His Birth? 30
The Role of Predestination in the Providence

The Meaning of "the Word"	30
Jesus Embodied the *Logos*	31
Predestination	32
Predestination and Personal Responsibility	33
Being Responsible Requires Spiritual Maturity	33
Predestination After the Crucifixion	34

5 Jesus Embodied the Mosaic Law 36
The Transition From Servant to Son

The Law Prepared Israel for the Messiah	36
The Evolution of Divinely-Inspired Laws	37
The First Legal System	37
The Radical Teachings of Jesus	39
A New Understanding of Circumcision	40
Differences Between Moses, the Prophets and Jesus	42

6 The Tabernacle and Temple Foreshadowed the Messiah 43
Establishing a Tradition of Obedience to Abel

The Tabernacle Was in the Image of the Messiah	43
The Levites Were Responsible to Uphold God's Word	45
The Temple Replaced the Tabernacle	46
The Tabernacle and Temple Had to be Kept Pure	47
The Temple Was Corrupted at the Time of Jesus	48
Finally the Actual Messiah Appeared	48

7 Jesus Belongs to the Order of Melchizedek 50
The Messiah is Both High Priest and King

The First Reference to Melchizedek	50
The Second Reference to Melchizedek	52
The Third Reference to Melchizedek	53
The Return of Melchizedek	55

8 Was Mary the Mother of God? 57
Seeking a Sinless Woman to Replace Eve

The Immaculate Conception	58
Zechariah and Elizabeth Supported Mary	59
Two Providential Families Prepared for the Birth of Jesus	61
Mary Risked Her Life to Follow Divine Instructions	62
Mary Substitutes for a Second Eve	63
The Holy Spirit as Divine Mother	63

9 Providential Women Risk all to Restore Eve. 65
An Old Testament History Leading to Mary

Abraham, Sarah and Hagar	66
Isaac, Rebekah, Esau and Jacob	71
Jacob, Leah and Rachel	74
Judah and Tamar	75
Lot and his Two daughters	78
Boaz and Ruth, Obed, Jesse and David	79
Esther and King Ahasuerus	81
Mary Inherited These Women's Foundation	84

10 Jesus Inherited the Missions of Moses and David 85
Combining the Roles of Priest and King

How Did Jesus Represent Moses and David?	85
The Importance of Being a Descendant of Levi and Moses	86
The Importance of Being a Descendant of Judah and David	87
Jesus' Disciples Said he was Descended from King David	91
But Jesus Rejected the 'Son of David' Identity	92
A Providential Perspective	92

11 Preparing a Nation and the World for the Messiah 95
Central and Supporting Providential Developments

The Importance of Abraham's Family	95
Jacob's Victorious Course as Abel and Adam	96
Rebekah's Victorious Role as Eve	97
Establishing a Nation to Receive the Messiah	98
400 Years of Slavery in Egypt	98
Moses Struggled With a Disobedient People	99
400 Years of Judges	102
The United Kingdom of Israel	103
The Divided Kingdoms and Babylonian Exile	104
Israel is Reconstituted	104
The Final 400-Year Preparation of Israel for the Messiah	106
The Axial Age: Worldwide Preparation for a Global Savior	107

PART II
The Providence Betrayed In The Crucifixion

12 Jesus' Difficult Early Life. 110
His Family Failed to Support Him

Jesus Was Targeted for Murder at Birth	110
Jesus Was Treated as an Ordinary, Non-Levitical Jew	112

Joseph and Mary Received Many Messages About Jesus	115
Jesus' Parents Failed to Grasp His Importance	118
Mary's Mission as a Good Eve and Mother	120
Joseph's Mission as Good Archangel and Son of David	121
The Family Did Not Help Jesus in his Public Ministry	122

13 The Sermon on the Mount 126
Teaching the Way of Abel

Jesus Begins his Ministry	126
Revealing the Depth of God's Parental Heart	127
A Revolutionary Message	127
The Sermon on the Mount: Teaching the Way of Perfected Abel	130
The Teachings of Jesus Superseded the Law	132
How Cain and Abel Can Be Reconciled on Abel's Terms	133
Love Was Jesus' Core Teaching	134

14 Parables and Miracles to Open Minds and Hearts 136
A Stubborn People Rejected Jesus' Message

Jesus Faced a Proud, Close-Minded People	136
Lessons Through Parables	137
Miraculous Healings	138
Healing Bodies; Purifying Spirits	140
A Stubborn and Ungrateful People	140

15 Jesus' Mastery of the Spirit World. 142
Cain and Abel Spirits and Angels Influence Our Lives

Cain-type and Abel-type Spirits and Angels	142
The Identity of Demons and Divines	143
The Conditions We Make Attract Good or Evil Spirits	143
A Failed Condition Requires a Greater Sacrifice to Restore it	144
Jesus Made Conditions for the World	146
Jesus Understood and Controlled the Spirit World	146
Evil Spirits Recognized Jesus	148
The Responsibility of Those Cleansed by Jesus	148

Table of Contents in Detail

The Disciples Inherited Jesus' Spiritual Powers	149
Ignorance of the Spirit World Persists	150

16 Persecution by Israel's Political Establishment 152
Herod and Pilate had Jesus Tortured and Killed

Herod's Illegitimate Dynasty	152
Herod Should Have Followed Jesus	153
The Herodian Dynasty Conspired to Kill Jesus	154

17 Persecution by Israel's Religious Establishment 158
The Wise Men of the Temple Rejected Jesus

Israel's Ossified Religious Establishment	158
Jesus and His Teachings Were Rejected by the Religious Leaders	159
Jesus Chastised the Religious Leaders for Their Failings	160
Jesus Identified His Persecutors as Cain-like	161
A Cain-type Lust to Kill Jesus	162
Cain's Self-righteousness	164
Only Jesus Understood the Heart of the Father	164

18 The Doubting Mind of John the Baptist 166
The Crucial Mission of Elijah Went Unfulfilled

The Miraculous Birth of John the Baptist	166
The Providential Person and Mission of John the Baptist	169
John's Mission Was Greater Than That of a Prophet	171
John and Jesus Went Down Different Paths	172
Why John Was So Important for the Success of Jesus	173
Why John's Association With Elijah Was So Important	173
Jesus Identified John as the Returned Elijah	174
But John Denied Being Elijah or a Prophet	175
John's Unrealistic Expectations for the Messiah	176
The Meaning of John Baptizing Jesus	176
Why John Didn't Follow Jesus After His Baptism	178
Jesus Rebuked John for His Lack of Faith	180

19 The Catastrophic Consequences of John's Failure 182
Moses and Elijah Confirm a Change in Jesus' Mission

A History of Small Mistakes with Huge Consequences	182
John's Mistakes Had Catastrophic Consequences for Jesus	184
Jesus Had to Redo John's Foundation	185
The First Temptation	186
The Second Temptation	186
The Third Temptation	187
Jesus Had to Do The Work of John	188
Jesus' Path Now Led to the Cross	189
A Providential Perspective: The Kingdom Delayed	191

20 Betrayal By His Disciples 192
Satan Invaded the Inner Circle of Jesus

Satan's Murderous Agenda	192
Satan Always Uses Those Closest to His Target	192
After John Failed, Jesus Chose 12 Disciples	193
Judas Became Satan's Tool	195
Jesus' Last Line of Defense: Peter, James and John	197
Only Peter Followed Jesus	198
Satan's Victory	199

21 The Tragic Death of Jesus on the Cross. 201
Cain-type Forces Conspired to Kill Christ

More Than a Lack of Understanding	201
The Cain-Like Conspiracy to Kill Jesus	202
The Unwitting Conspirators	203
The Witting Conspirators	205
The Significance of Jesus' Prayer in Gethsemane	207
The Profound Agony of Jesus	208
Evidence That the Cross Was Not God's Will	209
The Crucifixion Ended the Temple's Providential Purpose	210
Consequences for Followers of Christ	211

Table of Contents in Detail

PART III
Christians Inherit A Providential Mission From Jesus

22 Consequences of the Crucifixion 214
The Creation of an Otherworldly Kingdom

Repercussions from Jesus' Death on the Cross	214
A Spiritual Victory and Outpouring	214
The Spiritual Power Unleashed at Pentecost	215
An Otherworldly Kingdom	218
A Christian Heaven	219
The Way of Abel for Christians	220
Immeasurable Suffering Since Jesus	221
What if Jesus Had Not Been Killed?	221

23 The Meaning of Salvation Through the Cross 224
Why the Kingdom of Heaven Remains Elusive

Salvation is a Process, Not an Event	224
The Original Mind Seeks Salvation	225
Forgiveness of Sin and Salvation in the Old Testament	225
Forgiveness of Sin and Salvation in the New Testament	228
From Old Testament Servants to Adopted Children of God	231
The Limits of Salvation Through the Cross	232
Was Jesus Shedding Blood Important to Salvation?	234
Shedding Blood Does Not Remove Sin	236
Was the Crucifixion Pre-Ordained?	236

24 Inheriting the Mission of Jesus 238
The Path to Becoming One with Christ

The Imitation of Christ	239
Inheriting the Mission of Jesus	240
The Gifts of Christ For The Christian Providence	241
Purification And Empowerment Through Baptism	241

The Importance of Baptism with the Holy Spirit	243
The Disciples Were Empowered to Baptize	243
Infant Baptism Replaced Circumcision	246
The Importance of Adult Baptism	247
Becoming Christ-like Through the Eucharist	249
Blessings Come With Responsibilities	250

25 Inheriting the Mission of Israel............................251
Christians Must Learn from the Israelites' Mistakes

The Birth of a New Religion	251
The Providential Mission of Christianity	252
A New Iteration of Israel's Mission	253
Christians Can Expect to Suffer Like Jesus	254
Christians Must Not Repeat Israel's Mistakes	255

26 The Providence Unfolds Through Christianity 258
Preparing for the Second Coming of Christ

Christian Discipleship Requires Faith and Works	258
What Then is Predestination?	259
Predestination for Christians	260
Purification Through Cain-Abel Divisions	261
The Great Schism and Protestant Reformation	262
From Wycliffe to Luther	263
The Radical Reformation	264
The Protestant Work Ethic	265
The Counter-Reformation	265
The Pilgrims and America's Great Awakening	266
Preparing for a Second Coming of Christ	268

27 Christianity as Global Abel............................271
The Challenge to Save a Cain-Dominated World

The Blessings and Responsibilities of Abel	271
Christians and Fellow Christians	272
Christians and Members of Other Religions	272

Table of Contents in Detail

Christian Abels Must Give Light to the Whole World	273
Christians Together Must Create a New, Abel-type Israel	277
All Religion is Personal	277
The Kingdom of Heaven Has No Religions	278
Christians and Materialism	280
Christians and Materialist Ideologies	281
Christians, Science and Technology	281
Christians and Politics	282
Christians and Economic Systems	282

28 The Role of Christianity in Conflict and War 283
The Importance of Discerning Cain from Abel

The Christian Dilemma Over Use of Force	283
The Cain-Abel Paradigm and Conflict Resolution	286
Discerning Two Types of Cain	286
Cains Who Are Part of the Providence	287
Cains Bent on Destroying the Providence	289
Moses Purified Israel by Killing Internal Enemies	290
Moses Instructed the Israelites to Destroy Their Enemies	293
Jesus Was in No Position to Use Force	295
Jesus as Abel Sacrificed His Life to Save Cain	296
Christians Should Follow Jesus When Using Force	297
Christians Cannot Compromise with Evil	297
Christian Discernment of Cain and Abel	299

29 Christianity and Judaism 301
Becoming An Abel-Type Younger Brother

The Crucifixion Resulted in the Destruction of Israel	301
Jewish Messianism Lives On	303
A Bitter Relationship With Christianity	304
Christianity's Elder Brother in the Providence	306

30 Christianity and Islam 308
Becoming An Abel-Type Older Brother

The Root of Conflicts Among the Abrahamic Faiths	309
The Bitter Experience of Hagar and Ishmael	310
The Resentment of Hagar and Ishmael Burns in Muslims	313
Christians Are Tasked With Saving All People	314
Christianity Inherited the Mission to Love Ishmael and Esau	315
The Unexpected Advent of Islam	316
A Brief History of Mohammed and Islam	317
Islam and the Bible	319
The Abrahamic Faiths Must Unite as Abel to the World	320
The Shared Responsibility of the Abrahamic Faiths	321

31 Christianity and Marxism 323
Becoming a Resolute Abel to Defeat Cain

The Importance of Understanding Marxism	323
The Bloody French Revolution	324
Marxism Destroys Religion and Throttles Faith	325
Marxism is the Perfection of Anti-Christ Ideology	326
Marxism is Anti-Science	328
Marxism Destroys the Family	330
Marxism Demonizes Private Property	330
Marxism Offers False Utopias	332
Marxism's Utopian Seduction is Based on a Lie	333
Marxism Perfects the Ideology of Satan and Cain	335
How Marxists Are Born	336
The Bitter Truth About Socialism and Communism	337
Neo-Marxism Spreads The Cancer of Marxism	338
The Importance of Choosing God Over Mammon	340
The Fallacy of Christian Socialism	342
The Fallacy That Capitalism is Evil	343
The Fallacy of Supporting Social Justice Agendas	344
The Righteous Christian Response to Marxism	345
Christianity's Responsibility as Abel	346

32 Christianity and Science 348
Humanism Spurs Both Reformation and Renaissance
    Science and Technology Have Transformed the World   348
    But Science Cannot Quench Our Thirst for Truth and Love   349
    The Providential Advent of Modern Science   350
    The Christian Humanism of Petrarch And Erasmus   351
    The Intertwined History of the Reformation and Renaissance   352
    Freed From Church Dogma, Science Took Wing   354
    The Compatibility of Science and Religion   355
    The Moral Compass of Nature   357
    Christianity Should Harness Science for the Providence   359

33 Thy Kingdom Come on Earth. 361
Culmination of the Divine Providence
    Heaven Must Be Established on Earth   361
    Two Millennia of Christian Evolution   362
    The Futility of Just Waiting for Christ   363
    Use the Cain-Abel Paradigm to Recognize and Defeat Evil   365
    True Christian Discipleship   366
    Christianity's Mission as Abel is to Prepare for Christ's Return   368
    The Real Meaning of the End Times   369
    What Can We Know About the Time and Place?   370
    Building the Kingdom of Heaven on Earth   373

Acknowledgments. 374
Table of Contents in Detail 378
Index 390

Index

Abiathar 37
Abijah 166
Abijam 90
Abimelech 68, 69, 72, 97
Abishalom 90
Abu Bakr 318
Achaemenid 46, 81, 83, 105
Aenon 179
Africa 306, 315, 318, 342
Ahasuerus 81, 82
Alexander the Great 106, 108, 153
Alexandria 262
Alhambra Decree 305
Ali 318, 319
Amish 265
Ammon 96
Ammonites 79
Anabaptist 284, 342
Anabaptists 248, 264
Anaxagoras 107
Anaximander 107
Antichrist 326, 327
Antigonus II Mattathias 106
Antioch 262
Antiochus 47, 106
Antipater 152
Antithesis 329

Apostle xvi, 41, 91, 240
Apostles 19, 124, 216
Arab 152, 317
Arabia 314, 316, 318
Arabian Peninsula 308
Arabs 71, 95, 316
Aramaic 302
Aramean 71
Archangel 1, 11, 65, 68, 96, 121
Archelaus 154
Archimedes 107
Aristarchus ix, x, 107, 352
Aristotle 107
Ark 37, 44, 46, 89, 183
Artaxerxes 83, 84
Asher 75
Assyria 105
Assyrians 6, 104, 260, 290
Ataturk 318
Axial Age 107, 354
Babylon 6, 46, 47, 104, 107, 129, 271, 295, 301, 367
Babylonia 83
Babylonian exile 39, 104, 129, 218, 372
Babylonians 47, 83, 104, 153, 260, 290
Baghdad 318

Index

Barabbas 163
Bathsheba 90
Beatitudes 130, 131, 132, 134
Benjamin 75, 103, 104, 166
Bilhah 75, 292
Black Lives Matter 344
BLM 345
Blumhardt, Christoph 342
Boaz 52, 79, 80, 81, 112
Bolshevik 337
Bonhoeffer, Dietrich 367
Bourgeoisie 329, 330, 332
Bruderhof 342
Buddhism 107
Bukhari 318
Byzantine Empire 318
Caiaphas 195, 196, 202, 206, 207, 217
Caleb 99, 100, 101, 293
Caliph 318, 319
Caliphate 318
Calvin, John 264
Capitalism 108, 329, 330, 331, 332, 336, 337, 342, 343, 344
Capitalist 329, 332, 338, 342
Catholic Catechism 20, 57
Centurion 189, 244, 275
Chamberlain, Neville 298
China 107, 240, 255, 298, 299, 343
Circumcision 38, 40, 41, 42, 246, 247, 315
Cleisthenes 108
Communism 220, 240, 285, 326, 330, 333, 337, 338, 341, 343, 372
Communist 255, 285, 298, 299, 324, 326, 330, 331, 333, 334, 337, 338, 342, 343, 368
Communists 330, 331, 332, 337
Confucianism 107
Constantinople 19, 262, 288, 318
Copernican revolution x
Copernican theory x, 353
Copernicus, Nicolaus ix, 351, 352

Cornelius 244, 245, 248, 275
Counter-Reformation 19, 266, 352
Crusades 261, 263, 288, 305, 309
Cuba 338, 343, 363
Cyrus the Great 107
Damascus 51, 318
Darius 83, 84
Darwin 328, 329
Darwinism 329
Das Kapital 329
Democritus 107
Derrida, Jacques 339
Descartes 354
Devil 23, 187, 188, 244
Discipleship 215, 248, 250, 258, 366
Ecumenical Council 263
Edomite 106, 152, 207
Edomites 313, 314, 316
Edwards, Jonathan 267, 372
Einstein, Albert 356
Eleazar 294
Engels, Friedrich 324
Ephraim 79, 80, 102, 292
Ephrathah 25, 81, 111
Ephrathite 80, 81
Ephrathites 79, 112
Erasmus x, 266, 352
Eratosthenes 107
Esther 81, 82, 83
Eucharist 241, 250, 252
Euclid 107
Eudoxus 107
Fascism 285
Fascist 298, 324, 337
Fatalism 33, 259
Feudalism 329
Foucault, Michel 339
Fox, George 266, 372
Frankfurt School 281, 330, 339
Freud 339
Galilee 9, 58, 138, 154, 177, 243, 244
Galilei, Galileo x, 351

391

Gerar 68, 72
Gethsemane 28, 196, 198, 203, 205, 208, 219, 301, 362
Gettysburg Address 268
Gide, André 333
Gladiators 254
Gnosticism 19
Goliath 89
Great Diaspora 210, 289, 302
Hadith 318
Ham 15, 183, 184, 197, 367
Haman 82, 83
Haran 66, 71, 74, 75, 80, 96
Haskell, Edward 358
Hasmonean 106, 152, 153, 207
Hebrew 2, 24, 302
Heliocentric ix, 352
Heliocentrism x, 353
Herod Antipas 154, 155, 157, 177, 180, 193, 205, 207, 301
Herodian dynasty 53, 93, 153, 154, 206, 222, 316
Herod the Great 48, 106, 110, 152, 153, 154, 207
Hinduism 107
Hippocrates 107
Hitler 298, 299, 367
Humanism 266, 284, 350, 351, 352
Hus, John 19, 263, 351
Hutterite 265, 342
Idumea 106
Imam 319
India 107
Inquisition x, 240, 305, 353
Inter-faith 278
Inter-religious 309
Iscariot, Judas 195, 196, 207
Isnad 318
Jacobins 324
Jainism 107
Japheth 183, 184, 197
Jaspers, Karl 107

Jeremiah 2, 80, 104, 128, 227, 228
Jeroboam 90, 103
Jesse 52, 79, 81, 88, 112
Jesuit 266
John of the Cross 266
Jordan 102, 170, 177, 179, 204, 293, 294
Joshua 2, 88, 99, 100, 101, 102, 103, 284, 290, 293, 295
Judah 2, 6, 7, 25, 39, 46, 47, 59, 74, 75, 76, 77, 79, 81, 85, 86, 88, 90, 94, 103, 104, 106, 111, 115, 129, 153, 168, 227, 271, 288, 289, 290, 295, 367
Judaism 18, 38, 94, 253, 273, 300, 308, 314, 320, 321, 350, 370
Judea 59, 79, 83, 111, 116, 153, 154, 166, 169, 170, 179, 243, 244
Judeo-Christian 330, 344
Kadesh 68, 101, 260
King Louis XVI 324
Knox, John 264
Koestler, Arthur 333
Koran 308
Kutter, Hermann 342
Laban 74, 75, 96, 97
Lazarus 196
Leah 74, 75, 81, 88
Lenin, Vladimir 326, 337
Levi 7, 45, 51, 74, 94, 115, 158, 291
Levite 85, 86, 170, 172, 173, 207
Lewis, C.S. 364
Lincoln, Abraham 268, 277
Logos 30, 31, 32
Lot 50, 52, 78, 80, 96, 290
Loyola, Ignatius 266
Lubavitcher Hasidic dynasty 304
Luther x, 264, 265, 266, 351, 352, 353
Lutheran 246, 248
Maccabees 48, 106, 153, 207, 295
Maccabeus 106
Maimonides 303, 304, 305

Index

Malachi 6, 7, 73, 174, 253
Mammon 280, 341, 343
Manasseh 102, 292
Manicheism 19
Marcuse, Herbert 339
Marie-Antoinette 324
Mark Anthony 106, 152
Martyr 26, 40, 351, 368
Martyrdom 239, 241, 254, 367
Marxism-Leninism 337
Marx, Karl 323
Materialism 281, 292, 323, 328, 329, 339, 341, 370
Mattathias 106, 153, 207
Mecca 308, 317, 318
Melanchthon, Philipp x
Melchizedek 50
Mennonite 265, 342
Mesopotamia 355
Methodist 246, 267
Micah 25, 111, 112
Midian 293
Midianites 293
Moab 52, 78, 79, 80, 96, 294
Moabite 81
Monotheistic 300, 309, 316, 320, 321
Mordecai 82, 83
Morocco 303
Mount Ararat 183
Muslim 255, 286, 305, 308, 309, 310, 317, 318
Muslims 18, 71, 261, 288, 309, 310, 313, 316, 317, 318, 319, 320, 321
Naomi 79, 80, 81
Napoleon 325
NATO 285, 298
Nazi 297, 298, 306, 338
Nazism 372
Nebuchadnezzar II 6, 46, 271, 301
Nehemiah 2, 39, 46, 47, 83, 84, 104, 105, 106, 218, 295, 372

Neo-Marxism 281, 327, 330, 335, 339, 346, 347
Neo-Marxist 328, 331, 339, 342, 344, 347
Nestorianism 19
Newton 354
Newton, Isaac x
Nicaea 19
Noah xiv, 13, 15, 37, 85, 183, 184, 296
North Korea 255, 338, 343, 363
Obed 52, 81, 112
Ottoman Empire 306, 318
Pacifism 284, 285, 367
Passover 48, 118, 195, 197, 206, 302
Penn, William 267
Perez 77, 80, 81
Pericles 108
Petrarch x, 266, 351, 352
Pharaoh 43, 66, 67, 114, 154
Pharisees 37, 39, 48, 52, 92, 148, 155, 159, 160, 161, 162, 170, 178, 206, 347
Plato 107
Pope Clement VII ix, 353
Pope Francis 342
Pope Paul III ix
Postmodernism 281
Praetorium 54, 218
Predestination 32, 33, 34, 259, 260, 261
Priest-king 50, 52, 94
Protestant x, 239, 246, 248, 262, 263, 264, 265, 266, 288, 302, 350, 351, 352, 353, 367, 371
Protestantism 264, 265, 323, 353
Ptolemies 153
Putin, Vladimir 298, 363
Pythagoras 107
Quran 308, 318, 319, 320
Rachel 74, 75, 81, 166, 292
Ragaz, Leonhard 342
Rebbe 304

393

Reformation x, 108, 248, 263, 264, 265, 266, 278, 284, 288, 350, 352, 353, 371
Rehoboam 103
Reich, Wilhelm 339
Renaissance x, 108, 265, 266, 350, 351, 352, 353, 355
Reuben 74, 79, 102, 292
Revelation 44, 117, 159, 179, 227, 279, 280, 303, 369, 370, 373
Revelations 204, 206, 293, 308, 317, 320, 349
Robespierre, Maximilien 324
Rousseau, Jean-Jacques 324
Ruth 52, 79, 80, 81, 112
Sabbatai Zevi 304
Sabbath 36, 37, 160
Sacrament 241, 246, 248, 249, 250
Sadducees 48, 159, 170, 206, 217
Saint Augustine 239
Samuel 2, 88, 89, 103, 137
Sanhedrin 159, 190, 197, 202, 203, 208, 255, 303
Scribes 39, 48, 92, 111, 129, 156, 159, 160, 161, 162, 190, 206, 217, 228
Seleucid 47, 106, 153
Serpents 160, 162, 343
Seth 13, 183, 197
Shem 16, 183, 184, 197, 296
Shia 319
Smith, Adam 343, 354
Socrates 107
Sodom 78
Solon 108
Spencer, Herbert 328
Stalin 299, 333
Sunnah 319
Sunni 319
Suras 308
Tabernacle 38, 40, 44, 45, 46, 47, 48, 185, 210, 234

Tamar 75, 76, 77, 81
Taoism 107
Teresa of Avila 266
Thales 107
Theodosius I 315
Theophrastus 107
Torah 303, 320
Transgender 345, 349
Transgenderism 339, 345
Trinitarian 19, 21
Trinity 19, 20, 21, 57
Tutu, Desmond 342
Umar 318
Uncircumcised 26, 40, 247, 256
Uthman 318
Utopia 220, 285, 334, 335
Utopian 327, 330, 334, 336, 341
Vipers 160, 162, 170, 347
Weber, Max 265
Wesley, John 267, 372
Whitfield, George 267, 372
Wittenberg 264, 353
Wycliffe, John 263, 351
Xavier, Francis 266
Xi Jinping 363
Zinn, Howard 340
Zoroastrianism 107
Zwingli 264, 266, 352

www.ingramcontent.com/pod-product-compliance
Lightning Source LLC
Chambersburg PA
CBHW070457120526
44590CB00013B/669